Written with the Ba

Written with the Bayonet

Soviet Russian Poetry of World War Two

KATHARINE HODGSON

Liverpool University Press

First published 1996 by
LIVERPOOL UNIVERSITY PRESS
Senate House, Abercromby Square, Liverpool, L69 3BX

British Library Cataloguing-in-Publication Data
A British Library CIP Record is available for this book
ISBN 0-85323-710-7 *cased*
0-85323-720-4 *paper*

Text set in Sabon by
BBR, Sheffield

Printed and bound in the European Union by
Redwood Books, Trowbridge, Wiltshire

For my parents

Contents

Preface

During the Second World War, Soviet writers were urged to 'equate the pen with the bayonet', in other words, to use their literary talent as a weapon against the enemy. In its original context, Vladimir Maiakovskii's 1925 poem 'Domoi!' (Homewards!), however, it was not the idea of the word as a weapon which was uppermost in his comparison of pen and bayonet, but the idea of the mass production of poetry in accordance with the state's plan.[1] In the poem Maiakovskii expresses the wish that he should be given tasks for the year by Gosplan (the state planning agency), that his lips should be padlocked at the end of the working day, and that Stalin should report to the Politburo about recent increases in the understanding of poetry. The tone of the poem is humorous and ironic, but the readiness of the poet, even in jest, to give up his artistic freedom is alarming. The meaning of the desire to equate the pen with the bayonet can, therefore, be interpreted as a wish to write to order, a rejection of autonomy.

It is the aim of this book to explore the extent to which poets in wartime actually did 'write with the bayonet', producing work which conformed to official expectations, and also the ways in which poets were able to set their own agenda, taking advantage of the greater creative freedom the war afforded them. In order to show the characteristic features of Soviet war poetry, I have drawn on the work of a large number of poets who are little known in the West. Some of this poetry is only of historical interest, chosen to illustrate the cultural assumptions which dominated official Soviet life. More familiar names, such as Anna Akhmatova and Boris Pasternak, do appear, but in the foreground are poets who were closer to the literary establishment, such as Aleksandr Tvardovskii, Ol'ga Berggol'ts and Konstantin Simonov, whose work, immensely popular with contemporary readers, epitomises the way poetry changed during the war.

After a brief outline of Russian poetry on war themes between 1914 and 1941, the poetry of 1941 to 1945 is considered in a chronological survey, which places it in a historical and literary-political context. Three specific areas are then discussed in detail: the representation of heroes in relation to socialist realism; the portrayal of the common man; and the representation and self-representation of women. A final chapter looks at developments in post-war poetry on the war theme.

Although this study has aimed to show the wide range of poetry written during the war, it cannot hope to be comprehensive. Poetry in languages other than Russian is not included, but it is necessary to bear in mind the fact that war poetry was written in the languages of many Soviet nationalities, particularly in Ukrainian and Belorussian, but also in languages ranging from Armenian to Yiddish. A good deal of this poetry was published in Russian translation in wartime Soviet periodicals. Poetry by Russian emigre writers also lies beyond the bounds of this study, which is intended to explore the influences specific to the Soviet context on wartime poetry.[2]

The focus on the poetry's historical and cultural significance has meant that much more attention has been given to what is being said rather than how it is said. In a sense, this limitation, excluding detailed analysis of language, style and rhythm, is dictated by the poems themselves. As a whole, wartime poetry shows little evidence of formal innovation, something which had been effectively suppressed by campaigns against 'formalism' and in favour of 'classical simplicity', that is, the use of traditional forms and conventional rhymes. The most successful examples of war poetry are, on the whole, distinguished by simplicity, clarity and their effective use of colloquial speech. Tvardovskii's *Vasilii Terkin* is a significant achievement, a long narrative poem written in idiomatic, unpretentious language. Tvardovskii's poem might be tentatively compared with Pushkin's *Evgenii Onegin*; it covers multifarious aspects of the war without becoming monotonous, in spite of the apparent restrictions of meter and rhyme.

The question of the actual artistic value of Soviet wartime poetry is one which Soviet critics found difficult to address, as the high official status of its subject-matter has tended to lead to inflated assessments of its merits. Respect for the poetry's subject-matter can, indeed, get in the way of critical analysis, as Vera Sandomirsky noted in 1944. She felt that the expressions of suffering and endurance in many of the poems were so intense that 'it seems petty, indecent, almost impossible to approach it with the dissecting instruments of literary criticism'.[3] Scholars in the West seem to have taken her comments literally, since the subject has been virtually ignored, apart from a small number of articles published in the mid-1940s.[4] In the Soviet Union critics tended to repeat the opinions of their predecessors, examining the work of a narrow range of poets. Although this range gradually increased with time, the approach continued to be over-reverential, due, no doubt, to the war's status as a subject for commemoration rather than analysis. This privileged status has, in turn, made war poetry an area unlikely to be given much immediate attention in post-Soviet Russia.

There has been little critical reassessment of Soviet war poetry written between 1941 and 1945. While much of what was written confirms Western readers' worst prejudices about Soviet poetry, a quick glimpse into British wartime anthologies should remind them that works of lasting quality are the exception, not the rule. I do not set out to persuade them that Soviet war poetry as a whole is of an unusually high quality, but to convince them that it includes work of genuine artistic importance which was highly rated by contemporary readers and critics. This study aims to show that it is a topic worthy of attention, both as an influential period in the development of Soviet literature, and as a distinctive part of the body of poetry produced during World War Two.

NOTES

1 'Domoi', *Sobranie sochinenii*, 13 vols (Moscow, 1955–61), VII, 92–95.

2 See H. Iswolsky, 'Russian Emigré Literature in World War Two', *Russian Review*, 6, no.1 (1946), 69–76.

3 'Soviet War Poetry', *Russian Review*, 4, no. 1, (1944), 47–66 (pp. 52–53).

4 Vera Aleksandrova, 'Russia is Changing: Wartime Plays, Poetry, Novels Provide Proof', *American Mercury*, 56 (1943), 311–318; 'Soviet Poetry and Poets', *Voices: A Quarterly of Poetry (Maine)*, 124 (1946), 34–40; V. Sandomirsky, 'The Sad Armchair: Notes on Soviet War and Post-War Lyrical Poetry', *Harvard Slavonic Studies*, 3 (1957), 289–327; I. Segedi, 'Poets and Poetry in Wartime Russia', *Poetry Review* (October–December 1944), 311–19; E. J. Simmons, 'Soviet War Literature', *University of Toronto Quarterly* (April, 1944), 251–257; H. Slowchower, 'Fear, Tragedy and Humour in Soviet Literature', *Books Abroad*, 16 (1942), 246–251; F. D. Smith, 'The Spiritual Triumph of Russian Literature', *Southwest Review*, 31 (1945–46), 200–205.

Acknowledgements

I would like to thank Julie Curtis, who supervised the PhD dissertation on which this book is based, for her encouragement and attention to detail. Irina Kirillova and Jana Howlett both helped with the early stages of my research. Robin Milner-Gulland and Robert Porter, my examiners, made constructive observations on the original text. I am very grateful to Martin Dewhirst for his suggestions, particularly as far as the translations are concerned, and to Neil Cornwell for spotting some inconsistencies and omissions.

The original research was funded by the British Academy, and the book has been re-worked during a Postdoctoral Research Fellowship awarded by the Academy. The British Council funded an invaluable research visit to Leningrad and Moscow in 1989–90.

Particular thanks go to the poets of the 1941–45 war who granted me interviews: the late Margarita Aliger, the late Mikhail Dudin, Aleksandr Mezhirov, Lev Oshanin and Vadim Shefner. I would like to thank all those who were kind enough to offer me their opinions and advice: Svetlana Aleksievich, John Barber, Mariia Fedorovna Berggol'ts, Viktoriia Buznik, John Garrard, Simon Franklin, Aleksandr Kogan, Nina Koroleva, Svetlana Kovalenko, Lazar' Lazarev, Donald Piper, Mikhail P'ianykh, Aleksandr Rubashkin, Vitalii Shentalinskii, Shmuel Shwartsband.

Note on Transliteration

Russian names, with the exception of place names, such as Moscow, which have a commonly used English form, and titles of journals, newspapers etc. have been transliterated in accordance with the Library of Congress system.

The titles of journals and newspapers are given in transliteration, and not translated. Titles of books and poems are given in transliterated form, with translations.

Unless otherwise indicated, all translations are by the author.

Introduction

The Soviet fight against Nazi invaders is known in Russia as the 'Great Fatherland War', a title which evokes the 'Fatherland War' of 1812 against Napoleon. Both wars nearly proved disastrous for the state, but ended in resounding victory against an enemy believed by many to be invincible. The 1941–1945 war was enshrined as a central part of official Soviet culture, providing an enduring theme for writers and film-makers as well as sculptors and architects who designed vast and suitably-termed 'memorial complexes' constructed during the 1960s and 1970s to commemorate the suffering and courage of Soviet citizens. The memory of the past was kept alive to remind the population that the country's present was fought for at massive human and material cost, a reminder calculated to stifle potential dissatisfaction.

In 1985, forty years after the war ended, the poet Joseph Brodsky described this use of the war's legacy:

> State propaganda rubs the wounds of the nation with ghoulish intensity. Taking a cue from a line by Olga Berggolz (a Leningrad poet who survived the siege) which says 'No-one is forgotten and nothing is forgotten', it sets up hundreds and thousands of war memorials across the country ... finds and exhumes entire wartime graves, and reburies the remains of unknown and known soldiers with semi-religious pomp and ceremony ... If there is any nostalgia, it is that of the state for the only time it enjoyed a true rapport with the nation, for the only time about which it had reasons to brag.'[1]

Yet, Brodsky continues, there is another aspect to the war's cultural inheritance. It allowed Soviet writers, who had little opportunity to portray the social cataclysms of revolution, civil war and collectivisation, except in a carefully edited form, to address tragic themes openly for the first time:

> ... The point is that for about thirty years, as the country bled its way through great social changes, literature had to lie or keep its mouth shut about all these things ... Now the war produced the ultimate in bloodshed, yet this time it wasn't an inside job. So everything that had amassed in writers' psyches about human

> suffering, torment, heroism, stoicism, self-sacrifice, about death and betrayal, gushed onto the pages of post-war novels and poems.[2]

The war years did see a phase of rapid development in Soviet literature, particularly poetry, a genre which allowed a rapid response to events in progress. Writers discovered a level of autonomy which would have been unthinkable during the previous decade's intensification of state literary control. Censorship, of course, remained in place, but there was much less interference by functionaries attempting to prescribe what should be written about, and how. The writer's primary role was to mobilise enthusiasm for the war effort, and this allowed them to stray into previously forbidden territory for the sake of writing effective poetry. Once the victory, and therefore the survival of the state, seemed certain, official controls on writers were gradually re-asserted. Immediately after the war, young poets returning from the front were encouraged to move on to new subject matter, and the war theme was largely incorporated into the official culture of High Stalinism, where the foundations were laid for the verbal (and marble) monuments of the next thirty years.

There are, therefore, two main strands in Soviet representations of the war: one, blandly commemorative, emphasising victory; the other addressing awkward questions of moral responsibility and individual psychology, which are not without directly political and critical implications for the society in which they were written. The censors were not blind to the war theme's potential for controversy. Vasilii Grossman's novel *Life and Fate* only emerged in the Soviet Union once Gorbachev's policy of *glasnost'* was well established.[3] The author's comparison of Stalin's Russia with Hitler's Germany proved one of the reasons for it being placed on the index. Elsewhere, the war has been used as a metaphor for controversial events in Soviet history, as demonstrated in a poem by Aleksandr Mezhirov:

> ...Недолет. Перелет. Недолет.
> По своим артиллерия бьет...[4]

(Falling short. Overshooting. Falling short. The artillery is firing at its own men.)

In actual fact, such events were not unusual, and what is now termed 'friendly fire' is still a problem in modern combat. The poem's concluding lines, however, give the none too subtle clue to a second meaning. Mezhirov incorporates a saying commonly used to explain away the terror of the 1930s—'when you chop wood, chips fly'—making what would seem to be a war poem into a poem about the state's war against its own people. When recited, unattributed, in public by Evtushenko at a meeting during the 1950s, the poem provoked frantic activity on the part of Party functionaries who were trying to discover who had written the subversive lines. Mezhirov himself was unsuspected, although some of his contemporaries, including the poet Boris Slutskii, were questioned about the poem's authorship.[5]

It would, however, be over-simplifying the matter to say that the war theme was used in literature only as a vehicle for official propaganda or as a cover for critical comment. The war unleashed a powerful and complex emotional reaction among the Soviet people, amounting to a national trauma. Wartime losses, however calculated, were catastrophic. Areas which were occupied by invaders were devastated; much of the countryside was left unfit for cultivation, and in many villages the majority of the male population failed to return from the front. There was a real need for a focus for national mourning, as well as the reassurance that lives had been lost in the name of a worthy cause. It was also natural that those who had brought about the victory should wish to feel that their achievements had been recognised. The cult of the war, therefore, was not merely a set of artificial rituals imposed by the state, but founded on a real, popular desire to commemorate the dead and celebrate victory.

One enduring cultural legacy of the war is the vast number of songs which have enjoyed genuine popularity. Some of the poems to be discussed in this book were set to music, more than once in the case of some of the most popular, such as Konstantin Simonov's 'Zhdi menia' (Wait for Me). These songs were given mass exposure on the radio, and featured in some theatre productions and numerous films. Undoubtedly their popularity rests on their avoidance of political or ideological matters; they deal with universal feelings such as love of home and country, and the everyday experience of the soldier, faced with danger and longing for his wife and family. Their blend of nostalgia, sentiment and national feeling make them evocative symbols of the people's, rather than the Communist Party's war.

The capacity for war to promote national unity and popular self-esteem was discussed by Fedor Dostoevskii in the April 1876 edition of his journal *Diary of a Writer*. Dostoevskii put forward the theory of a character named 'Paradoxicalist' that war performed a useful function of reinforcing national unity and releasing creative energy. 'Paradoxicalist' claims that men do not go to war in order to kill, but to sacrifice themselves:

> ... they go to sacrifice their own lives—this must stand in the foreground. And this is altogether different. There is no loftier idea than to sacrifice one's own life, or even simply to defend the cause

> of one's own fatherland. Mankind cannot live without magnanimous ideas, and I am even inclined to suspect that mankind loves war precisely because it seeks to participate in a magnanimous idea.[6]

Dostoevskii's imagined interlocutor proceeds to discuss the general rise in people's spirits during wartime, the tendency of long periods of peace to foster hypocrisy and apathy. War, he claims, furthers science and, in the arts, the communication of simple, clear and vigorous ideas. Moreover, the prime beneficiaries of war are the people, who gain a temporary equality with their masters:

> War arouses the people's spirit and their feeling of self-respect. War equalises everybody during the battle and reconciles master and slave in the supreme manifestation of human dignity—in the sacrifice of life for a common cause, for everybody, for the fatherland.[7]

Although Dostoevskii treats his 'Paradoxicalist' with a certain detachment by calling him a dreamer, in his novels the author was not averse to putting his own ideas in the mouths of strange, even mad characters. His dreamer's comments on the beneficial effects of war seem to have considerable relevance to the Soviet Union's response to World War Two:

> To the masses war is a pretext for self-respect, and this is the reason why the people love war: they compose songs about it, and later, during long years, they listen with delight to war legends and stories ... Blood which has been shed is an important thing![8]

In the Soviet Union, war against an external enemy created a sense of national unity which revolution, civil war and terror had destroyed. The conditions of war demanded quick individual reactions to changing situations, providing an opportunity for people, soldiers and writers, to think and act independently, and to value their own contribution to the general good.

The historical context is essential to an understanding of the war's status in Soviet cultural consciousness. The war was preceded by the terror of the 1930s, which was founded on the concept of the 'enemy within'. Soviet society was engaged in rooting out foes, mainly imagined, on a scale which some estimate at many millions, with the number of victims perhaps rivalling the twenty-seven million who died as a result of the war. With the outbreak of war in 1941, the enemy was clearly and unambiguously identified. The gulf between the frightening reality of the 1930s and the public announcements that the Soviet people were enjoying happiness, prosperity and peace never before available to humanity created an atmosphere of stifling unreality. In Boris Pasternak's novel *Doctor*

Zhivago, Dudorov, one of Zhivago's friends who has been through a period of imprisonment in a labour camp, speaks of the war as an escape: '... compared to everything in the thirties ... the war came as a breath of fresh air, an omen of deliverance, a purifying storm'.[9] He reasons that the failure of the collectivisation of agriculture was covered by lies, that people, through fear, were weaned away from independent thought and were forced to draw conclusions which were contrary to the evidence of their own experience. War, he explains, is the return of reality: 'And when war broke out, its real horrors, its real dangers, its menace of real death, were a blessing compared with the inhuman power of the lie, a relief because it broke the spell of the dead letter'.[10]

Understanding how and why a people which had been systematically humiliated by its government was able and, apparently, willing to defend its own oppressors is perhaps made easier by Pasternak's words. Two crucial factors in determining the impact of the war and the people's motivation to resist invasion were the political alternative offered by the enemy, and the power of national feeling. Soviet citizens had been warned from the early 1930s of the fascist threat, and were, except for the brief period of the Nazi-Soviet pact between 1939 and 1941, encouraged to see Hitler as the arch-enemy of the Soviet Union. Hitler's fascism seemed little more attractive than Stalin's communism, particularly once it became clear that the Nazi view of Slav nationalities as racially inferior was to be used as a justification for slavery and brutality. As for national and patriotic emotions, although they had been dismissed in the initial post-revolutionary period in favour of internationalism, Russian patriotism was actively revived in the mid-1930s, providing a firm foundation for the wartime wave of national feeling which created enthusiasm for the defence of Russia, if not of communism.

In order to provide a contrast with Soviet war poetry, and perhaps to highlight some of it peculiarities, it is as well to look, briefly, at the British poetry of the time. In Britain the poets of World War Two are little known; the concept of the 'war poet' is related in the public imagination to the First World War, and suggests either Rupert Brooke's patriotic calls to arms, or the sombre view of war in the work of Wilfred Owen, Siegfried Sassoon and Isaac Rosenberg. Although the Second World War produced no single prominent war poet in Britain, there was a considerable amount of good poetry written during and about the war. The often disjointed and far-flung nature of the war, and the fact that an earlier generation had already revealed war's horrors, made it unlikely that one poet should emerge who could fulfil the role of a Brooke or an Owen. Yet somehow it was expected that the war should have its poets, or be condemned as 'unpoetic'. The question began to be asked: 'Where are the War Poets?', and a debate began over the poet's role in wartime and whether he (it was assumed that a war poet was, by definition, male) should not, in fact, keep silent.

Cyril Connolly's editorial in the May edition of *Horizon* for 1940 announced: 'The war is the enemy of creative activity, and writers and painters are wise to ignore it and concentrate their talents on other subjects'.[11] A soldier, Goronwy Rees, replied in July that artists had a responsibility to fulfil with regard to those involved in the war:

> The soldier has the right, in return for his blood and his life and his despair, for the crimes he must take on himself, to ask that those most qualified, by their sensibility, by their more lucid perception of values, by their release from belligerence, should comprehend, analyse, illuminate, commemorate his sacrifice and his suffering and the horror to which he is condemned.[12]

Keidrych Rhys wrote in his introduction to a 1941 anthology *Poems from the Forces* that circumstances for the poet on active service were hardly conducive to artistic success: 'Perhaps the poet who is fighting ... cannot write his very best when he is not being properly used and frustrated; ... therefore his output in the circumstances is forced to appear half-dead and loses much in spontaneity and spirit'.[13] Stephen Spender, writing on the poetry of 1941, evidently expected poets to rise above their difficulties, and confessed that he was not impressed with recent output:

> ... so far none of them seems to have created in imaginative terms 1) any major event of the war; 2) any statement of the nature of the struggle in which we are involved, either as suffering or as ideas; 3) any positive faith in the democracy for which we are fighting; 4) any effective statement against war.

Instead, Spender wrote, they had turned to 'the poetry of the bewildered victims of circumstances'.[14] Spender's criticisms were reported in *Literaturnaia gazeta* in May 1942.[15]

Mainstream Soviet poetry certainly fulfilled his first three requirements, while the fourth, the expression of anti-war feelings, was taboo, but Soviet poets did not enjoy the poetic freedom and individuality of their British counterparts. They also had a very different image of war, drawn more from romanticised portrayals of the civil war than from realistic descriptions of the battles of 1914–1918. War had none of the connotations of horror and futility which British poets such as Owen described. Although Nikolai Tikhonov's First World War poems express a similar alienation, these attitudes were set aside when the 1917 revolution and civil war decreed that fighting for a communist future made battle glorious and romantic.[16] There were no ambivalent feelings expressed when war broke out in 1941; the clash between communism and fascism had been long expected, and it was accepted that this would mean a fight to the death. Many young poets volunteered for active service, some to fight, while others were assigned to army newspapers to use their talents accordingly. A collective, rather than individual standpoint produced an attitude towards the war in which the individual was aware of his role as part of the whole country's effort. Critical pressure to conform made it almost impossible for the individual to express reservations about his participation in the war; moreover, the way the future war generation was brought up meant that they were unlikely to harbour doubts, or, still worse, pacifist ideas.

Perhaps Spender was expecting too much of British poets who were concerned with balancing their dual roles as servicemen and artists, often aware that circumstances forced them into the role of reporter in a narrow sector of war rather than that of a poet equipped with the leisure and range of information to make major pronouncements. Donald Bain wrote:

> We in our haste can only see the small components of the scene.
> We cannot tell what incidents will focus on the final screen.
> A barrage of disruptive sound, a petal on a sleeping face,
> Both must be noticed, both must have their place.
> It may be that our later selves or else our unborn sons
> Will search for meaning in the dust of long deserted guns,
> We only watch, and indicate, and make our scribbled pencil notes.
> We do not wish to moralise, only to ease our dusty throats.[17]

Such admissions were not entirely absent from Soviet war poetry. The nature of the war as a struggle to eliminate fascism was a fixed element in most poets' work. There was, however, a growing tendency, particularly among the younger writers, to share Bain's interpretation of the poet's role as an honest witness of events which existed below the level of the war's broad historical significance, recording details such as the 'petal on a sleeping face'. Both British and Soviet poets found that their work could provide a way for them to order their experience and create some small-scale statement on what the war meant, not as a historical event, but as a disruption of ordinary, private life. The reactions of Soviet literary critics to this approach were mixed, and as the war entered its final stages they called on poets to draw their conclusions from a historical perspective more appropriate to the significance of victory.

British poetry, compared with the Soviet poetry of the time, does indeed show a marked absence of comment on the nature and purpose of the war as a whole, or of the morality of war. Such questions are considered only as they relate to the individual, often bewildered, enduring the peculiar routine of army life and enforced contact with other similarly confused recruits:

> ... the stench
> Of breath in crowded tents, the grousing queues,
> And bawdy songs incessantly resung
> And dull relaxing in the dirty bar;
> The difficult tolerance of all that is
> Mere rigid brute routine; the odd
> Sardonic scorn of desolate self-pity,
> The pathetic contempt of the lonely for the crowd;
> And, as the crystal slowly forms,
> A growing self-detachment making man
> Less home-sick, fearful, proud,
> But less a man.[18]

Such is the ambivalent attitude of the poet Alun Lewis (1915–1944) towards army life. At the beginning of the war he considered registering as a conscientious objector. His intensely personal war poetry wrestles with the problem of love and war, and the paradox of:

> Love of mankind, impelling men
> To murder and to mutilate ...[19]

When Lewis decided to enlist, it was because he could accept more easily the possibility of being killed than killing, and discovered in war a sense of mission which meant abandoning selfishness and giving himself to the world. The surrender of self Lewis aspired to came close to the urge for self-annihilation; the neutrality and boundlessness of death had a mysterious appeal which strengthened when he was sent to serve in India in 1942. Two years later he died in an accident on active service. In his poetry, death became a welcome resolution of conflict:

> ... Or does the will's long struggle end
> With the last kindness of a foe or friend?[20]

A complete contrast to the reluctant soldier Lewis is another prominent poet, Keith Douglas (1920–1944), whose enthusiasm for military action impelled him to desert from a post at headquarters in Palestine to join the battle at El Alamein. For Douglas, battle was both a test of personal courage and a spectacle:

> I observed these battles partly as an exhibition, that is to say I went through them a little like a visitor from the country going to see a great show, or like a child in a factory—a child sees the brightness and efficiency of steel machines and endless belts slapping round and round, without caring or knowing what it is all there for. When I could order my thoughts I looked for more significant

> things than appearances; I still looked—I cannot avoid it—for something decorative, poetic or dramatic.[21]

His poetry often betrays the dispassionate, clinical eye of an observer, but at the same time he is able to identify with enemy soldiers, whose experiences he shares. The strange relationship between the killer and his victim is explored in 'Vergissmeinnicht'. A soldier, confronted with his victim's corpse, is reminded by a photograph of a girl that the dead man was both soldier and lover:

> ... We see him almost with content,
> abased and seeming to have paid,
> mocked by his durable equipment
> that's hard and good when he's decayed.
>
> But she would weep to see today
> how on his skin the swart flies move,
> the dust upon the paper eye
> and the burst stomach like a cave.
>
> For here the lover and killer are mingled
> who had one body and one heart;
> and Death, who had the soldier singled
> has done the lover mortal hurt.[22]

The closest any Soviet poet came to such a sympathetic contemplation of a dead enemy is in Mikhail Svetlov's 'Ital'ianets' (The Italian). The conventional Soviet portrayal of the German soldier made it impossible to acknowledge his humanity, but there was more sympathy for the Italians, often unwilling fighters, and poorly equipped to cope with the Russian winter. Svetlov begins with an appeal to the emotions, and to class consciousness:

> Черный крест на груди итальянца,
> Ни резьбы, ни узора, ни глянца,
> Небогатым семейством хранимый
> И единственным сыном носимый ...

(A black cross on the Italian's breast, without carving, embellishment or polish, kept by a poor family and worn by their only son.)

Svetlov's poem, by contrast to Douglas's, begins by recognising the enemy's humanity, but goes on to justify the speaker's right to kill those who threaten his country. At the very end, however, Svetlov returns to his original mood:

> ... Я не дам свою родину вывезти
> За простор чужеземных морей!
> Я стреляю—и нет справедливости
> Справедливее пули моей!
>
> Никогда ты здесь не жил и не был!..
> Но разбросано в снежных полях
> Итальянское синее небо,

Застекленное в мертвых глазах ...[23]
(I shall not let my country be taken away across the wide alien seas! I shoot—and there is no justice more just than my bullet! You have never been here, never lived here. But scattered over snowy fields are the blue Italian skies glazed over in dead eyes.)

For Douglas, the dead German is a fellow soldier and human being; for Svetlov, the dead Italian is a human being, but also an invader who must, in the name of justice, be killed. Soviet war poetry in general tends to dehumanise the enemy for ideological reasons. For Keith Douglas the nature and purpose of the war is of less concern than the exploration of the experience of war, where the absence of humanity becomes apparent in the self rather than the enemy. In 'How to Kill' the killer is so dehumanised by his profession that although he is rationally aware of his victim's humanity, he is emotionally unable to acknowledge it:

... Now in my dial of glass appears
the soldier who is going to die.
He smiles, and moves about in ways
his mother knows, habits of his.
The wires touch his face; I cry
NOW. Death, like a familiar, hears

and look, has made a man of dust
of a man of flesh. This sorcery
I do. Being damned, I am amused
to see the centre of love diffused
and the waves of love travel into vacancy.
How easy it is to make a ghost.

The weightless mosquito touches
her tiny shadow on the stone,
and with how like, how infinite
a likeness, man and shadow meet.
They fuse. A shadow is a man
When the mosquito death approaches.[24]

The experience of war, on such a fundamental level, was shared by British and Soviet poets alike. There is, perhaps, a faint echo of Douglas's 'How to Kill' in a less reflective, but equally detached poem by Georgii Suvorov, who, born in 1919, was one year older than Douglas:

На болоте блуждает светляк.
Луч луны закачался в ветвях.
Мрак лесной. Тишина. Блиндажи.
Майские ночи так хороши!

Пара глаз устремилась в лесок.
Мушка в прорези—на висок.
Палец плавно давит крючок.

На болоте погас светлячок.
Над болотом метнулась тень.
Мертвый немец свалился на пень.[25]

(A fire-fly wanders across the marsh. The moon's rays shiver in the branches. Forest dark. Silence. Dug-outs. How wonderful May nights are! A pair of eyes focus on the wood. Aim through the slit at the temples. A finger smoothly presses the trigger. On the marsh the fire-fly is extinguished. A shadow rushes by above the marsh. A dead German collapses onto a stump.)

Although the experience of war of the Soviet and the British people, and the conditions which governed their literary output, differed greatly, some of their responses to war were similar, and, perhaps, universal. While Soviet poets wrote from within the system of state-controlled literature, and British poets wrote in a somewhat disoriented literary world, in both countries the status of poetry rose considerably in wartime. More poetry was written as well as read. The boredom of periods of waiting, or of stagnation at the front, needed to be overcome somehow. The extreme circumstances of war demanded some kind of response from people who, through facing the possibility of death, needed to consider the significance of their own lives.

A curious footnote to this comparison is provided by poems written by Vladimir Lifshits, offered to the reader as translations of an English poet, James Clifford, who died fighting in Europe in 1944. Clifford, as Lifshits makes clear in his introduction to the 'translations', is an invented figure, but the attitudes to the war voiced by this *alter ego* suggest where a Soviet writer might suppose the differences to lie. The persona of Clifford, moreover, may have allowed Lifshits to say things which, as himself, he could not. Clifford complains of unreasonable commanding officers and the routine humiliations of army life. He also quotes the words of another, the common soldier Andy Smiles, who cynically compares barracks life with life in prison, mocks the corporal for being so busy that he has not had time to evolve from ape to human being, and states that if he dies, he will feel pity for the girls he hasn't yet managed to embrace. Clifford's defiant spirit emerges most clearly in what is presented as one of his last poems, 'Otstuplenie v Ardennakh' (Retreat in the Ardennes):

Ах, как нам было весело,
Когда швырять нас начало!
Жизнь ничего не весила,
Смерть ничего не значила.
Нас оставалось пятеро
В промозглом блиндаже.
Командованье спятило
И драпало уже.

Мы из консервной банки
По кругу пили виски,
Уничтожали бланки,
Приказы, карты, списки,
И, отдаленный слыша бой,
Я—жалкий раб господен—
Впервые был самим собой,
Впервые был свободен!
Я был свободен, видит бог,
От всех сомнений и тревог,
Меня поймавших в сети,
Я был свободен, черт возьми,
От вашей суетной возни
И от всего на свете!..
Я позабуду мокрый лес,
И тот рассвет,—он был белес,—
И как средь призрачных стволов
Текло людское месиво,
Но не забуду никогда,
Как мы срывали провода,
Как в блиндаже приказы жгли,
Как все крушили, что могли,
И как нам было весело![26]

(Oh, what fun we had when they began to throw everything at us! Life weighed nothing, death meant nothing. There were five of us left in the freezing cold dug-out. The commanders had lost their heads and had already legged it. Out of a tin we drank whisky in turns, destroyed forms, orders, maps, lists, and, hearing the distant battle, I—miserable sinner that I am—was myself for the first time, for the first time was free! I was free, God knows, from all the doubts and worries that had snared me in their net, I was free, devil take it, from your pointless fuss and from everything in the world!.. I shall forget the damp forest, And that dawn—it was pale,—And how between transparent tree trunks poured a mass of humanity, but I shall never forget how we ripped down wires, how we burned orders in the dug-out, how we ruined everything we could, and how much fun we had!)

Clifford's irreverence is combined with very colloquial language. The word he uses to convey the flight of his commanding officers is not one commonly found in Soviet war poetry, except perhaps when describing the actions of the enemy, certainly not of Soviet officers. The sense of freedom, found by Clifford in retreat and imminent danger may be seen, transplanted into a different context, as a reference to the desperate situation of the Soviet retreat in 1941, for many years a taboo subject in the USSR. His glee at the destruction of official documents, his disdain for the fleeing commanders and particularly his revelling in the liberation from trivial concerns brought by the prospect of death states clearly what other Soviet poets, writing 'as themselves', merely suggest: the war provided an escape from oppressive authority and an opportunity for self-discovery.

Official Soviet commemoration of the war had no room for

sentiments of this kind, preferring to project an image of monolithic devotion to the state. The collapse of the Soviet Union has shattered this monolith. Recent re-examination of Soviet wartime history has left the heroic myth looking rather tarnished, and confirmed that the baleful manifestations of Stalinism were not put on hold during the war years. The fact that the victory made the state stronger is enough to make some wonder whether defeat might not have been preferable. What is there left to celebrate in a victory that risks being rejected as a product of a system now vilified? In 1993 Daniil Granin defended the victory of 1945 as the one achievement of the Soviet state which could not be compromised. On the fiftieth anniversary of the victory, the editor of *Literaturnaia gazeta* called on his readership to celebrate the defeat of fascism, while recognising that the war in Chechnia and catastrophic price rises could hardly contribute to a festive mood.[27] The poetry of the war, for many years part of the school curriculum, risks being dismissed wholesale as part of the late, unlamented canon of Soviet literature. The best of this poetry does, however, show that writers were doing much more than mouthing triumphant slogans in response to instructions. The poems form a war memorial which, as Brodsky suggested, fused the previously repressed emotional reactions to the catastrophes which confronted the Soviet people before 1941 with the emotions unleased by the war itself.[28]

NOTES

1 'Literature and War: The Soviet Union', *TLS*, 17 May 1985, p. 544.

2 Ibid., p. 543.

3 *Zhizn' i sud'ba* was first published in the USSR in 1988 in the journal *Oktiabr'*, 1–4. For an account of the life and works of Grossman, see Frank Ellis, *Vasiliy Grossman: The Genesis and Evolution of a Russian Heretic* (Oxford, 1994); also by the same author 'Army and Party in Conflict: Soldiers and Commissars in the Prose of Vasiliy Grossman, in *World War Two and the Soviet People*, edited by John and Carol Garrard (London, 1993), pp. 180–201.

4 'My pod Kolpinom skopom stoim ...', *Izbrannoe* (Moscow, 1989), p. 561.

5 Related by Mezhirov at a talk given in Pembroke College, Cambridge, January 1991.

6 F. M. Dostoevskii, *The Diary of a Writer*, translated by Boris Brasol (Haslemere, 1984), p. 297.

7 Ibid., pp. 300–301.

8 Ibid., p. 301.

9 *Doctor Zhivago*, translated by Max Hayward and Manya Harari (London, 1988), p. 453.

10 Ibid.

11 'Comment', *Horizon*, 1, no.5 (May 1940), 309–314 (p. 314).

12 'Letter from a Soldier', ibid., 1, no.7 (July 1940), 467–471 (p. 468).

13 Introduction to *Poems from the Forces* (London, 1941), xiii–xxii (p. xx).

14 'Poetry in 1941', *Horizon*, 5, no.26 (February 1942) 96–111 (p. 97).

15 'Za rubezhom: angliiskaia voennaia poeziia', *Literatura i iskusstvo*, 5 September 1942, p. 3.

16 See the cycle of Nikolai Tikhonov's 1914–1917 war poetry, 'Zhizn' pod zvezdami-pokhodnaia tetrad'', in *Sobranie sochinenii*, 7 vols (Moscow, 1973–76), I, 61–77.

17 'War Poet', in *Poems of the Second World War: the Oasis Selection* (London, 1985), p. 25.

18 Alun Lewis, 'After Dunkirk', *Selected Poems of Alun Lewis* (London, 1981), p. 17.

19 Ibid., p.16.

20 'The Jungle', ibid., p. 100.

21 *Alamein to Zem-Zem* (London, 1946), p. 7.

22 *Complete Poems* (Oxford, 1978), p. 111.

23 *Sobranie sochinenii*, 3 vols (Moscow, 1974–75), I, 439–440.

24 *Complete Poems*, p. 112.

25 'Boloto', *Do poslednego dykhaniia: stikhi sovetskikh poetov, pavshikh v Velikoi Otechestvennoi voine* (Moscow, 1985), p. 296.

26 Vladimir Lifshits, 'Otstuplenie v Ardennakh', *Izbrannye stikhi* (Moscow, 1974), pp. 134–135.

27 'Daty, kotorye vsegda s nami', *Literaturnaia gazeta*, 23 June 1993, p.1; Arkadii Udal'tsov, 'Vechnaia voina posle Velikoi Pobedy', *Literaturnaia gazeta*, 9 May 1995, p. 1.

28 See note 2 above.

CHAPTER ONE

The War Theme in Poetry 1914–1941

The concept of war, conflict and struggle was a governing metaphor in the society which developed after 1917.[1] It was also a major part of twentieth-century Russian reality. The Soviet state originated in conflict and confrontation, in revolution and civil war, and continued to define itself in confrontational terms, beset by enemies beyond its borders, as well as those within. As hopes for world revolution receded, and as a new world war approached, sentiments of class solidarity with the international proletariat became overlaid with Russian nationalist attitudes. Increasing emphasis was placed on the unity of the Soviet people, standing proudly isolated in a world of hostile capitalist powers. The revolutionary state became a totalitarian state which required utmost clarity in defining its friends and, particularly, its enemies. The actual identity of the enemy changed with circumstances. During the civil war it was the White Army and foreign interventionists. During the 1930s, failures in industry and agriculture were blamed on 'wreckers', allegedly inspired by foreign powers, whose goal was to destroy all the achievements of the new society. The most rapid about-turn was performed in 1939 with the signing of the non-aggression pact between Germany and the Soviet Union, when yesterday's fascist enemy became an ally overnight. This preoccupation with enemies, although often used for domestic political manipulation, was far from being a groundless invention. The Soviet Union had few foreign friends. From the late 1920s, Soviet writers warned of a new, inevitable war against fascism; a generation grew up convinced that they were destined to take part in this war.

By 1932, with the creation of a single writers' union, Soviet writers were, without exception, assigned a partisan role and expected to prove their allegiance to the state by showing uncompromising attitudes and a lack of ambiguity. The theme of war was ideal for this purpose, and actual events provided an abundance of suitable raw material. The poetry to be considered in this chapter is based on a series of conflicts from the civil war of 1918–1921 up to the war with Finland in 1939–1940. The civil war brought internal chaos and foreign intervention, and left the country's economy in ruins. During the 1930s came an increasing threat of war from Western Europe, as fascism gained ground in Italy, Germany and Spain. The Spanish civil war captured public imagination as a re-run, in exotic settings, of their own civil war, or at least of the romantic version offered to Soviet readers. To the East, Japanese aggression sparked off battles in Mongolia during 1939. Further military activity took place in the same year due to the secret provisions of the Nazi-Soviet non-aggression pact, as Soviet troops moved into former Polish territories, now known as the Western Ukraine and Western Belorussia. In the winter of 1939–40 Soviet troops fought in Finland for a small territorial gain. The Second World War had lasted nearly two years by the time Hitler's armies massed near the Soviet border and the August 1939 pact was finally broken.

Before moving on to explore the ways in which war was represented by Soviet poets before 1941, a short survey of Russian poetry of World War One will provide some idea of the range of work written on the subject. The First World War was not a topic that merited much attention in the Soviet Union, as it was designated as an imperialist war, fought by nation states intent on territorial and financial gains. For in the vocabulary of the Bolsheviks there was no such thing as 'war' unqualified by the adjectives 'revolutionary' or 'imperialist'. The First World War was, in Soviet eyes, little more than a prelude to the October Revolution; the poetry written on the subject was little considered by critics until the 1930s, when it was examined for the dangerous germs of imperialism and pacifism. There was simply no way that Russian poetry of World War One could have the impact on later generations' perception and representation of war that British poetry had. And in fact it seems that much of what was written on the war in Russian supported the traditional portrayal of war as a heroic test of patriotism and masculinity.[2]

In Russia in 1914 it had seemed possible that the war might provide an opportunity for national reconciliation, as people and tsar joined forces against a common enemy, setting aside the divisive legacy of the 1905 Revolution. That year, poets of all political and artistic shades gave voice to patriotic and heroic evocations of war as Russia's chance to unite and reveal her true glory in battle. Many seem to have shared Rupert Brooke's enthusiasm for war as an escape from compromise and moral ambiguity.[3] It was notably non-combatant poets who spoke as soldiers who had found spiritual renewal on the battlefield, although Nikolai Gumilev, who had volunteered in the early days of the war, wrote of his battlefield experiences in equally glowing terms in his poem 'Nastuplenie' (The Attack):

Та страна, что могла быть раем,
Стала логовищем огня.
Мы четвертый день наступаем,
Мы не ели четыре дня.

Но не надо яства земного
В этот страшный и светлый час,
Оттого что господне слово
Лучше хлеба питает нас.

И залитые кровью недели
Ослепительны и легки,
Надо мною рвутся шрапнели,
Птиц быстрей взлетают клинки.

Я кричу, и мой голос дикий,
Это медь ударяет в медь,
Я, носитель мысли великой,
Не могу, не могу умереть.

Словно молоты громовые
Или воды гневных морей,
Золотое сердце России
Мерно бьется в груди моей.

И так сладко рядить Победу,
Словно девушку, в жемчуга,
Проходя по дымному следу
Отступающего врага.[4]

(The country that could have been paradise, has become a den of fire. We have been attacking for four days, we have not eaten for four days. But we have no need of earthly fare in this terrible and radiant hour, because the word of the Lord feeds us better than bread. And the weeks drowned in blood are blinding and light, above me shrapnel bursts, blades fly up faster than birds. I shout, and my savage voice is like the clash of cymbals, I, the bearer of a great idea, cannot, cannot die. Like thunderous hammers or the waters of angry seas, the golden heart of Russia beats evenly in my breast. And it is so sweet to deck Victory, like a young girl, with pearls, following the smoking trail of the retreating enemy.)

In other First World War poems by Gumilev and many others, religious motifs of assisting archangels, the arrival of heroes in heaven, and a messianic transformation of Russia through war are widespread. Claims of the type made in the poem just quoted, that earthly hardship is of no consequence to the man fighting for his beliefs recur in poetry of the revolution and civil war, with religious and nationalistic ideas being supplanted by those of communism. In both cases the representation of violence is overshadowed by the representation of heroics. As in later poems about the October Revolution and the civil war, the violent acts of the hero are aestheticised, or not represented as a matter of personal volition, as if the hero is subject to some elemental, external force. The hero, purified by his virtue and the rightness of his cause, declaims against a background of violence which, being transformed by its elevated purpose, is often seen in terms which recall more peaceful activities. Bal'mont celebrated the war as a 'festival of blood' which is to culminate in a glorious spring, while Gumilev manages to create something approaching a rural idyll in his evocation of battle as a harvest, transforming the sound of machine-gun fire into barking dogs, and the hum of bullets into that of bees, collecting 'bright red honey'.[5]

There were dissenting views about the war. Far from revelling in heroics, Marina Tsvetaeva and Maksimilian Voloshin saw the war as a tragic and unnecessary event. Tsvetaeva even on occasion expressed pro-German sentiment, unable to consider the people who had produced great works of art and music as the enemy.[6] The national tragedy of the war was expressed in poems by Anna Akhmatova and Aleksandr Blok, whose patriotic feelings were not associated with hatred of the enemy or visions of Russian heroes, but with restrained and profound awareness of national suffering.[7] Poets of the avant-garde, which had been at its height in 1913, expressed predictably unconventional and often contradictory opinions on the war. Igor Severianin, the prominent and fashionable ego-futurist, began the war with aggressive anti-German proclamations, but defended his noncombatant position as a poet dedicated to following his dreams, while Bal'mont wrote that the war was 'someone else's mistake' which had deluded the warring nations.[8] The futurist poet Velimir Khlebnikov, who had previously expressed aggressive nationalistic, anti-German opinions, came to declare war on war as a force which devalued human life and made human sacrifices out of the young Russians. An unwilling conscript, Khlebnikov later arranged to be discharged from the army on grounds of mental unfitness.[9] His fellow-futurist Vladimir Maiakovskii gradually changed his position too, from initial belligerent enthusiasm to rejection of war's senseless murder. Maiakovskii had at first revelled in the violence of war as a source of striking imagery; in a series of articles published in late 1914, he continually returned to the point that the war had put into practice the futurists' aesthetic credo of destruction.[10] Maiakovskii never saw battle, but came to change his ideas about war, if not his claim that only futurism provided the artist with the means to depict war adequately. His long anti-war poem 'Voina i mir' (War and the Universe) is full of gleefully horrific battlefield descriptions. By 1917 he expressed the position that the war was an irrelevant quarrel between capitalist nations. The 'imperialist' war, fought by workers in the interests of the rich, should be transformed into a civil war, in which workers fought in their own interests against those who wished to exploit them. He displayed his new political consciousness in 'K otvetu' (Call to Account):

...Во имя чего
сапог
землю растаптывает скрипящ и груб?
Кто над небом боев—
свобода?
бог?
Рубль?
Когда же встанешь во весь свой рост
ты,
отдающий жизнь свою им?
Когда же в лицо им бросишь вопрос:
за что воюем?[11]

(In the name of what does the coarse, creaking boot trample the earth? Who is above the sky of battles? Freedom? God? The ruble? When will you stand up to your full height, you who give up your life to them? When will you fling into their faces the question: what are we fighting for?)

Satirical poet Sasha Chernyi found little to mock in war; his poems offer realistic glimpses into the world of the front-line. As a medical orderly he was able to give graphic descriptions of battle casualties. The mundane experiences of front-line troops also found their place in Chernyi's work, which showed conscripts undergoing a medical examination, military training, and resting behind the lines.[12] Wider questions about the purpose of the war seem to be absent from the poet's perspective, that of an ordinary man caught up in the military machine and trying to survive with his humanity intact.

The violence of war as represented by contemporary poets appears to have a good deal in common with the violence of the 1917 October Revolution; in both cases violence is represented as a force for change and renewal, and is carried out in the name of a higher cause, whether this is victory against Germany or against the forces of Tsarism. In works written shortly after the October Revolution, particularly in Aleksandr Blok's 'Dvenadtsat'' (The Twelve), violence is an elemental force which sweeps away the past; it threatens to become uncontrollable, as Blok's Red Guards rampage around the city, but the poem's enigmatic ending, as Christ is seen leading them through the snow, suggests that their violence is sanctified, or at least sanctioned.[13]

Much of the poetry actually written during the civil war, from 1918 until the end of 1920, was printed in army newspapers as propaganda verse and has proved ephemeral. Circumstances dictated that the poetry written by supporters of the White Army has been all but forgotten, although Marina Tsvetaeva's cycle 'Lebedinyi stan' (Encampment of Swans) is an exception.[14] Poets who backed the Bolsheviks wrote poetry which dealt with immediate concerns of explaining the nature of the war and encouraging soldiers of the Red Army to fight. The aim was not to portray the ordinary soldier's experience of the war, but to influence his attitudes and behaviour. Dem'ian Bednyi, whose poems had appeared regularly on the pages of the pre-revolutionary *Pravda*, was at the height of his fame, as well as enormously productive, during this period. His didactic poetry uses simple, colloquial language and traditional verse forms. Bednyi's satirical verse ridicules the enemy. The White General Baron Wrangel is made to speak in a grotesque mixture of German and appalling Russian.[15] Apart from satire, the main verse genre of the civil war was the song, or march, which celebrated the heroism of the Red Army and exhorted the soldiers to still greater achievements. Vladimir Maiakovskii wrote both satire and heroic exhortations. His 'Levyi marsh' (Left march) of 1918 is an appeal to the sailors to 'strengthen the grip of the fingers of the proletariat around the throat of the world'. Maiakovskii composed verses in traditional folk styles for posters, putting forward reasons for accepting Soviet power, as he does in 'Pesnia riazanskogo muzhika' (Song of the Riazan' peasant) of 1919, or for mocking the enemy, which he does in the ballad of the same year entitled 'Ballada ob odnom korole i tozhe ob odnoi blokhe (on zhe Denikin)(Ballad about a king and a flea—alias Denikin), which depicts the White General Denikin as a flea leading an army of fleas, which the Soviet soldiers simply crush between their thumbnails. It is notable, however, that Maiakovskii's civil war satire closely resembles his anti-German verses dating from the early days of the 1914 war which were offered to Soviet readers in 1942.[16]

In the chaotic years of civil war which followed the October Revolution, poets portrayed Red Army soldiers in ways which recall the elemental violence identified with the Revolution. There is no realistic depiction of battle; it is represented through imagery which is dominated by ideas. The elemental force of the revolution is reflected in imagery of fire, molten lava or hurricane, natural phenomena which are unstoppable and beyond any criticism or moral argument. Bednyi's 'Na pomoshch' krasnym boitsam' (To the Aid of Red Soldiers) of 1920 gives the following typical evocation of battle:

Красные рати, не зная усталости,
Бьются с отвагой львиной,
Черную силу сметают без жалости

Неудержимой лавиной.[17]

(The Red armies, knowing no tiredness, fight with the courage of lions, they sweep away the black forces without mercy in an unstoppable avalanche.)

The strength of the united masses finds its expression in hyperbolic comparisons and the depiction of representative, larger than life figures. The Proletkul't poet Kirillov writes in 'Matrosam' (To the Sailors) of 1918:

Подобно утесам, вы встали, титаны,
На страже коммуны, на страже свобод.[18]

(Like cliffs you rose up, titans, to guard the commune, to guard freedom.)

Maiakovskii took such gigantomania to its logical conclusion in '150,000,000'. The title was taken from the 1919 population of the USSR, all of whom, claimed Maiakovskii somewhat unconvincingly, were co-authors of the poem. In the poem, which imitates the folk epic genre of *bylina*, a hyperbolical Russian hero 'Ivan' vanquishes the evil monster 'Woodrow Wilson'.[19]

Once the civil war ended, there was an increasing tendency for poets to create a nostalgic, romanticised image of the war in works which concentrated on individuals who epitomised the moral superiority of Soviet Man, rather than on armies, blindly propelled by elemental forces. The civil war, with its extremes of brutality, famine, confusion—it was not just a struggle between Reds and Whites, but Green peasant groups, local warlords, and various nationalists—was gradually transformed in poetry at least into a nostalgic myth of heroic national unity. There were obvious political reasons for loyal writers to project this image at a time when, in the early 1920s, popular support for the Party was waning due to the rigours of war communism. Poets could portray the recent past as a time when the people were united by a common ideal as well as against the menace of foreign armies, the significance of a civil war gradually fading from the picture. It was policy, however, not poetry, that went a long way towards restoring peasant support with the establishment of the New Economic Policy (NEP) during the early 1920s which allowed a certain amount of trading on the free market. But for many civil war poet-veterans, the era of NEP felt like a betrayal of what they had been fighting for. In their opinion there was nothing heroic about encouraging private enterprise. In contrast to the new, civilian, compromised form of existence, the war was a theme which allowed easy identification of friend and foe. The clear cut 'manliness' of battle and comradeship between soldiers offered a more palatable alternative to the rising tide of the bourgeoisie and the insidious menace of 'byt', everyday life which places emphasis on material rather than spiritual existence.

The civil war theme was used to considerable effect by Nikolai Tikhonov in the ballads he wrote during the 1920s which encapsulated the almost inhuman courage and devotion of the ideal Soviet Man. During World War One Tikhonov had served as a hussar; the poems he wrote about his experiences then present a war which offers no opportunity for heroism, but only indifference and inaction.[20] When, however, the poet perceives that the conflict is informed with high ideals, descriptions of war's pointless ugliness disappear. His collection *Braga* (Mead), containing poems from 1921 to 1924, includes the famous 'Ballada o gvozdiakh' (Ballad about Nails) about the crew of a submarine who obey orders to make an attack on the enemy from which they will not return. Their strength of purpose is what makes the author compare these men with nails. 'Ballada o sinem pakete' (Ballad about the Blue Parcel) is a laconically narrated story of an anonymous man who goes through danger and suffers injury in order to bring a written message to an important individual in the Kremlin. The message is delivered, stained with blood and dirt as evidence of the ordeals of its bearer, but it is too late; the recipient has heard the news already. Although the messenger has suffered in vain, Tikhonov makes no mention of his emotions on receiving this news.[21] Tikhonov's ballads have been generally described as 'romantic' by Soviet critics, but Efim Etkind disagrees with this definition, arguing that romanticism is essentially emotional, and Tikhonov's ballads exclude emotion, celebrating unconditional discipline instead.[22] The language used by Tikhonov is concise, factual, the language of commands and reports, with masculine rhyming couplets hurrying the reader towards the conclusion. More emotionally loaded are Mikhail Svetlov's nostalgic evocations of the war which describe heroes who are motivated by dreams and ideals to sacrifice their own lives. His enduringly popular 'Grenada' (Granada) of 1926 depicts a Russian soldier of the civil war, dreaming romantically of the peasants in Spain, for whose freedom he is fighting. His 'Dvoe' (Two) of 1924 describes two friends, inseparable in death, killed by the same bullet, their hands both tightly clasped round one machine gun, their faces showing an expression of 'terrible happiness'.[23]

Gradually, during the late 1920s and early 1930s, poetry began to present the civil war from an altered political perspective. The internationalist working-class solidarity prevalent in Svetlov's 'Grenada' was gradually supplemented, if not completely supplanted by Russian patriotism and a sense of pride in national achievements. This revision of values began as hopes for a world revolution were abandoned and replaced by Stalin's idea of socialism in one country. By the mid-1930s there had been far-reaching changes in Soviet society which can be broadly characterised as the move from revolutionary turmoil to the seemingly well-ordered totalitarian state. The old status quo had been successfully challenged; now the new order had to be consolidated and defended. Nationalistic sentiment was a natural development for a state which defined itself as proletarian. Antagonists of the USSR could be condemned both as capitalist states, and as foreign states. At a time when Russian nationalism was being encouraged, the civil war, thanks to foreign intervention, was able to take its place among other examples of how the Russian people united to repulse invaders such as the Tatars, the Poles, the Teutonic knights and Napoleon's army.

It was particularly important for Stalin to legitimise his position as leader, and the cult which had been built up around him. Where previously the collective had been treated as hero, it was the strong individual who now became the focus of attention. From the mid-1930s onward Russian history and cultural heritage were re-evaluated and rehabilitated; autocratic tsars were shown to have displayed exceptional qualities of leadership and wisdom, and their despotic excesses were overlooked. An emphasis on historical continuity and traditional patriotism was a logical development for a leadership which could no longer assert a credible claim to be faithful followers of Lenin's revolution. Stalin's dictatorship was therefore shown to be supported by historical precedent.

Towards the end of the 1920s the practically synonymous theme of war and heroism was taken up by a new generation of poets, some of whom were too young to have taken part in the civil war, others who were veterans of the war, and came to poetry relatively late via Party work, as did Aleksei Surkov, who was to play a major role in the Union of Writers, and as a poet of World War Two. With the advent of the First Five Year Plan in 1928, the depiction of heroism was particularly called for, and the civil war served admirably as a source of examples. Military metaphors were extensively applied to ostensibly peaceful endeavours, as if in obedience to Maiakovskii's advice to artists in 1914: 'Можно не писать о войне, но надо писать войною!'[24] (You do not have to paint about war, but you must paint by war!) The process of rapid industrialisation was likened to a battle, with 'attacks' launched on the various 'fronts' of industry.

Delegates at the First Congress of Soviet Writers in 1934 linked heroism of the civil war with that of the Five Year Plans, in order to call for more emphasis on the latter. Tikhonov complained that the heroes of industry were not depicted as strongly as the heroes of the war. He suggested that the reason for this was not that the 'bloody battle for Perekop' was a more fruitful source of artistic inspiration than the 'peaceful battle for Dneprostroi', but that the older poets were more emotionally involved with the war, and so could write about it with greater ease than about industry, with which they were only distantly acquainted.[25] Yet while some civil war poems, particularly those written after the event, became Soviet classics, poems of the first Five Year Plans faded into obscurity, having little literary merit to preserve them outside their original context. Like most of the poetry written while the civil war was in progress, verses of the first Five Year Plans were written for immediate propaganda purposes, to incite workers to greater achievements rather than to muse on these achievements in retrospect, distilling from them the ethos of a generation.

In the 1930s the civil war theme continued to play an important part in poems defining the nature and character of Soviet man. Aleksandr Prokof'ev, a veteran of the war who published his first collection of verse in 1931, ascribed a special quality to his generation who were forged by war's 'fiery squall':

Нам крышей служило небо, туманы с боков и мгла,
Мы пили такую воду, которая камень жгла.
Мы шли от предгорий к морю,—нам вся страна отдана,
Мы ели сухую воблу, какую не ел сатана![26]

(The sky was our roof, mists on all sides and darkness, we drank water which burned stones. We went from the foothills to the seas—the whole country is given to us, we ate dried Caspian roach, the like of which the devil never ate!)

Poetry on the civil war theme played a large part in creating images of Soviet heroism. The enemy and the actual waging of war were gradually overshadowed by the moral and physical resilience of the victors. As the civil war became transformed into a heroic legend, poets risked creating the illusion that the Red Army was invincible, a risk that was ignored until the prospect of new battles arose.

The theme of the threat of a new war began to emerge at the end of the 1920s. Maksim Gor'kii published an article in *Izvestiia* in July 1929, in which he expressed his belief that there would be a new war. He spoke of his revulsion against war in general, but then said that the fact that the working class had managed to build a new state made war inevitable: '...I too have become convinced that a fight to the death is inevitable'.[27] Iosif Utkin echoed Gor'kii's warning in 1930:

...И тиф,
　　и Деникин,
　　　　и нищета—
Все это,
　　товарищ,
　　　　за нами.
Но нам
　　не прощают,

нам пишут счета
На песню,
на трактор,
на знамя.
Враги не прощают
нам каждую пядь
Победы твоей
и работы.
Они заготовили,
отлили пять
Гаубиц
и
пулеметов.[28]

(Typhus and Denikin and beggary—all that, comrade, is behind us. But they haven't forgiven us, they want us to pay for a song, for a tractor, for a banner. The enemies won't forgive us even an inch of your victory and labour. They have produced and cast five howitzers and machine guns.)

The growing sense of the need to prepare for war was reflected in contemporary literature while civil war themes were still at the forefront. In 1927 Mikhail Golodnyi wrote 'Romanticheskaia noch'' (Romantic Night) in which the sleepless poet sees the shadow of war cast across his bed. A dream summons him to write about war, not love, and tells him that it has already woken Svetlov and Bagritskii, whose poetry was largely concerned with civil war themes.[29] The theme of approaching conflict did not displace the civil war theme, but reinforced it, only now the legend created by the veterans was taken up by poets too young to have been involved in the fighting. Among them was Boris Kornilov, who combined a romantic portrayal of the war's heroics with vivid immediacy and matter-of-fact, direct language.[30] In 1930, however, Kornilov writes of frightening premonitions of his own violent death in war, a war in which horror leaves no room for heroism:

На пять километров
И дальше кругом,
Шипя, освещает зарница
Насильственной смерти
Щербатым клыком
Разбитые вдребезги лица.
Убийства с безумьем кромешного смесь,
Ужасную бестолочь боя
И тяжкую злобу, которая здесь
Летит, задыхаясь и воя ...[31]

(Across five kilometres and further all round, hissing, a flash illuminates the faces, smashed to pieces by the chipped fangs of violent death. The mixture of infernal murder with madness, the terrible chaos of battle, and the heavy malice which flies here, panting and howling...)

This poem ends with the exclamation 'I protest!'. Quite different is the vision of death in Kornilov's later poem, using the same meter, 'Prodolzhenie zhizni' (Continuation of Life). Here a soldier calmly contemplates death in battle, knowing that his life will be continued by other soldiers. Death, he says, will only be complete when he sees the combines approaching his grave, a sign of victory and peace:

Я знаю себя и походку свою,
я молод, настойчив, не робок,
и если погибну, погибну в бою
с тобою, комвзвода, бок о бок.

Восходит сияние летнего дня,
хорошую красит погоду,
и только не видно тебя и меня,
товарищей наших по взводу.

Мы в мягкую землю ушли головой,
нас тьма окружает глухая,
мы тонкой во тьме прорастаем травой,
качаясь и благоухая.

Зеленое, скучное небытие,
хотя бы кровинкою брызни,
достоинство наше—твое и мое—
в другом продолжении жизни.

Всё так же качаются струи огня,
военная дует погода,
и вывел на битву другого меня
другой осторожный комвзвода ...[32]

(I know myself and my gait, I am young, persistent, not timid, and if I die I will die in battle side by side with you, platoon commander. The radiance of a summer's day shall rise, and make the good weather even better, but you and I will not be seen, nor will our comrades in the platoon. We have gone down headfirst into the soft earth, we are surrounded by dense darkness, and in the dark we shall sprout like fine grass, swaying and fragrant. A green, dull non-existence, if only a splash of blood falls, our dignity—yours and mine—is in another continuation of life. The streams of fire sway just as they did, the winds of war rise, and another me is led out to battle by another careful platoon commander ...)

The difference in attitude towards war in these two poems by Kornilov is easily explained by looking at contemporary thinking about war. There is no such thing as 'war', but there are different kinds of war, 'imperialist' and 'revolutionary'. The first is savage and hideous, waged for selfish ends of the type described in Kornilov's 'Voina' (War); the second is noble, and heroic. Among the aims of the literary group known by the acronym LOKAF (Literaturnoe Ob"edinenie Krasnoi Armii i Flota—Literary Association of the Red Army and Navy), created in 1930, was to encourage writers to spread such ideas through their work, and to prepare themselves and their readers for a future war. The division of war into two categories, 'imperialist' and 'revolutionary', meant that war was considered both bad and good; paradoxically, both pro- and anti-war sentiments were expressed. It was made clear, however, that pacifism was to be seen as an ally of militarism, part of the reactionaries' plot to fight the working classes. This dual perception of war led LOKAF to define its own literary preoccupation with military themes as the 'defence theme', while German war literature was felt to be aggressive.[33]

LOKAF was set up as the result of a meeting of writers called by the Political Direction of the Red Army; the first edition of the group's journal *LOKAF* was published in January 1931. Among early contributors were Vsevolod Vishnevskii, who became chief editor of *Znamia* in 1939, Vladimir Lugovskoi, Stepan Shchipachev, Dem'ian Bednyi, Aleksandr Bezymenskii, Mikhail Svetlov and Aleksandr Prokof'ev. Almost all of the contributors were civil war veterans, and the theme of the civil war made up a considerable part of the journal's output. Other subjects included the work of Soviet border guards and the history of the Red Army. Literary groups already existed in separate sections of the armed forces; LOKAF's role was to provide a single organisation which would both train writers within the forces and bring civilian writers into contact with military life, so that they could write about the army with expert knowledge. Organising writers to work on particular themes was not unknown in the Soviet Union; at the beginning of the Five Year Plans, writers had been assigned to factories in order to write about industrialisation. The attempted militarisation of literature promoted by LOKAF came at a time when the aggressive guardians of ideological purity, RAPP (Russian Association of Proletarian Writers), was making every effort to make writers follow the Party line, and shortly before writers were involuntarily conscripted into a single union of writers. The existence of LOKAF coincided, as has been pointed out, with the transition from a revolutionary to a totalitarian state.[34]

The journal *LOKAF* was set up with the aims of showing how the Soviet Union's defences were being strengthened, revealing imperialist preparations for war, and fighting what was termed 'remarkizm'—the attitude supposedly fostered in Erich Maria Remarque's book *All Quiet on the Western Front* that war was an inevitable and tragic part of human existence—and to show the Red Army both as it was in the present and in its heroic history. A contemporary review of the first two issues was basically favourable: 'One of the most powerful weapons—the writer's word—is increasingly mobilised into a fist to defend the first workers' state in the world. The arrival of the journal *LOKAF* is a vivid illustration of this.'[35] There were, however, serious obstacles to the success of the journal; many of the contributions were of a low artistic standard, and there were few serious critical essays. LOKAF's chief critic was N. Svirin, a collection of whose essays was published under the title of *Literatura i voina* (Literature and War) in 1932.[36] In these essays, Svirin discusses both theoretical questions on the subject of literature and war, and comments on literary works submitted to the journal. Svirin is insistent that the threat of war is real, that the danger of war demands that writers should take on their civic duty and produce literature which contributes to the country's defence, both by preparing the civilian population for war, and by firing the enthusiasm of the armed forces.

The group ceased to exist under the name LOKAF after April 1932, when all literary groups were disbanded by decree. The journal ceased publication for some months, but was re-launched as *Znamia* in January 1933, describing itself as a 'monthly literary and socio-political defence journal'. A year later the word 'defence' was dropped from this description; the journal explained that it had seen its theme too narrowly as literature concerned with the army, and that the 'defence' theme would henceforward include Soviet patriotism—a new concept to those used to internationalist sentiments and the rejection of purely national allegiance—the Motherland and the New Soviet Man. The 'class' element of war was not completely lost, but was reinterpreted: instead of being surrounded by potential class allies, the country was surrounded by imperialist powers, who could only be countered by a strong, united national group, but one which identified itself with the proletariat. During the latter half of the decade, *Znamia* published poetry and prose on the Spanish Civil War, on the wars in Mongolia and Finland, and on the fascist threat from Germany. Once the Nazi-Soviet pact had been signed in August 1939, it was France and England who were castigated as the aggressors.

Lokaf, later reconstituted as the journal *Znamia*, was by no means the only voice which called for literature to be involved in preparations for war. At the 1934 First Congress of Soviet Writers, Tikhonov declared that pacifism was alien to the spirit of Soviet poetry, and, in a discussion of Kornilov's 'Prodolzhenie zhizni' (Continuation of Life) quoted above, said that the logical attitude towards death in war was to understand it not as a failure, but as a contribution towards the future of socialism.[37] Aleksei Surkov made an impassioned appeal for the recognition of hatred as an aspect of humanism—a timely remark, with the first mass purges to begin after Kirov's murder at the end of 1934. Surkov rejected lyric poetry at a time when the atmosphere heralded war, and concluded by reminding his audience that poetry would soon be moving from the pages of the literary journals to those of the front-line newspapers.[38] In general it is remarkable how many of the writers at the congress used military metaphor when speaking of literary matters; Semen Kirsanov accused Bukharin, whose comments on some Soviet poets, particularly Maiakovskii, had provoked angry responses, of trying to 'take poetry away from front-line positions where it can take part in real life ... far behind the lines'.[39]

Poets did play their part in preparing the population for war. Vasilii Lebedev-Kumach, who provided the lyrics for countless popular songs of the 1930s and forties, placed the waging of war against the enemy alongside other heroic achievements of the Soviet people in aviation and exploration.[40] The official optimism of the times made war seem almost harmless, so that even a village girl who had learned to shoot rabbits felt that she was well prepared to face the enemy:

...И знаю я, когда придет, непрошен,
Заклятый враг в советские края,
Нас много встанет—девушек хороших,
И, может статься, первой буду я.[41]

(I know that when, uninvited, our sworn enemy arrives in Soviet lands, many of us—nice young girls—will rise up, and perhaps I shall be the first.)

In the meantime, the theme of the civil war was still widely used in poetry, although the hero was no longer simply an anonymous representative soldier, but a leader of exceptional stature. In 1934 Kornilov wrote 'Skazanie o geroe grazhdanskoi voiny tovarishche Gromoboe' (Tale of the Civil War Hero Comrade Gromoboi) which depicted the hero in legendary, super-human terms. Mikhail Golodnyi's 1935 song 'Partizan Zhelezniak' (Partisan Zhelezniak) describes the hero's burial mound and relates how he died leading his men into a successful attack. The same year brought Golodnyi's 'Pesnia o Shchorse' (Song about Shchors) about a famous civil war hero.[42] The cult of Stalin was accompanied by the proliferation of smaller personality cults, whether of exceptionally productive workers such as the miner Aleksei Stakhanov, eponymous founder of the Stakhanovite movement, or of local Party leaders. Essential to the cult was the belief that the cult figure possessed powers above those of the average human being, and the civil war hero was no exception.

The larger-than-life civil war heroes are in their exceptional strength and reckless daring similar to the Russian folk hero Il'ia Muromets, whose adventures are recorded in the traditional verse *bylina*. Their appearance on the scene was accompanied by the move, mentioned above, towards pre-revolutionary historical themes and characters, which were cited as guarantees of a heroic Soviet present and future. Vsevolod Vishnevskii, one of the founders of LOKAF, spoke at a meeting of writers in 1937 on the theme of war and history in literature. He called for writers to make a profound study of national history, and mentioned in particular the various attempts by enemies to invade Russia. Literature, Vishnevskii said, should depict the power of the Russian people and show Europe examples of their courage and endurance.[43]

Numerous poets found suitable material for work on the 'defence theme' in medieval subjects. Prokof'ev wrote on themes from the Igor Tale and concentrated on the figure of Iaroslavna grieving for her captured husband. Aleksei Nedogonov combined the medieval and modern in his 'Predchuvstvie' (Premonition), in which the poet dreams he is woken at night by high winds, goes outside and sees an army of Tatars from the times of Batu; when he wakes up in reality and goes outside, a squadron of Soviet soldiers rush by, a guarantee that the past will not be allowed to return. In Vladislav Zanadvorov's poem 'Shchit' (The Shield), an ancient shield found on the field of Kulikovo, site of the battle held to have been the first significant Russian defeat of the Tatars, is regarded with awe; the poet wonders how future generations will feel when contemplating a bayonet fragment found on a battlefield of the civil war.[44] Historical motifs of this kind were also much in evidence in the poetry written between 1941 and 1945.

It was not the wars of the past, but the vision of a new kind of mass destruction that the technology of a future war would bring, that fuelled Osip Mandel'shtam's 1937 'Stikhi o neizvestnom soldate' (Verses about an Unknown Soldier). The poem closes with the author among the ranks of doomed soldiers, his contemporaries:

...Наливаются кровью аорты,
И звучит по рядам шепотком:
—Я рожден в девяносто четвертом,
Я рожден в девяносто втором...—
И в кулак зажимая истертый
Год рожденья—с гурьбой и гуртом,
Я шепчу обескровленным ртом:
—Я рожден в ночь с второго на третье
Января в девяносто одном
Ненадежном году—и столетья
Окружают меня огнем.[45]

(Aortas fill with blood, and a whisper is heard among the ranks: 'I was born in ninety-four', 'I was born in ninety-two'... And clutching in my fist my worn date of birth—along with the crowd, the herd, I whisper through bloodless lips: 'I was born in the night of the second to the third of January in ninety-one, an untrustworthy year—and the centuries surround me with fire.)

Mandel'shtam, unable to publish his work for some years, nevertheless sent a copy of this poem to *Znamia*, and received a polite reply to the effect that the pacifism in itself was not worthy of approval.[46]

Those of a younger generation, born around 1920, were also concerned with a future war, but although they realised they were bound to be involved and not all would survive, the war they imagined was much less apocalyptic than Mandel'shtam's vision. The poets of this generation wrote stoically about their destiny. Some welcomed war as an escape from the petty world of 'domestic passions' into a world of adventure, a rite of passage into manhood:

...Теперь положено черстветь
рукам,
сжимающим винтовку,
и смерть берет на изготовку,
хотя ты прожил только треть.[47]

(Now it is time for the hands grasping the rifle to harden, and death is at the ready, even though you have lived only a third of your time.)

In a poem of 1940 Pavel Kogan describes the characteristics of his contemporaries as unquestioning endurance and loyalty. They accept hard work, even death, with equanimity:

...Мое поколение—
это зубы сожми и работай,
Мое поколение—
это пулю прими и рухни.[48]

(My generation—it's grit your teeth and work. My generation—it's take the bullet and drop.)

The prospect of an early death in battle reinforced the young poets' sense of destiny. A close contemporary of Kogan, Nikolai Maiorov, depicts his generation in the poem 'My' (We) as a remarkable generation who, although fated to die in war, will be looked upon as mythical heroes in times to come:

...Не все умрет. Не все войдет в каталог.
Но только пусть под именем моим
Потомок различит в архивном хламе
Кусок горячей, верной нам земли,
Где мы прошли с обугленными ртами
И мужество, как знамя, пронесли.[49]

(Not everything will die. Not everything will go into the catalogue. But may my descendant make out among the archive clutter under my name a piece of scorched and loyal earth where we passed by with charred mouths and carried courage like a banner.)

This generation, with their awareness of approaching war, did not meet this prospect as passive victims. They were resolved to put their ideals to the test with a characteristic lack of compromise and no trace of self-pity.[50] Death in battle is not feared, indeed, it confers a certain significant nobility on its victims, who would be sure to be remembered (unlike the countless victims who died in the camps and prisons). Perhaps this acceptance of death was seen, unconsciously, as an act of atonement for the arrests of the 1930s. In a culture which operated by seeing the world in terms of struggle between implacable enemies, it was necessary to accept death as part of the price of victory. As Svetlana Aleksievich puts it in her investigation of the phenomenon of suicide in the immediate post-Soviet era:

> It must be admitted that for a long time, too long we were ruled by the idea which you couldn't call anything but 'thanatology', the teaching of death. We were taught to die. We learned to die very well. Much better than we learned to live.[51]

By going back to the ethos of nineteenth-century Russian revolutionaries, it may be suggested that the prominence of self-sacrificial death in Soviet culture is descended from their insistence that the individual was of little importance, fulfilment being found only in self-denial. Indeed, one nineteenth-century woman revolutionary is said to have insisted that death was the best way of making a political point.[52]

To judge from the poetry of the younger generation, these ideals, ones worth dying for, are linked with the revolution and civil war, which they saw as a time of authentic heroism and self-sacrifice. Kogan calls his generation 'broad-browed boys of the unprecedented revolution'.[53] Mikhail Kul'chitskii approaches the coming war as a chance to prove allegiance to the revolution, and a chance to bring communism closer:

> ...Наперевес с железом сизым
> И я на проволку пойду,
> И коммунизм опять так близок,
> Как в девятнадцатом году.[54]

(Leaning forward with blue-grey metal I too shall go to the wire, and communism is once more as close as it was in 1919.)

The implication from these lines, clearly, is that communism was now felt to be not closer, but more distant, than in 1919. It was from the revolution, not from Stalin, that the younger poets derived their ideals. Some of them, however, reacted to the prospect of war with simple enthusiasm and affirmation of duty, as befitted the generation brought up on Tikhonov & co. At the age of eighteen Boris Smolenskii announced on behalf of his peers that they would go to war when summoned, leaving behind their studies and their families without a backward glance.[55] Yet in the same year, 1939, another short poem of his treats the theme of young men, presumably going to war, in a rather different, minor key:

Я сегодня весь вечер буду,
Задыхаясь в табачном дыме,
Мучиться мыслями о каких-то людях,
Умерших очень молодыми,
Которые на заре или ночью
Неожиданно и неумело
Умирали,
        не дописав последних строчек,
Не долюбив,
        не досказав,
                не доделав...[56]

(Today I shall spend the whole evening choking on tobacco smoke and tormenting myself with thoughts about some people who died very young, who at dawn or in the night, unexpectedly and awkwardly died, without having written their last lines, without having loved to the full, had their say, finished what they were doing...)

By the end of the 1930s some of Smolenskii's contemporaries had had their first taste of battle in Mongolia and in Finland. The reality of war did not completely correspond with their idealised version. Moreover, the expected final battle between communism and fascism had not materialised. To the younger generation's dismay, and not just theirs, the Soviet Union signed a non-aggression pact with Nazi Germany in August 1939, and censorship put an end to open anti-fascist statements. The sense of betrayal brought a new, tragic perception of war which had been stripped of its historical purpose. Another poem by Smolenskii dated 1939–1940 begins with the question:

Как лес восстановить по пням?
Где слово, чтоб поднять умерших?..[57]

(How can you restore a forest from tree stumps? Where is the word that can raise the dead?)

The dead had lost their lives, it seemed, for very little. A fragment written by Pavel Kogan in April 1941 suggests that he felt the prospects for his generation to be less glorious than he had once hoped:

Нам лечь, где лечь,
И нам не встать, где лечь.
....
И, задохнувшись «интернационалом»,
Упасть лицом на высохшие травы.
И уж не встать, и не попасть в анналы,
И даже близким славы не сыскать.[58]

(We shall lie down where we lie down, and we shall not stand up again where we lie down ... And, choking on the Internationale, we shall fall face down on the dried-up grass, and not get up again, nor make our way into the annals, and not bring glory even to our relatives.)

It is worth noting at this point that the motif of death and resurrection (a major element in the master plot of socialist realist novels, identified by Katerina Clark) features strongly in Soviet poetry of World War Two as an illustration of the hero's transcendence of material existence into a higher, spiritual plane.[59] In the lines just quoted above, this expected transformation is short-circuited. The necessary leap of faith is out of the question.

There were sober realisations among other young poets who, having faced battle in Mongolia and Finland, found that war was not at all like the descriptions given in poetry. Towards the end of the 1930s some critics complained that poetry on the theme of war showed too much confidence in the country's ability to defend itself, an illusion which had its roots in civil war poetry which ridiculed the enemy and presented hyperbolically heroic Soviet soldiers. It almost seemed as if a magical belief in the efficacy of the martial word might supplant details such as weapons and training. In the spring of 1938 a letter was published in *Literaturnaia Gazeta* from the commanders of the Red Army, who had detected an 'excessive, false and dishonest optimism' in the treatment of the war theme.[60] In the 1930s there was a tendency for poets to write of the Soviet Union's ability to repel an enemy with astonishing ease; Dem'ian Bednyi compared the country with a hedgehog, which could easily withstand attack, being protected by Red Army bayonets.[61] Semen Kirsanov's narrative poem 'Voina—chume!' (War on Plague!) likened enemy invasion to an infection of plague, but ended reassuringly by saying that their soldiers:

Стоят в двух шагах от Всюду,
В трех минутах от Везде![62]

(Stand two steps away from Everywhere, three minutes away from All Around!)

It was not long before such over-confidence was punctured by real battles. The work of Konstantin Simonov in the late 1930s shows the gradual development of a more realistic assessment of what war actually meant. In 1937 he first gained attention with a poem which fulfilled contemporary requirements to portray heroes and events from Russia's heroic past by describing Aleksandr Nevskii's defeat of invading Teutonic knights. The epilogue to 'Ledovoe poboishche' (The Battle on the Ice) is directed against German aggression of the present, citing examples of Germany's previous defeats at the hands of Russia, and promising heavy retribution for any future attack. In 1938–39 Simonov also wrote 'Suvorov', an account of the Tsarist general's last campaign. During the Spanish civil war Simonov's poems accentuated the adventure of revolutionary drama in a foreign setting. This was at a time when the decisive battle between fascism and communism appeared to have started, and Soviet poets reacted with excitement. Simonov gave a romantic evocation of the Republicans' heroism in poems like 'Rasskaz o spriatannom oruzhii' (A Story about the Hidden Weapons) and 'Izgnannik' (The Exile).[63] The virtues of iron discipline, as extolled in Tikhonov's civil war ballads, combine with an exotic setting. Il'ia Erenburg worked as a war correspondent in Spain, so unlike Simonov he saw the war at first hand. Erenburg's poetry shows a different war, ultimately tragic, bringing destruction and ending in defeat. A film about the Russian civil war hero Chapaev shown in a Spanish church brings conventional Soviet civil war imagery and inspires the poet with hope, but the film contrasts harshly with the heat, noise and chaos of the present.[64]

A radical change in Simonov's treatment of the war theme came when he wrote about battles that he witnessed at first hand. Conflicts in Mongolia (1937–39) and Finland (1939–40) brought many poets face to face with modern warfare and the realisation that victory was not as simple as had once been suggested. Simonov saw how the much vaunted powers of the Red Army were put to the test by fighting in Mongolia. The conflict ended in a Soviet victory in 1939, a victory which had not come easily, as testified to by Simonov in his numerous poems on the subject. One of the best known is 'Tank' (The Tank) in which the poet expresses his wish to set up a battered tank as a monument to the dead, to show how hard the battle had been:

...Невянущая воинская честь
Есть в этих шрамах, в обгорелых ранах.
На постамент взобравшись высоко,
Пусть как свидетель подтвердит по праву:
Да, нам далась победа нелегко.
Да, враг был храбр. Тем больше наша слава.[65]

(There is unfading martial honour in these scars and scorched wounds. Set up high on a pedestal, may it, like a witness, affirm by right: Yes, the victory was hard to gain. Yes, the enemy was brave. So much the greater our glory.)

In another of Simonov's Mongolian poems a grim picture is drawn of the battlefield strewn with corpses awaiting burial. There is a certain ambiguity in the use of the word 'eagle', used metaphorically in Russian of a 'proud, brave, strong man'.[66] This makes the poem open to interpretation as a veiled criticism of 'heroes' who stay behind the lines. Battle paintings, says Simonov, used to show eagles flying down to feed on the dead:

Но этот день я не сравню со вчерашним.
Мы, люди, привыкаем ко всему.
Но поле боя было слишком страшным:
Орлы боялись подлетать к нему.

У пыльных юрт второго эшелона,
Легко привыкнув к тыловым огням,
На вешках полевого телефона
Они теперь сидят по целым дням.

Восточный ветер, вешками колыша,
У них ерошит перья на спине,
И кажется: орлы дрожат, заслыша
Одно напоминанье о войне.[67]

(But I shall not compare today with yesterday. We, people, can get used to everything. But the battlefield was too terrible: the eagles were afraid to approach. By the dusty huts of the second echelon, easily accustomed to the lights of the rear, on the rods of the field telephone they now sit for days at a time. The east wind, rocking the rods, ruffles the feathers on their backs, and it seems as though the eagles tremble on hearing just a reminder of war.)

The poetry Simonov wrote as a result of his experiences in Mongolia laid down the foundations for what he was to write after 1941. His long narrative poem 'Daleko na vostoke' (Far Away in the East) is, in many ways, programmatic. It contains realistic descriptions of the harsh conditions in the desert where the battles took place, does not gloss over death in battle, and insists on the soldiers' right to think of home and loved ones without being considered weak or sentimental. Simonov rejects superficial celebrations of bemedalled heroes in favour of showing the less glamorous, but authentic side of heroism:

...Нам о славе судить,
Только зная,
Как она достается.[68]

(We can judge glory only if we know how it is attained.)

Simonov's work was recognised as playing an important role in the development of Soviet poetry on the theme of war. In a 1941 article 'War Lyrics of 1940', the critic D. Danin wrote that Simonov had made it possible to move from historical poems about war to 'living lyrical war poetry'.[69] Most of Danin's article is, however, concerned with poetry written during the war against Finland in the winter of 1939–1940. This war ended with Finland ceding territory of strategic importance to the Soviet Union, but in all other aspects the campaign was not a success. Soviet troops were poorly supplied; many were captured and casualties were high. The Soviet Union found itself threatened with international isolation after its act of unprovoked aggression. The harsh conditions under which the war was fought are reflected in the sombre tone taken by almost all of the poets who wrote on the theme from their own experience. No-one could now suggest that war was easy.

Poets already established in their literary careers such as

Tikhonov, Surkov and Tvardovskii, went to Finland as war correspondents. Tikhonov's poems chronicle the soldiers' heroic achievements in grandiose terms; soldiers fighting bravely against great odds are 'titans' engaged in 'legendary battle'.[70] Surkov's poetry gives a more realistic picture of soldiers lying in the snow waiting to attack and aware that they could be killed. Danin praises Surkov for his rejection of the falsely romantic: 'The harsh reality of war has passed with heavy tread across the canvas of countless sweet and pretty pieces of scenery of the kind which Surkov himself painted quite recently. War in its genuine threatening form scattered to the winds all pseudo-lyrical outpourings.' Danin does not reject outright the romantic aspects of war such as heroism and self-sacrifice. He is anxious about the trend towards superficial realism which contains the risk that '... the hardship of life at war, the tragic impressions of witnesses to war, the terrible injustice of death which poets have had the opportunity of observing, touching thoughts on home far away—these have become the main material and spirit of their poetry ... the genuine romance of war is often drowned in lyric poetry'.[71] Some poets have started to see death as tragic inevitability, he writes, instead of finding the 'proper' romantic side of death in the course of duty. The ending of Surkov's poem 'Zvenit pod lyzhami stekliannyi nast...' (The glassy crust of ice rings beneath the skis...) is quoted by Danin as an example of the correct attitude towards death:

...Есть высшее из всех гражданских прав:
Во имя жизни встретить ветер боя
И, если надо, смертью смерть поправ,
Найти в огне бессмертие героя.[72]

(The highest of all citizen's rights is this: in the name of life to meet the wind of battle and, if need be, having defeated death by death, to find in fire the hero's immortality.)

This romantic view of death in battle was not shared by one of the young poets who went to the front as volunteers. The younger generation had originally embraced the Finnish war as the beginning of their battle against fascism. Pavel Kogan went to the front, despite his poor eyesight, announcing, in an echo of Maiakovskii's 'My revolution', 'It's my war'.[73] Experience gradually brought the realisation that the Finns had not, after all, been waiting to be delivered from the evils of capitalism; there were doubts about the justice of such a war. Instead of indulging in sweeping generalisations about the nature and purpose of the war, young poets wrote of more immediate and prosaic concerns. Sergei Narovchatov's poems are made up of details which form a grim picture of days on end without sleep, corpses used to build protective barricades, bandages being valued as much as bullets. The irony in his laconic poetry is akin to that of Sassoon. In 'My sukhari ugriumo dozhevali...' (We grimly chewed up the dry bread...), letters from home promising the soldiers a speedy return are used for rolling cigarettes. Corpses built up as barricades are said to be serving despite death, and this thought reconciles the poet to his own death:

За ними укрываясь от огня,
Я думал о конце без лишней грусти:
Мол, сделают ребята из меня
Вполне надежный для упора бруствер.[74]

(Taking cover from fire behind them, I thought of the end without unnecessary sadness: The lads will make me into a thoroughly sound parapet to rest their weapons on.)

Aron Kopshtein describes how the experience of war altered the horizons of his friends and fellow students from the Literary Institute in Moscow. If there was any romance in war, it was in the survival of poetry, the works of Pasternak, Pushkin, and Blok recited at the front:

...Да, каждый стал расчетливым и горьким:
Встречаемся мы редко, второпях,
И спорим о портянках и махорке,
Как прежде о лирических стихах.
Но дружбы, может быть, другой не надо,
Чем эта, возникавшая в пургу,
Когда усталый Николай Отрада
Читал мне Пастернака на бегу.[75]

(Yes, each one has become careful and bitter, we meet rarely, hurriedly and argue over foot-cloths and tobacco as we used to about lyric poems. But perhaps there is no need for any other friendship than this, formed in a blizzard, when the exhausted Nikolai Otrada recited Pasternak to me as we ran.)

Narovchatov dismisses the conventionally literary, romantic picture of war with contempt:

Лгущая красивыми строками!
Мы весь ворох пестрого тряпья
Твоего, романтика, штыками
Отшвырнули напрочь от себя.[76]

(Lying in pretty lines! The whole jumble of colourful rags of yours, romance, we chucked away with our bayonets.)

Mikhail Dudin too was angered by the false depiction of war by an artist whose picture of an enemy sniper, clearly visible to approaching soldiers, was nothing like the reality he encountered in Finland.[77]

As in the case of Afghanistan forty years later, an awkward silence settled on the subject. In 1940 Ol'ga Berggol'ts wrote two poems, only published in 1988, about the unnatural silence after victory, and strangely muted celebrations:

...Откуда же молчанье на пире?
И чаши с вином не стучат,
И струны безмолвны на лире,
И гости, потупясь, молчат.[78]

(Why is there silence at the feast? And the goblets of wine do not clink, and the strings of the lyre are still, and the guests, lowering their eyes, say nothing.)

The silence of the battlefield was, for Berggol'ts, the unspoken and dreadful truth about the suffering and loss of life which had taken place there:

О друг, я не думала, что тишина
Страшнее всего, что оставит война.

Так тихо, так тихо, что мысль о войне
Как вопль, как рыдание в тишине.

Здесь люди, рыча, извиваясь, ползли,
Здесь пенилась кровь на вершок от земли...
Здесь тихо, так тихо, что мнится—вовек
Сюда не придет ни один человек...

Так тихо, так немо—не смерть и не жизнь.
О, это суровее всех укоризн.
Не смерть и не жизнь—немота, немота—
Отчаяние, стиснувшее уста.

Безмерно живущему мертвые мстят:
Все знают, все помнят, а сами молчат.[79]

(O my friend, I didn't think that silence was the most terrible thing that war would leave behind. It is so quiet, so quiet that the thought of war is like a wail, like sobbing in the darkness. Here people, snarling, writhing, crawled, here blood foamed an inch deep on the ground. Here it's quiet, so quiet that it seems—never again will anyone come here ... It is so quiet, so mute—neither life nor death. O, this is more severe than any reproach. Neither life nor death—muteness, muteness—despair which constricts the lips. The dead take their measureless revenge on the living: they know everything, remember everything, but are themselves silent.)

The silences associated with the subject of the war in Finland added a new and awkward resonance to the theme of war, which, up till then, had played the role of an uncontroversial, mainstream theme in Soviet poetry. Now war, or at least one particular war, had become one of the subjects not to be mentioned, along with the purges of the 1930s. In many poems about Finland, unpublished, naturally, at the time, war was presented without the qualifying adjectives 'imperialist' or 'revolutionary', war as such, destructive, ultimately pointless.

In Soviet literature war, maybe, had been a popular theme, but *the* war which began in September 1939 received little official attention. When Germany, the new ally of the Soviet Union, invaded

Poland, Soviet troops marched west to 'liberate', under the provision of secret protocols of the Non-Aggression pact, what they termed the Western Ukraine and Western Belorussia. There were few Polish troops available to oppose this second invasion. In the work of Soviet poets this invasion is presented as a liberation from the tyranny of Polish landowners; Soviet troops are greeted by a grateful population.[80]

From her position outside official literary circles, Anna Akhmatova watched the events of 1940 with foreboding. It was a time when:

> ... только могильщики лихо
> Работают. Дело не ждет!
> (Only grave-diggers work fervidly. No time to waste!)

She wrote of the London blitz as Shakespeare's twenty-fourth drama, written by time's 'dispassionate hand'.[81] Il'ia Erenburg was a witness of the fall of Paris, which he perceived as the death of the city.[82] In the official press, however, France and England were now seen as aggressors. Nikolai Aseev wrote of London financiers getting their just come-uppance in the blitz.[83] The invasion of 22 June 1941 forced a rapid adjustment of values; Germany was an enemy once more, and the reality of war, for so long masked by propaganda, was engulfing Belorussia and the Ukraine.

During the years between the October Revolution and the Nazi invasion, Soviet war poetry had developed its own traditions, rooted in the experience and the depiction of the civil war. By the end of the 1930s this tradition was being challenged by a younger generation of poets who tended towards a more personal portrayal of war, based on their own experiences. The civil war veterans favoured a depiction of war which emphasised its heroic aspects; they wrote little about their private experience, and instead created images which were coloured by their understanding of the civil war's political and ideological meaning. The younger generation was far from being apolitical, but they were more likely to create a sense of immediacy in their poetry, less likely to concentrate on exceptional heroism, more on everyday matters, such as friendship between soldiers. Their portrayal of war was often more realistic than their elders', even when being realistic meant including aspects which were rather less than positive. In the immediate pre-war years, however, published Soviet poetry on the war theme was dominated by the established writers. The divide between the generations emerged with force during the Second World War, and fuelled post-war literary debates.

NOTES

1 See E. Dobrenko, '"Stoi! Kto idet?" U istokov sovetskogo manikheistva', *Znamia*, 3 (1993), 180–189.

2 Though nineteenth century poems such as Batiushkov's 'K Dashkovu', *Sochineniia*, 2 vols (Moscow, 1989), I, 190–191, and Lermontov's 'Ia k vam pishu sluchaino,—pravo, ...' *Polnoe sobranie stikhotvorenii*, 2 vols (Leningrad, 1989), II, 56, had given vivid accounts of the horrors of war. Lermontov's 'Borodino', ibid., II, 9–13 and Pushkin's 'Poltava', *Sobranie sochinenii v odnom tome* (Moscow, 1984), pp. 187–200, are also influential examples of nineteenth century poetry on the war theme.

3 See Rupert Brooke, 'Peace', in *The Poems of Rupert Brooke* (London, 1987), p. 129.

4 Nikolai Gumilev, 'Nastuplenie', *Stikhotvoreniia i poemy* (Leningrad, 1988), pp. 234–235. For similar poems, see Fedor Sologub, 'Na podvig', *Voina v russkoi poezii*, edited by Anastasiia Chebotarevskaia (Petrograd, 1915), pp. 67–68; 'Obstrelian', ibid., pp. 68–69.

5 Konstantin Bal'mont, 'Prazdnik krovi', *Voina v russkoi poezii*, p. 79; Nikolai Gumilev, 'Voina', *Stikhotvoreniia i poemy*, pp. 213–214

6 See, for example, Marina Tsvetaeva, 'Ia znaiu pravdu! Vse prezhnie pravdy—proch'!', *Stikhotvoreniia i poemy*, 5 vols (New York, 1980-90), I, 194; Tsvetaeva's pro-German feelings are voiced in 'Germanii', I, 175. Maximilian Voloshin, 'Posev', *Izbrannye stikhotvoreniia* (Moscow, 1988), p. 133, also 'V eti dni', p. 134; 'Reimskaia bogomater'', pp. 135–136; 'Rossiia', pp. 142–143.

7 Anna Akhmatova's wartime poems include 'Iul' 1914', *Sochineniia*, 2 vols (Moscow, 1986), I, 100; 'Tot golos, s tishinoi velikoi sporia ...', I, 101; 'Uteshenie', I, 101–102; 'Molitva', I, 102, 'Pamiati 19 iulia 1914', I, 109–110. See also Aleksandr Blok, 'Petrogradskoe nebo mutilos' dozhdem ...', *Sobranie sochinenii*, 6 vols (Leningrad, 1980-83), II, 238; 'Korshun', II, 249.

8 Igor Severianin, 'Poeza vozmushcheniia', *Wictoria regia* (Moscow, 1915), p. 94; 'Poeza k Evrope', ibid., p. 96; 'Poeza o gunnakh', ibid., p. 99; 'Eshche ne znachit', ibid., 105–106; 'Moi otvet', ibid., p. 107; Konstantin Bal'mont, 'Voina–ne vrazhda', *Voina v russkoi poezii*, p. 77.

9 See 'Voina v myshelovke', *Tvoreniia* (Moscow, 1986), pp. 455–465.

10 See *Sobranie sochinenii*, 13 vols (Moscow, 1955-61), I, 302–332, 349–351.

11 'Voina i mir', *Sobranie sochinenii*, I, 211–242; 'K otvetu', I, 143–144. For a discussion of Khlebnikov and Maiakovskii's treatment of the theme of war and violence, see K. Hodgson, 'Myth-making in Russian War Poetry', in *The Violent Muse: Violence and the Artistic Imagination in Europe, 1910–1949*, edited by Jana Howlett and Rod Mengham (Manchester, 1994), pp. 65–76.

12 Sasha Chernyi, 'V operatsionnoi', *Stikhotvoreniia* (Leningrad, 1960), pp. 369–370; 'Sbornyi punkt', p. 366; 'Repetitsiia', pp. 367–368; 'Prival', pp. 368–369.

13 'Dvenadtsat'', *Sobranie sochinenii*, II, 313–324.

14 'Lebedinyi stan', II, 59–91.

15 'Manifest barona fon Vrangelia', *Sobranie sochinenii*, 8 vols (Moscow, 1963–65), III, 100–101. Dem'ian Bednyi is the pseudonym used by Efim Pridvorov (1883–1945).

16 'Levyi marsh', *Sobranie sochinenii*, II, 23–24. For a discussion of Russian avant-garde literature of the civil war, see Jana Howlett, 'Death, war, revolution: the literature of the Russian Civil War', *The Violent Muse*, pp. 88–99. 'Pesnia riazanskogo muzhika', III, 7–8; 'Ballada ob odnom korole ...', III, 26–27. Some of

Maiakovskii's World War One anti-German verses were published during World War Two, under the heading 'Satiricheskie stikhi 1914 goda', *Zvezda*, 3–4 (1942), 153–154.

17 III, 16–17.

18 *Antologiia russkoi sovetskoi poezii*, edited by V. A. Lugovskoi, V. O. Pertsov, A. A. Surkov, N. S. Tikhonov, 2 vols (Moscow, 1957), I, 163.

19 '150,000,000', II, 115–164.

20 See Tikhonov's cycle 'Zhizn' pod zvezdami', *Sobranie sochinenii*, 7 vols (Moscow, 1973–76), I, 61–77.

21 'Ballada o gvozdiakh', I, 117. The poem refers to officers, a captain and an admiral, perhaps rather surprisingly, as it is generally taken to deal with the Red Fleet, which had abolished the tsarist ranks. 'Ballada o sinem pakete', I, 119–120.

22 Efim Etkind, *Russische Lyrik von der Oktoberrevolution bis zur Gegenwart: Versuch einer Darstellung* (Munich, 1984), p. 81.

23 *Sobranie sochinenii*, 3 vols (Moscow, 1974–75), I, 152–158; I, 96.

24 'Bravshim kist'iu', I, 309. The verb 'pisat'' also means 'to write', and this advice was quoted by Soviet critics to writers in wartime.

25 *Pervyi vsesoiuznyi s"ezd sovetskikh pisatelei: stenograficheskii otchet*, facsimile reprint of 1934 Moscow edition (Moscow, 1990), speech by N.Tikhonov, p. 505 (future references to *Pervyi s"ezd*).

26 'Razgovor po dusham', *Stikhotvoreniia i poemy* (Leningrad, 1986), p. 105.

27 'O beschelovechii', *Sobranie sochinenii*, 30 vols (Moscow, 1949–55), XXV, 48–49.

28 'K rabochemu', *Izbrannoe* (Moscow, 1975), p. 111.

29 *Sbornik stikhov* (Moscow, 1943) pp. 324–326.

30 For example, 'Rasskaz moego tovarishcha', *Stikhotvoreniia i poemy* (Moscow–Leningrad, 1966), pp. 121–124; 'Rasskaz konnoarmeitsa', pp. 148–150.

31 'Voina', p. 101.

32 'Prodolzhenie zhizni', p. 153.

33 For information on LOKAF, see *Ocherki istorii russkoi sovetskoi zhurnalistiki*, edited by A. G. Dement'ev, 2 vols (Moscow, 1966, 1968), II, 340–362; L. A. Zamanskii, 'Tema zashchity Rodiny v russkoi sovetskoi poezii 30-kh godov', *Pobeda i mir: sbornik nauchnykh trudov*, edited by A. N. Iezuitov, A. I. Pavlovskii, V. A. Shoshin (Leningrad, 1987), 5–36 (pp. 10–13).

34 See E.Dobrenko, '"Stoi! Kto idet?": u istokov sovetskogo manikheistva', *Znamia*, 3 (1993), p. 80.

35 *Zemlia ovetskaia*, 6 (1931), p. 133.

36 *Literatura i voina: sbornik kriticheskikh statei* (Leningrad, 1932).

37 *Pervyi s"ezd*, speech by N. Tikhonov, p. 510.

38 Ibid., speech by A. Surkov, p. 515.

39 Ibid., speech by S. Kirsanov, p. 524.

40 See, for example, 'Marsh veselykh rebiat', *Izbrannoe* (Moscow, 1984), p. 251.

41 Mikhail Isakovskii, 'V lesnom poselke', *Sobranie sochinenii*, 5 vols (Moscow, 1981–82), I, 244–245. It must be said that during the 1930s many Soviet citizens, women included, received some kind of military training, and that when war did break out there were vast numbers of young girls who volunteered for front-line service. See John Erickson, 'Soviet Women at War' in *World War Two and the Soviet People*, edited by John and Carol Garrard (London, 1993), p. 60.

42 'Skazanie o geroe ...', *Stikhotvoreniia i poemy*, pp. 208–209. 'Partizan Zhelezniak', *Antologiia russkoi sovetskoi poezii*, 2 vols (Moscow, 1957), I, 389; 'Pesnia o Shchorse', ibid., I, 388.

43 'O dvizhenii nashei literatury', *Stat'i, dnevniki, pis'ma* (Moscow, 1961), pp. 198–203 (p. 201).

44 A. Prokof'ev, 'Slovo o polku Igoreve', pp. 197–200. A. Nedogonov, 'Predchuvstvie', *Izbrannoe* (Moscow, 1958), pp. 43–44. V. Zanadvorov, 'Shchit', *Do poslednego dykhaniia: stikhi sovetskikh poetov, pavshikh na Velikoi Otechestvennoi voine* (Moscow, 1985), p. 123.

45 'Stikhi o neizvestnom soldate', *Sochinenia*, 2 vols (Moscow, 1990), I, 245.

46 Ibid., II, 562–563.

47 Vsevolod Loboda, 'Dolg', *Do poslednego dykhaniia*, p. 217.

48 'Pis'mo', ibid., p. 166.

49 Ibid., p. 230.

50 See A. G. Kogan, *Stikhi i sud'by: frontovaia tema v sovetskoi poezii* (Moscow, 1977), pp. 46–48.

51 Svetlana Aleksievich, 'Zacharovannye smert'iu, *Druzhba narodov*, 4 (1993), p. 17.

52 See the words of Beta Kaminskaia quoted by Barbara Alpern Engel, *Mothers and Daughters: Women of the Intelligentsia in Nineteenth Century Russia* (Cambridge, 1983), p. 142

53 See note 48 above.

54 'Bessmertie', *Do poslednego dykhaniia*, p. 200.

55 'A esli skazhet nam voina: pora...', ibid., p. 281.

56 'Ia segodnia ves' vecher budu ...', ibid.

57 *Sovetskie poety, pavshie na Velikoi Otechestvennoi voine* (Moscow–Leningrad, 1965), p. 506.

58 'Nam lech', gde lech'...', *Do poslednego dykhaniia*, p. 167.

59 Katerina Clark, *The Soviet Novel: History as Ritual*, 2nd ed. (Chicago–London, 1985). The topic of death and resurrection will be discussed in Chapter Three.

60 *Literaturnaia Gazeta*, 10 April 1938, p. 2.

61 'Ezh', VII, 121–122.

62 *Sobranie sochinenii*, 4 vols (Moscow, 1974–76), III, 181.

63 'Ledovoe poboishche', *Sobranie sochinenii*, 12 vols (Moscow, 1979–87), I, 379–381; 'Suvorov', I, 382–410; 'Rasskaz o spriatannom oruzhie', I, 39–42; 'Izgnannik', I, 55–56.

64 'V kastil'skoi nishchenskoi zemle ...', *Stikhotvoreniia* (Moscow, 1982), pp. 51–52.

65 I, 78–79.

66 S. I. Ozhegov, *Slovar' russkogo iazyka* (Moscow, 1978).

67 'Orly', I, 70.

68 I, 472.

69 'Voennaia lirika sorokovogo goda', *Krasnaia nov'*, 5 (1941), 189–204 (p. 190).

70 'Tankisty', I, 422–424.

71 D. Danin, 'Voennaia lirika sorokovogo goda', 195–196.

72 *Sobranie sochinenii*, 4 vols (Moscow, 1965–66), I, 268. The phrase 'having defeated death by death' has strong biblical associations, being commonly used to refer to the Crucifixion.

73 Quoted by the critic A. G. Kogan, a contemporary, though not a relative, during an interview in Moscow, December 1989. There are echoes of Maiakovskii's 'Moia revoliutsiia', from 'Ia sam', his autobiographical work of 1928, I, 25.

74 'My sukhari ugriumo dozhevali ...', *Stikhotvoreniia i poemy* (Leningrad, 1985), p. 61; 'Zdes' mertvye stenoiu za zhivykh ...', p. 62.

75 'Poety', *Do poslednego dykhaniia*, p. 173.

76 'Lgushchaia krasivymi strokami! ...', ibid., p. 63.

77 '"Kukushka"', *Sobranie sochinenii*, 4 vols (Moscow, 1987–88), I, 26–27.

78 'Pochemu takoe molchanie?..', *Sobranie sochinenii*, 3 vols, (Leningrad, 1988–90), I, 197.

79 'O drug, ia ne dumala, chto tishina ...', I, 197–198. See also Aleksandr Tvardovskii, 'Velika strana rodnaia ...', *Izbrannye proizvedeniia*, 3 vols (Moscow, 1990), I, 214.

80 For example, Mikhail Matusovskii, 'Iz zapadno-belorusskikh stikhov', *Znamia*, 6 (1941), p. 144.

81 'Kogda pogrebaiut epokhu ...', *Sochineniia*, I, 195; 'Londontsam', I, 196.

82 'Parizh, 1940', pp. 74–78.

83 'Nad pasmurnym Londonom', *Novyi mir*, 9 (1940), p. 9.

CHAPTER TWO

Soviet Poetry 1941–45: A Chronological Survey

There is, it could be argued, a good deal more variety in Soviet war poetry than in British poetry written at the same time. Co-existing within the Soviet poetry are solidly Stalinist propaganda pieces, bitter reflections on the selfishness of government officials and grimly realistic evocations of the battlefield. Over time, the versions of 'Soviet war poetry' presented by scholars in the USSR have differed according to political circumstances. After Khrushchev's 1956 Secret Speech denouncing Stalin's crimes, wartime poems which portrayed Stalin vanished from the canon. Some poems printed during the war which expressed hatred of the enemy in particularly forceful terms have either been altered or excluded from later publications.[1] There have been many additions to the canon as a result of relaxations in censorship; the 'privileged' status of the war theme probably accelerated this process. Other works simply remained undiscovered for a time, for example poems found on the sites of former German concentration camps.[2] *Glasnost'* made it possible to publish poems which gave a completely unvarnished picture of battle, as well as work which introduced the subject of Soviet labour camps, political repression and the abuse of privilege in wartime.[3] Apart from written sources, the war produced a good deal of oral verse and song, some of which has been collected, but much of which has probably remained unrecorded.[4]

Although it is now possible to discuss the broad range of wartime literary output, political circumstances in the former Soviet Union have meant that the literature of the Second World War, which was once a staple for uncontroversial research, has been largely dismissed as a relic of the discredited past. The new range of material now available has yet to be used to augment existing studies. The words of the critic Aleksei Pavlovskii, writing in 1967, have not yet lost their relevance:

> The history of this most interesting period in our literature is

> limited to a few names and a few generally accepted titles which, to judge by the most recent works, seem unlikely to be expanded. Meanwhile the real evolution of Soviet wartime poetry, its swift but arduous progress cannot be properly explained without consideration of many and various factors which contributed to literary development, in particular the development of poetry.[5]

By drawing on material from wartime journals as well as poetry not published for many years after it was written, I have attempted to break down the rather monolithic image of Russian Soviet war poetry which has dominated critical discussion and to provide a sense of the range and development of poetry written in wartime. By considering the poetry in a chronological framework, I hope to show some of the forces which precipitated changes in the way poets wrote, with particular reference to the historical and literary-political context.

Setting out the case for a chronological examination of Soviet war poetry, Pavlovskii wrote:

> Sudden changes in the fortunes of war usually affected poets' work directly and at once in ways which were immediately obvious; in the course of a few days, events could create a perceptibly different intonation in poetry, and even call into literary existence images and themes which had been absent only days before.[6]

On the most obvious level, poets responded to the course of events, so that much of the poetry written during the war can in fact be read as a chronicle. Much of their work was produced for newspapers and journals, so poets learned to produce poems at high speed on relevant topics. In peacetime too, poets had been expected to write to order, but in wartime there was constant demand and very little time. Circumstances meant that poetry was often more involved in immediate reactions than in analysis, particularly in the early stages of the war. However, there is more to Soviet war poetry than a verse account of current events. It also charts, in parallel to the war's progress, the changes which occurred within people at war. In November 1944 Aleksei Surkov commented that the poems of the war fuse together to form a lyrical diary.[7] This diary traces the effect of war on the individual, the changes brought about by new circumstances and experiences, and the development of a new set of values. While poems marking significant events in the war tended to be superficial and standardised, those about the experiences of the individual at war often dealt with topics which might seem to be less immediately significant, but which raised questions such as individual suffering and responsibility which were difficult to raise in a more formal setting. This did not mean that events of national significance did not produce poetry which dealt with personal reactions to war. The siege of Leningrad and the battle for Stalingrad were both of tremendous symbolic importance as evidence of the Soviet people's heroism, but poets also showed the exceptional qualities, and suffering, of individuals fighting for physical and moral survival.

Broadly speaking, Pavlovskii traces the relationship between historical events and questions of genre. In his view, initial reactions to the outbreak of war, in the form of patriotic appeals and declarations, were followed by a tendency towards a documentary approach reporting on details of life at the front and on examples of real-life heroism. Poetry of 1941 was more concerned with immediate events than with wide-ranging analysis. Towards the end of 1941, lyric poetry became more prominent as poets began to focus on the feelings of the individual at war. The defeat of the German armies near Moscow that December brought the first taste of victory and new confidence. The summer of 1942, with renewed German advances, was marked by a return to the appeals, orders and declarations of the war's early phase. From the autumn of 1942 there was a tendency to approach the war theme on a larger scale, introducing historical and philosophical reflection. In 1943 the epic gained prominence, accompanied by an enhanced sense of history and the wish to sum up the meaning of the war on a universal, rather than local or personal, scale. Poetry written during 1944 and 1945, as the Soviet army advanced to Berlin concentrated on the theme of Russia's historic mission to liberate Europe, but due to the speed of the advance it was often rather superficial. Victory in Berlin was celebrated in oratorical poetry.

This outline gives a clear idea of how events at the beginning of the war acted as a catalyst for poetic development; it is less clear on the reasons behind the rise of epic forms from 1943 onwards, and shows a recurring lack of detail and focus regarding poetry written in the last two years of the war. Absent from the chain of cause and effect are, naturally, the workings of official literary controls. However, the contrast of Pavlovskii's occasionally sketchy treatment of the later poetry with his precise, detailed account of reactions to the invasion of 1941 may suggest to the reader the presence of unspoken questions. The way in which the state regulated writers and their work is, of course, one important factor which could not for many years be taken into account by mainstream Russian scholarship.[8] The system of control established in the 1930s prescribed a writer's theme and style; departures from the norm could be punished by fierce public attacks and the humiliating rituals of self-criticism. This went on under the aegis of the official literary method of socialist realism. A strict censorship scrutinised literary works for hints of political unorthodoxy. In wartime, the mechanisms of literary control did exercise a perceptible influence on what was actually published, although the system worked more effectively in Moscow than in the periphery and at the front. The Central Committee propaganda department, source of political and doctrinal orthodoxy, headed by G. F. Aleksandrov, was, for example, likely to block the publication, in book form, of work which had already appeared in army newspapers.[9]

While the apparatus of control continued to exist, however, there were clear indications that the expedient goals of winning the war meant that writers were temporarily allowed greater freedom to approach themes which had been marginalised before the war, such as the importance of private, individual concerns, particularly if these were integrated with the theme of Russian patriotism which had been officially encouraged since the mid-1930s. Paradoxically, while industrial workers were subject to draconian military discipline, the drive for total mobilisation produced a relaxation of prescriptive literary controls. This relaxation probably owed a good deal to the chaos of the war's early months, but it seems fair to detect a certain pragmatism in permitting poets to write on Russia, its landscape and history, of a soldier's bonds with his home and family, as these were more likely to evoke patriotic responses than talk of communist ideals in a population which had suffered under an authoritarian state. While the war was indeed a war of liberation from Nazi occupation, it was also fought by many with the hope of gaining freedom from home-grown oppression.

Once released from excessive interference from above, literature, and particularly poetry, developed rapidly, making the war years a fertile and productive stage in the growth of Soviet literature as a whole. Nevertheless, it would be an exaggeration to suggest that what happened was even comparable to the post-Stalin Thaw. The 'inner editor', the writer's own sense of what was officially permissible, continued to function as external literary controls relaxed. However, officially-sanctioned neglect of ideology allowed poets to be guided instead by their personal reactions to events.[10] Significantly, by the end of 1943, once the war had turned against the Germans and the Soviet state began to re-establish its authority, now as a major world power, critics again emphasised the need for the correct ideological content in literature. Lyrical and realistic trends were once more condemned, as they were felt to lack the epic breadth and grandeur appropriate to the supreme subject of Soviet victory over fascism. The change in mood is apparent in a number of critical articles written from 1943 onwards, but recent publications have offered some insight into the workings of the Party officials who set this process of stricter controls in motion.[11]

Before embarking on the main subject of this chapter, the chronological survey of wartime poetry, I shall enumerate the *dramatis personae*, the range of poets whose work is to be considered. The poets who were active, though not necessarily published, during the war years occupied a variety of positions within the Soviet literary establishment, or even outside it. Many of those on the edge of the 'new society' found that the war gave them a chance to return to the public arena, though the blameless patriotic sentiments of poets such as Boris Ruch'ev, then a prisoner in the camps, could only become known considerably later.[12] Some of the 'outsiders' were already established poets in 1917. Anna Akhmatova, after years of persecution and silence, returned to the literary scene with patriotic lyrics which were given a warm official welcome and published in *Pravda*.[13] Boris Pasternak, who had been forced to translate poetry from 1936 onwards, was allowed to publish two volumes of his own work during the war. Together with some poetry directly related to the war, which gained an ambivalent critical reception, Pasternak wrote on nature themes, on the changing seasons.[14] Most definitely on the margins of the literary scene was the young poet Nikolai Glazkov, whose unconventional works circulated among his friends and were 'published' by the author in home-made books or simply circulated in his letters.

Since 1917, Soviet writers had been classified according to their political allegiance, or lack of it. When the Soviet Union was threatened by a powerful enemy, ideological divisions temporarily lost their importance; even emigres like the writer Ivan Bunin felt committed to supporting a Soviet victory. The most striking division that emerged was not strictly along lines of political orthodoxy, although it did gain political overtones towards the end of the war. This was the divide between two 'war generations', each with its own way of writing about war. Older poets such as Nikolai Tikhonov, Iosif Utkin, Mikhail Svetlov, Aleksei Surkov and Aleksandr Prokof'ev had fought in and written about the civil war and, on the whole, wrote about the Second World War in similarly romantic and heroic terms. Those who were born around 1915 or later, among whom number Semen Gudzenko, Sergei Narovchatov, Mikhail Lukonin and Sergei Orlov, presented a more realistic picture of war which emphasised personal experience. While established poets largely adhered to the formulaic representation of events associated with the method of socialist realism, their aspiring successors recorded their immediate impressions with unprecedented directness and intensity.

Up till 1941, or, for those involved in the Finnish war, 1939, war had been for the younger generation a purely literary and romantic concept. When confronted with the reality of war, the young poets made every effort to avoid giving a 'literary' impression, and described a war in which blood and mud played a considerable role, as well as the sheer hard work of digging trenches and marching long distances. These realistic details did not, however, negate their search for meaning. It was a heightened reality rather than a higher reality that they described, which reflected the intensity of their experience and went hand in hand with a private, elevated vision of their generation as men of destiny on whom the future of the country depended. As Lev Anninskii noted in 1974: '... as the details became more realistic and coarse, so the symbolism concealed within them grew more powerful; war pinned their verses down on the ground, concentrating in them to the highest degree a thirst for the sky, a thirst for meaning'.[15] Few contemporary critics recognised that the younger generation had in fact retained the romantic attitudes found in civil war poetry, preferring instead to praise their honest realism, or, later in the war, to condemn their approach as 'naturalistic'. The romance of war perceived by these young writers, and encapsulated in the words of a young critic Mikhail Molochko, killed in the Finnish war, 'Romance is the future war that we are going to win', persisted in spite of grim realities.[16] Their work reveals the war as a major formative experience, and has a common theme of self-discovery, growing maturity and independence of outlook.

It is the work of the younger generation which has increasingly become the focus of critical attention, while the work of the older generation, often showing clear distinguishing marks of its origin in Stalinist culture, has been set aside. In an article marking the fortieth anniversary of the end of the war, Viktor Kochetkov emphasised poetry's resistance to grandiose language in describing a war which was heroic in a modest and unspectacular way: 'The routine nature of the war inevitably repelled any words of pathos or exclamation. War demanded language which was laconic, severe, restrained and exact.'[17] It is indicative that Kochetkov's article refers only to the work of the younger generation, a generation whose achievement was regarded with unambiguous pride throughout the Soviet era.[18] The generation that found a poetic voice in wartime was given a special place in the Soviet literary pantheon. Many anthologies have been devoted to the poetry of the young men who died at war, transplanting them, in a way, from what became the discredited context of the Stalin era. Their death in combat is implicitly an act of atonement, absolving them of guilt by association with their times. And yet at the end of the war, survivors from this generation, many of whom were later represented as pillars of the establishment, were regarded with suspicion and encouraged to seek new themes, or be silent.[19]

The older and younger generations' attitudes were influenced respectively by loyalty to the state they had helped to create, and by the intense impact of the war. Between these two generations were poets born around 1910. Events had not helped to provide them with a simple clarity of outlook. Their youth coincided with the public enthusiasm for the Five Year Plans and the collectivisation of agriculture, but they had also witnessed the state's coercive methods of bringing about socialism. In the most significant poets of this generation circumstances produced a tragic conflict between loyalty to the state and personal experience. Such tensions are rarely on view, however, in the work of Konstantin Simonov who, having made a successful literary debut before the war with narrative poems dedicated to the Soviet author and hero-figure Nikolai Ostrovskii and the Russian general Suvorov, progressed rapidly through the echelons of the literary hierarchy. Drawing on his experiences of war in Mongolia, Simonov focused increasingly on the concerns of the ordinary fighting man, and helped to re-launch lyric poetry as an acceptable genre in Soviet literature. His popularity with wartime readers testifies to the fact that his poems corresponded to overwhelming and previously unsatisfied public demand. Simonov was not without personal experience of the cataclysms in Soviet society before the war, as his step-father, a professional solder, had been imprisoned for some months in 1931, and other relatives were arrested in 1935. Aleksandr Tvardovskii, author of the extremely popular *Vasilii Terkin*, had seen his father denounced as a kulak and deported from his home village, and yet his convictions led him to write a long poem in celebration of the collectivisation of agriculture.[20] Ol'ga Berggol'ts wrote of her faith in victory while close to death in blockaded Leningrad, and throughout the war demonstrated her strong patriotic feeling. She had been arrested and imprisoned for several months in 1938, but wrote that the war had taken away her sense of hurt and injustice.[21] Both Tvardovskii and Berggol'ts produced some of their finest work during the war, and were popular with their readers. They showed a strong awareness of the tragedy which war brought to individuals, but wrote with determination about victory even in the bleakest days of the war.

The majority, although not all of the poets who wrote about the war did so from first-hand experience either as front-line soldiers, or from visits to the front as war correspondents. Leningrad poets who remained in the city during the siege are, as I have mentioned, a special case, as it lay on the front line where differences between soldier or civilian had little real meaning. The elderly and infirm were evacuated from Moscow and Leningrad as those cities became increasingly threatened by the German advance, and those writers had to rely on what they read in the newspapers to furnish them with material. Together with many others, Pasternak was sent to Chistopol' in 1941, returning to Moscow the following year. Akhmatova spent much of the war in Tashkent, worlds away from the Petersburg/Leningrad which had figured in so much of her work. Marina Tsvetaeva, who returned from emigration in 1939, was evacuated from Moscow on 8 August 1941, and took her own life in Elabuga on 31 August.[22] Many of those who were rejected as unfit for military service saw their writing as their contribution to the war effort; others managed to get accepted as war correspondents, despite poor health. From numerous wartime critical articles it seems clear that poetry was valued for its authenticity if its author had been at the front, although later in the war 'historical perspective', in other words, a correct political portrayal of the Soviet victors, was in demand. Front-line authenticity became a badge of the younger generation, most of whom began the war as soldiers. Later a number of them were transferred to work on front-line newspapers, often after wounds sustained in battle had made them unfit to fight. Those who worked for army newspapers had to supply poems on a given theme to order, and editors did not always look kindly on poets who wrote their 'own' work off duty. The young poet Mikhail Lukonin was told by his editor: 'You have no right to steal editorial time!'[23] Many established poets worked as war correspondents, and divided their time between working in Moscow, keeping the literary organisations running, and visiting soldiers in the front line to give readings of their own poetry and gather material. Some kept to their roles as visitors, while others fought alongside soldiers when occasion demanded.

From the Invasion of June 1941 to the Defence of Moscow

The German invasion of 22 June 1941 was seen as an act of treachery by a former ally. The question of whether such an alliance should have been concluded in the first place was not raised. The headline on the front page of *Krasnaia zvezda* two days later is representative of contemporary rhetoric:

> The bloodthirsty fascist bandits have attacked the Soviet Union. The Red Army and the Soviet people, united with the Party, government and great Stalin, have risen up to fight a Fatherland war for their country, for honour and for freedom.[24]

Poetry written immediately war broke out was founded on two central beliefs: that the war was a major event in Russian history, equal in status to the war against Napoleon, and that victory was certain. Most famous among the early war poems is 'Sviashchennaia voina' (The Holy War) published in *Izvestiia* on June 24 and set to music the following day. The style and sentiments of 'Sviashchennaia voina' are echoed in many other poems written at about the same time. Its combination of appeals and pledges evidently reflected the mood of the time, and the song became instantly popular:

Вставай, страна огромная,
Вставай на смертный бой!
С фашистской силой темною,
С проклятою ордой.

Пусть ярость благородная
Вскипает, как волна,—
Идет война народная,
Священная война![25]

(Rise up, vast land, rise up for a fight to the death! Against the dark forces of fascism, against the accursed horde. May noble fervour swell like a wave,—this is a people's war, a holy war!)

'Sviashchennaia voina' has been given pride of place in the official canon of Soviet war poetry, and has long been attributed to the popular and ideologically correct poet Vasilii Lebedev-Kumach, author of numerous 'mass songs' of the 1930s, including the famous 'Pesnia o Rodine' (Song of the Motherland) of 1935 which celebrated the country's freedom and happiness. A letter published in *Argumenty i fakty* in early 1991 claims, however, that 'Sviashchennaia voina' was written not in 1941, but in 1916, by a schoolteacher who sent it to Lebedev-Kumach in 1938, expecting some comments on the poem's literary merit.[26] The established figurehead of Soviet war poetry is thus revealed, perhaps, as the product of Tsarist Russia, slightly adapted to suit its new context. If 'Sviashchennaia voina' really was written in 1916, it is interesting to note that its sentiments and choice of words, comparable with other poems of the First World War, did not look out of place in the Second, even if the term 'holy war' was a little unexpected in an atheist state. In actual fact ecclesiastical terminology was not out of place in Stalinist culture; it emerged more explicitly in wartime, when greater official tolerance of the Orthodox Church was introduced.

While the origin of Lebedev-Kumach's contribution to early war poetry has been set in doubt, it is clear from contemporary literary journals and newspapers that poets reacted with great speed to a war which was, officially, unexpected. The war theme was, as we have seen, a significant element in the pre-war poetic repertoire, and a German attack had been expected from the early 1930s, even if attention had been directed elsewhere after the signing of the Nazi-Soviet pact. Most poetry published early in the war relies largely on simple formulae and is highly repetitive, showing a certain amount of inertia in portrayals of war as a brief, undemanding prelude to victory. It could be argued that this complacent approach had been fostered by LOKAF and its successor, the Defence Committee of the Writers' Union.[27] By contrast, poems written in the early months of the war but not published until later were more realistic, often bleak in their assessment of the situation.

But even during the first few months of the war there were signs that published poetry was changing. While some poets continued to write on uncontroversial themes such as the certainty of victory, the reality of war began to impinge on an otherwise highly selective view of events as others discarded their authoritative roles and spoke directly about the experiences they shared with their readers. It may have been pragmatism, or simply disorganisation that made editors more flexible in what they published, but in any case it would have been ludicrous to continue offering people the simplistic optimism which had dominated thoughts of war in the 1930s when it was obvious that things had gone badly wrong. That summer Pavel Antokol'skii appealed to the Germans to surrender before things got any worse for them.[28] In the ninth number of *Zvezda* another poet announced the good news:

И, слыша громы боевые,
Глядят народы на Восток,
Туда, где Красная Россия
Сдержала вражеский поток.[29]

(And, hearing the thunder of battle, the peoples look towards the east, where Red Russia has stemmed the enemy flood.)

The German advance continued at speed through the summer, and the risk of widespread disaffection in a wartime population who experienced one thing and read something completely different in the newspapers was evidently realised.

Writers, like the rest of the population, were expected to play their part in the war effort. *Literaturnaia gazeta* listed writers' contributions to the defence fund, exhorted its readership to acquire military expertise and to make themselves useful in whatever way they could.[30] Literature's didactic function and its role in mobilising the country was particularly emphasised.[31] Many poets used their work to instruct their readers in the art of war. Even Akhmatova contributed a poem aimed at producing enthusiasm for tasks such as digging vast defensive earthworks, something that was done by civilian women, often under repeated aerial attack:

Копай, моя лопата,
Звени, кирка моя,
Не пустим супостата
На мирные поля![32]

(Dig, my spade, ring out, my pickaxe, we shall not let the foe into our peaceful fields!)

The sudden re-adjustment demanded by war went beyond the purely practical. War brought with it its own mentality, and the sense of a new beginning, or, at least, of an immense psychological distance from the recent past. For the young soldier Mikhail L'vov, the brutal simplicity of war seems to reduce to nothing the concerns of his pre-war existence:

Я нынче страшным расстояньем
От мирной жизни отдален,
И вспомнить я не в состоянье
Театра свет, ряды колонн,
И лебединые страданья,
И лебединую беду,—
Я слышу тут одни рыданья
И вижу только лебеду,
И вспоминаю об искусстве,
Как о далекой старине,
Как о любви, о первом чувстве...
К ним не вернуться больше мне.

И снова зубы сжав до хруста,
Иду вперед и в грязь, и в ров.
И кажется, что нет искусства,
А есть железо, хлеб и кровь.[33]

(Now I am separated by a terrible distance from peaceful life, and I am in no state to remember the theatre's lights, the rows of columns, and the swan's sufferings and the swan's misfortune,—Here I only hear sobbing and see only goose-foot, and I reminisce about art as about old times long ago, as about the feeling of first love ... I shall never return to them again. And once more gritting my teeth till they grind, I go forward through mud and ditches. And it seems as if art does not exist, but what exists is iron, bread and blood.)

Konstantin Simonov wrote that he now saw the past as if through the wrong end of binoculars, yet the vision engendered by war only *appeared* to be distorted:

... Мы, пройдя через кровь и страдания,
Снова к прошлому взглядом приблизимся.
Но на этом далеком свидании
До былой слепоты не унизимся.

Слишком много друзей не докличется
Повидавшее смерть поколение.
И обратно не все увеличится

В нашем горем испытанном зрении.[34]

(... We, passing through blood and suffering, shall once more gaze back at the past. But in this distant encounter we shall not demean ourselves by our former blindness. Too many friends have been lost by a generation which has witnessed death. And not everything will regain its former size in our vision, tested by grief.)

Simonov's use of ternary meters, and especially dactylic rhyme in this poem is reminiscent of the work of the nineteenth century poet Nekrasov and of folk songs. Other early wartime poems by Simonov, most notably 'Ty pomnish', Alesha, dorogi Smolenshchiny ...', show similar characteristics.

The recent past, of course, had seen mass arrests and persecution in an atmosphere which encouraged the idea that enemies concealed among ordinary people were sabotaging Soviet society. Now an unmistakable 'enemy of the people' presented itself, and even those who had suffered in the purges felt that Hitler's dictatorship would be even more vicious than Stalin's, something that Nikolai Glazkov recognised in a wry prayer:

Господи! Вступися за Советы,
Сохрани страну от высших рас,
Потому что все твои заветы
Нарушает Гитлер чаще нас...[35]

(O Lord! Support the Soviets, preserve the country from superior races, because all your commandments are broken by Hitler more frequently than by us...)

Semen Lipkin, who translated poetry for a living while writing poetry for himself, had shown no inclination to eulogise the revolution. In August 1941 he wrote a poem 'Revoliutsiia' (Revolution). The revolution, personified as an enigmatic, sometimes violent but intriguing sorceress, now appeared in a different guise:

... Цвела, как весна, колдовская краса.
Казнила, гнала, продавала.
Но вот заглянула колдунья в глаза—
И ненависть к ней миновала.

Морщинами годы легли на челе,
И стóят иные столетий.
И мы расплодились на бедной земле,
Ее незаконные дети.

И пусть мы не смеем ее понимать,—
Ее осуждать мы не можем,
За грешную нашу беспутную мать
Мы головы с радостью сложим.[36]

(Like spring the enchantress's beauty bloomed. She executed, persecuted, betrayed. But now the enchantress has looked into our eyes—and hatred towards her has passed. Years, like wrinkles, have settled on her brow, and some are as burdensome as centuries. And we have multiplied over the poor earth, her unlawful children.

And though we may not dare understand her, we cannot condemn her, and for the sake of our dissolute mother we will gladly lay down our heads.)

These lines, as well as Simonov's poem quoted above, were, it hardly needs to be said, not published in the Soviet Union at the time.

In parallel to this private re-adjustment of attitudes towards the Soviet Union, there was a public campaign to change attitudes towards the Germans, who had for almost the last two years been seen officially as allies. Now they were cast as the Soviet Union's natural and age-old enemies. Internationalist class solidarity, which led some Soviet soldiers to sympathise with their opponents as conscripted workers, as well as respect for superior German culture and technology, had to be overcome.[37] There was a sudden proliferation of articles, many written by authors with Jewish surnames, which recounted the brutality and philistinism of Nazi Germany.[38]

In poetry, the enemy was portrayed as semi-human monsters or as pathetic targets of mockery, incapable of individual initiative.[39] Historical precedents were cited both in poetry and in essays, particularly the German occupation of the Ukraine in 1918, to give credence to this new image.[40] Aleksei Surkov produced numerous poems in 1941 which concentrated on the civilian population's suffering at the hands of the enemy in order to stir up vengeful feelings. Revenge is a dominant theme in the poetry of 1941, and Surkov made the theme his own, writing in a declamatory and straightforward style, using dramatic imagery. His poems follow a predictable pattern. First, the scene of desolation:

Лес притаился, безмолвен и строг.
Звезды погасли, и месяц не светит.
На перекрестках разбитых дорог
Распяты взрывами малые дети.

Глохнут проклятья истерзанных жен.
Угли пожарища теплятся скупо.
Воздух разбитых траншей заражен
Приторным тленьем забытого трупа.

(The wood has grown quiet, silent and severe. The stars have gone out and the moon does not shine. On the crossroads of shattered roads small children are crucified by explosions. The curses of tortured wives die down. The embers of fires glimmer sparely. The air of shattered trenches is poisoned by the sickly scent of decay from a forgotten corpse.)

Then the poem's horizons widen just enough to show the cause of all this carnage. An enemy soldier stands near by, regarding the scene with 'empty eyes'. The final stanza is a call for vengeance:

Руки убийцы в крови и в грязи.
Ржет он, клыки пожелтевшие щеря.
Мститель, над пламенем встань! Порази

В черное сердце пьяного зверя.[41]

(The murderer's hands are covered in blood and dirt. He cackles, baring yellowed fangs. Avenger, rise up above the flame! Strike the drunken beast to his black heart.)

The Soviet soldier commonly depicted in the poetry of 1941 is the heroic antithesis of his evil enemy. The enemy's deeds are shown in their full horror in order to produce a sense of anger and revulsion; his Soviet counterpart is a stranger to blood and dirt. Although the heroic exploits of real people were used as raw material, the resulting poems portrayed them as superhuman figures, paragons of virtue. Aleksandr Prokof'ev's 'Bilet No. 4 142 357' (Membership Card no. 4 142 357), the number of his central character's Komsomol membership card, is typical:

Шли суровой военной порою,
Громом пушек все перекричав,
Шли за власть Советскую герои,
Грозен был их путь и величав.

Презирая смерть во имя жизни,
Верные присяге до конца,
Верные незыблемо отчизне,
Бились комсомольские сердца.[42]

(They went in severe time of war, drowning everything in the thunder of their cannons, the heroes went out for Soviet power, terrible was their path and majestic. Scorning death in the name of life, faithful to the oath to the end, faithful, without wavering, to their country, beat their Komsomol hearts.)

Mainstream Soviet poetry's formulaic approach produced countless 'set pieces' in which heroes and villains were clearly identifiable. The course of almost any poem about a hero was predictable in plot and style, as was the poem-oath pledging vengeance or loyalty.[43] Needless to say, these poems were anything but realistic. Writers tended, quite understandably in the circumstances, to seize on isolated heroic acts, and present them as typical of the essence of the Soviet character, rather than trace the progress of the retreat. However, as well as poems cataloguing enemy atrocities and calling for revenge, Surkov began to write soberly realistic accounts of the effect of the war on soldiers and civilians. In this short poem describing civilians forced to flee their blazing city, Surkov lets the objects they carry, reminders of their ordinary, peaceful existence, accentuate their plight, rather than explicitly demanding an emotional response from the reader:

Толпы людей без конца и числа
Шли нам навстречу в предутренней рани.
Помню: старуха козленка вела,
Девочка в тонких ручонках несла
Маленький чахлый кустик герани.

Гнал их из города ужас ночной,
Пламя ревело за их спиной.[44]

(Crowds of people without end or number came towards us in the early morning dawn. I remember: an old woman was leading a goat, a little girl carried in thin hands a small, stunted geranium. The horror of the night drove them from the city, flames howled behind them.)

The military side of the summer retreats was not a common theme in poetry of 1941. This eloquent silence was scarcely broken until 1943, when poets with the advancing Soviet armies recalled the last time they had been in areas now being regained. Sergei Narovchatov, who had experienced military disaster already in Finland, recorded his impressions of summer 1941 in 'Otstuplenie' (Retreat), a chaotic scene of civilian refugees observed by a group of soldiers:

... Мы сидели в кузове машины,
Сгрудившись над картою измятой ...
Спутник наш, устало матерщиня,
Раздавал запалы на гранаты...[45]

(We were sitting in the truck crowded round a crumpled map ... Our companion, cursing wearily, handed out fuses for grenades ...)

Narovchatov saw the tragedy of war without inveighing against the enemy as the source of destruction. In the poem 'Oblaka krichat' (The Clouds Cry Out) he describes his reaction to the spectacle of a burnt-out village. The whole of nature echoes the poet's distress in a cacophony of sound:

... По земле поземкой жаркий чад.
Стонет небо, стон проходит небом!
Облака, как лебеди, кричат
Над сожженным хлебом.

Хлеб дотла, и все село дотла.
Горе? Нет ... Какое ж это горе...
Полплетня осталось от села,
Полплетня на взгорье.

Облака кричат. Кричат весь день!..
И один под теми облаками
Я трясу, трясу плетень
Черными руками.[46]

(Over the ground a hot gust blows. The sky groans, a groan passes across the sky! The clouds, like swans, cry out above the burned grain. The grain is burnt to ashes, the whole village to ashes. Grief? No ... What kind of grief is this ... Half a wattle fence is left of this village, half a fence on a rise. The clouds cry out. They cry out all day!.. And alone beneath these clouds I shake the fence in my black hands.)

As autumn approached, Leningrad was encircled. Moscow too came under threat, and there was mass panic in mid-October as people tried to leave the city. The fate of these two cities became another standard theme, along with the theme of the heroic soldier. In the form of an oath to defend their cities, poets wrote of Moscow, recalling Napoleon's failed attempt to capture it, and of Leningrad, drawing comparisons between the people's resistance during the civil war and in the present. Moscow carried extra symbolic significance as the seat of power and centre of the nation, which must be protected at all costs. One poem exhorted the city's defenders:

Вперед! В наступление! Назад ни шагу!
За нашей спиной Москва.[47]

(Forward! Attack! Not one step backwards! Moscow is behind us.)

Moscow's status as the country's political centre and home of Stalin was emphasised in the poems written to celebrate the anniversary of the 1917 Revolution. Simonov's 'Surovaia godovshchina' (Sombre Anniversary) printed in *Krasnaia zvezda* on 7 November is addressed to Stalin on behalf of all the soldiers who are far from Moscow and not on parade as usual in Red Square:

...В дни празднеств проходя пред тобою,
Не думая о горестях войны,
Кто знал из нас, что будем мы судьбою
С тобою в этот день разлучены?..
Так знай же, что в жестокий час разлуки
Лишь тверже настоящие сердца,
Лишь крепче в клятве могут сжаться руки,
Лишь лучше помнят сыновья отца.
Те, что привыкли праздник свой с тобой
В былые дни встречать у стен Кремля,
Встречают этот день на поле боя,
И кровью их окрашена земля.[48]

(On festive days passing before you, not thinking of the sadness of war, who among us knew that we would, by fate, be parted from you on this day?.. Know, then, that in this harsh hour of separation true hearts are even stronger, hands are clenched with greater firmness in the oath, sons remember their father still better. Those who are accustomed to mark their festival with you in bygone days at the Kremlin wall mark this day on the field of battle, and with their blood the earth is tinted.)

Simonov goes on to say that all who fall in battle on this day will see, in death, a fleeting vision of Red Square. Moscow is established as the centre of all things, powerful enough to transcend great distances.

The summer and autumn of 1941 in Moscow appear in a rather different light in poems by Dmitrii Kedrin, who received little recognition in his lifetime, but has since been appreciated as the author of historical poems with satirical relevance to his own times. Kedrin shows not heroism, but greedy speculation on the city's markets as food shortages began. Immediately after the mid-October panic in the city, he described what had happened:

Стоял октябрь, а всем казалось—март:
Шел снег и таял, и валил сначала ...
Как ворожея над колодой карт,
История загадочно молчала.

Сибирский поезд раздвоил пары,
В купе рыдала крашеная дама:
Бабье коробку паюсной икры
У дамы вытрясло из чемодана.

Зенитка била где-то у моста,
Гора мешков сползала со скамеек.
И подаянья именем Христа
Просил оборванный красноармеец.

Вверху гудел немецкий самолет,
В Казань бежали опрометью главки.
Подвыпивший малый на осклизлый лед
Свалился замертво у винной лавки.

Народ ломил на базах погреба,
Несли муку колхозницы босые ...
В те дни решалась общая Судьба:
Моя судьба, твоя судьба, Россия![49]

(It was October, but to everyone it seemed like March: snow fell and melted and fell heavily once more ... Like a soothsayer over a deck of cards, history was enigmatically silent. A train for Siberia redoubled its steam, in a compartment a painted lady sobbed: the womenfolk had shaken from the lady's case a box of pressed caviar. The anti-aircraft guns rumbled somewhere by the bridge, a heap of sacks was sliding off the benches and, in the name of Christ, a ragged Red Army man begged for alms. Up above a German plane droned, the bosses ran at full tilt to Kazan'. A drunken chap collapsed out cold on the slippery ice by the liquor shop. At the store the people broke into cellars, barefoot kolkhoz women carried flour ... In those days was decided the common Fate: my fate, your fate, Russia!)

The suggestion alone that women from collective farms went barefoot would have been enough to keep that poem out of the press. Kedrin wrote soberly about the war in poems which express uncertainty and a feeling of helplessness. His account of the early months of war is that of a civilian—because of poor eyesight, Kedrin was not accepted for military service—and gives unusual perspectives on events usually portrayed with emphasis on their military aspect. In 'Bab'e leto' (Indian Summer) written in October as the Germans threatened the city, he wrote with foreboding:

...Завтра хлынет дождик быстрый,
Тучей солнце заслоня.
Паутинкам серебристым
Жить осталось два-три дня.

Сжалься, осень! Дай нам света!
Защити от зимней тьмы!
Пожалей нас, бабье лето:

Паутинки эти—мы.[50]

(Tomorrow the swift rain will lash down, covering the sun with clouds. Silvery spiders' webs have two or three days left to live. Take pity, autumn! Give us light! Protect us from the winter's dark! Have mercy on us, Indian summer: these spiders' webs are us.)

An apocalyptic note sounds in many of Kedrin's poems of that summer and autumn, sometimes with black humour, as in his likening of the numbers written on the hands of people queuing to the marks placed by the Antichrist on sinners. He writes with ironic detachment of neighbours meeting for the first time when their house is destroyed by a 'democratic' bomb.[51] Other poems written in the early months of war show Kedrin's concern for the long-term effects of the war on traumatised children.

While the Red Army managed to turn back the German advance on Moscow in early December, Leningrad came under heavy enemy fire in September and was completely surrounded by early October. Natal'ia Krandievskaia-Tolstaia wrote sarcastically of those who used their Party and bureaucratic connections to be evacuated by air to places where even the hens refused a crust of bread.[52] Ol'ga Berggol'ts began broadcasting her poems on Leningrad radio, declaring the city's resolve to stand firm, but gradually introducing descriptions of what people there had to suffer. Privately, she despaired of the gap between the reality and what she was permitted to say: 'I am working furiously, writing "uplifting" poems and articles, and writing them from the heart, that's what is so surprising! But who will that help? Against the background of what is actually happening, it's just lies.'[53] Akhmatova gave a stark evocation of the starving city:

Птицы смерти в зените стоят.
Кто идет выручить Ленинград?

Не шумите вокруг—он дышит,
Он живой еще, он все слышит:

Как на влажном балтийском дне
Сыновья его стонут во сне,

Как из недр его вопли: «Хлеба!»—
До седьмого доходят неба ...

Но безжалостна эта твердь.
И глядит из всех окон—смерть.[54]

(The birds of death stand at the zenith. Who will come to help Leningrad? Make no noise around—it is still breathing, it is still alive, it can hear everything: it hears, on the damp bed of the Baltic, its sons moan in their sleep, and from its depths, the wails 'Bread!' rising up to the seventh heaven ... But this firmament is without mercy. And from all the windows death looks out.)

Nikolai Tikhonov, whose earliest wartime poems had been marked by florid rhetoric, wrote in muted tones which were more in tune with the mood of the hungry but determined city. A request to write a newspaper article commemorating the 1934 murder of the Leningrad communist leader Kirov led to the writing of 'Kirov s nami' (Kirov is With Us).[55] The poem, described as a 'a song through clenched teeth', follows the spirit of Kirov as he patrols the city, observing its defenders.[56] The poem is reminiscent of Zhukovskii's 'Nochnoi smotr' (Night Parade), in which the dead Napoleon rises from the grave at midnight to summon his ghostly armies.[57] Both share the same meter—amphibrachic trimeter, with no omitted stresses in the line, reinforcing a regular beat—and use lines as refrains, Tikhonov's 'В железных ночах Ленинграда' (in the iron nights of Leningrad) echoing Zhukovskii's 'В двенадцать часов по ночам' (At twelve o'clock each night). The first stanza of Tikhonov's poem is the most effective:

Домов затемненных громады
В зловещем подобии сна,
В железных ночах Ленинграда
Осадной поры тишина.
Но тишь разрывается боем,
Сирены зовут на посты,
И бомбы свистят над Невою,
Огнем обжигая мосты.
Под грохот полночных снарядов,
В железных ночах Ленинграда
По городу Киров идет.
В шинели армейской походной,
Как будто полков впереди,
Идет он тем шагом свободным,
Каким он в сраженьи ходил,
Звезда на фуражке алеет,
Горит его взор огневой,
Идет, ленинградцев жалея,
Гордясь их красой боевой.[58]

(The bulk of blacked-out buildings are in an ominous likeness of sleep, in the iron nights of Leningrad there is the silence of siege. But the quietness is shattered by battle, sirens summon people to their posts, and bombs whistle above the Neva, scorching the bridges with flame. Under the crash of midnight shells, in the iron nights of Leningrad, Kirov goes about the city. In a military greatcoat, as if before regiments he is walking with that free stride with which he went into battle, the star on his cap glows crimson, his fiery gaze burns, he walks on, pitying the Leningraders, taking pride in their martial glory.)

The war was turning out to be much more difficult than people had been led to believe, and the unexpected circumstances soon came to shape poets' responses. War's disturbing and uncomfortable unfamiliarity prompted many to look to values which offered some reassurance. Official ideology dictated that the guiding light came from the Party and from Stalin:

Страна моя—гордость и слава!
Великий советский народ
Стремительной огненной лавой
Фашистскую свору сотрет.
Сотрет!
　　　　И следа не оставит.
Отныне навеки сотрет!
Да здравствует Сталин,
Ведущий на битву народ,
Который и гордо и смело
Повсюду с оружьем встает
Сражаться за правое дело,
Священное дело свое.
И мужество, равное стали,
Пойдет нераздельно вперед.
Да здравствует Сталин,
Ведущий на битву народ![59]

(My country is my pride and glory! The great Soviet people in a headlong rush of fiery lava will wipe out the fascist gang. Wipe them out! And leave no traces. Will wipe them out for ever hereafter! Long live Stalin, who leads the people into battle, who both proudly and bravely rise up everywhere with weapons to fight for a just cause, for our sacred cause. And courage, equal to steel, will go forward united. Long live Stalin, who leads the people into battle!)

Most poetry of this type is not re-printed in collections published after 1956, and in any case its survival on purely artistic grounds is unlikely. Sentiments like those expressed in the above example were replaced to a considerable extent by subjects of genuine concern to the whole population. The critic Lazarev notes the growing awareness that poetry would have to change: 'Already in the early months of the war many poets realised that poems of that kind did not really achieve their aim, as they left their readers indifferent, and that this was not the way to break through to the reader's soul—they had to write differently'.[60]

The actual experience of war, whether from the point of view of a soldier at the front, or a civilian during an air raid, at first played little part in published poetry. Poets recorded their feelings nevertheless, and entered a private sphere free from ideological considerations. As time passed, poems were printed which offered a blend of personal emotion with wider concerns, no longer focused on specifically Soviet matters. Two of the best-known war poems were early signs of the renaissance, with the censor's permission, of love poetry, and of patriotic poetry which focused on traditional, rural Russia rather than the Soviet Union. They are Surkov's 'B'etsia v tesnoi pechurke ogon'...' (In the small stove a flame flickers), which became a popular song, and Simonov's poem, dedicated to Surkov, 'Ty pomnish', Alesha, dorogi Smolenshchiny ...' (Do you remember, Alesha, the roads near Smolensk...).

Surkov's poem, written to his wife, became immediately popular, despite reservations on the part of the literary, and even the military establishment. Love had been an unwelcome theme in Soviet poetry, as it was felt that too much attention to personal life would distract citizens from their social obligations. In wartime some thought morale would be undermined if soldiers were reminded of the women they loved. Surkov's poem was interpreted as a defeatist complaint; 'improvements' were suggested.[61] The poem was a success, though, with the mass readership, who accepted it without suspicion:

Бьется в тесной печурке огонь.
На поленьях смола, как слеза,
И поет мне в землянке гармонь
Про улыбку твою и глаза.

Про тебя мне шептали кусты
В белоснежных полях под Москвой.
Я хочу, чтобы слышала ты,
Как тоскует мой голос живой.

Ты сейчас далеко-далеко.
Между нами снега и снега.
До тебя мне дойти нелегко.
А до смерти—четыре шага.

Пой, гармоника, вьюге назло,
Заплутавшее счастье зови.
Мне в холодной землянке тепло
От моей негасимой любви.[62]

(A flame flickers in the small stove. The resin on the logs looks like tears, and in the dugout an accordion sings to me of your smile and your eyes. The bushes whispered to me of you in the snow-white fields near Moscow. I want you to hear how my living voice yearns. Now you are far, far away. Between us lie the snows. It is not easy for me to reach you. But death is only four paces away. Sing, accordion, to spite the blizzard, summon my straying happiness. In the cold dugout I am warmed by my inextinguishable love.)

Simonov's 'Zhdi menia' (Wait for Me), instructing his beloved to wait for him whatever happened, was similarly, if less controversially, successful. It will be discussed more fully in Chapter Four.[63] As well as playing an important role in the resurgence of love poetry, Simonov introduced another theme which became a key concept in patriotic poetry. Drawing on his experience as a war correspondent and witness of the long retreat through the Russian countryside, he wrote of his discovery of a different Russia which was rural and traditional. It was an encounter with the 'Rodina', the Motherland, which transcended the Soviet state and recent history to include Russia's past, its people and landscape, even its religious roots. The adjective 'russkii' (Russian) is heavily used. The emotional fascination of the theme, and Simonov's timely resort to it, combined to give the poem great popularity. Simonov emphasises the landscape's personal and emotional associations; the abstract concept of 'Russia' is concentrated within a few details:

> ... Слезами измереный больше, чем верстами,
> Шел тракт, на пригорках скрываясь из глаз.
> Деревни, деревни, деревни с погостами,
> Как будто на них вся Россия сошлась.
>
> Как будто за каждою русской околицей,
> Крестом своих рук ограждая живых,
> Всем миром сойдясь, наши прадеды молятся
> За в Бога не верящих внуков своих.
>
> Ты знаешь, наверное, все-таки родина—
> Не дом городской, где я празднично жил,
> А эти проселки, что дедами пройдены,
> С простыми крестами их русских могил ...[64]

(Measured more by tears than by versts, the road ran, disappearing from view behind the hills. Villages, villages, villages with cemeteries, as if they were the essence of all Russia. As if on the outskirts of every Russian village, protecting the living with the cross of their hands, our forefathers gathered all together to pray for their grandsons who do not believe in God. You probably know that the Motherland is not after all the city house where I lived a fine life, but those country lanes traversed by our grandfathers, with the simple crosses of their Russian graves.)

Traditional images of Russia, rural and religious, flooded into the poetry of late 1941, and persisted until the end of the war. While the Soviet Motherland had been hymned in panoramic evocations of its vast expanses, now the focus narrowed to small details, often apparently insignificant, but full of meaning to those who saw in them the essence of Russia.[65] This change of focus blended well with the attention given to the importance of home and family. The emphasis on Russian tradition also lent itself well to the first major success of the war in December, when the Germans had been turned back from Moscow. This event was celebrated by a good deal of verse which tended towards the grandiose in recalling Russia's past victories and inherent glory. Russian traditional patriotism was an effective means of uniting individuals' interests with those of their country in a way which allowed both the exploration of private concerns and an officially acceptable expression of national pride.

Colonel John Wilson
Editor, British Army Review and ADTN; Trenchard Lines, Upavon, WILTS SN9 6BE
armyreview@armymail.mod.uk; 01980 615056/ CGS-DGS ED BAR

Stephen,

I have Rodric Braithwaites 'Moscow 1941' – would you be interested in reviewing it?

John.

1942: Poets at the Front, Critics at the Rear

The successful defence of Moscow late in 1941 was followed by Soviet advances which lasted until March 1942. The ensuing period of relative quiet was brought to an end by the German summer offensive. During this breathing space, poets and critics began to take stock of the situation and gain a new sense of perspective before the German offensive drove back Soviet defenders into the Caucasus and across the Don to Stalingrad. As in 1941, desperate circumstances produced fiercely patriotic exhortations and declarations of hatred for the enemy. In August Prokof'ev's eulogy to the Russian people proclaimed:

Нет в мире подобных России раздольной,
Цветов наших ярче и крепче пород,
Бессмертен народ наш великий и вольный,
Наш русский, наш вечный, наш гордый народ![66]

(In the world there is no equal to vast Russia, no flowers brighter or breeds stronger than ours, immortal our people, great and vast, our Russian, eternal, proud people!)

Leaflets brought 'inspiring' verses to the troops:

Рвется на Юг
Немецкая дрянь.
Топчет пшеницу
Фашистская гадина.
Если отступим,
Наша Кубань
Будет растоптана
И раскрадена.
Немецкие руки
В русской крови...
Родина требует—
Останови![67]

(Tearing southwards is the German rabble. Trampling wheat is the fascist vermin. If we retreat our Kuban' will be trampled down and everything stolen. German hands are wet with Russian blood... The Motherland demands—stop them!)

Konstantin Simonov showed that his new prominence as a lyric poet had not weakened his ability to issue authoritative propaganda statements. 'Bezymennoe pole' (Nameless Field), written at the end of July, was a warning to retreating soldiers that their dead comrades could not rest easily in German-occupied ground, and that a horde of ghosts would follow the army until the retreat was over.[68] Also in July, Simonov produced the prolonged exhortation, 'Ubei ego' (Kill Him), countermanding the commandment 'Thou shalt not kill':

... Если немца убил твой брат—
Это он, а не ты солдат,
Так убей же немца, чтоб он

А не ты на земле лежал,
Не в твоем дому чтобы стон—
А в его—по мертвым стоял.
Так хотел он, его вина,—
Пусть горит его дом, а не твой,
И пускай не твоя жена,
А его—пусть будет вдовой ...[69]

(If your brother has killed a German—it is he, not you, who is a soldier, so kill a German, so that he, not you, lies on the ground, so that not in your house but in his the dead man is bemoaned. It was his choice, he is to blame—let his house burn, not yours, and let not your wife, but his, be a widow.)

While the reaction to the summer offensive produced poetry which, in its use of unoriginal exhortations, was strongly reminiscent of the previous summer's writing, in general the range of themes and moods in poetry broadened during the year, following changes in published poetry which had begun to be perceptible towards the end of 1941. Critics started to set down their response to work written since the outbreak of war, and were evidently less inclined to issue instructions than previously, although on occasion they would indicate that certain poems had gone beyond the bounds of the acceptable.

Fadeev and Surkov attacked the critics in February and March, deploring their inactivity, but as the year proceeded, the volume of their work increased.[70] At the end of the year, the critic Zoia Kedrina wrote: 'It is no exaggeration to say that after a year of war our poetry has made as much progress as would have been made in years of ordinary peacetime'.[71] Critics too made progress in bringing to attention the excessive rhetoric, repetitive language and general lack of originality in a good deal of war poetry. Shortcomings which had been ignored in 1941 were now identified as serious faults. An article, generally favourable, on the work of the loyal Party poet Prokof'ev, criticised the over-use of a single metaphor in one poem, and saw this as typical of a general problem:

> Here a widespread failing of a whole group of published work by our poets about the war makes itself felt: having found a more or less original image or turn of phrase, the authors burst into cold declamation. They do not consider it necessary or possible to create a lyrical interpretation of the chosen image or to "dissolve" it in their verse, so that it might crystallise as a lyrical formula, a fusion of thought and emotion. Their error is twofold: a naive certainty that an indisputable thought does not need to be keenly, lyrically felt and inwardly justified; a false idea of the specific nature of political poetry as a "special" genre.'[72]

Instead of prescribing an official line, critics observed and responded to new developments. They broadly welcomed the revival of lyric poetry. In March Pertsov wrote: 'Before the war there were certain people who were prepared to deny lyric poetry its existence on the grounds that it allegedly brought about enfeeblement of character and failed to mobilise our emotions in resistance to the enemy'.[73] Their objections, he continued, had been proved wrong. Towards the end of the year, in an article surveying poetry written since the outbreak of war, Miasnikov commented on the profound emotions which war had revealed, and which provided the 'engineers of the human soul' (a designation for Soviet writers, supposedly emanating from Stalin) with inspiring material.[74] Some voices from the literary establishment expressed certain reservations at the new trend. They agreed that the use of personal themes in poetry was a powerful means of mobilising patriotic enthusiasm, as long as they were seen to be part of universal emotions: 'The Great Fatherland war has elevated the patriotic theme and shown that it provides a central focus for all the themes of lyric poetry'.[75]

There is reason to believe, at least from entries in Berggol'ts's diary, that the censors were being a little more flexible as well as critics. On 26 May she wrote: 'We aren't being directed in the usual way,—I'll try to write from the point of view of someone finding their own way, someone who is deprived of direction, but dimly sensing the turns ahead'.[76] Poets, it appeared, had started to set their own agenda.

One of the principal items on this agenda was a more realistic representation of conditions at the front. As well as poems describing the experience of battle, which will be discussed shortly, plenty of poems were written in 1942 which presented 'domestic' scenes of the soldier's daily life, along the lines of this one by Iakov Khelemskii:

Здесь, под бревенчатым накатом,
Нехитрый фронтовой уют.
Солдаты, скинув маскхалаты,
Портянки сушат и поют.

Вот стол почти что настоящий,
Хоть и шатается слегка,—
Пять кирпичей, патронный ящик
И поперечная доска.

Буханка хлеба, горсть махорки,
Коптилка, каша в котелке,
Вода в брезентовом ведерке,
Три автомата в уголке.

Здесь пахнет дружбой, о которой
Красивых слов не говорят,—
Она на снеговых просторах

Огнем проверена стократ.

Пусть в эти мартовские ночки
С пургою борется весна,
Печурка из трофейной бочки
Здесь накалилась докрасна.

Пусть рядом смерть и пули свищут,
Ночных ракет тревожен свет.
Друзья, надежнее жилища
На свете не было и нет.[77]

(Here, beneath a layer of logs is simple front-line comfort. The soldiers, throwing off their camouflage capes, dry their foot-cloths and sing. Here's a table, almost a proper one, although it wobbles a bit,—five bricks, a cartridge box and a board across the top. A loaf of bread, a handful of tobacco, a kerosene lamp, porridge in the mess-tin, water in the canvas bucket, three machine-guns in the corner. Here it smells of friendship, about which no fine words are spoken,—it is tested by fire a hundredfold out on the open snows. Though on these March nights spring wrestles with the blizzard, the stove made out of a looted German barrel has become red-hot. Though death is near and bullets whistle, and the light of night-time rockets disturbs us, no safer house, my friends, has ever existed in the world.)

Like the settings they describe, poems of this kind are simple and unpretentious, offering a temporary refuge from a hostile environment. The early months of 1942, as the German army was hampered first by being ill-equipped for the cold weather, then by the thaw making roads impassable for their trucks, were successful ones for the Red Army. Their poets relished their own relative comfort, but also the discomfort of the enemy:

... На арийском на мерзавце
Не наряды бальные,—
С головы до ног—эрзацы,
Только вши—нормальные.

Юный фриц за старой кошкой
По деревне гнался с ложкой,
Кошка умная была,
Из кастрюли удрала...

... Фриц, дрожа от аппетита,
Жарит конское копыто,
Очень удивляется:
Почему не жарится?[78]

(The aryan scoundrel wears no ballroom get-up,—from head to toe he's dressed in ersatz, only the lice are normal ones. A young fritz chased an old cat round the village with a spoon, the cat was clever, it jumped out of the saucepan ... Fritz, trembling from his appetite, roasts a horse's hoof, he is very surprised: why isn't it cooking?)

Still, the war was in no danger of being reduced to a comparison of creature comforts. Poets moved from descriptions of the minutiae of soldiers' off-duty moments to equally detailed descriptions of their environment and state of mind in battle. The sensations and impressions of the ordinary man once more provide the focus. The actual experience of battle is something that plays an important role in the work of the younger generation of poets, writing as they were from familiar territory, and with a certain polemical edge. They rejected the romantic image of war with all the vehemence of fresh converts, scorning the cliched elegance of literary battles and focusing on unglamorous physical details. The startling descriptions in Semen Gudzenko's 'Pered atakoi' (Before the Attack) helped to launch his poetic career:

Когда на смерть идут—поют,
а перед этим
можно плакать.
Ведь самый страшный час в бою—
час ожидания атаки.
Снег минами изрыт вокруг
и почернел от пыли минной.
Разрыв—
и умирает друг.
И, значит, смерть проходит мимо.
Сейчас настанет мой черед.
За мной одним
идет охота.
Будь проклят
сорок первый год
и вмерзшая в снега пехота.
Мне кажется, что я магнит,
что я притягиваю мины.
Разрыв—
и лейтенант хрипит.
И смерть опять проходит мимо.
Но мы уже
не в силах ждать.
И нас ведет через траншеи
окоченевшая вражда,
штыком дырявящая шеи.
Был бой коротким.
А потом
глушили водку ледяную,
и выковыривал ножом
из-под ногтей
я кровь чужую.[79]

(When men go to their death they sing, but before this you are allowed to weep. The most terrible hour in battle is the hour spent waiting to attack. The snow all round is furrowed by mines and has turned black from their dust. An explosion—and a friend dies. And so death passes you by this time. Next it will be my turn. It is me alone they are chasing. Be accursed, year of 1941, and the infantry frozen in the snow. I feel as though I am a magnet and I am attracting the mines. An explosion—and the lieutenant croaks. And death passes by once more. But we no longer have the strength to wait, and we are led across the trenches by a frozen enmity which makes bayonet holes in enemy necks. The battle was short. And afterwards we poured icy vodka down our throats, and with my knife I scraped out another man's blood from under my fingernails.)

A poem by Mikhail Kul'chitskii, written at the end of 1942, aimed to shatter readers' illusions while deriding his own former naivety:

Мечтатель, фантазер, лентяй-завистник!
Что? Пули в каску безопасней капель?
И всадники проносятся со свистом
Вертящихся пропеллерами сабель.

Я раньше думал:
                    Лейтенант
Звучит
          «налейте нам»,
И, зная топографию,
Он топает по гравию.

Война совсем не фейерверк,
А просто—трудная работа,
Когда—
          черна от пота—
                              вверх
Скользит по пахоте пехота.

Марш!
И глина в чавкающем топоте
До мозга костей промерзших ног
Наворачивается на чоботы
Весом хлеба в месячный паек

На бойцах и пуговицы вроде
Чешуи тяжелых орденов.
Не до ордена.
Была бы Родина
С ежедневными Бородино.[80]

(Dreamer, fantasist, idle envier! What? Bullets on the helmets are safer than raindrops? And the horsemen dash past with a whistle of sabres revolving like propellers. I used to think that lieutenant sounded like 'pour drinks', and, as he knew topography, he stomped around on gravel. War is not a firework at all, but simply hard work, when, black with sweat, the infantry slithers up over a ploughed field. March! And the clay in the squelching tread of feet frozen to the marrow builds up on boots which weigh as much as a month's bread ration. The soldiers' buttons are like the scales of heavy medals. There's no time to think of medals. Just let our Motherland win a Borodino every day.)

Kul'chitskii, like his contemporaries, was far from dismissing the romantic view of war as an idealist's proving ground. The unglamorous surroundings did not, after all, make the war meaningless. In fact the emphasis on physical detail, mud, blood and so on, went side by side with determination and courage, both equally valid elements in their vision of war. Authentic detail, presented in a deliberately anti-aesthetic way, acts as a guarantee of emotional authenticity. The message seems to be that poets who are not afraid to reveal the truth about war may shock others, but are themselves undaunted by what they see.

The war that increasingly came to the fore in poetry of 1942 was not the elevated, heroic struggle portrayed in earlier days, but a difficult, dirty, somewhat prosaic slog, illuminated by camaraderie, thoughts of home, and the occasional heroic action. Poems which included details of soldiers' ordinary lives were welcomed by A. Leites: 'When you make a careful study of the poems which appear in the pages of our front-line army newspapers, your attention is caught most of all by those which reflect everyday army life, the heroism of the Soviet fighting man in all his down-to-earth uniqueness.'[81] Authentic detail came to be valued, and 'realism' (without the prefix 'socialist') was acceptable, within limits. Excessive preoccupation with unappealing detail risked being condemned as 'naturalistic'. Gudzenko's memorable lines about using a knife to scrape a dead man's blood from under his fingernails after a battle were a case in point.

Il'ia Sel'vinskii, working as a war correspondent, describes two constant aspects of the soldier's life—fear and fatigue—as if they were mild but chronic ailments, undramatic side-effects of war. Sel'vinskii explains patiently how the ordinary concept of sleep is altered at the front:

> ... От сна остается только слово:
> Не сон, а ощущение толчка.
> У застоявшего часового
> «Заснет», пожалуй, правая рука;
> Или майор в беседе засопит,
> Упустит нить и только взглянет тупо,—
> И это тоже сон. Война не спит.
> Тут спят по-настоящему лишь трупы.[82]

(All that is left of sleep is the word: not sleep, but the sensation of a jolt. The sentry who has been standing up for too long might have his right arm 'go to sleep'; or a major might start to snore in conversation, lose the thread and just stare dully,—and that too is sleep. War does not sleep. Here the only ones to sleep properly are the corpses.)

This kind of prosaic description, rooted in physical detail and without the 'justification' of heroic action, was not generally part of the poetic repertoire, even among the younger poets. Truthfulness may have been valued in the poetry of 1942, but not all versions of the truth were equally acceptable. Surkov's 'Kliuchi k serdtsu' (The Keys to the Heart) reads very much like a policy statement; as he was a poet of considerable official stature, the pronouncements it contained, such as:

Лишь слово правды, честное, простое,
Готовы мы принять в наши сердца.[83]

(Only words of truth, honest and simple, are we prepared to take into our hearts.)

can be taken as a hint of changing values. In his poem Surkov stresses the need for absolute honesty when addressing soldiers who had become acutely aware of any attempts to deceive them, and announces the simple truth to be of greater value than fine words. What the truth actually consisted of depended on the poet. While younger poets attacked falsely romantic notions of war, those adhering to Soviet literary orthodoxy looked for a 'higher' truth which was stripped of irrelevant and undignified details, revealing war's essentially heroic nature. When the establishment poets focused on prosaic matters, it was generally as a preliminary to the confident assertion that the boundaries between the ordinary and the extraordinary were very fragile, and that any man had the capacity to become a legendary hero. Mikhail Svetlov found monumental qualities in ordinary soldiers who were to him 'living legends':

Сидят товарищи меж нами
И вновь ведут, не торопясь,
Обыкновенными словами
Свой героический рассказ.[84]

(Our comrades sit among us and once more tell, unhurriedly, in ordinary words, their heroic stories.)

If the ordinary and the extraordinary could be said to have existed side by side during the war, then it was surely in Leningrad where the two were most closely linked. Daily life and work carried on in appalling conditions. During the winter of 1941–42, thousands died from starvation, in a city that was subject to heavy shellfire. It seems only natural that some of the most successful works on the siege were written by women civilians—Vera Inber, Zinaida Shishova and Ol'ga Berggol'ts—who continued living 'normal' lives, as far as conditions would allow, and whose work revealed the extraordinary physical and spiritual effort it took to maintain some degree of humanity. Three long poems by these women, who lived through the first and most terrible winter of the Leningrad blockade, explore a kind of heroism not usually portrayed by other writers at the time, the prosaic heroism of ordinary civilians, most of them women.

In Leningrad the extreme situation lent itself to more conventional representations, as civilians fought against hunger, cold and the enemy artillery. From the start of the siege, the city's resistance had been celebrated in short and heroic poems which consisted mainly of somewhat hackneyed phrases. The experience of many months in the blockade produced a more complex response. Vera

Inber's 'Pul'kovskii meridian' (Pulkovo Meridian) was written in the course of two years. The poem attempts to chronicle the city's resistance to cold, starvation and the enemy with documentary exactness. Inber compares her work with a filtering which captures the smallest particles of reality.[85] The second chapter observes with almost clinical detail the physical effect of hunger on the Leningraders:

> ...Как тягостно и, главное, как скоро
> Теперь стареют лица! Их черты
> Доведены до птичьей остроты
> Как бы рукой зловещего гримера:
> Подбавил пепла, подмешал свинца—
> И человек похож на мертвеца.
>
> Открылись зубы, обтянулся рот,
> Лицо из воска. Трупная бородка
> (Такую даже бритва не берет).
> Почти без центра тяжести походка,
> Почти без пульса серая рука.
> Начало гибели. Распад белка.[86]

(How painfully, and above all, how fast faces age now! Features are reduced to a bird-like sharpness, as if by the hand of some ominous make-up artist: add some ashes, mix in some lead, and a person looks like a corpse. Teeth are revealed, the mouth stretched taut, the face waxen. A corpse's beard (even a razor can't get rid of it). A gait almost without a centre of gravity, a grey hand almost without a pulse. The onset of death. Break-up of proteins.)

Zinaida Shishova's long narrative poem 'Blokada' (Blockade), like Inber's poem, was written during the course of two years. The poem focuses on a mother's efforts to keep her starving son alive, and contains minute descriptions of the physical effort needed to fetch water, the house without water, electricity, heating, as well as a summary of the values which helped keep people alive (reciting Pushkin, helping a child across the icy road, not falling upon the bread ration like a beggar).[87] The poem was broadcast on Leningrad Radio, against official wishes.[88] Ol'ga Berggol'ts produced two long poems containing episodes from the blockade which, at their best, are dramatic and unusual portrayals of people surviving a terrible ordeal.[89] Berggol'ts's work will be discussed in detail in Chapter Five.

At this point it is worth noting that civilians were little represented in Soviet war poetry as a whole. They had no clearly defined place in the conventional ideas of heroism, which really required a battlefield to work. Published poetry was mainly silent on the subject. Unpublished poetry was frequently less than complimentary. Writing in December 1942 in Stalingrad, Semen Lipkin described how he would dream of Moscow when life at the front became too hard to bear:

... Там с курятником посольство
Зажигает рядом свет,
Там несытое довольство
Полуголода сосед.

... Там торопится кутила
На метро попасть быстрей,
Там блюдут гвардейцы тыла
Наших жен и матерей...

Мир таких мечтаний гадок,
Но порой от них светло.
Есть, по крайности, порядок:
Свет и тьма, добро и зло.[90]

(There beside a hen-house an embassy turns on the lights, there insatiable prosperity is neighbour to half-starvation. There a high-living man rushes to get into the metro as fast as possible, there the guardsmen of the rear keep watch over our wives and mothers... The world of such dreams is vile, but sometimes they bring light. There is, at least, order: light and dark, good and evil.)

In conventional terms, this looks like a complete reversal of the situation—at the front there was a conflict between Good and Evil, at the rear, unity. In Lipkin's poem the conflict appears to be going on at home in a society divided between extremes of wealth and poverty, with the additional hazard of the secret police. The front, it seems, is too chaotic a place to provide any comforting sense of clarity of purpose. Dmitrii Kedrin was also rather dubious about the values governing wartime civilian society, which seemed rather similar to those of pre-war days. At the beginning of the year he wrote:

Я через лес к горящему селу
Не вел бойцов дорогою окольной.
Я видел то, что делалось в тылу...
По совести, и этого довольно!

Когда противник окружит лесок,
То у бойца, что бьется здесь за Тулу,
Есть пистолет, чтобы пустить в висок
Последнюю спасательную пулю.

А тут сиди и слушай, как течет
Яд трусости в двусмысленной беседе.
Свою судьбу ты знаешь наперед:
Упустят немцы,—выдадут соседи ...[91]

(I did not lead soldiers by a circuitous route through the forest to a burning village. I saw what was going on in the rear ... By my conscience, that was enough for me! When the enemy surrounds the copse, then the soldier fighting here for Tula has a pistol, so that he can fire a final, saving bullet into his temple. But here you have to sit and listen to the flow of cowardice's poison in an ambiguous conversation. You already know your own fate: if the Germans miss you, the neighbours will turn you in.)

The lyrical tendency in patriotic poetry, expressed clearly by Simonov in 'Ty pomnish' Alesha ...' became stronger. Historical parallels used since the outbreak of war, and reinforced by the victory at Moscow, were augmented by personal and somewhat unconventional declarations of love and attachment to Russia. Il'ia Sel'vinskii's 'Rossii' (To Russia) announces the poet's devotion to all things Russian and describes the inseparable bond between himself and his country. As we shall see, this poem was attacked in 1943, but on publication in 1942 it failed to provoke critical condemnation.[92] Kedrin's poems '1941' and 'Duma o Rossii' (Reflections on Russia) make historical comparisons between Russia's past and present, using archaic, elevated language and imagery,[93] but a more lyrical strain emerges in two poems which attempt to analyse his love of Russia. The country, embodied in the window of an inn lit by a torch, a dog howling at the moon, and Pugachev's cage, is no paradise on earth:

...Да, страна наша не была раем:
Нас к земле прибивало дождем.
Но когда мы ее потеряем,
Мы милей ничего не найдем![94]

(Yes, our country was no paradise: we were often lashed to the ground by rain. But when we lose it we shall find nothing dearer!)

There were signs of more varied, individual approaches to the theme of heroism as well as to patriotic themes. As in 1941, poets selected their subject-matter from life, but now began to write not just to commemorate certain figures and their achievements, but also to explore their personal response to them. Both Svetlov and Tikhonov chose the theme of the heroic resistance shown by twenty-eight men from General Panfilov's division during the battle for Moscow the previous November.[95] Ozerov praised Svetlov's work for its achievement in showing heroism as a 'phenomenon which is vivid and unique in its impact, but at the same time typical, repeated'.[96] The poems gained emotional force, wrote Ozerov, through their point of view—that of an involved contemporary observer—although this lyrical response would, he supposed, probably be surpassed by later work on an epic scale.

The lyrical and personal element is particularly strong in two long poems which commemorate two young people lost in the war. One of the heroes is the son of Pavel Antokol'skii, whose poem 'Syn' (The Son) is a requiem for his own son, killed in battle.[97] Margarita Aliger's 'Zoia', to be discusssed more fully in Chapter Five, commemorates the life and achievements of the young partisan Zoia Kosmodem'ianskaia, executed by the Germans.[98] The heroic and selfless qualities of these young people are seen by both poets as typical of their generation and the society which they grew up in, but in each case the central focus of the poem is the lyrical relationship between poet and hero. Aliger speaks to her heroine in a motherly way, and feels especially close to her when she relates how Zoia chose the pseudonym of Tania, the name of Aliger's own daughter, so as not to betray her true identity to German interrogators. Antokol'skii places his loss in a broader context by tracing the youth of a German boy, the antithesis of his son, but the poem is dominated by details of his own son's childhood, his interests, of the relationship between father and son, and of intense grief. Military and heroic considerations take second place to the emotional links between poet and hero.

This new focus on the inner world of the individual, on emotional responses to the war, was a significant element in poetry written about soldiers' experiences in the front line. Most lyric poetry written in 1942 was concerned with the everyday concerns of the ordinary fighting man. During the first months of the war, the figure of the superhuman hero dominated poetry. Although these heroes were based on real people, they were hardly characters with whom most readers could identify. Gradually poets turned to themes which had a more universal appeal, such as love and family. After the enemy retreat from Moscow, poets began to devote much more attention to the unexceptional figures who had played a major part in the city's defence.[99] Combined with the regeneration of lyric poetry, this shift in focus meant that the inner world of the ordinary soldier and the spiritual or psychological changes brought about by the experiences of war became a prominent theme. Nikolai Rylenkov, whose work was by nature quietly reflective, wrote that men had been made thoughtful and silent by the knowledge that they could be killed at any time.[100] Semen Gudzenko, one of the younger generation of poets, found that the harsh demands of war brought maturity which had not destroyed finer feelings:

Прожили двадцать лет.
но за год войны
мы видели кровь
                    и видели смерть—
просто, как видят сны...
...Стали на время
                    большой войны
мужественней сердца,
руки крепче,
                    весомей слова.
И многое стало ясней.
... А ты
                    по-прежнему неправа—
я все-таки стал нежней.[101]

(We have lived for twenty years. But in one year of war we have seen blood and death simply, as people see dreams. In time of a great war our hearts have become braver, hands stronger, words weightier, and much is now clarified. But you, as before, are wrong—I have, nevertheless, grown more tender.)

After Surkov had made love poetry officially acceptable and hugely popular with his poem 'B'etsia v tesnoi pechurke ogon'...', there were countless poems written about soldiers who were sustained in battle by the thought of their faithful wives waiting for them at home. No-one now thought to object that poems of this nature would somehow reduce men to sentimental despair; on the contrary, love poetry became accepted as an integral part of the broader patriotic theme. There were, however, some objections to Simonov's cycle 'S toboi i bez tebia' (With You and Without You).[102] The cycle traces the progress of an intense and sometimes unhappy love affair. The love between Simonov's hero and heroine is not the steady, reassuring devotion celebrated in the majority of love poems written at this time:

Пусть прокляну впоследствии
Твои черты лица—
Любовь к тебе—как бедствие,
И нет ему конца.

Нет друга, нет товарища,
Чтоб среди бела дня
Из этого пожарища
Мог вытащить меня.

Отчаявшись в спасении,
Сны видя наяву,
Как при землетрясении
Я при тебе живу.

Когда ж от наваждения
Себя освобожу,
В ответ на осуждения
Я про тебя скажу:

Зачем считать грехи ее?
Ведь не добра, не зла,
Не женщиной—стихиею
Вблизи она прошла.

И грозный шаг заслыша, я
Пошел грозу встречать,
Не став, как все, под крышею
Ее пережидать.[103]

(It may be I shall later curse the features of your face—my love for you is like a calamity which has no end. I have no friend or comrade who, in broad daylight, could drag me out of this conflagration. Losing all hope of rescue, dreaming while awake, I live alongside you as if beside an earthquake. When I free myself from this infatuation I shall say of you, in answer to censure: why consider her faults? She is neither good nor evil, and passed by not like a woman, but like a force of nature. And, hearing the fateful tread, I went to meet the storm, unlike everyone else, who was waiting beneath a roof for it to pass.)

Such tempestuous passions were not wholly acceptable to the literary establishment. Stalin himself is reported to have said that 'S toboi i bez tebia' should have been published in two copies only: one for 'him' and one for 'her'.

The literary event of the year proved to be the revival of a character created in humorous verse during the war with Finland. Vasia Terkin's adventures had been recorded by a team of writers including Tvardovskii, and from the outbreak of war in 1941 there had been several imitations of the good-natured hero. Tvardovskii began to publish 'Vasilii Terkin' in September 1942, although he had been writing a long poem about his Finnish war character in 1941 before the German invasion. Parts of this poem were used for his new work. The change of the hero's name from the diminutive signified that the work was likely to be more serious; the poem began light-heartedly, listing the soldier's essentials—water, food, humour —but soon showed itself to be more than mere entertainment in its choice of the most necessary thing of all:

... А всего иного пуще
Не прожить наверняка—
Без чего? Без правды сущей,
Правды, прямо в душу бьющей,
Да была б она погуще,
Как бы ни была горька.[104]

(But what is it without which, more than anything else, you can't survive? Without the essential truth, truth which strikes you right in the soul, as long as it is substantial, no matter how bitter it may be.)

Tvardovskii's early war poems are largely documentary in nature, concerned with battle incidents and boosting morale, but his treatment of two awkward subjects, usually left unmentioned, suggests a concern for the truth which refuses to submit to prejudice. In 'Ballada ob otrechenii' (Ballad about Renunciation) the theme of desertion, in official eyes equal to betrayal, is considered as a real moral dilemma for the deserter and his family.[105] 'Ballada o tovarishche' (Ballad about a Comrade) relates the tale of two soldiers who take refuge with a village woman during the summer retreat of 1941. One falls in love with her, and is presented with the dilemma of whether to stay with her or to rejoin his unit. The decision to leave is painfully reached.[106] In these two poems Tvardovskii had shown that he went beyond the normal, glib assumptions about the war.

'Vasilii Terkin', which will be discussed in Chapter Four, attained a scope and size unique in Soviet war poetry. In chapters published up until the end of the year Tvardovskii's hero was formally introduced to the reader, related his experiences of the 1941 retreat, swam across an icy river to deliver a message, was wounded, defeated a monstrous German soldier in single combat, shot down an enemy plane with a rifle and was awarded a medal. The voice of the author, sometimes addressing the reader directly, sometimes acting as narrator, complements his hero's voice and adds greater depth to what would otherwise risk being yet another narrative about a humorous but unconvincing hero. The language used in the poem is colloquial and unforced, and, above all, simple and accessible without being in any way patronising. The same meter, trochaic tetrameter, is used throughout, with subtle rhythmic variations which successfully avoid the danger of monotony, and while rhymes are generally alternating, patterns vary here too:

> ... Есть закон—служить до срока,
> Служба—труд, солдат—не гость.
> Есть отбой—уснул глубоко,
> Есть подъем—вскочил, как гвоздь.
>
> Есть война—солдат воюет,
> Лют противник—сам лютует.
> Есть сигнал: вперед!..—Вперед.
> Есть приказ: умри!..—Умрет.
>
> На войне ни дня, ни часа
> Не живет он без приказа,
> И не может испокон
> Без приказа командира
> Ни сменить свою квартиру,
> Ни сменить портянки он.
>
> Ни жениться, ни влюбиться
> Он не может,—нету прав,
> Ни уехать за границу
> От любви, как бывший граф.[107]

(There is a law—you serve your term, service is work, a soldier is no guest. When the all-clear sounds—he falls fast asleep, when reveille sounds—he jumps up like a nail. When there's war a soldier fights, if the enemy is fierce then he's fierce too. When the signal is 'advance!' he advances. When the signal is 'die!' he dies. At war there is no day or hour that he lives without orders, and without his commander's order he can never change his lodgings or his foot-cloths. Get married or fall in love he may not—he has no right to, or travel abroad out of love, like a former count.)

Critics welcomed Terkin as a new friend and archetypal Russian, although Ermilov took pains to point out that he had Soviet characteristics too. Discussion about Terkin's Soviet credentials continued throughout the war. Ermilov also expressed his reservations at what he felt to be a mismatch of a humorous hero with such a wide-ranging work.[108] Humour was more customary in satirical verse, or in verse which made no claims to be other than straightforwardly amusing. The combination of humour and seriousness in 'Vasilii Terkin' may have disconcerted Ermilov, but it certainly served to make the work very popular.

1943: Whose Victory at Stalingrad?

The turning point of the war came in early 1943 with the Soviet victory at Stalingrad, a city of great psychological and symbolic importance for both sides. As the city bearing his name was celebrated, there was also revival of poetry celebrating Stalin's inspiring example. It seems clear that his prestige was enhanced by the victory; until then there had been relatively few poems exalting the Great Leader in wartime, apart from a number in the summer of 1941. Yet the battle at Stalingrad had been won by ordinary soldiers, and poets continued to explore the heroism shown by the ordinary man, seeing Stalingrad as convincing proof of his value. During 1943 the tension between these incompatible points of view is reflected in an increasing division between poetry which focused on the stature gained by ordinary people through their own independent actions, and poetry which sought to divert the pride of individuals at their own actions into pride at the nation's achievement, epitomised in the figure of Stalin.

Conflicting attitudes are evident in poetry recording the advance which followed the German defeat at Stalingrad. Many poems celebrated the Soviet advance in general terms, evoking a particular mood rather then describing actual events:

Что такое шаг вперед?
Долгожданный час расплаты,
Песня мужеству солдата,
Это—поступь наших рот.

Это шаг в свою долину,
В бурю яростных атак,
Это шаг вперед—к Берлину!
Это так—и только так![109]

(What is a step forward? The long-awaited hour of vengeance, a song to a soldier's bravery, it is the tread of our companies. It is a step into our own valley, into the storm of fervent attacks, it is a step forward towards Berlin! It is that and only that!)

Such triumphant words were often combined with references to Stalin as the inspiration behind the army's success. His role in less propitious phases of the war was not mentioned. The post-Stalingrad trend towards a broader view of the war as a national and historical triumph was encouraged by critics. Although at the beginning of the year they continued to welcome the use of realistic detail which testified to the poet's experience of war, by the end of 1943 there were some calls for a more epic approach when dealing with elevated themes of victory, and for a wider historical perspective. Official triumphalist rhetoric, rare in 1942, now became more widespread, and contrasted sharply with the quieter tones of personal poetry. The small-scale, intimate approach which had evolved unbidden at a time of profound crisis was no longer officially needed once victory began to look certain.

Superficial celebration of the Soviet advance contrasts with a sober realisation of the suffering undergone both by those who lived under enemy occupation and by those who returned home only to find they had no home or family left. Gudzenko's 'Ballada o dome' (Ballad about Home) tells the story of one such homecoming. A young soldier rushes impatiently into battle to fight for his home village:

> ... И он рванулся
> по родной
> земле,
> знакомой с малолетства.
> Пошел под пули,
> как святой,
> Как завороженный.
> О, детство!
> О, дым,
> как небо голубой!
> О, дом,
> отцовское наследство!..

(And he rushed across the beloved ground, familiar since childhood. He walked off under bullets like a saint, like one enchanted. O childhood! O smoke, blue like the sky! O house, inherited from his father!)

Suddenly he falls, as if wounded, and kneels in the snow before a heap of ashes:

> Здесь было все ему родным.
> И сразу стало все понятным:
> И голубой
> бездомный дым,
> И красные на белом пятна.
> Мы дальше шли,
> но он берег,
> как завещанье,
> невесомый,
> жилья сожженного дымок—
> последнее дыханье дома.[110]

(Here everything was dear to him. And suddenly he understood it all: the blue, homeless smoke, and the red stains on white. We went on, but he kept, as a testament, weightless, a puff of smoke from the burned-out house, the last breath of his home.)

The price of victory, revealed in poems which observe events on a small scale, does not appear in poems concerned with Russia's mission to liberate the world from fascism. It can be argued that such an extension of the horizon is only natural when a sense of national pride is expressed. However, the tendency to exclude concrete details in favour of abstractions played down the extent of damage and loss sustained by the country and its people. Russia, the 'Motherland', becomes an abstract concept, no longer a definite landscape, but a national spirit fulfilling a messianic role:

Союз Советских Республик!
Реки его блеснули.
Бор его стал чернее
в лучах штабного авто.
Есть державы-деляги,
есть державы-плясуньи.
Лазутчики есть державы.
А эта держава—кто?
Слушайте голос отчизны:
на рубежах укрепиться,
Новую выстоять муку
и навалиться горой.
Верю! Верую! Знаю!
рухнет держава-убийца
и снова цветную Европу
спасет держава-герой.[111]

(The Union of Soviet Republics! Its rivers glistened. Its forest became blacker in the lights of the staff car. Some powers are wheeler-dealers, some are dancers, some are spies. But who is this power? Hear the voice of your fatherland: stand firm on the front, ready to withstand new suffering and to crash down like a mountain. I trust! I believe! I know! The murderous power will collapse, and once more many-coloured Europe will be saved by the hero-power.)

The author of this poem, Il'ia Sel'vinskii, was one of the main targets of critical attacks launched in 1943 which marked an attempt by the literary establishment to reassert its authority following a public display of disarray earlier in the year. At the end of March, the Union of Writers organised a five-day symposium on literature and the war, during which critics were publicly censured for the sparseness and poor quality of their work. The keynote address on poetry by the critic A. Leites was described in *Literatura i iskusstvo* as a weak and contradictory attempt to analyse recent developments in poetry.[112] Pavel Antokol'skii said: 'Our critics are working to no purpose, they make no attempt to analyse a work of art profoundly and seriously, but simply label it according to genre'.[113] Reports of the meeting in *Literatura i iskusstvo* and *Novyi mir* commented disparagingly that it was left to the writers to analyse current trends, something which threatened to undermine the critic's role in the system of literary controls.[114]

At the March symposium, writers themselves were far from unanimous in their assessments of wartime poetry. Simonov was the target of criticism for more than one speaker, though admissions of his popularity with readers may suggest a little professional jealousy, and Iosif Utkin thought that criticism of Simonov might in actual fact be criticism aimed at his readers who were supposed not to want to read the love poetry he wrote.[115] Pavel Antokol'skii called for literature to represent the tragedy of war, which he described as a 'school of suffering', not of heroism. Gusev spoke of the 'blossoming' of poetry,[116] while Nikolai Aseev thought that it had little to distinguish it from poetry of the First World War: 'The same vocabulary, the same patriotic declamations which do nothing to reveal the new meaning of this patriotism, the same rhythms and meters, the same return to archaisms...'[117] He did, however, praise the work of young soldier-poets for its 'convincing truthfulness'.

A former futurist colleague of Maiakovskii, Aseev repeated Maiakovskii's 1914 trick of combining separate stanzas by different war. poets to emphasise their stylistic monotony.[118] The poem put together by Aseev was made up of four stanzas from separate poems in an anthology celebrating the twenty-fifth anniversary of the October Revolution:

Еще такой суровой годовщины
Никто из нас не знал за жизнь свою,
Но сердце настоящего мужчины
Лишь крепче закаляется в бою.

И день и ночь, на суше и на море,
И в зной и холод, в бурю и в пургу,
Герои мстят за муки и за горе,
Повсюду смерть несут они врагу.

С тех пор злодеев полегло немало,
Навек нашли убежище свое,
Повсюду гибель их подстерегала,
Хотя они не видели ее.

Над миром ночь бездонна и темна,
Но в скрежете, в гуденьи, в звоне стали,
Клянемся, что отомстим врагу сполна,
Что за отчизну биться не устали![119]

(As yet no such sombre anniversary none of us has known in his lifetime, but the heart of a real man is tempered more strongly by battle. In the daytime, at night, on land and sea, in heat and cold, in storm and blizzard, the heroes avenge suffering and sadness, everywhere they bring death to the enemy. Since then no small number of villains has fallen, they have found their eternal shelter, death lurked in wait for them everywhere, though they did not see it. Above the earth the night is fathomless and dark, but in the rumble, crash and clang of steel we swear that we shall avenge ourselves fully on the enemy, that we shall not weary of fighting for the fatherland!)

Literatura i iskusstvo does not, sadly, record how this patchwork epitome of official verse was greeted by the assembled writers, but it did print Vera Inber's riposte that she could easily produce a single poem from works by Maiakovskii, Kirsanov and Aseev.[120] That may well have been true, but Aseev's criticism that poets were failing to use words which were 'unexpected and passionate, not fitting in with the rules of a textbook on versification, not imitative and repeating things already well known and understood, but revealing new phenomena, thoughts new to minds and hearts blinded by the thunderous explosions of reality' was more than borne out by the identikit poem he quoted. The meter, iambic pentameter, has been the most popular meter in Russian twentieth-century poetry, and the composite poem uses the most common rhythmic variants, omitting stresses most frequently on the fourth ictus, and only once adding an extra syllable after the caesura in the penultimate line. The rhymes are a conventional alternation of feminine and masculine, with the order reversed in the final stanza. The vocabulary is predictable, particularly in the lists of the second stanza. Formal regularity is accompanied by banal sentiment and standardised exclamation. Of course, the example presented by Aseev is extreme, but it is hardly unrepresentative of wartime poetic output as a whole. His own work, it must be said, is somewhat more original in its use of meter and rhyme, showing complex sound patterns and unusual images. Aseev daringly attributed the uniformity found in wartime poetry to the fact that the basic rule of art—independence—had been forgotten. He could have added that the regimentation of Soviet literature had actively discouraged formal innovation, labelling it as 'formalism', and that a poem's accessibility and 'message' were more valued than originality of style.

The meeting, as reported in the press, certainly gives the impression that the 'official' sector, that is, critics, were failing in their task as envisaged by socialist realist standards of instructing writers in their work. This state of affairs was not allowed to continue for long. *Literaturnaia gazeta* in July 1993 contains an interesting account of the machinations of the Central Committee Department of Agitation and Propaganda, under G. F. Aleksandrov. Another article published in the same year provides more details from the former Party archives.[121] Both authors see the events of 1943 as a prelude to Zhdanov's campaigns in 1946. In 1943 a planned book by Aseev was banned, because it contained 'political mistakes'; it is not unlikely that his speech in the spring had something to do with this. In late autumn a resolution was presented to the Central Committee Secretariat concerning 'mistakes' in the work of the poet Il'ia Sel'vinskii. This resolution was not upheld; apparently it was not considered sufficient to attack only one poet for only three poems, so Aleksandrov organised a trawl through the work of other writers, and, together with his deputy A. A. Puzin and A. M. Egolin, head of the Department's literature section, presented the Central Committee Secretariat with a memo which attacked a number of writers, Sel'vinskii included. The resulting series of secret Central Committee resolutions in December 1943 named the offending writers and criticised the journals which had published their work. Control over the work of literary journals was tightened: Aleksandrov was given responsibility for the journal *Novyi mir*, while his deputies were assigned to *Znamia* and *Oktiabr'*.

Il'ia Sel'vinskii was one of the main targets for critical attacks, particularly for two patriotic poems, 'Rossii' (To Russia), written in 1942, and 'Kogo baiukala Rossiia' (Those whom Russia Cradled) of 1943. In the proposed Central Committee Resolution that autumn, 'Rossii' was criticised for its 'ridiculous and vulgar discussion of our Motherland'.[122] There are numerous differences between the version published in his 1943 collection *Ballady i pesni* and the one which appears in subsequent collections. Striking images from the original are replaced by ones which are altogether more conventional. The first stanza in the original began:

Хохочет, обезумев, конь!
Фугасы хлынули косые ...

(Losing its mind, a horse laughs! Incendiaries crash down diagonally)

This was replaced by the less startling:

Взлетел расщепленный вагон.
Пожары... Беженцы босые...

(The shattered railway carriage exploded. Fires... Barefoot refugees...)

The second stanza was altered in all but one line (the third). The original reads:

Я твой. Я сын твоей любви,
Детеныш русской Марсельезы!
Твоя волна в моей крови,
В моих костях—твое железо!
Нервинкой каждою скорбя,
Оглохший от бомбометанья,
Люблю тебя! Люблю тебя
До стона и до бормотанья!

(I am yours. I am the son of your love, the offspring of the Russian Marseillaise! Your wave is in my blood, in my bones—your iron! Grieving with every nerve, deafened by bombs, I love you! I love you until I groan and mumble!)

The last line was mentioned specifically in the draft resolution, as well as in subsequent attacks on Sel'vinskii, as an example of the poem's vulgarity. It was replaced by the line 'Всем пламенем и всем дыханием'(with all my fire and breath), altogether more conventional. The 'Russian Marseillaise' of the second line is replaced by the declaration 'Я жизнью за тебя в ответе!' (I answer for you with my life). The grief and trauma of lines five and six are diminished in the later version:

> Гордясь тобой или скорбя,
> Полуседой, но с чувством ранним ...

(Proud of you or grieving, half grey-haired, but with early emotion...)

Another line singled out in public attacks came in the stanza which praises the birds of Russia; the poet expresses his love for the 'грачей, разумных, как крестьяне' (rooks, reasonable as peasants), which was felt to be an insult to Russian peasants.[123] This was replaced by the inoffensive and suitably martial 'Военный строй в гусином стане' (the martial ranks of a flock of geese). Russian women appear in a somewhat different light in the later version, tame creatures compared with those in the original:

> Какая молния взрастила
> Казачью удаль их любви?

(What lightning flash nurtured the Cossack daring of their love?)

becomes:

> Какая песня в них взрастила
> Самозабвение любви?

(What song nurtured in them the selflessness of love?)

Sel'vinskii's understanding of Soviet society was evidently found to be faulty too; the intelligentsia was accorded four lines in the original, and described as the 'fermenting froth of the revolution', but the lines are cut to two, and the intelligentsia is simply 'enduring in battle'. A stanza on poetry, recognising Pushkin and Pasternak as his teachers, and stating that fools cannot understand them, is thoroughly altered, so that the poetic impulse is seen more broadly as a revolutionary one, linking the Decembrists with the Communists. The poem's final four lines are also completely changed, from:

> Пускай рыданья и гроба
> Чернят простор моей Отчизны—
> Бессмертно трепетанье жизни!
> Зовуща
>   русская
>   труба!

(Though there are sobs and coffins blackening the spaces of my fatherland—the quiver of life is immortal! The Russian trumpet summons!)

to:

В удушье денежного века,
Где низость смотрит свысока,
Мы окрыляем человека,
Открыв грядущие века.[124]

(In the airlessness of the money age, where baseness looks down haughtily, we give wings to man who opens up future centuries.)

These changes illustrate very clearly what was not acceptable—signs of deep crisis, even if accompanied by unshakeable loyalty—and what was required—a pronounced ideological stance, emphasising the moral superiority of Soviet people over capitalist nations.

The other patriotic poem by Sel'vinskii which was attacked was 'Kogo baiukala Rossiia' (Those whom Russia Cradled), in which the essence of Russia is seen as its combination of tenderness towards the weak and defenceless, and savage resistance towards its enemies. The quality of compassion towards the 'urod', the freak, was felt to be a slander on the Russian people and a serious ideological mistake.[125]

But while official circles began to take a renewed interest in the ideological correctness of literature, many poets wrote with not so much as a nod in the gesture of political dogma. Victory at Stalingrad appeared to provide an appropriate occasion for the re-introduction of 'official' rhetoric and imagery connected with the Soviet state. It was nevertheless open to less conventional interpretation, as in Semen Lipkin's 'Ruiny' (The Ruins), a poem full of biblical echoes:

Как тайны бытия счастливая разгадка,
Руины города печальные стоят.
Ковыльные листы в парадных шелестят,
Оттуда холодом и трупом пахнет сладко.

Над изваянием святого беспорядка
Застыл неведомым сиянием закат.
Но вот из-за угла, где рос когда-то сад,
Выходит человек. В руках его тетрадка.

Не видно жизни здесь.
Как вечность, длится миг.
Куда же он спешит? Откуда он явился?
Не так ли, думаю, наш праотец возник?

Не ходом естества, не чарой волшебства,—
Внезапно вспыхнувшим понятьем Божества
От плоти хаоса без боли отделив.[126]

(Like a happy solution to the mystery of existence the sad ruins of the city stand. The leaves of feather-grass rustle in doorways, from where comes the sweet smell of cold and corpses. Above the sculpture of sacred disorder the sunset is frozen in unknown splendour. But from round the corner where once grew a garden a man emerges. There's a notebook in his hands. There is no sign of life here. The moment lasts like an eternity. Where is he hurrying to? Where did he appear from? Was that not how, I think, our forefather sprang up? Not by any process of nature or the charms of magic,—but by a concept of the Divinity, suddenly flaring up, separating from the flesh of chaos without pain.)

Out of the chaos and destruction of war, suggests Lipkin, man is metaphorically re-created. The physical collapse of the pre-war world offered a potential for spiritual renewal and change. Those who served at the front and enjoyed an unprecedented degree of independent action had begun to realise the scale of their achievement; it seemed only reasonable to hope that this would be recognised and rewarded by the state, itself renewed and purified by its ordeal. While some poets noted the moral renewal of men in war in rather general terms, others made pointed comments on the shortcomings of those who had avoided battle or might in future forget their experiences. Aleksandr Gitovich, who in the course of his work as a war correspondent took part in bombing raids, expressed his contempt for editors who:

> За мирными приемниками сидя,
> По радио прослушивают войну.[127]

(Sitting by their peaceful wireless sets, listen to the war on the radio.)

Simonov's 'Dom v Viaz'me' (The House in Viaz'ma) is one soldier's plan to ensure the survival of wartime values by rebuilding a house in which he and his friends spend the night before a battle. There, faced with death, they embrace truthfulness, loyalty and generosity for all time:

> И если кто-нибудь из нас
> Рубашку другу не отдаст,
>
> Хлеб не поделит пополам,
> Солжет или изменит нам,
>
> Иль, находясь в чинах больших,
> Друзей забудет фронтовых,
>
> Мы суд солдатский соберем
> И в этот дом его сошлем.[128]

(And if one of us will not give his last shirt to a friend, will not share his bread, lies or betrays us, or, having reached high rank, forgets his friends from the front, we shall assemble a soldiers' court and exile him to this house.)

As the end of the war came into sight, poetry could begin to consider what the prospects were for the soldier returning home. Poets repeatedly wrote that war had revealed which values were truly important. Stalin had no place in their list. In Tvardovskii's view, army life was a revelation of what was essential:

> Когда пройдешь путем колонн
> В жару, и в дождь, и в снег,
> Тогда поймешь,

Как сладок сон,
Как радостен ночлег.
Еще поймешь порой,
Как хлеб хорош
И как хорош
Глоток воды сырой.

Когда пойдешь таким путем
Не день, не два, солдат,
Еще поймешь,
Как дорог дом,
Как отчий угол свят.
Когда—науку всех наук—
В бою постигнешь бой,
Еще поймешь,
Как дорог друг,
Как дорог каждый свой.[129]

(When you follow the columns in heat and rain and snow you will realise how sweet sleep is and how joyful a lodging for the night. You'll also realise at times how good bread is and how good a mouthful of cold water. When you follow that path, not just for a day or two, soldier, you'll also realise how dear your home is, how sacred your father's home. When—highest knowledge of all—in battle you comprehend battle fully, you will also realise how dear a friend is, how dear each one of our men.)

Younger poets celebrated the friendship and mutual trust they found at the front. Gudzenko's 'Ballada o druzhbe' (Ballad about Friendship) describes the intensity and preciousness of a bond which could lead one man to sacrifice his own life for a friend. His comparisons are taken from the battlefield:

Так
        в блиндаже хранят уют
коптилкой керосиновой.
Так
        дыхание берегут,
когда ползут сквозь минный вой.
Так
        раненые кровь хранят,
руками сжав культяпки ног...

Не зря мы дружбу берегли,
как пехотинцы берегут
метр
        окровавленной земли,
когда его в боях берут.[130]

(Like this they preserve comfort in the dug-out with a kerosene lamp. Like this they preserve their breath, when they crawl through the howl of mines. Like this wounded men preserve their blood, pressing their hands to the stumps of their legs... Not for nothing did we preserve our friendship, like infantrymen preserve a metre of bloodied earth when they take it in battle.)

The absolute lack of what would have been recognised as political content in such evocations of soldiers' values shows the continuation of a trend which had begun late in 1941. The state and its ideology was gradually replaced by aspects of private life which were valued for themselves and not as a fragment of a more significant whole. The experience of war was presented as something separate from life in pre-war society, an autonomous zone which generated its own norms and values. This 'new' morality was given validity because it was shown to have originated in extreme circumstances, where it was impossible to dissemble. Whether this was actually true or not, a significant number of poets did present this picture of moral renewal through war which seemed to have no connection with official pre-war values. The poets' silence on overtly political themes suggested a tacit rejection of the system, so often praised in empty words.

Boris Pasternak, always an outsider in the 'new society', had made his living through translations since the mid-1930s rather than risk danger by writing his own poetry. In 1943 he wrote the beginning of a narrative poem, 'Zarevo' (The Glow). The introduction was printed in *Pravda* in October; the first chapter appeared only in 1965. Pasternak describes the homecoming of a soldier who has distinguished himself in battle. What he finds is hardly a home 'fit for heroes'; the children have run wild and his wife is entertaining a strange man, apparently a black-market dealer. Descriptions of civilian life in the rear were uncommon throughout the war; the subject lacked the simple clarity of battle and risked revealing the hardship faced by those at home. Pasternak's hero Volodia finds it difficult to reconcile petty domestic concerns with the transforming effect of war:

... Он надышался смертью, порохом,
Борьбой, опасностями, риском,
И стал чужой мышиным шорохам
И треснувшим горшкам и мискам.

Он не изменит жизни воина,
Бесстрашью братии бродячей,
Лесам, стоянке неустроенной,
Боям, поступкам наудачу!

А горизонты с перспективами!
А новизна народной роли!
А вдаль летящее прорывами
И победившее раздолье![131]

(He has breathed in death and gunpowder, struggle, danger, risk, and has become alien to the rustle of mice and cracked pots and bowls. He will not betray the soldier's life, the fearlessness of the wandering brotherhood, the forests, the roughly-built quarters, the battles, the hazarded actions! And the horizons and vistas! And the novelty of the people's role! And the victorious expanses stretching far off in a series of breakthroughs!)

In a dream, Volodia is faced with his 'double'—the antithesis of military virtue—whose complaints reveal political repression, material shortages, and the authorities' unrealistically high demands from the workforce. Angrily, Volodia dismisses his treacherous inner voice:

... Нытьем меня своим пресытили,
Ужасное однообразье.
Пройди при жизни в победители
И волю ей диктуй в приказе.[132]

(I have had more than enough of your whining, the dreadful monotony of it. Go on and be a victor in life, and impose your will on it as an order.)

Mariia Petrovykh, living in Chistopol' as an evacuee, also wrote of the new beginning and independence that war offered:

... Не в расточительном ли детстве
Мы жили раньше? Не во сне ль?
Лишь в грозный год народных бедствий
Мы осознали нашу цель.

И можем быть вполне в ответе
За счастье встреч и боль потерь...
Мы тридцать лет росли, как дети,
Но стали взрослыми теперь...

... Живи же, сердце, полной мерой,
Не прячь на бедность ничего
И непоколебимо веруй
В звезду народа твоего.

Теперь спокойно и сурово
Ты можешь дать на все ответ,
И скажешь лишь два кратких слова,
Два крайних слова: да и нет.

А я скажу: она со мною,
Свобода грозная моя!
Совсем моей, совсем иною
Жизнь начинается, друзья![133]

(... Did we not live earlier in wasteful childhood? In a dream? Only in a terrible year of national disaster did we realise what our aim was. And we can be completely responsible for the joy of meetings and the pain of losses ... For thirty years we grew like children, but have grown up now ... Live then, heart, to the full, don't save up for a rainy day and believe firmly in the star of your people. Now calmly and severely you can give an answer to everything, and you will say only two short words, two extreme words: yes and no. And I will say: it is all mine, my formidable freedom! A life is beginning now, my friends, which is totally my own, totally new!)

Although literature had been permitted more freedom than before the war, direct criticisms of Soviet society could not be published. If the future was to be considered at all, then it must be in generalisations, usually about how the war would be remembered. In

1942 poetry had begun to use a wider perspective to encompass varied and more detailed aspects of the war, but in 1943 perspectives were extended beyond the immediate present to speculation on the war's historical significance to future generations. Prokof'ev, as usual responsive to convention, foresaw the creation of legends about Leningrad; others wrote of the discovery of relics on former battlefields.[134] Aleksei Surkov too seemed to think that the legends would be created later; nevertheless he gently mocked this tendency in his poem 'Zhizn' i mechta' (Life and Dreams):

Умолкнет гром, пройдут года,
Мы постареем вдвое, втрое,
И будет сложена тогда
Легенда-сказка о герое.

Как шел он, не жалея сил,
Против жестокого теченья,
И в смертный час произносил
Высокопарные реченья,

Как предавался он мечте
В ночи, перед кровавой сшибкой...
Мы будем слушать сказки те
С веселой старческой улыбкой.

Ведь мы к героям тех годин
В землянки запросто входили,
И ели с ними хлеб один,
И из одной баклажки пили.

Без нимба светлого на лбу,
Глотая пыль, топча порошу,
Они несли свою судьбу,
Как кирпичей тяжелых ношу.

Таскали сумки на горбах,
Со смертью в прятки не играли,
И с грубым словом на губах,
Когда случалось, умирали.

Их явь и их ночные сны
Цвели цитатами едва ли.
А вот судьбу своей страны
Они в обиду не давали.

Пусть их прикрасят—не беда.
Воображенье любит мощи.
Ведь человечья жизнь всегда
Была грязней, святей и проще.[135]

(The thunder will cease, the years pass by, we shall age two or three times over. And they will create a fairy-tale legend about a hero. He went, not sparing his strength, against a fierce current, and in the hour of his death pronounced high-flown utterances, he gave himself over to dreams at night before a bloody clash... We shall listen to those fairy-tales with a cheerful old man's smile. We quite simply walked into the dug-outs to see the heroes of those times, and shared their bread and drank with them from the same flask. Without a bright halo on their brow, swallowing dust, trampling down new snow, they bore their fate like a load of heavy bricks. They carried kitbags on their backs, did not play hide and seek with death, and, when it came to it, they died with a coarse word on their lips. Their waking life and their dreams at night hardly blossomed with quotations. But they did not let their country's fate be harmed. Let them be embellished—that is no calamity. Imagination loves holy relics. We know that human life always was more dirty, sacred and simple.)

In July 1943 Surkov delivered a report on his recent work to the Union of Writers, placing considerable emphasis on the importance of a realistic portrayal of the war. Writers, he said, had been taught by experience that the best way to reach their readers was to speak directly and honestly.[136] By raising the matter of how poets turned real human beings into falsified legendary figures, Surkov evidently touched a raw nerve—the process of turning the war into a heroic myth was already under way, and would become well established not long after the war was over.

Tendencies towards the monumental were more than balanced by publication of poems which took the everyday details of war as their inspiration, as, for example, this poem by Aleksandr Petrov:

Нам для песни слова подсказали
Медный голос рожка на вокзале,
Дальний гул торопливых колес,
Свет коптилки в блиндажном окошке
И раздумье солдатской гармошки,
И печаль облетевших берез.

Я услышу знакомые строчки
В пулеметной стремительной строчке,
В перестуке тяжелых подков,
В лязге гусениц, в чортовой тряске,
По дорогам разбитым и вязким
Громыхающих грузовиков.[137]

(The words for our songs were dictated by the brazen voice of the station loud-speaker, the distant rumble of hurrying wheels, the light of an oil lamp in the dug-out window and the reveries of a soldier's accordion, and the sadness of birch trees that have lost their leaves. I hear familiar lines in the swift rattle of machine-guns, in the pounding of heavy hoofs, in the grinding of tank tracks, the infernal jolting of roaring trucks over muddy, shattered roads.)

Here, it seems, is a claim of authenticity; the poem is inspired directly by the physical circumstances of war rather than by any official promptings from a world far away from the realities of the front. Nikolai Rylenkov too promotes authenticity as the highest aim of his work in a poem which voices objections to poetry which was loudly triumphant and took no note of the sorrow of war. His own poems might not, he wrote, be included in the 'chronicle of war' or be part of victory celebrations, but his would be read by a contemporary as he would his own diary:

Про себя прочтет и скажет—есть в них
Дым войны, что в душу мне проник ...[138]

(He shall read them to himself and think—in them is the smoke of war which has penetrated my soul.)

A curious phenomenon in poetry of 1943 is the short poem which creates, then dashes, the reader's expectations. War-weariness might offer part of the explanation for this; it may also have been a retort to the instructions issuing from above for the production of 'monumental canvases' with a future-oriented historical perspective. In his memoirs Il'ia Erenburg recalls Moscow writers' less than enthusiastic response to such appeals.[139] The tone of these poems is mostly humorous, but shows a distinct sense of disillusion. Dmitrii Kedrin looks to the end of the war, describing a man's feelings of relief at having survived:

«Теперь,—ты думаешь—жизнь будет длинной!
Спокойной будет старости пора».
И вдруг у ног твоих взорвется мина,
Саперами забытая вчера.[140]

(Now, you think, my life will be a long one! My old age will be peaceful. And suddenly at your feet a mine explodes, one the sappers forgot the day before.)

Tvardovskii subverts the conventional treatment of two popular subjects: the woman who hides an army banner during enemy occupation and is rewarded for her actions, and the kindness of a stranger to an orphan child. His heroine receives a medal, but would rather be given a calf; the boy by the roadside prefers cigarettes to sympathy.[141] A similar discrepancy between conventional expectations and reality is found in Narovchatov's 'Frontovaia pochta' (Mail at the Front). The letters soldiers receive, he writes, give them great joy and enable them to forget the miserable weather. It seems that all is as it should be, but the poem ends:

Хорошие письма! Вам этот стих!..
Но конец его будет случаен,—
Ни я, ни товарищ мой писем таких
Чтой-то... не получаем!..[142]

(Fine letters! This poem is for you!.. But its end shall be accidental,—neither I nor my friend, for some reason or other, get letters like that!..)

In 1943 poetry shows a strange mixture of hope and uncertainty. It is clearly felt that people have been altered by war, and for the better. There is hope that society too will change. At the same time there is a sense of anxiety, not drowned out by the loud confidence of official hymns to victory, that such expectations are likely to be betrayed. That year's developments in the official literary sphere certainly justified their fears.

1944: Optimism in Private and in Public

The invading German armies were driven out of Soviet territory during 1944, and by the end of the year Soviet forces had nearly reached Warsaw and Budapest. In the Soviet press a mood of optimism prevailed, a sense of pride at the country's military achievements, but also at the progress made in literature. The last number of *Zvezda* for the year contained an article by Vissarion Saianov, claiming that the country was on the threshold of a great literary epoch. Gone were the quarrels of the 1920s and 1930s: 'Artificially created schemes have vanished, literary schools have collapsed,— there is more individual talent in literature'.[143] The war, Saianov wrote, had raised the general level of culture, and *Zvezda* was to respond by becoming a journal in the old Russian tradition, dealing with literature, criticism, social and political matters. Such ambitions were, as it turned out, already undermined by the Central Committee Resolutions of late 1943, and would be finally dashed by the resolutions of 1946, in which *Zvezda* was named one of the chief malefactors.

Throughout the year, in articles and reviews of collections of poetry, critics commented favourably on wartime literary achievements. Many of the younger poets who published their first books in 1944 were praised for the sincerity and truthfulness of their work. Most prominent among them was Semen Gudzenko. Il'ia Erenburg wrote of his book *Odnopolchane* (The Men of my Regiment): 'This tiny book takes the place of many long poems which are full of water coloured to look like blood. Here are only a few drops, but they are blood, not water.'[144] In a variety of articles, the younger poets were welcomed as the major poets of the future.[145]

There were, however, signs of official anxiety over some wartime developments. At the end of 1943, as we have seen, the Central Committee passed a number of resolutions concerning 'mistakes' in literature. In January 1944 Fadeev, president of the Union of Writers, was replaced by Nikolai Tikhonov. His first major engagement in this new role was at the 9th Plenum of the board of the Union in February, and he was, apparently, thoroughly briefed as to whom he should praise and criticise.[146] In his speech Tikhonov gave a survey of recent literature, incorporating the criticisms made in the December Resolutions regarding the work of the literary journals, and he drew particular attention to a lack of political awareness which had allowed the publication of Zoshchenko's story 'Pered voskhodom solntsa' (Before Sunrise) and Sel'vinskii's 'Kogo baiukala Rossiia' (Those whom Russia Cradled). Apparently, though, Tikhonov's criticisms were not put forcefully enough, and Aleksandrov, the head of the Central Committee for Agitation and Propaganda, had to intervene with attacks on Sel'vinskii, Zoshchenko and so on. The same names, including Aseev's, featured in a note sent to Zhdanov by the People's Commissar for State Security that October. Aseev was criticised for his slanderous representation of the Soviet rear as Asiatic and backward, presumably in his poems about his evacuation to Chistopol'.[147] During 1944 there was continued concern that the literary journals were still working badly, in other words, they were failing to maintain the desired ideological line. *Znamia* was singled out for particular criticism of its low ideological and literary standards, and managed to be reprimanded for pieces which it had not even printed.[148]

The Soviet literary establishment began to reassert its prescriptive powers as attention focused less on the actual events of the war, but more on its historical significance for the Soviet state, then emerging as a major world power. The most significant event recorded by poets in 1944 is the reaching of the Soviet Union's pre-war border. Many describe the sense of having come full circle as they head west across territory lost in the retreat of 1941, and, on reaching the border, give the impression that the *real* war is over. Long accounts of battles, by Pavel Shubin and Mikhail L'vov, trace the progress of the advance as far as the border. L'vov is more concerned to convey the experience from the soldier's point of view, and uses original similes to suggest his perceptions of battle. Shubin gives more attention to the overall picture of events, and to the drawing of historical parallels.[149] In both works the reaching of the border brings the action to a close, and acts as a cue for reflections on the war, as if it were already over. Neither poet pays much attention to the enemy, who, having been a bloodthirsty monster in poetry of 1941, is in 1944 almost non-existent, appearing either as a corpse and symbol of German defeat, or as a despised prisoner of war.[150]

Once the border is crossed, images of Russia impose themselves on poets' perceptions of foreign countries, Germany in particular. In poems that deal with the Soviet advance into German territory, the theme of revenge returns with force. Burning Russian villages are remembered as poets state that it is now time for the enemy to experience what they inflicted on others:

> ... Как занялся огнем твой дом,
> Ты увидал впервые,
> А нам тот запах так знаком

И дым тот очи выел.[151]

(You have seen for the first time fire taking a hold on your house, but to us that smell is so well known, and that smoke has eaten away our eyes.)

In 'Vozmezdie' (Retribution) Tvardovskii explains Soviet intentions, which have a moral purpose and expressly exclude territorial ambitions:

... И мы не с тем сюда пришли,
Чтоб здесь селиться хатой.
Не надо нам твоей земли,
Твоей страны проклятой.
Нас привела сюда нужда,
Неволя—не охота.
Нам только надо навсегда
Свести с тобою счеты.[152]

(We have not come here to settle. We do not need your land or your accursed country. We have been brought here against our will, not willingly, by necessity. All we need to do is to settle scores with you for ever.)

The liberation of Eastern Europe from Nazi occupation was seen as a time of renaissance. Poets, almost in unison, compared the Soviet advance with the coming of spring. Boris Pasternak uses spring as a metaphor for universal renewal. The poet and the natural world share equally in spring's vitality; nature is animated, endowed with human emotions:

... Иначе думается, пишется,
И громкою октавой в хоре
Земной могучий голос слышится
Освобожденных территорий.

Весеннее дыхание родины
Смывает след зимы с пространства
И черные от слез обводины
С заплаканных очей славянства.

(One writes and thinks differently now, and like a loud octave in the choir is heard the mighty voice of the earth from liberated territories. The vernal breath of the motherland washes the traces of winter from all around, and the streams black with tears from the tear-stained eyes of the Slavs.)

The blossoming of spring flowers appears as a metaphor for the liberation of European countries from tyranny, but is also related to the broader context of the fantastic world of fairy tales and traditional art. This renaissance is rooted firmly in ancient tradition:

... Сказанья Чехии, Моравии
И Сербии с весенней негой,
Сорвавши пелену бесправия,
Цветами выйдут из-под снега.

Все дымкой сказочной подернется,
Подобно завиткам по стенам

В боярской золоченой горнице
И на Василии Блаженном.

(The tales of Czechia, Moravia and Serbia, with vernal abundance breaking through the shroud of injustice, sprout like flowers from beneath the snow. Everything is covered in a fairy-tale haze, like the patterns on the walls of the boiars' gilded chamber and of St Basil's cathedral.)

Poets more conventional than Pasternak see Moscow, of which St Basil's cathedral is, of course, a famous landmark, in its more modern guise. Pasternak's enthusiasm for Moscow is, he emphasises, a romantic attachment to the city as a seat of tradition, not of political power, although the final two lines are perhaps a little ambiguous on this account:

Мечтателю и полуночнику
Москва всего милей на свете.
Он дома, у первоисточника
Всего, чем будет цвесть столетье.[153]

(To the dreamer and midnight thinker Moscow is dearer than everything in the world. He is at home, by the prime source of everything by which the age will blossom.)

It is more common to find Moscow unambiguously depicted as a symbol of Soviet power. Poets write from abroad of visions of the distant Kremlin towers; Moscow is the ultimate source of truth, light and reality.[154] The political message to the liberated peoples of Europe, and to Soviet citizens at home, was that Soviet troops, representatives of a superior political system, have brought freedom and enlightenment to their benighted brother Slavs. Moreover, the Russians as liberators could lay claim to seniority, a message implicit in the word-play of Sergei Narovchatov's 'Pol'skie stikhi' (Polish verses):

... Беломостье нам платье машет,
Белым платом, омытом в крови,
Истомился по нас Томашев,
Ждет Любашев нашей любви.

Нам идти по путям подзвездным,
Чтобы плечи Плоцк распрямил,
Чтобы познала свободу Познань,
Чтобы Поморье узнало мир ...[155]

(Belomost'e waves a cloth at us, a white cloth soaked in blood, Tomashev longs for us, Liubashev waits for our love. We shall go along roads beneath the stars, so that Plotsk straightens its shoulders, so that Poznan' shall know freedom, so that Pomor'e shall know peace ...)

The Russian language becomes the source of meaning to which other languages defer, as, for example, in the third line quoted, where the verb is**tomi**t'sia, to long for, gives the place name **Tom**ashev the implicit meaning of a town in a state of longing.

Evgenii Dolmatovskii takes a rather more direct approach in his poem 'Parol'' (The Password), stating proudly that 'я русский' (I am Russian) is a universally recognised password. Dolmatovskii offers mild, though ideologically impeccable criticism of social inequalities in the capitalist world, perhaps in an attempt to remind Soviet troops that their country's supposed moral riches are superior to foreign material wealth.[156] Although nothing is explicit, poems of this kind were surely intended to make Soviet 'imperialist' designs on Eastern Europe seem right and natural.

The 'post-war' atmosphere is furthered in poems which deal with themes of reconstruction and of soldiers returning home. Here the tone is optimistic, making light of the destruction and trauma of war. Soldiers are shown returning to their happy families and to work.[157] Mikhail Lukonin's poem 'Pridu k tebe' (I shall come to you) first suggests, then dismisses, the possibility of being unable to adjust to civilian life:

> ... Потом
> меня
> сведет с ума
> непривычный уют.
> Будешь к завтраку накрывать,
> а я усядусь в углу.
> Начнешь,
> как прежде,
> стелить кровать,
> а я
> усну
> на полу.
> Потом покоя тебя лишу,
> вырою щель у ворот,
> ночью,
> вздрогнув,
> тебя спрошу:
> —Стой! Кто идет?
> Нет, не думай, что так приду.
> В этой большой войне
> Мы научились ломать беду,
> Работать и жить вдвойне ...[158]

(Then I'll go mad from the unaccustomed comfort. You'll set the table for breakfast, and I'll go and sit in the corner. You'll begin, as before, to make up the bed, and I'll go to sleep on the floor. Then I'll deprive you of peace, I'll dig a trench by the gate, and at night, trembling, I'll ask you: "Halt! Who goes there?" No, don't you believe that I'll return like that. In this great war we have learned to overcome misfortune, to work and live for two...)

It was the boast of Soviet critics that after this war there would be no 'lost generation' of disillusioned young men as there had been in Europe after the First World War, no Soviet Remarque to produce a new *All Quiet on the Western Front*.[159] The potential difficulties that might be faced re-integrating into society large numbers of young men who saw themselves as liberators deserving of greater freedom themselves were not mentioned, but it seems reasonable to assume that they were not overlooked. There was perhaps rather more attention paid to the war dead, rather than to the young men who were going to return. Increasingly, such poetry commemorated the dead with little consideration of the enormity of the country's loss or the suffering of grieving relatives. At the centre of such poems was a generalised, anonymous 'unknown soldier'. Critics now required of poets a historical perspective, meaning a view of the war which went far beyond its effects on individuals.[160] Specific attainments were swamped by the grandeur of approaching victory. Isakovskii hymned Russia's achievements with suitable expansiveness:

Ты—выше всякой славы,
Достойней всех похвал!
И все народы мира,
Что с нами шли в борьбе,
Поклоном благородным
Поклонятся тебе;
Поклонятся всем сердцем
За все твои дела,
За подвиг твой бессмертный,
За все, что ты снесла;
За то, что жизнь и правду
Сумела отстоять,
Советская Россия,
Родная наша мать![161]

(You are above all glory, more worthy than any praises! And all the peoples of the world who went alongside us in the struggle will bow to you with a noble bow; they will bow with all their hearts in recognition of all your deeds, of your immortal victory, of all that you withstood; because you were able to defend life and truth, Soviet Russia, our dear mother!)

Sometimes the pursuit of historical perspective meant that the present, and therefore the specifically Soviet aspects of the country's achievement were lost from sight, to the displeasure of some critics. It seems debatable whether Nikolai Glazkov's lines of 1944 can be taken at face value:

Счастлив, кто врага разит,
Совсем не страшась контратак.
От ВРАГ БУДЕТ РАЗБИТ
До БЫЛ РАЗБИТ ВРАГ
Легла пятилетка войны.
Ее за четыре года
Выполнили сыны
Трудового народа!
Победа как никогда близка:

Даже время не кажется длинным.
Наши доблестные войска
Встали в очередь за Берлином![162]

(Happy he who smashes the enemy with no fear of a counter-attack. From THE ENEMY SHALL BE CRUSHED to THE ENEMY WAS CRUSHED lay the five year plan of war. It was fulfilled in four years by the sons of the working people! Victory is near as never before: even time does not seem long. Our glorious forces have joined the queue for Berlin!)

It seems doubtful whether a Five Year Plan would have been considered of sufficient stature to convey the grandeur of victory; Glazkov's disproportionate comparison suggests lurking irony. The Plans had been compared to a war, but this comparison was not generally inverted. The historical perspective critics were increasingly demanding was oriented towards the future and towards creating a monument to a victory won by Soviet man. The perspective adopted in 1941 looked back at the past, at Russian tradition, and had been welcomed at the time. Now the 'timeless' figures of Russian soldiers 'of all great wars and ages' were no longer in favour.[163] Tikhonov had already warned that Vasilii Terkin, although a traditionally Russian character, showed insufficient signs of his Soviet background.[164] Many poets portrayed their heroes as timeless figures. In Pavel Shubin's poem 'Gvardiia' (The Guardsmen) Soviet soldiers gathered around a campfire are transformed into Russian veterans of campaigns both ancient and modern:

... А сапоги до голенищ сносились,
А седина в усах осела хмуро:
Они еще под Куннерсдорфом бились,
Шли, не сгибаясь, в пламя Порт-Артура.

А может быть, они еще древнее
И подлинны, как грубый миф Эллады,
И в их морщинах залегла, темнея,
Святая пыль развалин Сталинграда.[165]

(But their boots are worn down to the tops, and grey has settled grimly in their moustaches: they fought before at Kunersdorf, and advanced unbowed into the flames of Port Arthur. But perhaps they are even more ancient and genuine, like a crude Hellenic myth, in their wrinkles the sacred dust from the ruins of Stalingrad has settled darkly.)

Opinions on the status and value of current poetry varied. Critics began to look to the future and agreed that the epics of the war would come later. Pertsov considered the work of Inber, Berggol'ts and Shishova as valuable human documents, but also pointed out that not all work which helped people in the present to gain an awareness of their strength would continue to be effective in future.[166] Surkov was convinced that the poetry to come would supersede most wartime works, which would be mainly of sentimental value: 'As time passes, new, major, talented works about the heroism of our people will be written. They will be refined in form and broad in the range of events depicted. But the works written now will remain dear to readers' hearts.'[167] Before the war had even finished, critics began to sum up wartime developments in poetry, creating a retrospective interpretation of its smoothly linear progression from a belief in victory in 1941 to the certainties of the present. War poetry was portrayed as a monolithic whole, an expression of national unity: 'Across huge distances the voices of poets quite unlike one another mingled because in them spoke one and the same voice, the voice of the people's heart, beating in the firm rhythm of confidence in the justice and immortality of our cause'.[168] The rush to draw conclusions can be seen as part of an ideologically motivated drive to bring literature back into line. For some, the debate was not yet closed; poets in particular had plenty to say about the nature and significance of their work.

1945: Perspectives on Victory

Literary criticism, however, had by 1945 definitely returned to its business of looking out for ideological 'mistakes' and informing writers of the 'correct' attitude. Much of what poets were actually writing was far from being in accordance with official expectations of new epics. The Leningrad poet Vadim Shefner's narrative poem 'Vstrecha v prigorode' (Meeting in the Suburbs), written during 1944 and 1945, begins with a warning to the reader:

Не ждите здесь широких обобщений,—
Еще кипит военная страда,
Мы помним дым пылающих селений
И взятые с боем города.
Мы помним встречи, имена и даты,
Разлуки, битвы, номера полков,—
Но мы не летописцы, мы солдаты,
Мы не ведем на марше дневников.
Немудрено,—мы в битве, в самой гуще,
Лишь свой участок боя виден нам.
Чтоб не отстать от впереди идущих,
Мы не должны глазеть по сторонам.[169]

(Don't expect broad generalisations here,—the toil of war is still seething, we remember the smoke of blazing villages and the towns taken in battle. We remember meetings, names and dates, partings, battles, numbers of regiments,—but we are not chroniclers, we are soldiers, we do not keep diaries on the march. No wonder—we're in the thick of battle, we can only see our sector of the fight. So as not to fall behind those ahead we may not stare to either side.)

Shefner echoes Donald Bain's reservations about the task of a war poet; he records his experiences without attempting to draw conclusions about them.[170] Similarly the young poet Aleksandr Mezhirov, looking back on the first winter of the war from the vantage point of 1945, concentrates on evoking a certain atmosphere, exploring a single incident, rather than drawing conclusions from the experience amassed in the meantime.[171] In 1945 critics were demanding, more then ever, the 'broad generalisations' which Shefner and many others felt unable to provide.

The change in tone was becoming increasingly clear from critical articles and from the speeches at the 10th Plenum of the Writers' Union in May 1945. Nikolai Tikhonov said:

> Socialist realism is our strength. There are people who are not fully aware of this. The writer is the voice of his times. And the critic should follow the writer with the same attention and readiness to explain his achievements and mistakes as Belinskii followed the development of Lermontov.[172]

The term 'socialist realism' had scarcely been mentioned throughout the war. Now critics repeatedly conveyed the message that victory was to be celebrated as an achievement of socialist man, and not of some timeless and archetypal Russian soldier. It was claimed that socialism had created people who, for the first time, acted in complete consciousness of their historical role.[173] Some of the younger poets, as will be shown below, were aware of their part in history, but did not attribute their achievements to the influence of socialism.

Aleksei Surkov addressed the problem of the 'war generation' in his speech at the 10th Plenum. By now the lack of historical perspective was a common criticism of their work. Surkov praised the way they drew on their experience of war, their ability to write without rhetoric and with courage, but warned of the dangers of excessive realism. The mere fact of having taken part in the war, said Surkov, did not place a poet above criticism.[174] Sergei Orlov, a soldier since 1941, felt that critics had no right to comment on work created in the heat of battle:

> Пускай в сторонку удалится критик:
> Поэтика здесь вовсе ни при чем.
> Я, может быть, какой-нибудь эпитет—
> И тот нашел под огнем.
> Здесь молодости рубежи и сроки,
> По жизни окаянная тоска...
> Я порохом пропахнувшие строки
> Из-под обстрела вынес на руках.[175]

(Let the critic step aside: poetics isn't important here. It may be I found some epithet, and that under fire. Here are the borderlines and terms of youth, a desperate yearning for life... I carried in my hands, from under fire, lines imbued with the smell of gunpowder.)

Like Orlov, Evgenii Vinokurov, who entered the army aged eighteen in 1943, protested the authenticity of his poetry. Implicit in his words is the claim that work organically linked with real experience needed no additional 'historical perspective' to be considered valid:

Я эти песни написал не сразу.
Я с ними по осенней мерзлоте,
С неначатыми,
по пластунски лазал
сквозь черные поля на животе.

Мне эти темы подсказали ноги,
уставшие в походах от дорог.
Добытые с тяжелым потом строки
Я, как себя, от смерти не берег.[176]

(I did not write these songs at once. With them, not yet begun, I crawled on my belly across frozen ground in autumn, across black fields. These themes were dictated by my legs, weary from marches over rough ground. I did not hide these lines, procured with heavy sweat, from death, as I did not hide myself.)

Victory was naturally the dominant theme of poetry in 1945. The advance through Europe was given little attention except as a prelude to the capture of Berlin. As in the previous year, the actual events of the war were scarcely mentioned. Semen Gudzenko continued to concentrate on immediate impressions in poems charting his progress through Hungary and Rumania.[177] More commonly, poets chronicled the march towards Berlin and to victory, condemning the evil done by the Germans and praising the virtue of their own army in undistinguished and formulaic verse. A cycle of poems by Vissarion Saianov gave an exhaustive account of his travels with the advancing army in the spring of 1945, recording, among other things, the horror of a concentration camp and the day of capitulation in Berlin.[178] Russia's mission to liberate Europe is a recurring theme treated in symbolic terms. Sergei Narovchatov's 'Soldaty svobody' (The Soldiers of Freedom) portrays a small barefoot girl running to greet Soviet soldiers. Her name is Europa.[179]

As Soviet troops advanced through Eastern Europe, poetry began to focus either on the future victory in Berlin, or on the past, on Russia's suffering under enemy occupation rather than on the effects of the Soviet advance. The major beacons by which poets oriented themselves were the desperate battles of 1941, the heroic defence of Stalingrad, and the capture of Berlin. The impossibility of giving honest and realistic descriptions of the Soviet advance through Europe was further compounded by the absence of a pre-ordained scheme for the depiction of the advance. Once Soviet troops restored their country's former border, the cycle of retreat and return underlying many poems written between 1941 and 1944 became obsolete. The lack of a framework created perspectives which were disconcertingly large:

... Взглянул солдат вокруг окопа:
в траве земля,
в дыму трава.
Пред гребнем бруствера—
Европа,
за гранью траверса—
Москва![180]

(The soldier looked around the trench: the earth covered in grass, the grass covered in smoke. In front of the parapet's mound—Europe, behind the line of the traverse—Moscow!)

The greater the distance from Moscow, the less real the surroundings. Germany is perceived at several removes; its alien appearance relates it to something seen only in pictures:

Я это видел в детстве на гравюрах:
под черепицей двухэтажный дом
и готика таинственных и хмурых
старинных зданий над прудом.[181]

(I saw this in my childhood in engravings: a two-storey house with a tiled roof, and the Gothic style of mysterious, gloomy, ancient buildings by a pond.)

Evgenii Dolmatovskii, who as a war correspondent travelled with Soviet forces through Europe, writes from abroad of his memories of Russia. He is unable to write about what he sees—a restriction imposed apparently from within, rather than as the result of external persuasion—as images of Stalingrad and the suffering of people in Russia are more persistent than details of 'exotic' foreign lands:

Я хотел написать о Балканах,
О румынском прохладном вине,
О костелах за Вислой, о странах,
Где прошли мы в дыму и огне.
Но на белых страницах тетради
Возникают иные края—
Тот разбитый блиндаж в Сталинграде,
Где окончилась юность моя,
Да кривой городок Новозыбков,
Где однажды пришлось ночевать.
Там до света над крохотной зыбкой
То ли пела, то плакала мать.[182]

(I wanted to write about the Balkans, about cool Romanian wine, about the churches beyond the Visla, about the countries we passed through in smoke and fire. But on the white pages of my notebook other places rise up—that shattered dug-out in Stalingrad where my youth ended, and the crooked little town of Novozybkov, where I once had to spend the night. There a mother was either singing or crying over a tiny cradle until dawn.)

Between the past and future lay a no-man's land. In another poem Dolmatovskii describes East Prussia as a nameless, alien and apparently godless country, in implicit contrast with 'holy' Russia where the atheist state had sought the support of the Church it had previously persecuted:

Дьявол придумал такую
в атласах мира неназванную страну.[183]

(The devil thought up such a country, not named in any atlases of the world.)

The only living creatures mentioned in this poem are Soviet soldiers, one of whom encounters his own wife among a group of captive foreigners. The only suffering involved in this war, implies the poem, is that of the Soviet victims of Nazi aggression. However, according to Lev Kopelev's account of Soviet activities on the East Prussian front, the defeaters of fascism indulged in looting, rape, arson and the indiscriminate murder of civilians. Kopelev's complaints that such behaviour was unworthy of the soldiers who defeated Hitler were interpreted as an undue expression of sympathy towards the enemy, and led to his arrest.[184]

By the time the Soviet army celebrated victory in Berlin, the theme had already been current in poetry for several months, and, it seemed, it was not easy finding something new to say about it. Aleksei Surkov resorted to vague and tautological rhetoric:

Не умолкает гром орудий.
Бушует пламя в дымной мгле.
И говорят друг другу люди:
—Есть справедливость на земле!

И ныне перед всей вселенной
Той справедливости закон,
Святой, незыблемый, нетленный,
Отвагой смелых утвержден.

Мы—совесть мира. Нам отмщенье,
Прошедшим сквозь огонь и ад.
Тот высшей правды воплощенье -
Бесстрашный сталинский солдат.[185]

(The guns thunder unceasingly, flames rampage in the smoky darkness. And people say to one another "there is justice in this world!" And now before the whole universe stands the law of justice, sacred, unshakeable, unfading, confirmed by the courage of the brave. We are the world's conscience. Vengeance is ours, who passed through fire and hell. The embodiment of the utmost truth is the fearless soldier of Stalin.)

Aleksandr Tvardovskii refrained from showing his hero Terkin entering Berlin in triumph, describing only how soldiers took a bath before setting off on the last stages of the campaign. Terkin had, characteristically, fought his war very much on the periphery of events, not in major battles, and now he was seen outside the noisy rhetoric surrounding the battle for Berlin. Throughout the poem the business of waging war had been referred to as work, using expressions and vocabulary from peaceful occupations to describe the soldiers' actions. Taking a bath marked the end of a job well done.[186]

Tvardovskii evidently found it less easy than Surkov to produce a fluent instantaneous response to the end of the war:

Не в самый полдень торжества
Приходят лучшие слова...

И сердцу радостно и страшно
Себя доверить той строке,
В которой лозунг наш вчерашний
Сегодня—ноша на штыке.

Отчизна, мать моя, сурово
Не осуди, я слов ищу,
И я лишь первые два слова
Об этом празднике пишу.

Я их сложил, как мог, в минуты
Волненья, что лишают слов,
Когда гремел салют салютов
Из всех, какие есть, стволов.

С твоими равными сынами
Я плакал теми же слезами,
Слезами радости, твой сын.

Берлин, о Родина, за нами,
Берлин, товарищи, Берлин![187]

(The best words come not at the very zenith of the triumph... My heart feels joyful and anxious about trusting itself to the line in which our slogan of yesterday is now a burden on a bayonet. My country, my mother, do not judge me severely, I am looking for words, and I am writing only the first couple of words about this celebration. I composed them as best I could, in minutes of excitement which took my words away, when the salute of salutes roared out of every gun barrel. With your equal sons I, your son, wept the selfsame tears, tears of joy. Berlin, o Motherland, is ours, Berlin, comrades, Berlin!)

The suspicion of glib and verbose reaction which appears to be implicit in Tvardovskii's poem is more clearly given in a short poem by Mikhail L'vov. For him and his fellow-soldiers, joy at winning the war is tempered by the thought of the millions of lives lost, and they are unable to join in the festivities:

... А нам нельзя и раскричаться—
У нас в зубах песок.
А нам нельзя и целоваться—
Песок к губам присох.

Мы отвечали, как умели,
Восторгам шумных сел.

Но только танки все шумели—
Водитель молча вел.

Еще мы павших не забыли,
И больно нам кричать.
Пусть нас простят.
Мы победили.
Нам можно помолчать.[188]

(But we cannot shout out—we have sand in our teeth. And we cannot kiss—the sand has dried on our lips. We responded as best we could to the exultations of noisy villages. But only the tanks made a noise—the driver drove in silence. We haven't yet forgotten the fallen, and it is painful for us to shout. Let people forgive us. We have won. We are allowed to be silent.)

The price of suffering exacted by the war, in loss of life and in terrible memories, is strongly evoked in 'Pobeda' (Victory), a poem written by Vladimir Bobrov, a paratrooper whose work was not published until after his death in 1977:

Был я там, где рвались мины.
Слышал рядом свист свинца.
Долю фронтовой судьбины
честно вынес до конца.

Рад бы память не тревожить,
да забыть я не могу
вшей на заскорузлой коже,
кровь и трупы на снегу,

и карболовое счастье
лазаретов, где я гнил,
и оскаленные пасти
наспех вырытых могил,

и перед броском минуты...
Знаю, какова она—
отгремевшего салюта
настоящая цена.

И мне думается, рано
подводить боям итог.
Нерубцующей раной
мир лежит у наших ног.[189]

(I was there where mines exploded, heard beside me the whistle of lead. I honourably bore to the last my front-line fate. I'd be glad not to trouble my memory, but I cannot forget the lice on coarsened skin, the blood and corpses on the snow, or the carbolic-scented happiness of field hospitals where I rotted, or the gaping jaws of graves dug hurriedly, or the minutes before the parachute jump ... I know what it was, the real price of the salute which has just died down. And it seems to me too early to draw conclusions about the battles. Like a wound which won't heal over, the world lies at our feet.)

Although mainstream Soviet poetry was eloquent on the subject of the positive inner transformation which war brought about, it had little to say about the physical or mental damage inflicted on soldiers. Sergei Orlov, whose face was disfigured by burns sustained in a blazing tank, was left physically marked and painfully aware of other people's attitudes of horror or pity. The taboo of physical scars has, it seems, even more force than that of psychological damage, as such poems are rare:

Не таким, не в войну, с полпути,
Я мечтал в этот домик прийти.
Щеки в шрамах, в багровых рубцах
(Нету прежнего больше лица),
Руку скрюченную неся,
Кисть багрова, как лапа гуся.
Смотрит с жалостью женщина: вот
С фронта новый калека идет.[190]

(Not like this, not in wartime, from half way did I dream of coming back to this house. My cheeks are scarred with crimson scabs (my former face no longer exists), I carry a twisted arm, my hand is purple like a goose's foot. A woman looks at me with pity: there's another cripple back from the front.)

The soldier's problems were by no means over even if he arrived home unscathed. Among many accounts of the joyful reunion of husband and wife, Mikhail Isakovskii's 'Vragi sozhgli rodnuiu khatu...' (The Enemies Burned his Family Home...) was a sober reminder that the soldier could not leave the war behind by leaving the front. Like the hero of Isakovskii's poem, many soldiers who survived the ordeal of battle found that their homes and families had been destroyed by war. Victory and medals lose their meaning when the soldier comes home to find nothing but his wife's grave:

Он пил—солдат, слуга народа,
И с болью в сердце говорил:
«Я шел к тебе четыре года,
Я три державы покорил...»

Хмелел солдат, слеза катилась,
Слеза несбывшихся надежд,
И на груди его светилась
Медаль за город Будапешт.[191]

(He drank—a soldier, servant of the people, and with pain in his heart he said: "I spent four years coming back to you, I conquered three powers ..." The soldier became drunk, a tear rolled down, the tear of disappointed hopes, and on his breast there shone a medal for the city Budapest.)

The indignant reaction to Isakovskii's poem confirmed an unspoken rule: it was not permissible to portray Soviet man as a victim of war. It was, however, allowed to show Jews as victims of German wickedness. Although anti-semitism was revived soon after the war in an official campaign, during 1945 the press voiced horror at Nazi atrocities and sympathy for their victims. The war correspondent and novelist Vasilii Grossman published a stark eye-witness report on the concentration camp at Treblinka. *Literaturnaia gazeta* announced that a book chronicling Nazi treatment of the Jewish population in occupied countries was to be produced jointly by American writers and the Jewish Antifascist Committee in Moscow.[192] Sergei Narovchatov wrote a poem about Soviet soldiers adopting a boy who had escaped from the Warsaw ghetto, and declared that the Soviet people were a family which took no notice of nationalities, only of shared humanity:

> ... Без семьи, без родных, без народа ...
> Стань же мальчику в черный год
> Ближе близких, советская рота,
> Вместе с ротой—советский народ!
>
> И сегодня, у стен Пулутска,
> Пусть в сердцах сольются навек
> Оба слова—еврей и русский—
> В слове радостном—человек![193]

(Without a family, relatives, a people... Soviet troops, be to this boy in a dark year closer than relatives, and together with the troops, the Soviet people! And today, by the walls of Pulutsk, may there be joined in our hearts for ever two words—Jew and Russian—in the joyful word—man!)

It was permissible to show Jews as victims of the war in 1945, but to suggest that Soviet soldiers had been in any way traumatised by their experiences invited criticism. Nikolai Tikhonov expressed strong misgivings about the young poets' feelings of sadness at a time when the 'sunlight of victory' should predominate. The death of friends was, Tikhonov said, an inevitable theme for the young soldier-poets, but one which threatened to dominate their work to the exclusion of new themes: 'I am not calling for displays of high spirits over the graves of friends, but I do object to the cloud of sadness which is obscuring our path ahead'.[194] Others were prepared to accept the emotional legacy of war. Vera Inber found the young men's feelings only natural.[195] Ol'ga Berggol'ts put a strong case for not excluding all mention of wartime suffering. She was herself criticised by Prokof'ev for writing too much on the Leningraders' suffering during the blockade,[196] but replied:

> There is a one school of thought whose adherents protest against the portrayal and depiction of the great trials which the people as a whole and every person individually have undergone on the way to our tremendous victory. But why should the people's achievements be devalued? And why diminish the enemy's crimes, after they have forced our people to suffer so many terrible and burdensome things?'[197]

Meanwhile, in August 1945 Egolin presented a document to Malenkov, naming poets, including Vladimir Lifshits, Ol'ga Berggol'ts, Mikhail Dudin and Vsevolod Rozhdestvenskii, whose work, published in *Zvezda*, was 'shot through with images of suffering, death and feelings of doom'. Writers such as Aseev, Zoshchenko and Sel'vinskii had 'begun to revise Soviet views on reality and social relations'. Even worse, writers had been complaining of restrictions placed on them by censors and editors, while Vsevolod Vishnevskii had publicly demanded 'bourgeois artistic freedom', saying 'We have been to war and fought, now give us freedom of speech'.[198]

Looking at the work of the younger poets, it seems more reasonable to assume that the real cause of anxiety among literary bureaucrats was not in fact a preoccupation with sadness. Demands, implied or openly expressed, for post-war freedoms were much more worrying. A closer look at the poetry which may have given rise to Tikhonov's complaint shows it to be poorly founded. The sadness he condemned is present, but it is far from despairing. While the young veterans mourned the death of friends, they refused to see themselves, the survivors, as victims of the war. Their realisation of the dreadful price of victory did not tempt them to self-pity, and they expected no pity from others. As Gudzenko wrote:

> Нас не нужно жалеть, ведь и мы никого б не жалели.
> Мы пред нашим комбатом, как пред господом богом, чисты.
> На живых порыжели от крови и глины шинели,
> на могилах у мертвых расцвели голубые цветы...
>
> ... Нас не нужно жалеть, ведь и мы никого б не жалели.
> Кто в атаку ходил, кто делился последним куском,
> тот поймет эту правду—она к нам в окопы и щели
> приходила поспорить ворчливым, охрипшим баском.
>
> Пусть живые запомнят, и пусть поколения знают
> эту взятую боем суровую правду солдат—
> и твои костыли, и смертельная рана сквозная,
> и могилы над Волгой, где тысячи юных лежат...
>
> Это наша судьба, это с ней мы ругались и пели,
> подымались в атаку и рвали над Бугом мосты.
> ... Нас не нужно жалеть, ведь и мы никого б не жалели.
> Мы пред нашей Россией и в трудное время чисты...
>
> ... Мы поклонимся в ноги родным исстрадавшимся людям,
> матерей расцелуем и подруг, что дождались, любя.
> Вот когда мы вернемся и победу штыками добудем—
> все долюбим, ровесник, и ремесла найдем для себя.[199]

(There is no need to pity us, we wouldn't have pitied anyone else. We are pure before our commander, as before the Lord God. On the living the greatcoats are rusted with blood and clay. On the graves of the dead blue flowers have blossomed. There is no need to pity us, we wouldn't have pitied anyone else. Those who went into attacks, who shared their last crust of bread will understand this truth—it came into our trenches and ditches to argue in a grumbling, hoarse bass voice. Let the living remember, and let the generations know this severe soldiers' truth which we won in battle—and your crutches, and the fatal piercing wound, and the graves by the Volga where thousands of young men lie... It is our fate, we cursed and sang with it, with it we rose up to attack and blew up the bridges over the Bug. ...There is no need to pity us, we wouldn't have pitied anyone else. We are pure before our Russia even in hard times... We shall bow down to the ground before the dear people who have suffered so much, kiss our mothers and girlfriends who waited lovingly for us. When we come back and secure victory with our bayonets—we will live to the full, my contemporary, and find a trade for ourselves.)

This poem, 'Moe pokolenie' (My Generation) does indeed read like an anthem for a generation, with its challenging bluntness and the assertive rhythm of the long five-foot anapestic lines. It circulated in manuscript form at the end of the war; the final stanza's promise to return home and procure victory with the bayonet seems to be a sufficiently clear expression of dissatisfaction with the *status quo*. The war experiences of the younger generation had made them more resistant, not less, although their resilience was soon to be tested by renewed Stalinist repression:

> ... Эпоха воспитала цепких, жестких,
> Нас, не согласных стяг склонить хоть раз,—
> Мы знали, командиры и подростки:
> Эпоха недействительна без нас.[200]

(The epoch raised us to be tenacious and tough, to refuse to lower the banner even once,—we knew, commanders and youths, that the epoch was not valid without us.)

The poets of the 'war generation' confidently declared their own importance for the country's present and future, and announced their willingness to continue fighting for a new, better life. The work of some young poets has lines which read like a protest, although a careful ambiguity is retained. Mikhail L'vov asserts the strength of his own will and that of his generation, saying: 'А раз не хотим мы, то кто нам прикажет' (if we do not wish it, who shall order us?), which suggests rebellion, although the poem was ostensibly about the poet's refusal to die when severely wounded.[201] After the victory L'vov wrote the ambiguous lines:

> Мы с боем шли по водам и по сушам,
> И дождь хлестал нас острый, как резьба,
> И мы себе заглядывали в душу
> И там не обнаружили раба.[202]

(We went in battle over sea and land, and rain lashed us, sharp as blades, and we looked into our souls and did not find slaves there.)

According to L'vov's poem, a whole generation had realised that they were free and independent, slaves to no-one, not Hitler, and probably not Stalin either. For young soldiers returning from the front, the war appeared to have the status of a process of moral purification, an atonement for the moral collapse of the pre-war years. Semen Gudzenko, as early as 1942, had written that the war generation would fight on, using words for ammunition:

Нам дня не жить
без битвы и оружия,
И будет порох
словом заменен.

(We cannot live one day without battles and weapons, and gunpowder shall be replaced by the word.)

A later version, published in 1961, some years after the poet's death, altered the final line to 'без шелеста простреленных знамен' (without the rustle of shot-through banners), which removes the aggressive self-assertiveness of the original.[203]

The experience of war had taught many young people, both men and women, that they were capable of taking on responsibility and carrying out difficult tasks. They had grown used to seeing their actions influence events. Both in the case of the army veterans and those who lived through the nine hundred days of the Leningrad siege, the existence within a relatively small and exclusive group had produced a greater sense of solidarity and mutual dependence than had been possible in life before the war, in which fear and suspicion was used as a method of social manipulation. War veterans had found their way independently to new moral values, adapted to a different way of life, and had gradually moved away from the idea of the pervading control of the state. While soldiers were absent carrying out their task of putting an end to fascism, in the name of freedom, the relative freedom at home had begun to look ephemeral. Ironically, these same young soldiers were laying down the basis for the renewal of state authority, unaware of the wider consequences of their achievements. Stalin clearly realised that their awareness of a discrepancy between hopes of new freedom and the reality of renewed repression was a threat to his authority. Potentially rebellious soldiers returned from the front, but some, particularly those who had been prisoners of war abroad, went home only after serving a sentence in the Gulag. Stalin, presumably, was reminded of those who returned from the defeat of Napoleon and later took part in the Decembrist conspiracy against the tsar, and took preventive measures accordingly.

Although critics had welcomed the new generation of poets as the future of Soviet literature, their subversive potential as a united but unofficial voice in post-war Soviet society was evidently recognised. Within a short time they faced official criticism for continuing to write about the war when they should have been writing about post-war reconstruction.[204] The need to mobilise patriotic feeling had brought about concessions in literature which were seized upon by the new generation, who, however, by 1945, were unwilling to give up their freedom.

NOTES

1 Compare, for example, the 13 stanza version of Nikolai Tikhonov's 'Rastet, shumit tot vikhr' narodnoi slavy ...' in *Zvezda*, 1–2 (1942), 3–4 with the nine stanza version in *Sobranie sochinenii*, 7 vols (Moscow, 1973–76), I, 445.

2 For poems found on the site of former German concentration camps, see *Sovetskie poety, pavshie na Velikoi Otechestvennoi voine* (Moscow–Leningrad, 1965), pp. 659–669; *Stikhi za koliuchei provolokoi* (Moscow, 1953). See also the poems of the Tatar poet Musa Dzhalil', held prisoner and executed in Berlin, in *Izbrannoe* (Moscow, 1966). Also Stepan Zlobin's poems written in a German prisoner of war camp, in *Sovetskie pisateli na frontakh Velikoi Otechestvennoi voiny*, 2 vols, Literaturnoe nasledstvo, 78 (Moscow, 1966), II, 145–146.

3 For critical poetry, see Natal'ia Krandievskaia-Tolstaia, 'Iz tsikla "v osade"', *Rekviem: stikhi russkikh sovetskikh poetov* (Moscow, 1989), p. 42; Viktor Bokov, 'Pis'mo Stalinu iz lageria', ibid., pp. 207–208 (a parody of Simonov's 'Surovaia godovshchina').

4 See M. Azadovskii, *Frontovoi fol'klor* (Moscow, 1944); *Russkii fol'klor Velikoi Otechestvennoi voiny*, edited by V.Gusev (Moscow, 1964); V. IU. Krupianskaia and S. I. Mints, *Materialy po istorii pesni Velikoi Otechestvennoi voiny* (Moscow, 1953).

5 A. I. Pavlovskii, *Russkaia sovetskaia poeziia v gody Velikoi Otechestvennoi voiny* (Leningrad, 1967), p. 207.

6 *Russkaia sovetskaia poeziia v gody Velikoi otechestvennoi voiny*, p. 4.

7 'Predchuvstvie pobedy', *Literaturnaia gazeta*, 7 November 1944, p. 3.

8 Recent publications using archival material have begun to open up this area. See in particular Denis Babichenko, *Pisateli i tsenzory: sovetskaia literatura 1940-kh godov pod politicheskim kontrolem Ts.K* (Moscow, 1994), especially Chapter Two, pp.64–102, on the war years. See also Denis Babichenko, 'Zhdanov, Malenkov i delo leningradskikh zhurnalov', *Voprosy literatury*, 3 (1993), 201–214; Iurii Zhukov, 'Preliudiia', *Literaturnaia gazeta*, 28 July 1993, p. 6.

9 See George Reavey, *Soviet Literature To-Day* (London, 1946), Chapter Two, 'The Life and Organisation of Writers', pp. 30–44, and Chapter Seven, 'The Writer and the Critic', pp. 111–118, for a contemporary description of literary controls.

10 From a conversation with the Soviet critic Mikhail P'ianykh, Leningrad, March 1990.

11 See note 8 above.

12 See Boris Ruch'ev, *Sobranie sochinenii*, 2 vols (Cheliabinsk, 1978-79), for 'Stikhi o dalekikh bitvakh', I, 160–162, and 'Nevidimka', II, 22–35.

13 See, for example, 'Kliatva', *Sochineniia*, 2 vols (Moscow, 1986), I, 198; 'Muzhestvo', I, 199.

14 See the conflicting opinions over Pasternak's 1945 collection *Zemnoi prostor* in P. Gromov, 'Boris Pasternak: *Zemnoi prostor*', *Zvezda*, 5–6 (1945), 157–159, and A. Tarasenkov, 'Novye stikhi Borisa Pasternaka', *Znamia*, 4 (1945), 136–139.

15 Lev Anninskii, 'Glubina fronta: eticheskaia tema v lirike voennogo pokoleniia', *Novyi mir*, 4 (1974), p. 222.

16 Quoted by L. Lazarev in *Eto nasha sud'ba* (Moscow, 1983), p. 77.

17 'Poeziia velikoi voiny', *Nash sovremennik*, 5 (1985), 169–174 (p. 171).

18 Certain members of the war generation were, however, attacked for their 'cosmopolitan' views in an article by Stanislav Kuniaev, 'Radi zhizni na zemle: sovetskaia poeziia o Velikoi otechestvennoi voine', *Molodaia gvardiia*, 8 (1987), 246–267.

19 For more on the immediate post-war treatment of the younger generation, see Chapter Seven.

20 See 'Strana Murav'ia', *Izbrannye proizvedeniia*, 3 vols (Moscow, 1990), II, 5–78. According to the poet Aleksandr Mezhirov, during a conversation in Moscow, January 1990, Tvardovskii is said to have commented on this disjunction between his life and his art: 'There are two truths. I shall follow the one that the people follow'.

21 See 'My predchuvstvovali polykhan'e...', *Sobranie sochinenii*, 3 vols (Leningrad, 1988-90), II, 7. Also 'Iz dnevnikov Ol'gi Berggol'ts', *Vremia i my*, 6, no.57 (1980), 276–302 (p. 300).

22 For Akhmatova's Tashkent poems, see 'Luna v zenite', *Sochineniia*, 2 vols (Moscow, 1986) I, 203–215; 'Kogda lezhit luna lomtem chardzhuiskoi dyni ...', I, 207; 'Eto rys'i glaza tvoi, Aziia...', I, 207–208; 'Tashkent zatsvetaet', I, 208. See also Roberta Reeder, *Anna Akhmatova: Poet and Prophet* (London, 1994), pp. 249–282 for an account of Akhmatova's life during the war, and the reminiscences of Zoia Tomashevskaia, 'Ia—kak peterburgskaia tumba', in *Ob Anne Akhmatovoi*, edited by M. M. Kralin and I. I. Slobozhan (Leningrad, 1990), pp.417–438.

For Pasternak's wartime letters to his wife, see *Vtoroe rozhdenie: pis'ma k Z. N. Pasternak* (Moscow, 1993), pp. 154–199; see pp.301–331 of the same volume for his wife's wartime memoirs. The wartime correspondence between Pasternak and Ol'ga Freidenberg is included in *Perepiska Borisa Pasternaka* (Moscow, 1990), pp. 184–212. The recently published collection of memoirs relating to Pasternak, *Vospominaniia o Borise Pasternake*, compiled by E. V. Pasternak, M. I. Feinberg (Moscow, 1993), contains several items related to Pasternak's life during the war. See in particular Aleksandr Gladkov, 'Vstrechi s Pasternakom', pp. 326–241; Valerii Avdeev, 'Vspominaia Pasternaka', pp. 342–346; Viktor Bokov, 'Sobesednik roshch', pp. 350–352; Emma Gershtein, 'O Pasternake i Akhmatovoi', pp.395–397. The same volume also contains some of the poet's wartime correspondence: Tamara Ivanova, 'Boris Leonidovich Pasternak', pp.243–248; Daniil Danin, 'Eto prebudet s nami', pp.316–317. See also Lazar Fleishman, *Boris Pasternak: the Poet and His Politics* (Cambridge, MA and London, 1990), pp. 223–246.

An account of Tsvetaeva's life after her return to the USSR is given in Mariia Belkina, *Skreshchenie sudeb*, 2nd edition (Moscow, 1992). See also Irma Kudrova, 'Tret'ia versiia: eshche raz o poslednikh dniakh Mariny Tsvetaevoi', *Novyi mir*, 2 (1994), 205–229.

23 Introduction by Lev Anninskii to Mikhail Lukonin, *Stikhotvoreniia i poemy* (Leningrad, 1985), p. 17.

24 *Krasnaia zvezda*, 24 June 1941, p. 1.

25 Vasilii Lebedev-Kumach, *Izbrannoe* (Moscow, 1984), p. 337, but see below on disputed authorship.

26 'Pesnia o Rodine', *Izbrannoe*, pp. 253–254. N. Derevianko, 'Kto napisal "Sviashchennuiu voinu"?', *Argumenty i fakty*, 13 (1991), p. 7. The previously accepted version of the poem's origins, including photographs of manuscripts, can be found in M. M. Sitkovetskaia, 'Iz istorii pesni "Sviashchennaia voina"', *Sovetskie pisateli na frontakh Velikoi Otechestvennoi voiny*, I, 433–443.

27 See discussion of LOKAF in Chapter One.

28 'Nemetskim soldatam', *Oktiabr'*, 7–8 (1941), p. 11. See also V. Bershadskii, 'Tupoi fashist, soobrazhai, kuda zadumal lezt'...', ibid., p. 150.

29 Nikolai Oksenov, 'K sviashchennoi mesti', *Zvezda*, 9 (1941), p. 31.

30 *Literaturnaia gazeta*, 30 June 1941, p. 1; 13 August 1941, p. 1; 3 September 1941, p. 1.

31 N. Stepanov, 'Boris Lavrenev: Veter s moria', *Zvezda*, 9 (1941), p. 107.

32 *Sochineniia*, I, 322.

33 *Sobranie sochinenii*, 3 vols (Moscow, 1987–88), I, 37.

34 'Slovno smotrish' v binokl' perevernutyi ...', *Sobranie sochinenii*, 12 vols (Moscow, 1979–87), I, 91.

35 'Gospodi! Vstupisia za Sovety ...', *Izbrannoe* (Moscow, 1989), p. 355.

36 *Volia: stikhi* (Ann Arbor, 1980), p. 16.

37 See Il'ia Erenburg's memoirs, *Liudi, gody, zhizn'*, 3 vols (Moscow, 1990), II, 247–248.

38 See, for example, V. Golant, 'Korichnevaia chuma nad Evropoi', *Zvezda*, 7–8 (1941), 143–151; T. Khmel'nitskaia, 'Smert' kul'tury', ibid., 152–153; E. Gollerbakh, 'Iskusstvo v okovakh', ibid., 66–74; Z. Rabinovich, 'Protiv fashistskogo varvarstva', ibid., 169–178; I. Zil'berfarb, 'Germaniia Gitlera protiv Germanii', *Novyi mir*, 9–10 (1941), 158–173; I. El'vin, 'Kannibaly', *Oktiabr'*, 7–8 (1941), 190–197; M. Rozman, 'Germanskii narod pod igom fashizma', ibid., 198–204; M.Korotnev, 'Sterilizatsiia dukha', *Znamia*, 7–8 (1941), 158–163.

39 See Aleksei Surkov, 'Rasplata', *Krasnaia zvezda*, 13 December 1941, p. 3; A. Gatov, 'Po zver'iu—ogon'', *Novyi mir*, 7–8 (1941), p. 26; Elizaveta Polonskaia, 'Razgovor v adu' and 'Vzbesivshiisia volk', *Leningrad*, 3–4 (1941), inside back cover; Anatolii Mariengof, 'Dva germantsa', *Zvezda*, 9 (1941), 43–44.

40 See the article 'Kak nemetskie okkupanty grabili Ukrainu v 1918 god', *Novyi mir*, 7–8 (1941), 179–184, and the poems by Aron Kopshtein, 'Tysiacha deviat'sot vosemnadtsatyi god', ibid., 148–149; Pavel Zheleznov, 'Nazad!', *Krasnaia nov'*, 6 (1941), p. 20.

41 'Les pritailsia, bezmolven i strog ...', *Sobranie sochinenii*, 4 vols (Moscow, 1965-66), I, 306.

42 *Stikhotvoreniia i poemy* (Leningrad, 1986), p. 217.

43 For examples of poems about heroes see N. Tikhonov, 'Ballada o leitenantetankiste Iukhniche', *Zvezda*, 7–8 (1941), p. 8; Mikhail Svetlov, 'Ballada o starshem leitenante Kuz'mine', *Krasnaia zvezda*, 2 July 1941, p. 2; 'Kliatva', ibid., 25 September 1941, p. 3.; Mikhail Golodnyi, 'Podvig kapitana Gastello', ibid., 6 July 1941, p. 2, Konstantin Simonov, 'Prezrenie k smerti', ibid., 24 July 1941, p. 4; Iurii Inge, 'Ballada o Mikhaile Martyshchenko', *Pobeda* (Leningrad, 1970), pp. 205–206. The treatment of the hero in poetry is discussed fully in Chapter Three.

For examples of the poem-oath, see Aleksei Surkov, 'Prisiagaem pobedoi', I, 300–301; 'Opiat' etot dolgii, preryvystyi voi ...', I, 311; Vadim Shefner, 'Svoi dolg ispolnim', *Lichnaia vechnost'* (Leningrad, 1984), pp. 21–22; Ol'ga Berggol'ts, 'Pesnia o soldatskoi materi', II, 11–12.

44 I, 307.

45 *Stikhotvoreniia i poemy* (Leningrad, 1985), p. 73.

46 Ibid., pp. 71–72.

47 A. Surkov, 'Za nashei spinoi Moskva', I, 302.

48 *Stikhi, p'esy, rasskazy* (Leningrad, 1949), pp. 107–108.

49 Dmitrii Kedrin, '16 oktiabria', *Izbrannoe* (Moscow, 1991), pp. 74–75. See also his 'Polustanok', p. 73; 'Nepogod'', p. 75; 'Istoriia', p. 77; 'Tolkuchii rynok', p. 79.

50 Ibid., p. 72.

51 'V ocheredi', ibid., pp. 77–78; 'Dom', p. 152.

52 See note 3 above.

53 Diary entry for 13 September 1941, 'Blokadnyi dnevnik', *Aprel'*, 4 (1991), p. 132; for mentions of censorship, see pp. 135 and 137.

54 I, 199.

55 'Kirov s nami', II, 266–270. See Tikhonov's account of how the poem came to be written in 'Iz perezhitogo', in *Riadom s geroiami*, compiled by A. M. Beilin (Leningrad, 1967), pp. 7–10.

56 Aleksei Tolstoi, 'Nikolai Tikhonov', *Sobranie sochinenii*, 10 vols (Moscow, 1958–61), X, 520–522 (p. 522).

57 V. Zhukovskii, 'Nochnoi smotr', *Izbrannye sochineniia* (Moscow, 1982), pp. 139–140. The same rhythm is also used by Lermontov in his 'Vozdushnyi korabl'', *Polnoe sobranie stikhotvorenii*, 2 vols (Leningrad, 1989), II, 48–50, in which the ghost of Napoleon rises from the grave.

58 'Kirov s nami', II, 266.

59 Boris Shmidt, 'Da zdravstvuet Stalin, vedushchii na bitvu narod ...', *Leningrad*, 13–14 (1941), p. 13.

60 *Eto nasha sud'ba*, p. 46.

61 A. Verkin, 'Tsennoe oruzhie', *Literatura i iskusstvo*, 17 October 1942, p. 2.

62 II, 347.

63 I, 158–159.

64 'Ty pomnish', Alesha, dorogi Smolenshchiny ...', I, 88–89.

65 This point will be developed in Chapter Four on The Common Man.

66 'Bessmerten narod nash', p. 231.

67 Quoted by I. Eventov, 'Stikhotvornye listovki', *Zvezda*, 5–6 (1942), 189–191 (p. 190).

68 I, 108–110.

69 I, 105–107.

70 See 'Soveshchanie literaturovedov i kritikov', *Literatura i iskusstvo*, 28 February 1942, p. 4; also A. Surkov, 'Tovarishcham kritikam', ibid., 8 March 1942, p. 2.

71 'Ispytanie ognem', *Oktiabr'*, 12 (1942), 85–93 (p. 85).

72 D. Zolotnitskii, 'Oruzhie agitatora-pesnotvortsa', *Zvezda*, 5–6 (1942), 183–185 (p. 184).

73 'O lirike', *Literatura i iskusstvo*, 28 March 1942, p. 2.

74 'Literatura i voina: 16 mesiatsev', *Oktiabr'*, 11 (1942), 136–144 (p. 136).

75 V. Pertsov, 'Zametki o sovetskoi poezii nashikh dnei', *Literatura i iskusstvo*, 14 March 1942, p. 2.

76 'Iz dnevnikov Ol'gi Berggol'ts', *Zvezda*, 6 (1990), p. 162. See also p. 166, p. 168, p. 171, for her remarks on relaxation in censorship.

77 Iakov Khelemskii, 'Blindazh', *Izbrannoe* (Moscow, 1983), p. 53.

78 Pavel Shubin, 'Pod garmon'', *Izbrannoe* (Moscow, 1988), pp. 251–252.

79 *Stikhi slagalis' na khodu* (Moscow, 1990), pp. 72–73.

80 *Do poslednego dykhaniia*, pp. 204–205.

81 'Novye stikhi A. Surkova', *Novyi mir*, 3–4 (1942), 241–245 (p. 243).

82 'Son', *Sobranie sochinenii*, 6 vols (Moscow, 1971-74), I, 369–370. See also 'Strakh', I, 370–371.

83 I, 375.

84 'Zhivye legendy', *Sobranie sochinenii*, 3 vols (Moscow, 1974–75), I, 429.

85 *Dusha Leningrada* (Leningrad, 1979), p. 17.

86 Ibid., p. 18.

87 *Blokada* (Moscow, 1943).

88 See the entry for 25 July in 'Iz dnevnikov Ol'gi Berggol'ts', *Zvezda*, 6 (1990), p. 170.

89 'Fevral'skii dnevnik', *Sobranie sochinenii*, II, 34–39; 'Leningradskaia poema', II, 40–49.

90 'Mechtaniia', *Volia: stikhi*, pp. 29–30.

91 'Tyl', *Izbrannoe*, pp. 83–84.

92 I, 366–368.

93 *Izbrannoe*, pp. 86–88; pp. 97–99.

94 'Khochesh' znat', chto takoe Rossiia? ...', ibid., p. 92; see also 'Ia ne znaiu, chto na svete proshche ...', p. 93.

95 M. Svetlov, 'Dvadtsat' vosem'', I, 405–416; N. Tikhonov, 'Slovo o dvadtsati vos'mi gvardeitsakh', II, 271–281. Recent research suggests that the events portrayed in these works may not have taken place; see John Barber, 'The Twenty-Eight Panfilovtsy and the Battle of Dubosekovo Siding: the Making of a Soviet Myth', unpublished paper, CREES, University of Birmingham, March 1993.

96 'Poemy Mikhaila Svetlova', *Literatura i iskusstvo*, 22 August 1942, p. 2.

97 *Sobranie sochinenii*, 4 vols (Moscow, 1971–73), II, 40–62.

98 *Sobranie sochinenii*, 3 vols (Moscow, 1984–85), I, 277–321.

99 See, for example, A.Surkov, 'Podoshla voina k Podmoskov'iu ...', I, 336; 'V dymu pozhara tonet dal' sedaia ...', I, 338.

100 'V surovyi chas razdum'ia nas ne tron'te...', *Stikhotvoreniia i poemy* (Leningrad, 1981), pp. 164–165.

101 'Prozhili dvadtsat' let ...', *Stikhi slagalis' na khodu ...*', p. 46.

102 The cycle was published in *Novyi mir*, 11–12 (1941), 18–24; *Krasnaia nov'*, 1–2 (1942), 30–34; *Novyi mir*, 11–12 (1942), 109–113.

103 I, 185.

104 *Vasilii Terkin*, *Izbrannye proizvedeniia*, II, 80.

105 *Sobranie sochinenii*, 6 vols (Moscow, 1976–83), II, 71–75.

106 *Izbrannye proizvedeniia*, I, 235–241.

107 'Vasilii Terkin', ibid., II, 136.

108 'Russkii voin Vasilii Terkin', *Literatura i iskusstvo*, 31 October 1942, p. 2.

109 A. Prokof'ev, 'Shag vpered', p. 244.

110 *Stikhi slagalis' na khodu ...*, pp. 77–78.

111 I.Sel'vinskii, 'Nad kartoi Evropy 1943 goda', I, 385–386.

112 'Literatura Velikoi Otechestvennoi voiny: na tvorcheskom soveshchanii v soiuze sovetskikh pisatelei', *Literatura i iskusstvo*, 3 April 1943, p. 3. For the text of the speech by Leites, see 'Poeziia sviashchennoi voiny', ibid., 23 February 1943, p. 3.

113 Ibid., p. 3.

114 'Literatura Velikoi Otechestvennoi voiny: na tvorcheskom soveshchanii', ibid,; P. Skosyrev, 'Otveta ne posledovalo: o kritike v nashi dni', *Novyi mir*, 4 (1943), 118–123.

115 Iosif Utkin, 'Pisatel' i chuvstva naroda', *Literatura i iskusstvo*, 17 April 1943, p. 2.

116 Pavel Antokol'skii, 'Chuvstvo istorii', *Literatura i iskusstvo*, 10 April 1943, p. 2; Viktor Gusev, 'Rastsvet sovetskoi poezii', ibid, 3 April 1943, p. 3.

117 Nikolai Aseev, 'O chuvstve novogo', *Literatura i iskusstvo*, 3 April 1943, p. 3.

118 In his 1914 article 'Poety na fugasakh', *Sobranie sochinenii*, 13 vols (Moscow, 1955–61), I, 306, Maiakovskii combined stanzas by Briusov, Bal'mont and Gorodetskii.

119 See note 117 above.

120 'Boesposobnost' stikha', *Literatura i iskusstvo*, 3 April 1943, p. 3.

121 See note 8 above.

122 Iurii Zhukov, 'Preliudiia', see note 8 above.

123 A. M. Egolin, *Sovetskaia literatura v dni Otechestvennoi voiny* (Moscow, 1944), p. 13.

124 'Rossii', later version and variants in *Stikhotvoreniia i poemy* (Leningrad, 1972), pp. 194–196; pp. 897–899.

125 A. M. Egolin, *Sovetskaia literatura v dni Otechestvennoi voiny* (Moscow, 1944). p. 14.

126 *Volia*, p. 36. See also 'Metamorfozy', pp. 30–32; 'Imena', pp. 33–36.

127 'Voennye korrespondenty', *Izbrannoe* (Leningrad, 1973), pp. 46–47; see also 'Poety', p. 48.

128 I, 135–136.

129 *Izbrannye proizvedeniia*, I, 256.

130 *Stikhi slagalis' na khodu ...*, pp. 78–81.

131 *Sobranie sochinenii*, 5 vols (Moscow, 1989–92), II, 53–54.

132 II, 55.

133 'My nachinali bez zaglavii ...', *Izbrannoe* (Moscow, 1991), pp. 38–39.

134 A. Prokof'ev, 'Vot voidut v legendy, v byli ...', p. 245; Aleksandr Iashin, 'Kanava', *Sobranie sochinenii*, 3 vols (Moscow, 1984–86), I, 95–96.

135 'Zhizn' i mechta', I, 539–540.

136 'Tvorcheskii otchet na zasedanii voennoi kommissii soiuza pisatelei', *Sovetskie pisateli na frontakh Velikoi Otechestvennoi voiny*, I, 335.

137 *Zvezda*, 5–6 (1943), p. 47.

138 'Kak polyn'', mne khleb razluki gorek ...', *Stikhotvoreniia i poemy*, pp. 171–172.

139 Il'ia Erenburg, *Liudi, gody, zhizn'*, II, 316.

140 'Posle voiny', *Izbrannoe*, p. 101.

141 'Nagrada', *Izbrannye proizvedeniia*, I, 281; 'V pilotke mal'chik bosonogii ...', I, 280.

142 *Stikhotvoreniia i poemy*, pp. 89–90.

143 'Dnevnik pisatelia: Zvezda v 1945 godu', *Zvezda*, 7–8 (1944), 107–108 (p. 107).

144 'Stikhi soldata', *Znamia*, 5–6 (1944), 219–221 (p. 219).

145 For example, Konstantin Simonov, 'Podumaem ob otsutstvuiushchikh', *Literatura i iskusstvo*, 19 August 1944, p. 3; Aleksei Surkov, 'Molodye golosa', *Literaturnaia gazeta*, 2 December 1944, p. 3; I. Erenburg, 'Stikhi Mikhaila L'vova', ibid., 25 November 1944; P. Gromov, [review of Gudzenko's *Odnopolchane*], *Zvezda*, 7–8 (1944), 192–193; T. Khmel'nitskaia, [review of Dudin's *Koster na perekrestke*], ibid., 193–194. A less positive opinion was given by L.Ozerov in 'Pravda zhizni i literaturnye kanony', *Literatura i iskusstvo*, 26 August 1944, p. 3.

146 Iurii Zhukov, 'Preliudiia', see note 8 above. Nikolai Tikhonov, 'Otechestvennaia voina i sovetskaia literatura', *Novyi mir*, 1–2 (1944), 180–189. Apparently Tikhonov was too mild in his criticism, and Aleksandrov had to intervene to attack Zoshchenko, Sel'vinskii, Dovzhenko and Aseev.

147 A. M. Egolin, *Sovetskaia literatura v dni Otechestvennoi voiny* (Moscow, 1944), p. 14. Egolin may have been referring to Aseev's poems 'Moskva-Kama', *Sobranie sochinenii*, IV, 351–354, and 'Gorodok na Kame', IV, 359–364.

148 Babichenko, 'Zhdanov, Malenkov i delo leningradskikh zhurnalov', p. 203.

149 M. L'vov, 'Doroga', I, 57–71; P.Shubin, 'Bitva na Sviri', pp. 505–521.

150 See, for example, Mikhail Dudin, 'Vesna', I, 129; Pavel Shubin, 'V novgorodskom lesu', p. 314; Dmitrii Kedrin, *Izbrannoe*, 'Plennye', pp. 221–222.

151 A. Tvardovskii, 'Vozmezdie', *Izbrannye proizvedeniia*, I, 291.

152 Ibid., p. 292.

153 'Vesna', II, 71.

154 See, for example, Evgenii Dolmatovskii, 'Voskhod solntsa', *Sobranie sochinenii*, 3 vols (Moscow, 1978–79), I, 302; Mikhail L'vov, 'Moskva, Moskva! Kakoi dalekoi ...', I, 82.

155 'Pol'skie stikhi', p. 112.

156 'Parol'', I, 321; 'V etom domike sred' ruin ...', I, 317.

157 See, for example, Mikhail Isakovskii, 'Vozvrashchenie', *Sobranie sochinenii*,

5 vols (Moscow, 1981-82), II, 93–95.

158 *Stikhotvoreniia i poemy* (Leningrad, 1985), p. 72.

159 E. Troshchenko, 'Poeziia pokoleniia, sozrevshego na voine', *Novyi mir*, 10–11 (1943), 164–171 (p. 171). Third in a series of articles on Aliger, Simonov & Dolmatovskii.

160 See I. Grinberg, 'Vzgliad v budushchee', *Zvezda*, 7–8 (1944), 153–160 (p. 156); P. Gromov, 'S. Gudzenko: Odnopolchane', ibid., 192–193 (p. 192).

161 'Slovo o Rossii', II, 103.

162 'Fantasticheskie gody', *Izbrannoe*, p. 362. Sergei Narovchatov recorded that Tikhonov appeared to have detected Glazkov's irony—*Vospominaniia o Sergee Narovchatove* (Moscow, 1990), p. 33.

163 Aleksandr Tvardovskii, 'Boitsu iuzhnogo fronta', *Izbrannye proizvedenia*, I, 227.

164 'Otechestvennaia voina i sovetskaia literatura', p. 182.

165 *Izbrannoe*, p. 352. Kunersdorf—battle of the Seven Years' War in which the Russian army fought; Port Arthur—site of Japanese attack on the Russian fleet which began the Russo-Japanese War (1904–05).

166 'Literaturnye zametki', *Znamia*, 3 (1944), 156–160 (p. 156).

167 'S narodom i dlia naroda', IV, 205–233 (p. 229).

168 A. Surkov, 'Predchuvstvie pobedy', *Literaturnaia gazeta*, 7 November 1944, p. 3.

169 *Lichnaia vechnost'*, p. 37.

170 See note 17, Introduction.

171 See, for example, 'Pesnia', *Izbrannoe* (Moscow, 1989), pp. 456–457; 'Na zimnem polustanke', pp. 434–436; 'Na rubezhakh', pp. 444–453.

172 'Pered novym pod"emom', *Literaturnaia gazeta*, 17 May 1945, p. 2.

173 See L. Subbotskii, 'Oruzhie pobedy', *Znamia*, 5–6 (1945), 161–167 (p. 165); A. Surkov, 'Poeziia naroda-pobeditelia', *Literaturnaia gazeta*, 17 May 1945, p. 2; N. Tikhonov, 'Pered novym pod"emom', ibid.; V. Pertsov, 'Podvig i geroi', *Znamia*, 9 (1945), 118–132 (p. 132).

174 'Poeziia naroda-pobeditelia', p. 2.

175 'Rukami, ogrubevshimi ot stali ...', *Izbrannoe* (Moscow, 1988), p. 151.

176 'Ia eti pesni napisal ne srazu ...', *Sobranie sochinenii*, 3 vols (Moscow, 1983–84), I, 11.

177 See, for example, 'Nikogda ia ne zabudu ...', *Stikhi* (Moscow, 1961), pp. 99–100; 'Chudesa', pp. 104–109; 'Posle marsha i nochnoi ataki', p. 110; 'Vo khmeliu', pp. 119–121; 'Vot kolesa po graviiu skripnut ...', pp. 122–123.

178 Vissarion Saianov, 'Vesna 1945 goda: pokhodnaia tetrad'', *Zvezda*, 5–6 (1945), 72–78.

179 *Stikhotvoreniia i poemy*, pp. 125–126.

180 A. Nedogonov,'Vesna na staroi granitse', *Izbrannoe* (Moscow, 1958), p. 118.

181 S. Gudzenko, *Stikhi*, p. 115.

182 'Ia khotel napisat' o Balkanakh ...', I, 310. See also 'Osen'', I, 306; 'Noch' na beregakh Visly', I, 315.

183 E. Dolmatovskii, 'Vstrecha', *Oktiabr'*, 1–2 (1945), p. 124.

184 *Khranit' vechno*, 2nd edition (Ann Arbor, 1978).

185 'Den' torzhestva', I, 596.

186 'Vasilii Terkin', *Izbrannye proizvedeniia*, II, 218–224.

187 'Berlin', ibid., I, 301.

188 'Pervyi den'', ibid., I, 91.

189 *Poeziia moia—ty iz okopa* (Moscow, 1985), pp. 38–39.

190 *Izbrannoe*, p. 123. See also 'Pobeda', p. 124; 'Vot chelovek—on iskalechen ...', p. 125.

191 'Vragi sozhgli rodnuiu khatu ...', II, 118.

192 V. Grossman, 'Treblinskii ad', *Znamia*, 11–12 (1945), 121–144. For references to *Chernaia kniga*, see *Literaturnaia gazeta*, 22 January 1945, p. 4; interview with Grossman, ibid., 13 October 1945, p. 4.

193 'Volchonok', p. 118.

194 See note 172 above.

195 'Preniia po dokladu N. Tikhonova', *Literaturnaia gazeta*, 22 May 1945, p. 1.

196 Ibid., p. 2.

197 'Put' k zrelosti', II, 357–358.

198 D. Babichenko, 'Zhdanov, Malenkov i delo leningradskikh zhurnalov', p. 205.

199 'Moe pokolenie', *Stikhi slagalis' na khodu ...*, pp. 128–129.

200 M. L'vov, 'Pokolenie', I, 93.

201 'Ia zhiv', I, 49.

202 'Posle voiny', I, 96.

203 'Put'', *Odnopolchane* (Moscow, 1944), p. 5; *Stikhi*, p. 27.

204 See Chapter Six, 'No-one is Forgotten and Nothing is Forgotten', for details on critics' treatment of the young generation of poets after 1945.

CHAPTER THREE

Heroes and Leaders: Socialist Realism in Wartime Poetry

Much of the work produced by Soviet writers in the Stalinist period can be criticised for being repetitive and formulaic, and the principal reason for this fault is usually identified as socialist realism, the literary method imposed on writers by the state. Although there were signs of change and originality in some of the poetry written and published during the war years, a good deal of it conforms to expectations by dealing with a narrow range of themes in standardised language. The most consistently-used theme in Soviet poetry during four years of war, and one associated with a markedly formulaic treatment, was that of heroism. The heroism evoked is not that of the faceless masses, but of individuals whose actions are performed in the spirit of self-sacrifice. A typical poem by Sergei Vasil'ev, not a major poet, adopts the theme, widespread in wartime poetry, of the signaller who dies while repairing communications lines. His corpse is found, as so often in poems on the subject, with the wires clenched between his teeth. Some poets restrict themselves to this proof of devotion to duty after death, but Vasil'ev includes a plethora of other details as supporting evidence:

> ... Его нашли, когда уже смеркалось.
> В руках винтовка, поднятый прицел.
> В зубах был провод. Связь не прерывалась.
> Вблизи валялась груда мертвых тел.
> Он тихо умер, чуть назад отпрянув,
> Прижавшись к ели и оледенев,
> Но на лице его, спокойном и упрямом,
> Не ужас был, а ненависть и гнев.[1]

(They found him when dusk was already falling. A rifle was in his hands, raised in aim. The wire was between his teeth. The connection was unbroken. Nearby lay a heap of dead bodies. He died quietly, leaning back slightly, pressed against the spruce tree, icy cold, but on his face, calm and determined, there was not horror, but hatred and anger.)

Not only has the dead man done his duty, he has also killed a large number of enemy soldiers single-handed before succumbing, with his gun still at the ready. His facial expression gives additional information about his state of mind when he died. Descriptions of this kind are legion in poetry published during the war years. It may be, of course, that what we have here is nothing more than an example of undistinguished verse, and that the circumstances of war engender a good deal of repetitious portrayals of heroic soldiers. The possible influence of socialist realism, specific to Soviet literature, should, however, be considered when asking what, apart from a poverty of imagination or the limited nature of the subject-matter, the formulae associated with the portrayal of heroism might mean.

The present chapter will examine the ways in which socialist realism may have acted as a guiding force in wartime poetry. In considering the primary function of socialist realist literature as the purveyor of ideological content, the paradigms used to depict the figure of the hero and the leader will be investigated as an expression of basic cultural ideas fostered by the state. The fundamental significance of these paradigms will be discussed, as will their adaptation to include concepts from outside the official culture. This is to be considered as a paradoxical result of literature's function in Soviet society at the time: it was adherence to outer forms, rather than belief in ideological content, that made literature acceptable to the authorities.[2] In wartime some of these paradigms were so altered in significance, particularly through the overt introduction of religious imagery (secularised religious references played a significant role in pre-war literature too), as to suggest that literary controls had become less rigid, and that poets were no longer restricting themselves to their role as preservers of the system's orthodoxy. It is also worth bearing in mind that critics, particularly during the first two years of war, adopted a 'hands off' approach, for which they were publicly rebuked in 1943.[3]

If heroic deeds and heroic deaths are the stock-in-trade of Soviet war poetry, then the motifs which dominate the poetry of Nazi Germany, or of Britain, are rather different. An anthology of poetry published in the *Sunday Times* newspaper between 1939 and 1945 reveals two major preoccupations. The actual events of the war feature less than evocations of English landscapes, tradition and values. These are presented as things to be protected from war's ravages, but more frequently as the source of people's resistance to the enemy. One author imagines the scene after invasion; a group of partisans leave their blazing village, led by a mysterious man whose identity as the King Arthur of legend is suggested by the Excalibur-like glitter of his bayonet.[4] The image of England is predominantly rural and unchanging, a long way from contemporary reality and therefore a potent symbol of the nation's continuity, untouched by historical cataclysms.[5] In poems directly concerned with the waging of war, the figure of the airman predominates. It is his fate to soar, bird-like, until his luck runs out. Fatalism, it seems, has taken the place of heroism. The final stanza of Lord Derwent's 'Spitfire' is representative:

> ... I am a flake of flame,
> The gull's pinion.
> At Death's impeccable aim
> I tremble, but cannot care;
> I am hardly, hardly there.
> That hit can be but a miss;
> All Heaven waits with a kiss,
> For I am the colour of air
> And the sky's minion.[6]

Here nature and destiny combine to produce not heroism, but a cool acceptance of death and a sense of being at one with the elements. Terrestrial battle, entrenched in the mud and barbed wire of the First World War, is left behind for a cleaner world, where death depends on a gamble and is instantaneous. In the air at least, war preserves a certain amount of romance. The main values promoted by the pieces in the *Times* anthology are those of tradition and self-effacing fatalism, values which reflect a nostalgic search for security and the re-evaluation of ideas about heroism in warfare after the Great War.

While the British poetry is politely vague about ideological matters, the poetry produced by writers of the Third Reich clearly reflects National Socialist ideology. There are, naturally, numerous poems extolling the Führer, which will be compared later in this chapter with Soviet verses on Stalin. The poets' central theme is the unity and destiny of the German nation, surrounded in mystical, pseudo-religious imagery. Sons of the soldiers defeated in 1918 are continually summoned to fulfil their fathers' hopes as a glorious new day dawns.[7] Individual heroism is precluded by a sense of obliteration of the self by dissolving into the unit of the *Volk*, bound together by duty. Unquestioning obedience provides the refrain for Gerhard Schumann's 'Lied der Kämpfer'—'Wir fragen nicht. Wir sind des Führers Faust' (Song of the Fighters—We do not ask questions. We are the Fuhrer's fist), while Hans Baumann's 'Eid des Fähnrichs' (Oath of the Standard-Bearer) presents a declaration of irrational loyalty against an apocalyptic background:

> Über tapferer Männer Beben,
> über meines Herzens Not
> werde ich, vom Leid umloht,
> händelos die Fahne heben.

Wenn die Lüfte jäh zerspringen,
wenn der Strom erschrocken steht,
werde ich, vom Krieg umweht,
mit verstummten Munde singen.

Tausend fallen, tausend türmen
zum Gebirg der Leiber Feld.
Ich werd, tausendmal gefällt,
auf den Knien stehn und stürmen.[8]

(Above the trembling of brave men, above the anguish of my heart I shall, when suffering blazes around me, raise the flag though I have no hands. When the air rapidly explodes, when the stream stands still in horror, I shall, buffeted by war, sing, though my mouth is dumb. Thousands fall, thousands are heaped up on the field with the mountain of corpses. Though felled a thousand times, on my knees I shall rage.)

This is, as we shall see, a long way from the behaviour of standard Soviet heroes; poets record specific feats of courage, as in Vasil'ev's poem about the signaller quoted above. Here the paradoxical fanaticism of Baumann's poem is rejected in favour of calm rationality and precisely directed action. On both sides of the conflict, sacrifice through death is a recurrent theme. Soviet poems tend to find significance in the act preceding death, but in German poems death has a purpose of its own, that of *Blutopfer* or blood sacrifice. The soldiers who fall in battle become the foundation for national unity and territorial gain. The death of the individual can have no greater significance than this:

... Hier schöpfe! Wer hier trinkt, wird viel erkennen ...
Und ob er tötet, ob er stirbt, er weiss:
Dies alles sind nur Saaten künftiger Liebe.
Viel Blut, viel Blut muss in die Erde sinken;
nie wird sie sonst den Menschen heimatlich.[9]

(Here create! He who drinks here shall learn much ... And whether he kills or dies, he knows that all this is but seeds of future love. Much blood, much blood must sink into the earth, else it shall never feel like home to man.)

Indeed, for a man to imagine that his life is worth preserving runs the risk of separation from the *Volk*:

So kostbar ist kein Leben jetzt,
um nicht im Feld zu enden.
Von jedem, der zu hoch sich schätzt,
wird ab das Volk sich wenden.

Die Stunde fragt nicht nach Talent,
nach Stellung nicht, nach Namen.
Sie fragt, wer Pflicht und Anstand kennt.
Zieh aus und kämpfe! Amen.'[10]

(There is no life now so precious that it cannot end on the battlefield. The People shall turn away from everyone who esteems himself too high. The hour asks not for talent or high position or name. It asks who knows duty and decency. Go forth and fight! Amen)

Self-sacrifice and renunciation of identity in the name of the Fatherland is preached in rather ecclesiastical language:

Nun werde Stahl, du deutsches Herz!
Denk nicht an Nöte, nicht an Schmerz!
Vergiss dein kleines Erden-Ich,
das nahe, enge Ich und Mich
und weite deine Seele!
Dass sie, für jedes Opfer frei,
sich über sich erhebe
und dir die erste Waffe sei,
auf dass die Heimat lebe.
Im Schicksal bist du nicht allein;
ein jeder wird dein Bruder sein.

Ein jeder isst das gleiche Brot,
und jeden trifft die gleiche Not,
das gleiche Glück, die gleiche Ehr.
Sei du ein Glied im grossen Heer!
Gib dich mit Herzen, Hirn und Hand,
gib ganz dich deinem Vaterland,
gleich ob du lebest oder fällst,
wenn du die heilige Flamme hältst,
so wirst du, lebend oder tot,
mit eingehn in das Morgenrot
der fessellosen Zeit,
der deutschen Ewigkeit.[11]

(Now turn to steel, you German heart! Think not of trouble, nor of pain! Forget your little earthly self, the close, narrow I and me and broaden your soul! So that it, free for all sacrifices, rises above itself and becomes your first weapon which will let your homeland live. In hardship you are not alone; each man will be your brother. Each eats the same bread, each is touched by the same trouble, happiness and honour. Be you a member in the great army! Give yourself with heart, brain and hand, give yourself completely to your Fatherland, and whether you live or fall, if you hold the holy flame you shall, living or dead, enter the morning glow of unshackled time, of German eternity.)

The examples of German war poetry given above should demonstrate clearly enough that it was used primarily as a vehicle for promoting official ideology, while the British examples illustrate a less well-defined set of cultural assumptions, in which the overt expression of ideology was anathema, and nature and tradition were offered as an 'innocent' substitute. In both cases, however, the way in which published poets approached the subject of the war expresses values and ideals central to society, or, at least, to the ruling elite. Stalin's Russia, like Hitler's Germany, was a totalitarian state, so it would be reasonable to assume that, in both systems focused on conflict with The Enemy, recurring images in wartime poetry were governed by ideological concerns. Yet while German poets stuck mainly to exhortation or to declarations of faith, their

Soviet counterparts reproduced a condensed narrative of heroic death and transfiguration. Both German and Soviet works focus on acts of self-sacrifice, one seeking obliteration in the mass of the *Volk*, the other culminating in personal immortality achieved by a conscious act in the name of a higher ideal. The National Socialist hero is presented with the emphasis on irrational exaltation, the socialist realist hero with the emphasis on rational decision.

From the examples given it seems fairly straightforward to see how German wartime poetry reflected the beliefs of National Socialism. In order to determine the ideological significance of Soviet poetry's representation of the hero, it is necessary to look at the literary method which was the main vehicle of ideological control—socialist realism. At this point there might be objections to dignifying socialist realism with the title of 'literary method', arguing that it was little more than a smokescreen for the oppressive, prescriptive censorship that suffocated Soviet literature for twenty years. Certainly the pronouncements made by Andrei Zhdanov at the First Congress of the Soviet Writers' Union in 1934 do not add up to a literary method:

> Truthfulness and historical concreteness of artistic representation must be combined with the task of ideological renewal and education of the workers in the spirit of socialism. Such a method of literature and literary criticism is the one we call the method of socialist realism.[12]

Zhdanov saw a writer's highest value in his effectiveness as an 'engineer of human souls' or, as Andrei Siniavskii put it: 'The poet doesn't just write poems, but also by his poems helps to further the building of Communism'. Socialist realism may have set out to reflect reality, but it was also deeply concerned with changing it.[13]

Perhaps the most significant defining feature of socialist realism is this attempt to meld two views of the world normally held to be mutually exclusive—the realistic and the ideal, or, in the words of the Writers' Union Constitution, 'Socialist realism ... demands from the author a true and historically concrete depiction of reality in its revolutionary development'.[14] Socialist realism sought to combine a recognisable, historically concrete picture of the world with a vision of what lay beyond mundane and flawed reality. If the 'realism' component of socialist realism was rather unusual, the concept of the 'typical' was similarly unconventional. It was taken to mean not so much what was most representative of society as a whole, as what corresponded most closely to expected developments; the atypical could, with the application of the future perspective, be portrayed as the norm. Consequently the idea of heroism in wartime was depicted as typical. In practice, the attempt to bridge the gap between the real and the fantastic, to create a higher reality, led literature to adopt particular strategies. Special emphasis had to be placed on the level of symbol, which led to the creation of a system of recurring plot elements and imagery which can be shown to have had a particular ideological significance.

In practice, socialist realism defined itself through a set of canonical examples, many of which pre-dated the method. Critics played an important role in identifying works which could be incorporated into the canon and those which failed to conform. They took on the status of ideological guardians to 'misguided' writers, identifying their 'mistakes', but rarely commenting on matters of form or technique. Speaking at the 1934 Congress, Nikolai Bukharin, on the other hand, suggested that more should be done to improve poets' technical skills in order to compare with the very best in world literature. Bukharin's vision of poetry as a dynamic, evolving entity was in conflict with his opponents' attempts to construct a canon against which all subsequent works should be measured. As it turned out, admission to the canon depended very little on a poet's technical expertise; stylistic innovations were treated with suspicion, as the preferred qualities were simplicity and accessibility to the average reader. Bukharin's criticisms drew angry responses from many of the delegates at the 1934 Writers' Congress. An indication of just how controversial some of his remarks had been was the fact that on the final day he submitted a written apology which was read to the delegates at the beginning of the last session.[15] Bukharin himself was executed in 1938; his erudite exposition of the tasks facing Soviet poetry was suppressed, together with the entire transcript of the 1934 congress.

If the prime concern for socialist realism was to produce literature which would convey ideology effectively, then that would help to explain the importance of simplicity and accessibility, the privileging of content over form, even the prevalence of formulaic plots and one-dimensional heroes. What it does not explain is why certain types of plots and heroes came to be predominant in literature assigned to the official canon. The answer, as we shall see, must lie in the nature of the ideology being communicated. Katerina Clark has given a convincing account of the relationship between the socialist realist canons and Marxist-Leninist ideology in her book *The Soviet Novel: History as Ritual*. Using comparisons from the anthropological study of myth, Clark likens the role of the Soviet novel to that of myth or ritual, in that it turns the abstract beliefs, fundamental to a certain society, into a narrative. The actions of the socialist realist, or 'positive', hero, are, according to Clark, governed by the interaction of two dialectically opposed forces, 'spontaneity' and 'consciousness'. Clark identifies these as the main factors in shaping the typical plot of the Soviet novel, which plays out the Marxist-Leninist idea of society's eventual transformation, through a series of syntheses, to a Communist society. The motivating forces behind this transformation, 'spontaneity' and 'consciousness', are concepts peculiar to Russian Marxism.[16] 'Consciousness' is understood as the force guiding actions which are disciplined and based on political awareness, while 'spontaneity' is related to anarchic actions, or to the working of impersonal historical forces. Through a series of syntheses, society moves towards an ever higher state of 'consciousness', until the opposition between the two ceases to exist, and 'natural' impulses are in harmony with political awareness. In the novel, this process is shown through the biography of a single character, who must master his own 'spontaneity', that is, wilfulness, and achieve greater 'consciousness' by gaining political awareness and complete self-control. The 'conscious' individual moves beyond selfish actions and becomes part of a collective. Hans Günther's study *Die Verstaatlichung der Literatur* considers Clark's approach to be fruitful, although he questions the validity of a comparison which could be felt to neglect the fundamental difference between the conventions of medieval art and myth, which belong to pre-autonomous art based on consensus, and those of socialist realism, which deprived art of autonomy and imposed the canon by attacking deviations from it.[17] Whatever the origins of uniformity, however, it seems reasonable to see socialist realist literature, like medieval art, as the embodiment of what were supposed to be a society's ruling beliefs.

Clark's study is concerned with the Soviet novel, particularly with the analysis of plot and representation of character. I hope to show that a similar approach can be used in an analysis of Soviet poetry. Most of the poems about wartime heroes are particularly concerned with presenting a condensed narrative, which bears comparison with the plot of a typical socialist realist novel. Prose was undoubtedly the preferred medium of socialist realist literature, as it is less subject to ambiguity than poetry and emphasises content rather than form. As a result of campaigns during the 1930s against 'formalism' and stylistic experimentation in poetry, stylistic elements were reduced to regular rhyme and meter, summed up in the virtue of 'classical simplicity'. As content became Soviet poetry's primary concern, the 'mass song', which expressed enthusiasm for the many achievements of socialism, became a preferred and very simplified form. This is not to say that formal differences between poetry and prose were reduced to a minimum; the attributes which distinguished poetry, such as rhyme and meter, were adhered to;

nevertheless, they were not subject to much variation, as content took precedence.

In wartime, stylistic innovation as such was not demanded by critics, although they did express the concern that most poetry was too rational and limited in its approach to evoke the people's heroism appropriately. The most extreme objections came from the ex-futurist Nikolai Aseev in 1943. He complained that the poetry of the current war showed no progress in style or originality from that of the First World War. In Aseev's opinion, very little of value had been written at all during the war.[18] Others were less sweeping in their judgements, although complaints about stylistic monotony appeared regularly. In 1942 one critic writing on Prokof'ev found that most poems were marred by a repetitive use of imagery, by a declamatory tone, were too much concerned with thought and not enough with a lyrical fusion of thought and feeling.[19] In the same year another pointed out the unoriginal choice of vocabulary in an anthology of recent poetry:

> The choice of words could be richer. It is true to say that bullets 'whistle', tanks 'roar along', the enemy is 'evil' and 'cunning', glory is 'immortal' and so on; but you hardly need to be a poet to say that—any reader would express his thoughts and feelings using more original and vivid language.'[20]

Such poverty of expression was not simply a sign of literary incompetence; the repetitive and conventionalised use of language was symptomatic of Soviet literature's official role as the vehicle for conveying ideology. According to Hans Günther, official discourse of the time was concerned not with conveying information, but with expressing the state's monopoly on the interpretation of reality; communication was replaced by domination. The proportion of actual content to verbiage was therefore low, and the bulk of the discourse was taken up by redundant repetition and tautology.[21] As there was no need to persuade the reader of the validity of any claims put forward, they could afford to be transmitted with an excess of language which was there not to convince but to saturate the reader with familiar phrases. Boris Grois states that Stalinist culture was interested in shaping the reader's consciousness without revealing the mechanisms behind the manipulation. Slogans endlessly repeated were no longer consciously perceived, but subconsciously ever-present.[22] The fact that critics were prepared, in wartime, to draw attention to stereotyped language, and, as we shall see, stereotypical heroes perceptible as such strongly suggests that the ideological outlook conveyed in literature no longer held the monopoly. Their criticisms may be seen as an attempt to revitalise language in order to reassert this outlook or, what seems more likely, a move away from the ideology that was contained in these previously 'invisible' formulae.

The theme of war presented an ideal field in which the conventions of socialist realism could function. Socialist realism, based on Marxist dialectics, naturally adopted the concept of progress through conflict of opposites. The most common type of symbolism used in socialist realist literature is that of conflicting polarities; the paradigmatic plot is that of confrontation, in which the hero, a representative of absolute good, overcomes obstacles in order to create a new, better order, both in himself and in society. This literary method was developed in a society deeply entrenched in confrontation, both internal and with the outside world, and in which definite commitment to the side of justice, that is, the revolution, left no room for seeing the world in tones other than black and white. Of course the literature produced by this outlook could not show confrontation between forces of equal validity, nor was it aimed at converting those readers who did not hold the views promoted by the author. The function of the representation of conflict in socialist realist literature was to strengthen convictions already held by author and reader.

A Russian specialist on wartime literature, Aleksandr Kogan, when questioned about the influence of socialist realism on Soviet literature, replied that it was now common for people to point to the corpse of socialist realism and claim, falsely, that it had always been a corpse.[23] While it is true to say that a considerable number of poets began to write more realistically in wartime, socialist realism remained a powerful shaping force in literature. The poet Konstantin Simonov, in an article on Tikhonov, considered the problem of how the truth of war should be depicted in literature, and put forward a recognisably socialist realist point of view:

> Writing about war is difficult. You mustn't write about it only as an easy, triumphant parade, that will be a lie. If you write only about difficult days and nights, only about the mud of the trenches and the cold of snowdrifts, only about death and blood, then that will be a lie too, for while all that does exist, writing only about these things means that you forget the soul, the heart of the man fighting this war, who in moments of exhilaration in battle forgets about blood and death, and mud and cold, and believes only in one thing—in the victory ahead.[24]

Instead of debating the question of whether awkward objective facts should be denied or acknowledged by writers, Simonov looks to a higher truth to resolve the dilemma. His rejection of earlier images of war which were simplified and over-optimistic was in line with current official thinking, as was his suspicion of a new trend in literature which threatened to reveal too much about the war's uncomfortable reality. The concept of the heroic found in socialist realist literature relies on a similar emphasis on the spiritual at the expense of physical reality.

The presence of an underlying ideological structure in socialist realist literature meant that it was obliged to approach reality selectively, including only those elements which conformed to pre-existing patterns. The actual circumstances of the war were, of course, infinitely more complex than mainstream poetry suggested. In general, the war was portrayed as a clash of absolute opposites, of light against darkness, good against evil, a concept carried mainly in the stereotypical depiction of both Soviet and German soldiers. The Positive Hero confronted an absolutely evil enemy. Anatolii Chivilikhin's 'Iz dnevnika' (From My Diary) shows them as representatives of an absolute polarity:

> ...И было здесь два средоточья силы,
> Две воли, как два полюса враждебных:
> Тот дрессировщик властный и надменный
> И наш—людей суровый повелитель.
> И оба твердо знали, что к рассвету
> Из них двоих останется один.[25]

(And here there were two concentrations of force, two wills, like two hostile polarities: that powerful and arrogant animal tamer and our man—a severe commander of people. And both knew firmly that towards dawn only one of the two would be left.)

In Antokol'skii's poem 'Syn' (The Son) the author compares his own son with the son of his German contemporary. To the German father he says: 'My boy is a human being, but yours is an executioner'.[26] Few more subtle attempts were made to explore the German's inner nature. Poets relied on external features, usually a low forehead and lots of red hair, to suggest his violent and primitive nature. In poetry the enemy is rarely dignified with the word 'soldat' (soldier). Instead he is given the ignoble name of 'ubiitsa' (murderer) or 'palach' (executioner) and compared with an animal, generally a wolf. Psychological details are restricted to the motivating forces of pride and greed. The typical German, described by a Soviet poet, is nothing like the Nazi theorist's Aryan ideal, but an embodiment of his country's evil, sometimes ridiculed as physically degenerate and incapable of individual thought. The Soviet hero, on the other hand, was physically and psychologically strong; his actions revealed selfless initiative.

The image of a clash of absolute good and evil was, of course, a thoroughly simplistic view of the war. Grey areas, such as the fate of prisoners of war, were excluded from public discourse. Volunteers from among Soviet prisoners of war, apart from helping German soldiers or being sent to work in Germany, were organised in groups such as the Russian Army of Liberation, created under German authority, but eventually fighting against both Nazi and Soviet forces. The existence of these armies was quite unmentionable in an official context, until some of the leading figures were rounded up and tried.[27] Nationalist groups, Ukrainians and Cossacks, were also sponsored by Germany. The pro-Soviet partisan movement was fraught with ambiguities; partisans did not hesitate to commandeer food from occupied villages, force specialists to work for them, or to exact summary justice on those suspected of treachery. Another awkward topic which did not quite fit the official scheme was that of desertion by Soviet soldiers. Not quite so unmentionable as the Vlasov army, desertion was condemned in poems in which a soldier's wife threatened to disown her husband if he were to desert.[28] Few ventured beyond the realms of the hypothetical, except Aleksandr Tvardovskii in his 'Ballada ob otrechenii' (Ballad about Renunciation).[29] He shows the moral and emotional dilemma of parents who learn that their son has come to them not on leave, but as a deserter, believing that he must save his own life for their sake. The fact of desertion is condemned, but the poet has his hero repent of his action and return to his unit, hoping for mercy. Tvardovskii's poem conveys the 'correct' message that desertion is unacceptable, yet by revealing the emotional conflict it produces, his poem loses the linear simplicity found in other poems on the same theme. By introducing an element of emotional ambiguity, Tvardovskii sets his work apart from the usual propaganda designed to deter potential deserters.

It is important in this context to note that the Russian use of the word 'propaganda' has more positive connotations than the English equivalent. Implicit in the effective functioning of propaganda is the absence of ambiguity. Tvardovskii's refusal to deliver a cut and dried judgement on the deserter by recognising his parents' genuine conflict of interest sets his poem apart from those which conveyed certain beliefs and standards as fixed elements in an absolute system of good and evil. The complex reality of war therefore had no place in mainstream Soviet poetry if it was to function in its proper role. Mere appearances were often held to be less significant than the 'higher' truth which lay behind them. One critic commented in 1957 that the complex truth about the war, the initial retreats, was now known, but that this was much less important than the higher truth, that the people and Party together had destroyed the German blitzkrieg.[30] Many poets in reality were unwilling to impose a framework on their interpretation of the war. Dmitrii Kedrin's poem

'Glukhota' (Deafness), written in September 1941, describes the poet's inability to shut out the voice of human suffering. By likening the war to a symphony, Kedrin appears to accept the presence of an underlying order which will, after a series of modulations and variations, reach a suitable resolution in victory. He is, however, unable to hear most of the orchestra. Due to his supposedly impaired hearing, all he hears is the soldiers' wives weeping:

Война бетховенским пером
Чудовищные ноты пишет.
Ее октав железный гром
Мертвец в гробу—и тот услышит!

Но что за уши мне даны?
Оглохший в гуле этих схваток,
Из всей симфонии войны
Я слышу только плач солдаток.[31]

(War writes monstrous music with Beethoven's pen. The iron thunder of its octaves can be heard even by a dead man in his coffin! But what kind of ears are mine? Deafened by the rumblings of these battles, out of the whole symphony of war I can hear only the weeping of soldiers' wives.)

Kedrin's 'deafness' turns out in fact to be a heightened perception of suffering; the real 'deafness', it is implied, belongs to those whose senses are dulled by the grandiose music of war.

The subordination of immediate reality to pre-ordained patterns implicitly criticised by Kedrin makes Soviet war poetry comparable with myth, as it shares myth's function of transmitting fundamental beliefs, and its concern for revealing an absolute truth and reality beyond everyday existence. The Rumanian scholar of myth, Mircea Eliade, has described aspects of traditional myth relating to time, place and ritual actions which are echoed in the conventions used in Soviet wartime poetry and in socialist realist literature in general.

Eliade describes a typical element of myth as the division of time into two categories: one, which he terms Profane Time, is ordinary historical time, perceived, he claims, by traditional man as a succession of inexplicable catastrophes such as floods and famine;[32] the other, Great Time, is in absolute contrast to the apparent chaos of Profane Time. In Great Time nothing is arbitrary or incomprehensible, as all actions either imitate acts which were performed in a mythical time of origins, or which pre-figure the messianic age which is to come.[33] Great Time is re-created whenever archetypal acts are performed. The performance of archetypal acts abolishes ordinary historical time and attributes value to the present because it either imitates some significant event of the heroic past or prefigures the future.

In the case of Soviet literature, the heroic past consists of the events of the 1917 Revolution and the civil war, and was extended backwards in the mid-1930s to include events from Russia's earlier history, such as the defeat of Napoleon. The messianic age is, of course, the coming of Communism. Like the primitive cultures described by Eliade, the orthodox socialist realist canon rejected the view of history as a succession of unforeseeable and generally calamitous events. Literature belonging to the canon promotes instead the idea of history as a repeated cycle of archetypal events which are interpreted according to categories rather than as a unique combination of circumstances. In wartime, mainstream Soviet critics appeared to share what Eliade terms 'an aversion to history' by rejecting the idea of literature as a chronological record of events. In July 1942 Aleksei Surkov said that the poetry of the early months of the war could be divided into work which looked at the present for signs of future developments, and work which recorded only the events as they happened: 'If a poet was, at that time, writing poems which simply recorded and responded to episodes as they happened, he was therefore caught up in the whirlwind of events, losing his head, unable to see beyond mere empiricism'.[34] What mattered was not the chronological succession of events, but those events which bore a special significance by detaching themselves from the merely chronological and becoming a part of the heroic age, existing above ordinary reality. From the beginning of the war, poets selected those examples of heroic behaviour which pointed to an eventual victory, rather than events which were representative of how the war in general was progressing. Critics later looked back on the poetry of 1941, using the benefit of hindsight to guide their selection, and identified the certainty of eventual victory as its guiding principle:

> In the days of battle which were most difficult for the people, Soviet poetry resounded with the belief in victory. This belief allowed us to look the terrible prose of war in the eye, directly and boldly. From this belief we drew strength and confidence.[35]

In depicting the war then in progress, poets filtered their immediate impressions through a system of historical precedents. The 'rehabilitation' of Russian history which took place during the 1930s proved an invaluable resource. Specific events of the present war were incorporated into a pantheon of victories which included the victory over foreign intervention in the civil war, the defeat of Napoleon, and the country's liberation from Tatar rule. In December 1941 Vera Inber set the blockade of Leningrad, then entering its most severe phase, in its rightful place:

> ... К плеяде столь прославленных имен,
> Как Измаил, Полтава, Севастополь,

Прибавится теперь еще и он,
Град Ленина, о чей гранитный цоколь
Разбилась боевая мощь врага,
Зарывшегося в русские снега.[36]

(To the pleiad of such glorious names as Izmail, Poltava, Sevastopol' now this one too shall be added, the city of Lenin, on whose granite pedestal has been shattered the martial might of the enemy, now buried in Russian snows.)

United by their qualitative similarity, historical events transcend the bounds of history, so that past, present and future become irrelevant concepts. The chaotic force of historical time is neutralised; future events become predictable.

Together with a dualistic and hierarchical view of time, in which ultimate reality and truth are to be found outside historical time, Soviet wartime poetry demonstrates another feature of traditional myth described by Eliade—a hierarchy of place.[37] Ancient cultures designated sacred places, which were perceived as the centre of the earth and a zone of absolute reality. This idea appears in the work of many wartime poets, for whom Moscow, being the seat of Soviet government, was just such a place. In October 1941, when the enemy was approaching the capital, its position as a focus of patriotic emotion was emphasised:

Москва!
До последних патронов,
До дольки последней свинца
Мы в битвах!
Твоя оборона
Идет через наши сердца![38]

(Moscow! To the last bullet, to the last scrap of lead we are in battle! Your defence goes through our hearts!)

Once Soviet forces reached foreign soil Moscow's mystical status was enhanced. It was seen as the source of all reality and of light. Distance cannot separate the soldier from its mysterious presence, as demonstrated by Narovchatov's poem 'Na chuzhbine' (In a Foreign Land). The poet denies the force of distance, which is more than bridged by the significance of the day, being the anniversary of the October Revolution, a central event of the 'heroic age':

... Чужое небо светится над нами,
Чужая речь ручьем вокруг течет.
И снова перед нашими глазами
Отчизна наша светлая встает.

Пускай мы от нее сейчас далеко,
Чужая окружает нас земля,—
По-прежнему нам светит свет с востока,
Высокий свет родимого Кремля.[39]

(An alien sky gleams above us, an alien language flows around us in streams. And once more before our eyes rises up our bright Fatherland. Though we are now far away, and an alien land surrounds us—as before the light from the East illumines us, the sublime light of our beloved Kremlin.)

Both time and distance can be transcended in the knowledge of this higher reality, made accessible through the mediation of symbolic events and places.

The conventions used in poetry of the war show an idealised world which is internally coherent. There is no possibility of contradiction or ambiguity; everything is as it should be. In this ideal world, convention determines the course of history and the pattern of individuals' actions—it specifies how a hero should think, act, even die. Everything is ultimately predictable, nothing is arbitrary, meaning is assigned to everything, in other words, it is ritualised. This world has striking similarities to the world presented in medieval Russian chronicles, which related important historical events, and described the lives of saints and princes. Theirs is also a very formulaic version of history, concerned with showing events and characters in accordance with established patterns, rather than creating a faithful record of what actually happened. The main figures appear only in specific situations, performing public acts, such as the victorious return to their city after battle. Positive qualities are attributed only to the heroes, usually through standard epithets which express the hero's relationship to external bodies such as the Church, his soldiers and his subjects. The enemy is shown to be completely wicked, and most frequently depicted in ignominious flight from defeat.[40]

During the war, Soviet poets returned to medieval chronicles about battles against the Tatars and the Poles, and imitated their archaic style of language. They sometimes drew direct parallels between the present and the past, indicating a common heroic spirit.[41] While Soviet poets drew on historical precedent in order to convey a sense of a higher reality, the medieval chronicles had a higher reality of their own, derived from religion. Religious belief is shown as the ultimate source of victory, especially when the enemy were the 'heathen' Tatars. Faith is shown to enable the medieval heroes to fight their enemies to the death, as they believe both in the rightness of their cause and in eternal life. Together with the structure of religious belief came an element of the fantastic, as visions, prophecies and miracles intervened in the course of ordinary life. The night before a battle was a likely time for a soldier on watch to see apparitions of helpful saints assuring victory.[42]

The explicitly religious route to a higher reality was not available as such to Soviet writers, although they borrowed the vocabulary of religion and folklore to transcend ordinary reality. Certain concepts belonging to Christianity took on a powerful resonance in the literature and culture of the 1930s. As Katerina Clark says:

> Thirties values comprised a belief system in which the notion of transcendence was central: going "higher", going beyond the this-worldly and the mundane, beyond the realm of mere appearance. It was in effect a neoreligious doctrine of salvation and rebirth.[43]

Because Christian symbolism was out of the question as a means to express these ideas, Soviet writers resorted to folklore for imagery and language which might help to communicate a new sense of higher order reality.

Pre-war culture promoted the idea that ordinary physical reality could be transcended by faith. The concept of two orders of reality, the ordinary and the extraordinary, which applied to time, place, and people, had become established during the 1930s when official rhetoric promoted the idea of a fantastic age in which 'fairy-tales have become reality'. Fundamental to this sense of the fantastic was the belief in Soviet man's unlimited capacity to go beyond the 'normal' limits of time, space and physical endurance. This belief found its expression in the celebration of two types of hero: the Stakhanovite worker and the aviation pioneer. It was, of course, axiomatic that Stalin possessed the ultimate in wisdom. The Stakhanovites and the aviators made up for what they lacked in insight by their daring challenge to rational expectations. The achievements of Soviet aviators such as Chkalov, who made the first non-stop flight between the United States and the Soviet Union in 1937, and of Arctic explorers, particularly the Cheliuskin expedition of the same year, were celebrated as the breaching of boundaries which others, limited by mere reason, had considered absolute. This ethos was particularly evident in the Stakhanovite movement, founded in 1935, which encouraged workers to emulate the miner Aleksei Stakhanov by overfulfilling their production quotas. The words of Vasilii Lebedev-Kumach 'We conquer space and time' encapsulate the heroic qualities attributed to these paragons of New Soviet Manhood.[44]

During the war, folklore continued to provide writers with an 'enabling language' which would emphasise the heightened significance of events described.[45] Motifs were drawn from other traditional sources besides the chronicles, including fairy-tale and the oral epic *bylina*, which provided ways of presenting events of the war in simplified form as a duel between a hero and an evil monster. As official attitudes towards the Orthodox Church became more tolerant during the war, the incidence of religious symbolism in poetry increased. There were few direct imitations of the religious vision before battle favoured by chronicle writers, though Surkov did create a secular equivalent in a soldier's dream of the appearance of Lenin and Stalin together.[46] The motif of death in battle, to be discussed in detail later, was closely associated with Christian concepts of death and transfiguration. Through death even the most humble soldier could be elevated to divine status. If Antokol'skii's son can be described as a 'demigod' in life, in death the hero of Iaroslav Smeliakov's poem 'Sud'ia' (The Judge) attains full divinity.[47] Smeliakov looks ahead to the Day of Judgement, when the 'stern boy from Moscow' who died in battle clutching a handful of Russian soil will deliver judgement on everyone:

> ... Он все узнает оком зорким,
> с пятном кровавым на груди,
> судья в истлевшей гимнастерке,
> сидящий молча впереди.[48]

(He shall see all with his piercing eye, the judge in a tattered army tunic, with a bloody stain on his breast, sitting silently before them.)

An ordinary Soviet soldier is elevated to the level of God sitting in judgement—an extreme way of expressing his country's moral superiority. Soviet virtue is amalgamated with overtones of a Russian messianism, which began to appear in poetry from 1943 onwards, accentuating Russia's historical role as saviour of the West from the Golden Horde, Napoleon, and now Hitler. It is worth noting that the motif of the Judgement Day recurs more frequently as the end of the war approaches, depicting the Germans as sinners about to be cast into the outer darkness.[49] Semen Kirsanov went so far as to portray the entire war in his poem of 1945, 'Edem' (Eden), in terms of the Old Testament story of man's expulsion from Paradise and his efforts to regain it. In this, Kirsanov follows the example of his hero Maiakovskii, whose poem about the First World War, 'Voina i mir' (War and the Universe), ends with paradise and peace restored to a perfect world.[50] Maiakovskii's poem would probably have been more acceptable to Soviet critics, who were by then beginning to find the number of religious references in literature disturbing, as it uses religious imagery to present an anti-theist message. The hero, who is of course Maiakovskii himself, is so outraged by the horrors of war that he storms the heavens to order God to put a stop to it. As God is absent, Maiakovskii takes on himself the task of redeeming the world by sacrificing himself as a Christ substitute.

Kirsanov's approach, by contrast, can hardly be called violently iconoclastic. He uses biblical imagery as a means of interpreting his experiences and, it would seem, drawing comparisons with appropriately significant events. The poet casts himself as Adam separated from Eve by war, though this time it is the forces of hell which drive them out of paradise. He also uses the image of the rainbow as the sign of a new covenant of peace. Kirsanov makes it clear that, although he comes to believe in hell's embodied forces, he does not believe in God; in times of danger his prayer is the name of the woman he loves. His vision of the war is populated by figures who seem to be ordinary people, yet at the same time bear the identity of angels and saints; the enemy soldiers are expressly portrayed as the agents of hell, while the people's suffering is symbolised in Christ's crucifixion:

> ...Дрожит Вселенная от топота, народы на полях распяты,
> лежат с разрезанными выями и обожженными глазами,
> Сын Человеческий растоптан, кровоточат его стигматы,
> бегут Иосифы с Мариями, Петры уходят в партизаны.[51]

(The Universe trembles from the trampling footsteps, the peoples are crucified in the fields, they lie with slit necks and scorched eyes. The Son of Man is trampled underfoot, his stigmata bleed. Josephs and Marys flee, Peters go to join the partisans.)

Only the religious context of apocalypse and salvation seems to provide Kirsanov with the scope for communicating the fantastic intensity of war. The implicit religious content in the portrayal of the war as a clash between absolutes of good and evil routinely used by mainstream poetry emerges in 'Edem' in a kaleidoscope of biblical imagery, woven together rather incongruously. What, one is forced to speculate, was the sin committed by the inhabitants of paradise, or the Soviet Union, that they should receive such punishment? The explicit religious references are, in many ways, close to the system of opposing good and evil used in other contemporary works, but connected with them is a self-contained philosophy alien to state ideology. Shared symbols do not necessarily have the same meaning.

Soviet critics have scarcely mentioned Kirsanov's poem. They have also largely ignored the question of religious symbolism in war poetry, which, unmentioned at first, became the subject of disapproving comment later on in the war. Tikhonov found religious references 'strange'.[52] Surkov felt such things were inappropriate for the good Soviet writer:

> The poet is, of course, free to write as he wishes, but I am not sure whether the deliberate or involuntary cultivation of ecclesiastical-religious imagery and mysticism should form part of the ideas of people who lay claim to the title of engineers of the souls of Soviet people.[53]

It is perhaps difficult to tell whether the use of religious symbolism in Soviet wartime poetry reflects an upsurge in religious belief. What seems likely is that official tolerance of the Orthodox Church, a pragmatic move in order to enlist national support for the state, was accompanied by the acceptance of a certain amount of religious symbolism in literature. Appeals to Marxism-Leninism took second place, as shown in the previous chapter, to references to Russian tradition.

If in the 1930s the ability to transcend ordinary reality was ascribed to extraordinary individuals, in wartime it expanded to include the whole fighting population, all of whom were considered potentially capable of acts of supreme heroism. It was a very short step from the ordinary world to the world of legend, as heroes' exploits moved rapidly from the newspaper report to the poem. A review of one such poem stated:

> These simple people with simple Russian names are turning into heroes before our eyes. Unexpectedly, but unstoppably newspaper reports are transformed into fairy tales, legends, just as these nine men who died in one trench won immortality.[54]

Nikolai Tikhonov's poem recording the heroic resistance and deaths of the twenty eight Panfilov guardsmen, who had held up the enemy advance on Moscow in November 1941, was noted by Antokol'skii in 1942 as 'an attempt to touch on an event which immediately became legend'.[55] The ordinary existed side by side with the extra-ordinary: 'Our times are terrible and sublime. Average people become heroes'.[56]

The 'fantastic age' of the 1930s was a time when 'spontaneity', the ability to transgress boundaries, was highly valued in hero figures like the aviator Chkalov and Stakhanov the miner. Greater emphasis was laid in wartime on the importance of 'consciousness' in the hero, the ability to let his actions be guided by a correct understanding of the situation. He could not be shown in the grip of the kind of blind, elemental force associated with the enemy's regressive, violent behaviour. As it turned out, it was no easy task for poets to depict heroes who possessed the correct balance between the two forces. Most commonly, especially during the early months of the war, 'consciousness' drowned out any hint of 'spontaneity' in heroes portrayed in poems which were criticised for their monotony and lack of drama.

These 'hyper-conscious' heroes, although wartime equivalents of the Stakhanovites, being soldiers and, particularly, airmen, who had overfulfilled the norm for destroying enemy tanks and planes, did not share their predecessors' reputation as 'spontaneous' supermen. The model war hero displayed an exemplary attitude towards his exploits. In August 1941 *Literaturnaia gazeta* instructed writers to use the examples of real-life heroes to illustrate the Soviet national character:

> Writers are provided with plenty of material by the thousands of occurrences of individual and collective heroism shown by the Red Army and Fleet. A writer should use his skill to create generalisations from these facts so as to reveal artistically in every example of heroism the national character of Soviet people, the nobility of their ideas, which inculcate a scorn of death and hatred of the enemy.[57]

Poems of this type were usually straightforward, repeated the hero's name several times, described his feat, and concluded with an exhortation. Stress was placed on the way in which the heroes weighed up the situation carefully and reached a conscious decision in favour of self-sacrifice for a greater good. Konstantin Simonov provided a representative example in July 1941. 'Prezrenie k smerti' (Scorn of Death) was written to commemorate gunner Poliakov, who had destroyed five enemy tanks before meeting his death. Simonov sets the scene: tanks are advancing on three sides, but the Red Army soldiers are all brave, none more so than Poliakov, who is renowned for his ability to conceal his gun until the enemy is close at hand. Poliakov's calm words of encouragement punctuate the development of the tale:

> ... А враг все ближе подходил,
> Всего пятьсот шагов...
> Но не привык считать врагов
> Наводчик Поляков.
> —Пускай крепка у них броня,
> Пускай идут они.
> В груди есть сердце у меня
> Покрепче их брони.
> Из стали скованы сердца
> У нас, большевиков.—
> Так говорил своим друзьям
> Наводчик Поляков.

(The enemy kept coming closer, only five hundred paces away... But counting the enemy is not the habit of gunner Poliakov. 'Their armour may be strong, let them come. In my breast I have a heart stronger than their armour. We bolsheviks have hearts forged from steel.' Thus to his friends spoke gunner Poliakov.)

Eventually Poliakov dies, crushed by the fifth tank. His success in slowing down the enemy's advance is held up as an example to the reader:

> ... Учись, товарищ, делать так,
> Как сделал Поляков!
> Учись, как надо презирать
> Опасности в бою,
> И если надо—умирать
> За Родину свою.[58]

(Learn, comrade, to act as Poliakov did! Learn how it is necessary to scorn danger in battle, and if need be, to die for your Motherland.)

The drama of the event is subordinate to the hero's calm attitude in the face of danger and death. This lack of drama was seen by some critics as a shortcoming. Sergei Spasskii thought that many poems failed to enhance the impact of the newspaper items on which they were most frequently based: 'A poem placed on the second or third page talks about the same thing, but in more abstract language. It tries to illustrate a command, but looks like an infinitely faded copy of that command.'[59] Another critic remarked on the superficial depiction of heroes who all seemed identical to one another:

> At the moment authors often use the method of superficial enumeration. In some poems the heroes are named, but not explored or even shown ... Often authors, in their concentration on universal, fundamental characteristics, forget about individuals. So that man is a hero, and this one, all heroes turn out looking the same, just in the same way as all the enemies are identical; images are replaced by the stereotype.[60]

Although these poems used the heroes' real names repeatedly, there was in fact nothing to distinguish the hero of one poem from that of another, or, for that matter, one poem from another.

This procession of identical heroes shows the artistic problems inherent in the paradoxical concept of the heroic then current, which defined it as a 'vivid, exceptionally forceful phenomenon, but at the same time typical, recurring'.[61] This, of course, was consistent with the contradiction inherent in socialist realist literature as a means of combining the ordinary present with the ideal future. Dmitrii Kedrin, an outsider who criticised the Stalinist regime through historical allegories, felt that the modern soldier was stripped of all romantic and exceptional attributes by the technological trappings of twentieth-century warfare and made into a prosaic factory worker:

> Гусар, в перестрелки бросаясь,
> Стихи на привале писал.
> В гостиных пленяя красавиц,
> Бывал декабристом гусар.
>
> А ныне завален по горло
> Военной работой солдат.
> Под стать пневматическим сверлам
> Тяжелый его автомат.
>
> Он в тряском товарном вагоне
> Сидит, разбирая чертеж,
> В замасленном комбинезоне
> На сварщика чем-то похож.
>
> Ну, что же! Подсчитывай, целься,
> Пали в механических птиц!

Ты вышел из книги Уэльса—
Не с ярких толстовских страниц.

С гусарами схож ты не очень:
Одет в меховые штаны,
Ты просто поденный рабочий
Завода страданий—войны.[62]

(The hussar, who threw himself into skirmishes, wrote verses in camp. He captivated the beauties in drawing rooms, the hussar was a Decembrist. But now the soldier is up to his neck in the work of war. His heavy machine gun is the size of a pneumatic drill. In a jolting goods van he sits, examining a diagram, in oily overalls, looking rather like a welder. Oh well! Make your calculations, take aim, fire at mechanised birds! You have come out of a book by Wells, not from Tolstoy's vivid pages. You are not much like a hussar: dressed in fur trousers, you are simply a hired labourer in the factory of suffering—war.)

References to the Decembrists drew a further parallel between Russian soldiers of the past and their present counterparts, who appeared to have been deprived of any spark of rebellion by repressive state control. Kedrin's lament for lost 'spontaneity' was not echoed by many other poets, who saw plenty of scope in the war and its heroes for the romantic, particularly the romance of discipline favoured by Tikhonov. Kedrin had imagined war to be governed by technical expertise. This idea found little favour with established poets, who preferred to shy away from the war's mechanised aspects, or to translate them into more acceptably archaic terms. The conventional war hero had to be inspired and inspiring, depicted in scenes of high drama, in single combat with an enemy soldier or fighting alone against a large enemy force, and without the scientific security of calculations and sophisticated equipment. Trust was not to be placed in mere technology, particularly as the German forces had superior equipment and numbers. The truth was to be found by those who had sufficient 'consciousness' and the insight to perceive what lay beyond the purely material. In 1941 Dem'ian Bednyi confessed his belief in victory in spite of the desperate situation:

... Пусть приняла борьба опасный поворот,
Пусть немцы тешатся фашистскою химерой,
Мы отразим врагов. Я верю в свой народ
Несокрушимой тысячелетней верой.[63]

(Though the struggle has taken a dangerous turn, though the Germans amuse themselves with the fascist chimera, we shall repel our enemies. I believe in my people with an indestructible thousand-year faith.)

Boris Pasternak, an outsider whose work was considered too obscure and ideologically uncommitted, gave an evocation of heroism in a poem of 1941 which did not coincide with current opinion on the proper balance of 'consciousness' and 'spontaneity'. The variations in critical reaction to the poem indicate the less than efficient functioning, in terms of the socialist realist method, of wartime criticism.[64] In 'Smelost'' (Bravery) Pasternak began by emphasising cold expertise at a time when 'noble fervour' was required by the literary establishment:

Вы брались рукой умелой—
Не для лести и хвалы,
А с холодным знаньем дела—
За ружейные стволы.

И не только жажда мщенья,
Но спокойный глаз стрелка,
Как картонные мишени,
Пробивал врагу бока.

(You put your skilful hand to the barrel of your gun, not for flattery or praise, but with a cold knowledge of the task. And it was not just thirst for revenge, but the marksman's calm eye that bored through the enemy's side as though through cardboard targets.)

The reduction of the enemy to cardboard targets, instead of monsters of depravity, was too dispassionate to be acceptable. Pasternak then compounded his ideological 'mistake' by showing his heroes' mood moving suddenly from cold calculation to reckless daring. The denial of self shown by his heroes seems to be based more on desperation than on conscious choice:

Между тем слепое что-то,
Опьяняя и кружа,
Увлекало вас к пролету
Из глухого блиндажа.

Там в неистовстве наитья
Пела буря с двух сторон.
Ветер вам свистел в прикрытье:
Ты от пуль заворожен.

И тогда, чужие миру,
Не причислены к живым,
Вы являлись к командиру
С предложеньем боевым.

Вам казалось—все пустое!
Лучше, выиграв, уйти,
Чем бесславно сгнить в застое
Или скиснуть взаперти.

Так рождался победитель:
Вас над пропастью голов
Подвиг уносил в обитель
Громовержцев и орлов.[65]

(Meanwhile something blind, intoxicating and dizzying, drew you to break out from the confines of the dug-out. There in a frenzy of inspiration the storm sang on all sides. The wind whistled to you under cover: you are protected from bullets by a spell. And then, alien to the world, not numbered among the living, you reported to the commander with a suggested battle plan. It seemed to you as though everything was trivial! It was better, having won, to leave rather than to rot ingloriously in stagnation or grow stale under lock and key. Thus was a victor born: above the chasm of heads you were carried off by your heroic deed to the habitations of thunderers and eagles.)

In order to conform to accepted practice, such transcendence of self had to be depicted as a conscious, clear-headed act, but Pasternak's heroes appear to be possessed by some external and elemental force. But the clear-headed hero did not easily emerge as an exciting or charismatic figure; he was often a colourless, faceless creature for whom poets expressed their somewhat stilted admiration. Vsevolod Rozhdestvenskii writes of a boy who died bombing a German staff car in revenge for the destruction of his collective farm:

Такая смерть прекрасна и проста
(Such a death is beautiful and simple.)

The poem ends with a generalisation:

В такие дни становятся героем
От мала до велика—весь народ.[66]
(In such days the whole people, from least to greatest, become heroes.)

In order to escape such bald statements and show the extraordinariness of their heroes' achievements, some resorted to comparisons with heroes of legend. Stepan Shchipachev described one such 'like an ancient Russian knight'; Nikolai Tikhonov's tank-driver hero is 'like a legendary horseman', while another tank-driver 'smashes the enemy like a hero of epic song'.[67] These gestures in the direction of the legendary proved to be a transitional phase leading towards a portrayal of the hero which transported him into a world of pure legend, as comparison was gradually replaced by the wholesale adoption of the formulae peculiar to myth. Symbol replaces the poet's commentary.

Coinciding with this leap into the legendary, the portrayal of the hero underwent a significant alteration. Real-life figures almost vanished, and were replaced by anonymous and fictitious figures, whose dramatic potential was not subject to the limitations of reproducing a real event. The new type of hero operated in a world of symbolic gesture. The ballad became the preferred genre for relating heroic exploits, a genre which, wrote a Soviet critic in 1963, allowed an elevated, romantic style and a dramatic content bordering on the fantastic.[68] Commenting on the characteristics of the wartime ballad, another Soviet critic showed an awareness of the peculiarities of the portrayal of heroes in war poetry: 'Even with all their realistic qualities they do not live a "prosaic" life, which to some extent surrounds people at "ordinary" times. All their thoughts and actions take place in the sphere of higher national interests.'[69] The hero, freed from a specific identity, could take on timeless qualities and participate fully in a higher reality.

Poems concerned with the portrayal of the hero are constructed around a central motif of transformation and transcendence, depicting the hero's rite of passage as he is translated to a higher state of 'consciousness'. Although the move towards greater 'consciousness' was implicitly present in poems such as 'Prezrenie k smerti', it was not actually shown. Simonov's hero, depicted retrospectively in the light of his achievements, seems already to have reached the desired level, and is a static, rather than a dynamic figure. Rozhdestvenskii's poem quoted above deals with the common theme of self-sacrifice during a heroic attack on the enemy, but his hero is not shown to undergo any qualitative change in the process.

As the first year of the war passed, poems began to indicate the hero's inner transformation by emphasising some symbolic outer change, perhaps a wound, or just a new expression of the eyes, to show that the encounter with death in battle has given the hero greater maturity and understanding. As in a rite of passage, performed to mark the transition from youth to maturity, an ordeal must be undergone which leaves a visible sign which can then be seen as proof of the new status. If the hero dies, this sign symbolises his transition into a timeless sphere, most often through the comparison of the hero at the moment of death to a statue. The encounter with death provides an entry to the realm beyond the restrictions of the physical and temporal, the ultimate 'higher reality'. Since many of the Soviet pantheon of heroes had passed through death, the war hero's symbolic death and resurrection denoted that he too had access to the insight they possessed.

One commonly found motif is the hero who uses his own blood from enemy-inflicted wounds as a living banner which soldiers follow into battle. The blood from a wound imitates the colour of the Soviet flag, and so has intensified symbolic qualities in addition to potential religious significance, transforming the hero into a living embodiment of patriotic and self-sacrificial fervour. This image may also echo Maiakovskii's repeated poetic attempts at self sacrifice, particularly in his 'Oblako v shtanakh' (A Cloud in Trousers), in which he bears his trampled soul as a banner.[70] Georgii Suvorov, one of the younger generation whose work became known and published before the end of the war, provides a typical example:

> ... Сквозь боль ты видел их... И перед ними встал,
> Чтоб мужеством своим расправить смерть-старуху,
> И поднял над собой, как знамя, как сигнал,
> Осколком окровавленную руку.[71]

(Through your pain you saw them. And in front of them you stood up, so as to spite the old woman death with your courage, and raised above your head, like a banner, like a signal, your hand, bloodied by a shell fragment.)

A variant of the same theme uses fire instead of blood, as the commander of a burning tank leads the infantry into battle:

... Как знамя живое из огненной ткани,
Зовущее в бои вперед и вперед.[72]

(Like a living banner of fiery cloth, summoning onward, onward into battle.)

The changes which occur in the heroic soldier may not always be so dramatic. For example, Aleksei Nedogonov's machine gunner who successfully fights off an enemy attack is shown to have completed a rite of passage from youth to maturity which leaves no physical scars:

... Был он совсем молодой лицом,
Но как-то по-взрослому молодой;
За пулемет
он прилег юнцом,
Поднялся мужчиною с бородой.[73]

(His face was quite young, but somehow young in a grown-up way; he lay down at the machine gun a young lad, stood up a man with a beard.)

One of the most prominent signs of heroism is the hero's transition at moments of great significance into a sphere beyond the temporal. Pavel Shubin, describing a hero going into attack, calls attention to this cessation of time:

Мгновенье, стой!
Стой!
Запечатлей на века
Славу солдата-большевика ...[74]

(Moment, stop! Stop! Preserve for ever the glory of the bolshevik soldier...)

The idea of transformation is reinforced when the hero is shown at the moment of self-sacrificial death. At the centre of the portrayal of death is the concept of immortality, which is signified in different ways. Sometimes there is the suggestion that the hero's work continues, in actual fact or symbolically, after his death. A gunner is transformed in death into an integral part of his machine gun, which continues to fire:

... человек, приросший к пулемету,
мертвым был.
Но продолжал стрелять.[75]

(The man, who had become as part of the machine gun, was dead, but carried on shooting.)

The device of death and resurrection is sometimes exploited rather more literally, and even with a touch of humour, as in the first-person narrative of Surkov's 'Razvedchik Pashkov' (Scout Pashkov), who relates how he was captured, interrogated and shot, but discovered, when he was buried, that he was not dead at all:

> ... В десять тридцать враги меня погребли,
> А в одиннадцать я воскрес.
> Через день после первых моих похорон
> Я про раны свои забыл
> И опять досылал в патронник патрон,
> И своих могильщиков бил.[76]

(At ten-thirty the enemy buried me, but at eleven I rose again. The day after my first funeral I forgot my wounds and once more sent cartridges into the chamber and shot my grave-diggers.)

This same pattern of death and resurrection is used symbolically in poems which suggest not literal escape from death, but the creation of something new and superior. In Sel'vinskii's 'Russkaia pekhota' (Russian Infantry) a soldier's death is a source of glory:

> Он падет. Но встанет слава.[77]

(He shall fall. But glory shall arise.)

Even inanimate objects can undergo a symbolic death and resurrection. Aleksandr Iashin describes a tank which appears to 'die' of engine failure when stuck in a marsh, but when the Germans begin to tow it away, the engine is miraculously revived. A less dramatic version of the same theme is given in the same poet's account of the retrieval of a flag, shot from off a boat crossing the Volga to Stalingrad. The bullet hole which speaks of its 'ordeal' gives the flag greater significance than it had before.[78]

Most commonly the transformation from life into death and immortality is represented not by the suggestion of a dynamic continuation in the temporal world, but by the image of the living man suddenly changed into a statue. Also used as a symbol for the heroic endurance of soldiers who stand their ground under fire, the image of the statue is most commonly found at the moment of death as a sign of qualitative change and the move to a sphere beyond time and movement:

> ... И пораженный насмерть командир
> на самом гребне высоты на миг
> как памятник застыл. И пал за гребень ...[79]

(The commander, fatally struck, stood for an instant on the very crest of the hill like a statue. And fell behind the crest.)

The soldier as statue is endowed with a double significance. He is simultaneously transported into timelessness, and into a permanent existence in time, captured in the moment of his ultimate fulfilment. Bodies left after a battle, as described by Anatolii Chivilikhin, are like statues, whose poses still reflect the intensity with which the soldiers fought:

> ... Мороз и смерть свое творили дело,
> И застывали павшие. Тела их
> Вмиг бронзовели в напряженных, страстных,
> Порывистых, неповторимых позах.
> О, изваянья страшные! Над ними
> Уже клубился вечности дымок ...[80]

(Death and frost did their job, and the fallen stiffened. Their bodies instantly turned to bronze in intense, passionate, violent, extraordinary poses. O terrible sculptures! Above them already swirled the haze of eternity...)

Boris Slutskii writes as a soldier who finds that he is resurrected to serve as his own monument—a further development of the death and transformation motif—and given a new resonance by the fact that he is transformed into a real statue, the expression on his face smoothed out by the sculptor:

> ... Гримасу лица, искаженного криком,
> Расправил, разгладил резцом ножевым.
> Я умер простым, а поднялся великим,
> И стал я гранитным,
> а был я живым.[81]

(The grimace on my face, distorted by a shout, he straightened and smoothed out with a chisel. I died a simple man, but rose up a great one, and I have become granite, but I was alive.)

Art has achieved a transformation which bestows greatness, yet the transition from living soldier to granite statue, flattering though it may be, seems to suggest the possibility of art creating a false image of reality.

The paradigms of death and transformation which were applied to heroes lower down in the Soviet hierarchy were largely redundant when it came to portraying the figures at its head, most of whom were already dead. The image of the statue is, however, common to both groups, with one important difference: the soldiers are transformed into a statue at the moment of heroic death, and stand as an inspiring monument, while the dead leaders, present in the form of statues, are re-animated and step down from the pedestal to influence events directly. One figure not represented as a statue was of course Stalin, still alive, and standing at the pinnacle of the Soviet hierarchy. He had been built up as a focus for public adulation during the 1930s. While the average person was largely ignored, the strong individual, exemplified in Stalin, was elevated to great heights. The hierarchical state gave exalted status to heroes of production and those such as explorers and aviators, who made special achievements in fields which displayed the daring adventurous qualities of Soviet man. Stalin himself possessed wisdom and bravery which far outstripped those of possible rivals; his position as leader was undisputed, no ordeal was required to test his strength. He was surrounded by a mystique which emphasised his insight, stretching far beyond the confines of ordinary logic. It was doubtless very convenient to discourage any attempt at a critical analysis of the career of a man who, although continuing to proclaim himself as Lenin's successor, pursued objectives which had no basis in Leninist principles, and who consolidated his position as leader by removing 'Old Bolsheviks' while claiming to uphold the beliefs which they represented. Adulation of Stalin was complemented by irrational fear and hatred of 'enemies of the people', paraded in show trials as scapegoats for industrial and agricultural failures.

Soviet man's admiration for and loyalty to Stalin were shown to be boundless. Mikhail Isakovskii wrote a song in 1936 about Stalin's selfless efforts to bring happiness to a people utterly devoted to him. Among other things, Stalin was responsible single-handed for the defence of the country:

> ... Границы от вражьих нашествий
> заделал он в броню литую,
> закрыл их стальными ключами
> великих и славных побед.[82]

(He has clad the borders in cast bronze against enemy invasions, he has locked them with the steel keys of great and glorious victories.)

War, when it came, showed Stalin's devotion to the defence of the country to be less effective in life than in literature. During the early days of the war he temporarily disappeared from public view, and left the business of breaking the news of Germany's attack to his Foreign Minister, Molotov. The state's lack of preparedness for war was made obvious by the speed of the retreat. After an initial spell of inertia, as Stalin was routinely praised, poets made little mention of their leader, preferring to celebrate the deeds of heroes lower down the scale.[83] During 1942 Stalin more or less gave way to Russia and the Motherland, universally invoked by poets as patriotic symbols which retained their power throughout the war. The Communist Party, little mentioned even in 1941, did not reassert itself until after the victory at Stalingrad, with its powerful symbolic connotations, helped restore Stalin to a more prominent position in war poetry. In 1943 the output of Stalin poems appears to have peaked; poems marking the end of the war tend to emphasise the unity between Stalin and the people, Stalin and the Motherland, rather than singling out his contribution to the victory as being decisive. There were few poets already established who did not mention Stalin in wartime: as far as I can tell, Tvardovskii managed to avoid his name.

Berggol'ts does, in 1941, make some references to bolsheviks; thereafter Leningrad and the Motherland take centre stage, though Stalin is mentioned once in her 1945 version of a poem in a stanza removed from subsequent editions.[84] The 'generation gap' between older poets such as Tikhonov and Surkov, and the younger generation such as Gudzenko and Narovchatov, reveals itself in the elders' regular attention to the leader and their juniors' almost complete ommission of his name.[85]

The hierarchy of heroism, which ran in descending order from Stalin, places most value on the transcendence of reality and the attainment of a state which is purely spiritual. Access to this state, with the exception of Stalin, is through death, which figures such as Lenin and Kirov have already passed through. Even the ordinary soldier achieves a considerable shift of consciousness in death:

> ... Мертвый, мертвый ...
> он лежит и слышит
> все, что недоступно нам, живым:
> слышит—ветер облако колышет,
> высоко идущее над ним.
>
> Слышит все, что движется без шума,
> что молчит и дремлет на земле;
> и глубокая застыла дума
> на его разглаженном челе ...[86]

(Dead, dead... He lies and hears everything which is inaccessible to us, the living: he hears the wind ruffling a cloud passing high above him. He hears everything that moves noiselessly, that is silent and slumbers on the earth; and a profound contemplation is fixed on his smoothed-out forehead...)

If all this is possible to achieve as a young soldier, then the heroes from higher up in the hierarchy have unlimited capabilities: omnipresence and the ability to transcend death in order to help, either by inspiration or direct intervention, in the struggle against the enemy. Curiously—or perhaps not so surprisingly after all, given the risks involved in producing a 'lifelike' portrait of Stalin—of the three most prominent leaders depicted in Soviet wartime poetry, the only one alive, Stalin, seems to be the most disembodied. The figures of Lenin and Kirov, both dead, are depicted as real, physical presences in the world, usually, but not always, as statues. Death has brought them immortality; Stalin appears to have achieved immortality by circumventing death altogether. His portrayal suggests his divinity; lesser beings such as Lenin have lived and died, but for Stalin such concepts have no meaning. The mere suggestion that Stalin would one day die was tantamount to blasphemy, and poets, even when evoking the leader's status as an immortal, could not associate Stalin with death.

Stalin is so elevated as not to appear in person, but he manifests himself through his words and his portraits, which are frequently cited as sources of inspiration. He is described, in 1945, as the voice of history, existing beyond the confines of space and time:

Вы слышали? Опять провозгласила
Нам формулу железную свою
Вся прямота его, вся страсть и сила,
Вся вера в тех, кто победил в бою.

Где он витает, замыслом орлиным?
Где гнев солдата, мысль большевика?
Там, далеко на запад, за Берлином?
Там, далеко в грядущем, сквозь века?

Или под звук воинственного марша
Он вспомнил тех, кто пал за Сталинград?
Иль ветеранам улыбнулся маршал
Улыбкой друга, лучшей из наград?

Где бы он ни был, с нами он навеки.
В огне фронтов, в любом конце страны
В простом и сильном человеке
Все без изъятья воплощены.

Вы слышали? Так вслушайтесь же снова,
Чтоб вникнуть силой сердца и ума
В живое слово, в сталинское слово.
Так говорит История сама.[87]

(Have you heard? Once more all his directness, all his passion and strength, all his faith in those who conquered in battle proclaim to us his iron formula. Where does he soar in his thoughts, like an eagle? Where is the soldier's anger, the Bolshevik's thoughts? There, far in the west, beyond Berlin? There, far in the future, through the ages? Or to the sound of the military march does he remember those who fell for Stalingrad? Or has the marshall smiled at veterans with the smile of a friend, the best of all rewards? Wherever he may be, he is with us for ever. In the fire of the front, in any part of the country, everyone, without exception, is embodied in this strong and simple man. Have you heard? Then listen once more so as to penetrate with heart and mind the living word, Stalin's word. So speaks History itself.)

Vadim Shefner wrote that the leader's word was:

Искренне, правдиво и сурово,
Негасимый излучая свет.[88]

(Sincere, truthful and stern, radiating an inextinguishable light.)

Even the name of Stalin has a talismanic quality attributed to it:

Как знамя, мы имя любимое—Сталин
Над светлой земле пронесем.[89]

(Like a banner we shall bear the dear name of Stalin above the radiant earth.)

Stalin is described in terms which give him a god-like stature. Man is made in his image, according to Antokol'skii's poem quoted above. The close bonds between the leader and his devoted people appear to transcend the material, and exist on a spiritual level. As the inspiration of heroism, he is seen by those who throw themselves on enemy guns in battle, where, although absent in body, he is present in spirit:

К его душе, невидимые глазу,
Идут с фронтов прямые провода.[90]

(From the front direct lines, invisible to the eye, lead towards his soul.)

The spiritual link is so strong that the troops seem to be manifestations of Stalin's thoughts:

Бряцая знамени, сталью звуча,
Идут полки, как могучие мысли
Глядящего
в будущее
вождя.[91]

(With the rattle of banners and the clang of steel the regiments march like the mighty thoughts of the leader as he looks into the future.)

In the imitation *byliny* composed by Marfa Kriukova, granddaughter of a famous White Sea folk poet, Stalin occupies the niche which is traditionally filled by Vladimir, Prince of Kiev. Kriukova's Soviet folklore represents Hitler, the evil antithesis of Stalin, as a monster worse than the Serpent Gordynovich, a stock *bylina* villain:

... Гитлер лютый змей да страшный зверь,
Как откроет пасть свою змеиную,
А из пасти-то его да дым густой валит,
Дым густой валит, да искры сыплются,
Хочет он народ да весь советский-то,
Кого хочет он да все огнем сожжечь,
Кого хочет он, злодей, да все водой залить,
Кого хочет змеиным дымом отравить же он,
Кого хочет он забрать в свои же хоботы змеиные,
Он ведь хочет унести да в свои норы-то ...[92]

(Hitler is a savage serpent and a fearsome beast, when he opens his serpent's jaws, from his jaws wells thick smoke, thick smoke wells and sparks fly, he wants all the Soviet people, some he wants to burn with fire, some he wants, the villain, to drown in water, some he wants to poison with his serpent's smoke, some he wants to take away in his serpent's tentacles, he wants to carry them away into his lair.)

Hitler is rarely represented as an individual; his name is not often mentioned. He does not share Stalin's status as a leader, even as a leader of enemy forces. When he is portrayed, it is as a target of ridicule. Semen Kirsanov describes the Führer's desperate attempts to falsify statistics in order to make German forces seem larger and Soviet forces less imposing.[93] Like the Germans in general, Hitler is seen more as an animal than a human being. A satire on Nazism, 'Vzbesivshiisia volk' (The Mad Wolf), begins:

Случаются на свете чудеса,
Взбесился волк и—книгу написал ...[94]

(Miracles happen on earth, a wolf went mad and wrote a book.)

One of Surkov's early war poems speaks of Hitler's inhumanity:

Нет твари бессердечней и бесчестней,
Чем злобный Гитлер, враг моей земли.[95]

(There is no creature more heartless and dishonourable than vicious Hitler, the enemy of my land.)

Hitler's comparative absence from Soviet war poetry makes it clear that he is a figure of little importance. Usually the enemy is depicted as an impersonal horde of savage soldiers, and Hitler is essentially the same as they are, or an exaggerated version of the average Nazi. Stalin therefore has no individualised counterpart on the enemy side, but appears as the powerful personality set against primitive, faceless masses. In relation to his own subordinates, Stalin is depicted as being qualitatively different, not just an amplified version of the Soviet man's virtues, but an embodiment of super-human virtue. His lone dominance is not challenged by the depiction of other Allied leaders. Churchill and Roosevelt are conspicuously absent from the scene, together with the theatres of war under their control. Churchill appears only in poetry once the war is over, portrayed as a belligerent figure with a slight German accent.[96]

At this point it should be said that poems written in German celebrating Stalin's former ally Adolf Hitler ran along somewhat similar lines to Soviet poems in praise of Stalin, though the mystical link between people and leader, being a central tenet of National Socialist ideology is, if anything, intensified. There is a considerable amount of christian imagery used to represent Hitler as the saviour of the German people, sometimes implicitly through the choice of vocabulary—some poems refer to him as his people's 'redeemer' and 'saviour'—or it is explicitly claimed that he is sent by God.[97] Hitler is presented as the man who roused the people from sleep and united them in the creation of a new Germany. This task is sometimes portrayed as the building of an enormous cathedral; one example borrows the christian symbolic interpretation of Christ and the Church as groom and bride in a mystical marriage of Hitler and the *Volk*.[98]

There is a tinge of religious symbolism in wartime poems about Lenin. A little lower down the hierarchy than Stalin, he puts in several posthumous appearances as a figure leading troops into combat, with or without the symbolic armoured car of 1917. His inspiring presence is otherwise felt in statues and in banners which represent him.[99] Lenin inspires affection where Stalin inspires wonder. He is altogether more human than Stalin, even though he appears in the world through the medium of inanimate objects. If Stalin is a remote and awesome god, Lenin is his intermediary on earth, and can be imitated by human beings without offending against his divine status. An interesting combination of the heroic death and transformation motif with 'Leniniana' is found in Sel'vinskii's 'Ballada o leninizme' (Ballad about Leninism) which relates the removal of a statue of Lenin by the enemy, and the hanging of a young political worker on the empty pedestal. At the moment of death, the young man is transformed by imitating the statue's gesture of the outstretched arm. Through this ritual gesture he becomes a replacement for the missing statue and releases the emotions of the hitherto silent crowd:

... Этим движеньем
От плеча,
Милым видением
Ильича
Смертник молоденький
В этот миг
Кровною родинкой
К душам приник ...
Так над селеньем
Взмыла рука
Ставшего Лениным
Политрука.[100]

(By this movement from the shoulder, by the dear vision of Il'ich, in that moment the young condemned man pierced their souls to the very quick... So above the village shot up the hand of the political officer who had become Lenin.)

'Ballada o leninizme' shows a symbolic similarity to the story of the crucifixion which reinforces the relative status of Stalin as god and Lenin, embodied in the German's victim, as a Christ figure, whose sacrifice 'redeems' the crowd from their stupor.

Lower down the scale of merit than Lenin, theologically more comparable with a local saint, is Sergei Kirov. Kirov was the leader of the Leningrad Communist Party whose murder in 1934 was used as a pretext for the beginning of widespread arrests and may almost certainly have been planned deliberately by Stalin who saw in Kirov a dangerously popular rival. Kirov appears in the works of Leningrad poets, most notably in Tikhonov's 'Kirov s nami' (Kirov is With Us), in which he patrols the streets of the besieged city and sees that the citizens of Leningrad, including the sailors who crew the ship bearing his name and the Kirov factory workers, are upholding his revolutionary values.[101] Vadim Shefner writes of metal, which, having been intended for a statue of Kirov, is used for weapons instead, as if the great man himself stepped off his pedestal to help:

... Не тенью и не символом бесплотным,
А—как живой—лицом к лицу с судьбой,
Упорный, грозный и бесповоротный,
Он нас ведет в большой и трудный бой.
Покуда вражья сила не разбита,
На площади пустует пьедестал,—
Как будто Киров сам сошел с гранита,
Когда для нас тяжелый час настал.[102]

(Not a shadow or an unfleshed symbol, but like one alive, face to face with fate, stubborn, threatening, unyielding, he leads us into a great and difficult battle. While the enemy's strength is not yet broken, the pedestal on the square remains empty, as if Kirov himself stepped off the granite when our dark hour came.)

Death and resurrection, of different orders, are available to rank and file heroes, and to leaders; both can be accommodated in the set of formulae peculiar to socialist realist literature. But the result was often all too monotonous and unconvincing, as wartime critics noted. Moreover, the ideological message that had inhabited recurring motifs of the rite of passage and resurrection did, for a certain period during the war, seem to lose its importance. The representation of heroes and heroism became an area full of difficulty. According to Miasnikov in 1942: 'It is a most difficult problem in art to portray a heroic act which is always original and distinctive'.[103] Also in 1942 V. Nikonov wrote that poets tended to write about heroes in highly abstract terms, paying no attention to surrounding circumstances.[104] In 1943 came the resounding declaration: 'Today the Soviet soldier expects from his poets the qualities of concreteness, breadth and directness, not abstract symbolic phraseology and high-flown eulogies'.[105] Yet by the end of the war, heroically elevated abstractions were once more in demand, and these reservations were conveniently forgotten. The term 'socialist realism', which had been out of use since 1941, was restored to the critical arsenal.

For a time, at least, critical debate had noted the problems inherent in portraying the 'typical' socialist realist war hero. Meanwhile, poets had largely turned their attention to more mundane creatures, the ordinary men and, occasionally, women, who faced the war with the resources of mere human beings. When, in 1945 Sergei Spasskii wrote: 'It would seem that the heroic theme is especially appropriate in times like ours. Undoubtedly it now has great significance. But on further reflection it can be seen that its sphere of action is limited', he was only repeating what numerous poets had been saying over the last three years or so.[106]

The paradigms associated with heroes were closely identified with the culture which had produced them, and, as has been shown, were symbolic expressions of the state's ideology. The values upheld in poetry of this type, then, did not have a universal appeal; the need to mobilise the whole population for war meant that poetry had to address themes which did. Spasskii, in the wake of poetic practice, recognised this need and commended lyric poetry for its attention to the ordinary man at the centre of events. This change of focus, from the heroic and superhuman to the ordinary, lay at the heart of developments in poetry which emerged from early in the war, when it expanded its thematic range beyond the heroic or vengeful tones of summer 1941.

NOTES

1 'Sviazist', *Radi zhizni na zemle*, compiled by S. Podelkov (Moscow, 1975), p. 98. For other poems on this theme, see Il'ia Erenburg, 'Byvala v dome, gde lezhal usopshii ...', *Stikhotvoreniia* (Moscow, 1982), p. 92; Semen Gudzenko, 'Sviazist', *Stikhotvoreniia* (Moscow, 1985), 40–43; Aleksei Surkov, 'Sviazist', *Sobranie sochinenii*, 4 vols (Moscow, 1965-66), I, 334.

2 Hans Günther, *Die Verstaatlichung der Literatur: Entstehung und Funktionsweise des sozialistisch-realistischen Kanons in der sowjetischer Literatur der dreissiger Jahre* (Stuttgart, 1984), p. 173.

3 See P. Skosyrev, 'Otveta ne posledovalo: o kritike v nashi dni', *Novyi mir*, 4 (1943), 118–123; P. Antokol'skii, 'Chuvstvo istorii', *Literatura i iskusstvo*, 10 April 1943, p. 3.

4 Edward Shanks, 'If It Happened Here', *War Poems from the Sunday Times* (1945), pp. 20–21.

5 A particularly clear example is B. R. Gibbs, 'To a Country Boy', ibid., pp. 49–50.

6 Lord Derwent, 'Spitfire', ibid., pp. 24–25.

7 See Lulu von Strauss und Torney, 'Licht! Licht!', in Loewy, *Literatur unter dem Hakenkreuz: Das Dritte Reich und seine Dichtung—Eine Dokumentation*, 2nd ed. (Frankfurt am Main, 1969), p. 158, Ina Seidel, 'An den Strassen', in *Deutschland, Deutschland: politische Gedichte vom Vormärz bis zur Gegenwart*, compiled and edited by Helmut Lamprecht (Bremen, 1969), pp. 452–453, Kurt Eggers, 'Kamerad!', ibid., p. 454.

8 Gerhard Schumann, 'Lied der Kämpfer', in Loewy, *Literatur unter dem Hakenkreuz*, p. 287; Hans Baumann, 'Eid des Fähnrichs', in A. Schöne, *Über politische Lyrik im zwanzigsten Jahrhundert* (Göttingen, 1972), p. 31.

9 Hans Carossa, 'Der Himmel dröhnt von Tod ...', quoted by Ernst Loewy in *Literatur unter dem Hakenkreuz*, p. 197.

10 Rainer Schlösser, '31.August 1939', *Deutschland, Deutschland*, p. 451.

11 Hellmund, 'Im Opfer frei', ibid., pp. 453–454.

12 *Pervyi vsesoiuznyi s"ezd sovetskikh pisatelei: stenograficheskii otchet*, facsimile reprint of 1934 Moscow edition (Moscow, 1990), speech by A. Zhdanov, p. 4.

13 Ibid., speech by Zhdanov, p. 5. Abram Terts (pseudonym of Andrei Siniavskii), 'Chto takoe sotsialisticheskii realizm?', in *Fantasticheskii mir Abrama Tertsa* (New York, 1967) p. 403.

The belief in the prerogative of art to change reality is seen as an important element connecting the Russian avant-garde with Socialist Realism. See Boris Grois,

The Total Art of Stalinism: Avant-Garde, Aesthetic Dictatorship and Beyond (Princeton, 1992); E. Dobrenko, 'Levoi! Levoi! Levoi! Metamorfozy revoliutsionnoi kul'tury', *Novyi mir*, 3 (1992), 228–240.

14 *Pervyi s"ezd*, p. 712.

15 Ibid., declaration to the Congress presidium by N. Bukharin, p. 671.

16 K. Clark, *The Soviet Novel: History as Ritual*, 2nd ed. (Chicago–London, 1985), p. 16.

17 Günther, p. 179; p. 174.

18 'O chuvstve novogo', *Literatura i iskusstvo*, 3 April 1943, p. 3.

19 D.Zolotnitskii, 'Oruzhie agitatora-pesnotvortsa', *Zvezda*, 5–6 (1942), 183–185 (p. 184).

20 V.Nikonov, 'Poeticheskii dnevnik Otechestvennoi voiny', *Znamia*, 7 (1942), 157–159 (p. 158).

21 Günther, pp. 175–176.

22 Boris Grois, *The Total Art of Stalinism*, pp. 43–45.

23 From an interview in Moscow, December 1989.

24 'Soldatskoe serdtse', *Literatura i iskusstvo*, 16 April 1942, p. 2.

25 'Iz dnevnika', *Golos vremeni: stikhotvoreniia i poemy* (Moscow-Leningrad, 1964), p. 30.

26 'Syn', *Sobranie sochinenii*, 4 vols (Moscow, 1971–73), II, 48.

27 See Catherine Andreyev, *Vlasov and the Russian Liberation Movement: Soviet Reality and Emigre Theories* (Cambridge, 1987); also Aleksandr Solzhenitsyn, *Arkhipelag GULag*, 3 vols (Paris, 1989), I, 229–258.

28 For typical poems on the theme of desertion, see Vera Inber, 'Zhenshchine', *Dusha Leningrada* (Leningrad, 1979), p. 41; E. Sheveleva, 'Pis'mo na front', *Krasnaia zvezda*, 4 January 1942, p. 3.

29 'Ballada ob otrechenii', *Sobranie sochinenii*, 6 vols (Moscow, 1976-83), II, 71–75.

30 E. Kolpakova, 'Literatura na voine', *Voprosy literatury*, 8 (1957), 59–72 (p. 62).

31 'Glukhota', *Izbrannoe* (Moscow, 1991), p. 69.

32 Mircea Eliade, *Le mythe de l'éternel retour—archétypes et répétition*, 2nd edition (Paris, 1949), p. 139.

33 Ibid., p. 167.

34 'Stikhi v stroiu', IV, 183–204 (p. 196).

35 A. Surkov, 'Predchuvstvie pobedy', *Literaturnaia gazeta*, 7 November 1944, p. 3.

36 'Bessmertie', *Dusha Leningrada*, p. 48.

37 Eliade, p. 30.

38 A. Prokof'ev, 'Moskve', *Stikhotvoreniia i poemy* (Leningrad, 1986), p. 218.

39 'Na chuzhbine', *Stikhotvoreniia i poemy* (Leningrad, 1985), p. 111.

40 See D.S.Likhachev, *Chelovek v literature drevnei Rusi* (Moscow–Leningrad, 1958), pp. 33–42.

41 See, for example, Mikhail Dudin, 'Aleksandr Nevskii', *Leningrad*, 3–4 (1942), p. 155; Nikolai Ushakov, 'Krestonostsy', *Stikhotvoreniia* (Moscow, 1988), p. 183; Iakov Shvedov, 'Na Zadonshchine', *Samoe zavetnoe: pesni, stikhi, poemy* (Moscow, 1976), p. 56.

42 For examples of religious omens before battle, see 'Zhitie Aleksandra Nevskogo', in *Pamiatniki literatury drevnei Rusi: XII vek* (Moscow, 1981), pp. 428–431; 'Skazanie o mamaevom poboishche', in *Pamiatniki literatury drevnei Rusi: XIV—seredina XV veka* (Moscow, 1981), pp. 168–171.

43 K.Clark, *The Soviet Novel*, p. 151.

44 'Marsh veselykh rebiat', *Izbrannoe* (Moscow, 1984), p. 251.
45 See note 43 above.
46 'Rasskaz gvardeitsa', *Oktiabr'*, 3–4 (1944), p. 2.
47 'Syn', II, 51.
48 'Sud'ia', *Stikhotvoreniia i poemy*, second ed. (Leningrad, 1979), p. 164.
49 See, for example, Dmitrii Kedrin, 'Den' suda', *Stikhotvoreniia i poemy* (Moscow, 1974), pp. 204–206.
50 'Voina i mir', *Sobranie sochinenii*, 13 vols (Moscow, 1955-61), I, 211–242.
51 'Edem', *Sobranie sochinenii*, 4 vols (Moscow, 1974–76), I, 198.
52 'Pered novym pod"emom', *Literaturnaia gazeta*, 17 May 1945, p. 2.
53 'Poeziia naroda-pobeditelia', ibid.
54 V.Reizov, 'Il'ia Avramenko: Noch' nakanune bessmertiia', *Zvezda*, 4 (1943), 119–120 (p. 120).
55 'Nikolai Tikhonov', *Krasnaia nov'*, 3–4 (1942), 139–144 (p. 144). It is possible that the events transformed into legend by Tikhonov never actually happened; see note 95, Chapter Two.
56 Il'ia Erenburg, 'V boevom poriadke', *Znamia*, 5–6 (1943), 235–238 (p. 237).
57 'Mesto literatora v Otechestvennoi voine', *Literaturnaia gazeta*, 20 August 1941, p. 1.
58 'Prezrenie k smerti', *Krasnaia zvezda*, 24 July 1941, p. 3.
59 'Pis'mo o poezii', *Zvezda*, 1 (1945), 118–123 (p. 118).
60 See note 20 above.
61 L. Ozerov, 'Poemy Mikhaila Svetlova', *Literatura i iskusstvo*, 22 August 1942, p. 2.
62 'Soldat', *Stikhotvoreniia i poemy* (Moscow, 1974), pp. 158–159.
63 'Ia veriu v svoi narod', *Sobranie sochinenii*, 8 vols (Moscow, 1963–65), VIII, 17.
64 For criticism of 'Smelost'', see 'O novykh stikhotvoreniiakh Borisa Pasternaka', *Novyi mir*, 7–8 (1943), 157–160; for an opposite view, see P. Gromov, 'Boris Pasternak: Zemnoi prostor', *Zvezda*, 5–6 (1945), 157–158.
65 'Smelost'', *Sobranie sochinenii*, 5 vols (Moscow, 1989–92), II, 43–44.
66 'Rasplata', *Zvezda*, 5–6 (1942), p. 34.
67 'Boets Sadokha', *Literatura i iskusstvo*, 1 January 1942, p. 2; 'Ballada o leitenante-tankiste Iukhniche', *Zvezda*, 7–8 (1941), p. 8; Aleksandr Gitovich, 'Tankist Zinovii Kolobanov', *Pobeda: poety o podvige Leningrada v Velikoi Otechestvennoi voine* (Leningrad, 1970), p. 129.
68 A. V. Kulinich, *Russkaia sovetskaia poeziia: ocherk istorii* (Moscow, 1963), p. 295.
69 P. S. Vykhodtsev, *Istoriia russkoi sovetskoi literatury* (Moscow, 1970), p. 402.
70 *Sobranie sochinenii*, I, 185.
71 'Komsomolets Durdy', *Vesna pokhozha na pobedu* (Omsk, 1985), p. 12.
72 A. Shmigel'skii, 'Tankist', *Literatura i iskusstvo*, 18 December 1943, p. 2.
73 'Pulemetchik', *Izbrannoe* (Moscow, 1958), p. 93.
74 'Russkii soldat', *Izbrannoe* (Moscow, 1988), p. 292.
75 A. Nedogonov, 'Gnezdo', p. 102.
76 'Razvedchik Pashkov', I, 319.
77 'Russkaia pekhota', *Sobranie sochinenii*, 6 vols (Moscow, 1971–74), I, 395.
78 'Ballada o tanke', *Sobranie sochinenii*, 3 vols (Moscow, 1984–86), I, 75; 'Flag', I, 85–87.
79 Sergei Podelkov, 'Vysota', *Radi zhizni na zemle*, p. 124.
80 'Iz dnevnika', p. 29.

81 'Pamiatnik', *Sobranie sochinenii*, 3 vols (Moscow, 1991), I, 84.

82 'Pesnia o Staline', *Sbornik stikhov* (Moscow, 1943), p. 445.

83 See John Barber, 'The Image of Stalin in Soviet Propaganda and Public Opinion during World War 2', in *World War Two and the Soviet People*, edited by John and Carol Garrard (London, 1993), pp. 38–49. Also Rosalind Marsh, *Images of Dictatorship: Stalin in Literature* (London, 1989).

84 Stalin is mentioned in Berggol'ts's poem 'Vstrecha', *Tvoi put'* (Leningrad, 1945), p. 122, but not in the later version 'Vstrecha s pobedoi', *Sobranie sochinenii*, 3 vols (Leningrad, 1988–90), II, 300–301.

85 Without reading all the army newspapers and civilian press, it is difficult to state conclusively which poets did not mention Stalin. Most poems about the leader did appear in the press, but failed to survive, a sign, presumably, of their routine nature and lack of artistic merit.

86 Ol'ga Berggol'ts, 'Pamiati zashchitnikov', *Sobranie sochinenii*, II, 71–72.

87 Pavel Antokol'skii, 'Govoril Stalin', *Znamia*, 5–6 (1945), p. 9.

88 'Slovo vozhdia', *Zvezda*, 5–6 (1943), back cover.

89 Liudmila Popova, *Zvezda*, 7–8 (1941), p. 63.

90 Vladimir Lifshits, 'Stalin', *Leningrad*, 2 (1942), inside front cover.

91 Il'ia Sel'vinskii, 'Chitaia Stalina', *Lirika i drama* (Moscow, 1947), p. 101.

92 'Rastrevozhilas' da vsia zemeliushka ...', *Zvezda*, 1 (1943), p. 13.

93 'Naschet podscheta', *Krasnaia zvezda*, 1 July 1941, p. 2.

94 Elizaveta Polonskaia, 'Vzbesivshiisia volk', *Leningrad*, 16 (1941), p. 12.

95 'Detei ne zhdet teplo rodnogo krova...', I, 304–305.

96 Il'ia Sel'vinskii, 'Otvet g. Vinstonu Cherchilliu', I,. 600

97 See Hermann Burte, '1940', in Ernst Loewy, *Literatur unter dem Hakenkreuz*, p. 298; Josef Weinherr, 'Dem Führer', ibid., pp. 301–302; Hermann Claudius, 'Deutscher Spruch', ibid., p. 302; Will Vesper, 'Der Führer', in Joseph Wulf, *Literatur und Dichtung im Dritten Reich* (Gütersloh, 1963), p. 367.

98 Hanns Johst, 'Dem Führer', *Literatur unter dem Hakenkreuz*, p. 304. For other poems on the Third Reich/cathedral-building theme, see Lulu von Strauss und Torney, 'Licht! Licht!', ibid., p. 158; Ina Seidel, 'Lichtdom', ibid., pp. 300–301; Max Wegner, 'Gelöbnis', in Joseph Wulf, *Literatur und Dichtung im Dritten Reich*, p. 367; Gerhard Schumann, 'Sieg, 1940', in Helmut Lamprecht, *Deutschland, Deutschland*, pp. 456–457.

99 Boris Likharev, 'Leninskii bronevik', *Pobeda*, p. 251. For other poems on a similar theme, see Vera Inber, 'Lenin', p. 57; Ol'ga Berggol'ts, 'Pervyi den'', II, 8; Nikolai Tikhonov, 'Leninskoe znamia', *Sobranie sochinenii*, 7 vols (Moscow, 1973–76), I, 443–444; Semen Gudzenko, 'Ballada o znameni', *Stikhi* (Moscow, 1961), pp. 67–73; Dem'ian Bednyi, 'Lenin s nami', *Znamia*, 1–2 (1944), p. 1.

100 'Ballada o leninizme', I, 358.

101 'Kirov s nami', II, 266–270.

102 'Pamiatnik Kirovu', *Zvezda*, 5–6 (1942), p. 47.

103 'Literatura i voina: 16 mesiatsev', *Oktiabr'*, 11 (1942), 136–144.

104 See note 20 above.

105 A. Leites, 'Poeziia sviashchennoi voiny', *Literatura i iskusstvo*, 23 February 1943, p. 3.

106 See note 59 above.

CHAPTER FOUR

The Common Man

The most enduring and popular figure in Soviet war poetry was not one of the many heroic exemplars portrayed in the high socialist realist tradition, but a character presented as an emphatically ordinary Russian man. This is, of course, Aleksandr Tvardovskii's Vasilii Terkin. Terkin began his existence during the war against Finland as the collective creation of several poets, Tvardovskii included. Known then as Vasia Terkin, he was a soldier who combined humour with the fantastic in his improbable exploits. Between 1941 and 1945 several figures of this type featured in the humour section of army newspapers, but Terkin's new and more serious incarnation appeared in September 1942 under the heading of 'literature' rather than 'humour', and he was now dignified by the use of his full name Vasilii. The new Terkin retained his predecessor's sense of humour, but lost his more fantastic qualities. In his previous incarnation he was described as 'extraordinary'; now Terkin was introduced to the reader as a perfectly ordinary man:

... Парень просто сам собой
он обыкновенный.[1]
(He is simply an ordinary chap.)

Just how ordinary Terkin was is difficult to say; at times in the poem he seems to take on the larger-than-life stature of what Tvardovskii calls a 'russkii chudo-chelovek', a Russian miracle-man. There is something of the folklore hero about him, but no sign of the superhuman socialist realist hero. His characteristics and his virtues are on a human scale. Perhaps the relationship between the Terkin of 1942 and his earlier self has something in common with the resurrected hero of a 1945 poem by Leonid Martynov:

Мне кажется, что я воскрес.
Я жил. Я звался Геркулес.
Три тысячи пудов я весил.
С корнями вырывал я лес.
Рукой тянулся до небес.
Садясь, я ломал спинки кресел.
Но умер я... и вот воскрес:

Нормальный рост, нормальный вес—
Я стал как все. Я добр, я весел.
Я не ломаю спинки кресел ...
И все-таки я Геркулес.[2]

(It seems to me that I have risen again. I lived. I was called Hercules. I weighed three thousand poods. I tore out trees at the root. I stretched my hand as far up as the heavens. When I sat down I broke the backs of chairs. But I died ... and now I have risen again: normal height, normal weight—I have become like everyone else. I am kind and cheerful. I do not break the backs of chairs ... And all the same I am Hercules.)

Although the typical socialist realist hero was, like Terkin, portrayed ostensibly as an ordinary man, they had little in common. It was officially claimed during the 1930s that the new socio-economic conditions had altered human character. The result was the New Soviet Man, an extraordinary creature given to selfless dedication in his work for the state, for whom personal life was irrelevant. Heroism was the New Soviet Man's bread and butter, and the war provided him with plenty of opportunities to demonstrate his devotion to the state. As the previous chapter's discussion of the paradigms used to portray heroes suggested, this process involves a transcendence of time, space, and identity. The world of the everyday is set at a distance. Terkin, by contrast, is rooted in ordinary reality. He depends on good food and fresh water rather than the rarefied atmosphere of the heroic, and makes his judgements on the basis of common sense rather than political conviction. The New Soviet Man is an exemplary figure to be admired and emulated; Terkin is a figure with whom readers could identify, an instantly recognisable type who inspired trust and affection. Tvardovskii's hero is associated from the start of the poem with the truth, which is named as the main requirement of every soldier, along with food, water and humour. Of course, under existing conditions it was not possible for Tvardovskii to reveal the whole truth about the war. Even so, according to Solzhenitsyn, who witnessed soldiers' reactions to the work at the front, Tvardovskii had stopped short of telling lies, and so produced a miracle, a timeless work written with courage and a rare sense of proportion.[3]

Vasilii Terkin was far from being the only common man to appear in wartime poetry. Indeed, a large proportion of wartime poetry was concerned with the views of the common man, for whom family and home were more important than Stalin and the Communist Party. While heroic exploits continued to be an important theme in poetry, there was a clear shift of perspective away from the grandiose and impersonal towards the domestic and individual. This chapter will examine how the common man was used as a relatively unproblematic figure to promote individual responsibility and national unity.

Family relationships were presented as a paradigm for wider society, which allowed poets to portray personal concerns as an integral part of the war effort, and to equate the common man with the New Soviet Man. It will also explore the way in which themes of love and death challenged this model by emphasising the uniqueness of personal relationships and the vulnerability of the family in wartime. The introduction of a more intimate perspective coincided with the revival of lyric poetry dominated by the themes of love and the soldier's perception of the realities of battle. In poems on the latter theme, particular emphasis is placed on the authenticity of personal experience rather than on exceptional events or virtues. Above all, the common man, whether as object or subject of poetry, is associated with the truth, including the tragedy of war, and as such stands in implicit opposition to the likes of the heroes discussed in Chapter Three. The implications of this kind of approach were evidently understood by critics, particularly in the later stages of the war, who tried to bring writers into line by demanding of them a more clearly-defined historical perspective. Finally we will return to the poetry of Tvardovskii who, in *Vasilii Terkin*, portrays not one common man, but two: the eponymous hero and the narrator.

It was undoubtedly works like *Vasilii Terkin* which the expert on Russian literature E. J. Simmons had in mind when he claimed in 1944 that contemporary Russian war literature was unique among all other literature on the theme:

> In general, the horrors, heroics and pathos of war in fiction and poetry have an ancient dullness about them; they stifle rather than stimulate human response. Always the living seem to go on dying, and the dead are forever dead ... In order to stir and not surfeit the emotions, war literature must preserve the simple values of common people amid the heroics and pathos of clashing armies. A good deal of Soviet war literature does just that.[4]

In British war poetry of the time, in which the perspective of the ordinary man dominated, the appeal to the 'simple values of common people' was nothing new. In pre-war Soviet poetry, however, the values attributed to the mass of ordinary people were imposed from above. Whatever values the people might actually hold belonged to a stratum of existence which did not signify in a state which only acknowledged the importance of individual life as part of society's movement, on a collective-historical level, towards a perfect future.[5] In wartime, however, poetry began to celebrate the largely apolitical values of ordinary people, rooted in tradition and personal experience.

This change of focus from the elevated to the mundane can be seen in poems of the time which attribute value to everyday scenes and objects previously dwarfed by the grandiose visions of the 1930s. Before the war, poets had expressed patriotic feelings by creating panoramic views of the country and its achievements, seen from an aerial perspective. One of the best known songs by Vasilii Lebedev-Kumach began 'Shiroka strana moia rodnaia ...' (Wide is my Native Land).[6] War brought the poets back down to earth. This is graphically demonstrated by M. F. P'ianykh who compares two versions of Simonov's poem 'Rodina' (Motherland), one written before, one after the German invasion. The version written in 1940 begins:

Дойдя до трех великих океанов,
Она лежит, раскинув города,
Вся в черных обручах меридианов.
Огромная земля. Огромная вода.[7]

(Stretching between three great oceans she lies, her cities spread out far and wide, covered in the black hoops of meridians. A vast land. Vast waters.)

This large-scale approach was very much in tune with the times, and is echoed in a similarly expansive view in a poem by Pavel Kogan, written between 1940 and 1941:

... Но мы еще дойдем до Ганга,
Но мы еще умрем в боях,
Чтоб от Японии до Англии
Сияла Родина моя.

(But we shall yet reach the Ganges, we shall yet die in battle so that from Japan to England my Motherland shall shine.)

This part of Kogan's poem was cited in 1987 by the poet and critic Stanislav Kuniaev as a sign that some members of the war generation were insufficiently attached to the national traditions of Russia.[8] Kuniaev's objections to this generation's enthusiasm for world revolution have, one may suspect, more to do with anti-semitic objections to 'cosmopolitanism'. Casting doubt on Kuniaev's point is his failure to mention that Kogan's 'internationalist' sentiments are prefaced by lines declaring his love for Russia:

... Я—патриот. Я воздух русский,
Я землю русскую люблю.
Я верю, что нигде на свете
Второй такой не отыскать,
Чтоб так пахну́ло на рассвете,
Чтоб дымный ветер на песках ...
И где еще найдешь такие
Березы, как в моем краю!
Я б сдох, как пес, от ностальгии
В любом кокосовом раю.[9]

(I am a patriot. I love the air and the land of Russia. I believe that nowhere in the world can one find another land with the same breezes at dawn, with the same smoky wind over the sands... And where can you find such birch trees as there are in my country? I would die like a dog from nostalgia in any coconut palm paradise.)

Returning to Simonov's pre-war version of the poem 'Rodina', it can be seen that Simonov, like Kogan, devotes several lines to the beauties of Russian nature. Here the nature theme develops as a tentative contrast to the grandiose panorama, as the 'other Motherland':

> ... Боясь так громко называть ее,
> От посторонних глаз ее оберегая,
> Считаем мы за личное свое
> Клочок земли, припавший к трем березам.[10]

(Afraid to name it so loudly, protecting it from outsiders' eyes, we consider as something of our very own the patch of land beneath three birch trees.)

The private world of the common man is acknowledged, but Simonov's hesitant tones contrast with the confident presentation of the whole country in the opening stanza. This reticence is absent from the 1941 version, in which, after an almost identical beginning, Simonov energetically asserts the value of the private world, where everyday objects are made significant by the associations they hold for the individual:

> ... Но в час, когда последняя граната
> Уже занесена в твоей руке,
> И в краткий миг припомнить разом надо
> Все, что у вас осталось вдалеке,
>
> Ты вспоминаешь не страну большую,
> Какую ты изъездил и узнал,
> Ты вспоминаешь родину—такую,
> Какой ее ты в детстве увидал.
>
> Клочок земли, припавший к трем березам,
> Далекую дорогу за леском.
> Речонку со скрипучим перевозом,
> Песчаный берег с низким ивняком.[11]

(But in the hour when the last grenade is already raised in your hand, and in a short moment you instantly remember everything that you have left far away, you remember not the large country you travelled through and came to know, but you remember your homeland as you saw it in childhood. The patch of land beneath three birch trees. The distant road beyond the wood. The little river with the creaking ferry, the sandy bank with low-growing willows ...)

When the country came under threat it was not the panoramic image of 1930s' poetry which was offered to people in order to stimulate their patriotic feelings. The image of a small piece of land, into which all associations with childhood were concentrated, was presented as something which had to be defended, not just eulogised. The country's image in patriotic poems became fragmented at a time when orders were made to preserve every last patch of ground from invasion. At the same time, while many soldiers of the Red Army were either killed or captured, the monolithic image of Soviet man was gradually whittled down to more human proportions. In 1939 Vasilii Lebedev-Kumach had written that the Soviet people would rise up as one man to defend their country:

Если завтра война, если враг нападет,
Если темная сила нагрянет—
Как один человек, весь советский народ
За любимую родину встанет.[12]

(If there is war tomorrow, if the enemy attacks, if dark forces descend—like one man the whole Soviet people shall rise up to defend their beloved Motherland.)

Such colossal figures were the ultimate symbol of a united people living in social harmony; they could not experience any conflict between personal loyalties and loyalty to their country. Lebedev-Kumach had evoked a figure of Titanic proportions and invulnerability which, in the summer of 1941, failed to materialise. The figures depicted in the desperate defence of their country did retain some monumental qualities, but they also assumed a more ordinary identity. Personal responsibility, it was implied by the emergence of these more modest figures, was not after all to be superseded by the collective will. Towards the end of 1941, Aleksei Surkov described a young soldier standing guard near Moscow, then under threat of invasion. Against the background of the hectic movement of troops and armaments the soldier stands completely still:

... У околицы пулеметчик
С темной рощи не уводит глаз.

Будто руки окаменели,
Будто он вкопан в грунт, во рву.
Этот парень в серой шинели
Не пропустит врага в Москву.[13]

(At the city's outskirts a machine gunner does not shift his gaze from the dark wood. It seems as though his arms have turned to stone, as though he is rooted in the earth, in the ditch. This lad in the grey overcoat will not let the enemy into Moscow.)

This lone soldier is depicted like a statue, with all the connotations of the heroic that implies, and can therefore be interpreted as a symbol of the country's resistance or the embodiment of the strength of the national spirit.[14] The poem's penultimate line, however, presents a more mundane image of a young man in a grey overcoat. The word 'paren''—lad—, not normally used to refer to soldiers, has connotations both of youth and informality which appear to contradict the poem's monumental imagery. Significantly, Surkov's soldier is not presented performing any single spectacular heroic action. It is his qualities of endurance and determination which are accentuated.

Surkov's poem shows clear signs of a retreat from ritualised heroics to a more authentic representation of war; the common man became a symbolic guarantee of the poem's authenticity.

This apotheosis of an ordinary soldier represented a reversal of the idea, propagated during the 1930s, that the common man was little more than a cog in a machine. While Surkov's criticism of this attitude is implicit, Aleksandr Mezhirov makes his position quite clear in his post-war 'Zashchitnik Moskvy' (Defender of Moscow). His soldier is small and slightly-built, not made for heroism, but absolutely indispensable and uniquely valuable:

> ... Пот по капельке вытек,
> Кровью выкрасил снег—
> Человек, а не винтик!
> Человек ... Человек ...
> Был он тихий и слабый,
> Но Москва без него
> Ничего не смогла бы,
> Не смогла ничего.[15]

(He poured out his sweat drop by drop, coloured the snow with his blood—a man, not a cog! A man ... A man ... He was quiet and weak, but without him Moscow could have done nothing, could have done nothing at all.)

During the early stages of the war, most of the ordinary men described in Soviet poetry are ordinary only in that their acts of heroism are narrated in a way which is very prosaic indeed. By contrast, the common man inhabits a world which is unashamedly ordinary. He has a home, a family, often comes from a specific locality, and his allegiances are governed by these factors rather than by abstract loyalties to a political ideal. He is still heroic, but less given to self-sacrifice—death accompanies the idealised hero discussed in the previous chapter, but the ordinary man is a survivor whose exploits are related with attention to realistic detail. Unlike his apparently disembodied predecessor, he can feel fatigue and pain. He is also possessed of an inner life, something foreign to the likes of Simonov's hero Poliakov discussed in the previous chapter.[16]

The conventional Soviet hero demonstrated the importance of initiative by his exemplary behaviour, but his lack of identity or human emotions made it difficult for the reader to identify with him. Tvardovskii produced a suitably modified hero in 'Serzhant (Sergeant) Vasilii Mysenkov' of 1941. His poem seems to be a rewrite of Tikhonov's civil war piece 'Ballada o sinem pakete' (Ballad about a Blue Package); both heroes are entrusted with the delivery of a vitally important package, and both fulfil this task at considerable personal risk and suffering. But while Tikhonov's messenger arrives too late, and finds that his ordeal is unappreciated, Tvardovskii's hero reaches his destination in time and enjoys the satisfaction of duty done. Another important difference between the two is that Mysenkov's own voice is heard in the poem as he encourages himself, under enemy fire, by addressing his opponents defiantly:

... Моя земля. Моя трава.
Мой луг, и лес, и рожь.
Ты здесь найди меня сперва,
Возьми-ка. Хрен возьмешь!

(My land. My grass. My meadow and woods and rye. You'll have to find me here first, and catch me. Like hell you will!)

This is no formal speech, carefully composed, but a sequence of brief, fragmented, perhaps breathless exclamations. Equally informal is Tvardovskii's treatment of the physical signs of heroism. Far from reaching the realms of the immaterial, Mysenkov is depicted sweating, unshaven, exhausted:

... Да, все иначе на войне,
Чем думать мог любой,
И солью пота на спине
Проступит подвиг твой.

Щетиной жесткой бороды
Пробьется на щеке
И кровью ног босых следы
Отметит на песке ...[17]

(Yes, everything in war is different from what you might think, and it is in the salt of sweat upon your back that your great achievement will be shown. In the bristles of your prickly beard it will break through on your cheek, and the traces of blood from your bare feet will mark it on the sand.)

Some remnants of the socialist realist paradigms of the heroic do persist here nevertheless; Mysenkov's shining eyes are an outer sign of his inward transformation.[18] The emphasis in Tvardovskii's poem and elsewhere on the common man's capacity for heroism and responsibility can be seen as a pragmatic reaction to the circumstances of the war's first months. Personal commitment, not blind loyalty to the leadership, is the theme of a short poem of 1941 by Surkov. It suggests the inner state of a young soldier who, on seeing his grey-haired reflection, an external sign of his reaction to the horrors he has witnessed, vows revenge:

Человек склонился над водой
И увидел вдруг, что стал седой.
Человеку было двадцать лет.
Над лесным ручьем он дал обет
Беспощадно, яростно казнить
Тех убийц, что рвутся на восток.
Кто его посмеет обвинить,
Если будет он в бою жесток?[19]

(A man bent over the water and suddenly saw that his hair had turned grey. The man was twenty years old. Above the forest stream he made an oath to execute, mercilessly and zealously, the murderers rushing eastward. Who would dare blame him if he is cruel in battle?)

Here is no external, authoritative voice exhorting the soldier to act. His motivation is shown to come from within, not from the upper reaches of the hierarchy. Surkov's poem is a sign that the common man was to be trusted to think and act appropriately in war. How far this trust actually extended in practice is debatable, as political surveillance was maintained at the front, and Soviet soldiers who had escaped from German captivity were interrogated under suspicion of espionage. Taking individual responsibility for the conduct of the war was encouraged implicitly in the images discussed above, and more explicitly in satirical verses such as 'Don't rely on your neighbour, kill a fascist yourself...', which mocked a soldier who was too busy admiring his comrades' fighting to fire a shot himself.[20] Aleksandr Tvardovskii's 'Rasskaz tankista' (A Tankman's Story) of 1941 tells how even a small boy can play a decisive role in a battle by guiding a Soviet tank to enemy artillery positions.[21] The cultivation of the ordinary hero figure contained the message that anyone could make a significant contribution to beating the German army. Early in 1942 a poem in *Krasnaia zvezda* declared the value of the individual in war:

... И будет человек цениться
по этим дням войны.[22]

(Man will be valued according to these days of war.)

The implicit suggestion of these lines is that this had not been the case before the war. The need for appeals to individual initiative and responsibility suggests that years of apparently arbitrary terror had convinced much of the population that their own actions were powerless to change the course of events. A passive population, which was an asset to the state in peacetime, became a liability in a war which threatened to destroy the country. Now it was the enemy soldiers, though, who were represented as being bereft of initiative; their shortcomings were claimed as evidence of the ruinous effects of tyranny.

The surest way of making the soldier's responsibility clear to him was to appeal to his family loyalties. Instead of exhorting him to emulate the actions of faceless heroes in the name of socialism, poets reminded him of his duty to protect his wife and children, at the same time reassuring him that he could draw on thoughts of love and home for new strength. Contemporary critics classified this material under the general category of the 'lichnaia tema' (personal theme).

Their reaction towards it was ambivalent, and altered as the nature of the war changed from defensive to offensive. The 'lichnaia tema' had not been an acceptable ingredient in pre-war Soviet poetry, because it suggested a separation of public and private life. In wartime, however, as literary controls were relaxed, love poems like Simonov's 'Zhdi menia' (Wait for Me) and Surkov's 'B'etsia v tesnoi pechurke ogon'' (A Flame Flickers in the Small Stove) were published and received with enthusiasm by the reading public. Some critics were sceptical of these poems' value, but the majority of poets followed Surkov's and Simonov's example, being convinced that the 'lichnaia tema' was not only popular, but also raised morale. The poet Iosif Utkin pointed out at a Writers' Union meeting in March 1943 that for the soldier the concept of the motherland was embodied in Russia, love meant the love for wife, mother and children, and the concept of the nation meant the soldier's own ancestors.[23]

Critics were, in short, confronted with a fait accompli. According to Surkov's report to the Writers' Union War Commission in the summer of 1943, war had obliged writers to 'take into account the emotional needs of fighting people whom the war has snatched from familiar surroundings'.[24] The only thing critics could do was to place a suitable interpretation on the new phenomenon which, by focusing on the exclusive relationships of the family, threatened to exclude the wider context of the state. Only when private emotion was seen as an integral part of higher patriotic feelings could critical opinion give its wholehearted approval, as in this article of late 1942:

> Soviet man, fighting with all his might, a disciplined soldier, now perceives love in a special way, we can say, in a way that is more pure and profound. Love of women, of his mother, of children fuses with intense love of the Motherland, becoming a part of that great emotion we call patriotism.[25]

Comments of this kind carried the unspoken reminder that personal concerns were significant only when they were linked with those of the nation. The 'lichnaia tema' was favoured only when it used family happiness as a source of reassurance; when it came to death and bereavement, as will be shown below, it was as unacceptable as ever.

Essential to critical tolerance of the 'lichnaia tema' was the fact that it used an already established symbol of unity in the family. During the 1930s the family had been used as a paradigm of the ideal relationship between the individual and the state. The 'greater family' of the Soviet state imitated the ordinary family unit, but its claims were more binding than those of blood relationships. This was illustrated in the case of Pavlik Morozov, made a child-hero for denouncing his own father as a kulak. He was subsequently murdered by outraged relatives. For the New Soviet Man, happiness was to be found only in the collective, the archetype of which was the family. A poem of 1939 by Vadim Strel'chenko is a happy reflection by the author on the sense of recognition felt when he meets people on the street, and on everyone's resemblance to everyone else.[26]

When war broke out, the theme of the family continued to serve its former purpose. The priority of the state over the 'real' family is upheld in two poems of 1941 by Ol'ga Berggol'ts. 'V gospitale' (In the Hospital) describes a nurse ministering to a wounded and delirious soldier who calls in turn for his mother, wife and sister. Each time the nurse answers him, assuming the part of his relatives:

> ... Я здесь, жена твоя, сестра и мать.
> Мы все с тобой, защитником отчизны.[27]

(I am here, your wife, sister and mother. We are all with you, defender of the fatherland.)

'Nachalo poemy' (Beginning of a Poem) shows the declaration of war exerting a sudden and dramatic influence on a husband and wife reconciled after a quarrel. The wife immediately re-defines her relationship with her husband in terms of the wider family of the nation:

> ... Еще ты муж, но больше—брат ...
> Ступай, родной ...
> И ты—солдат,
> ты соотечественник мне,
> и в этом—всё.
> Мы на войне.[28]

(You are still my husband, but more—my brother ... Off you go, my dear. And you are a soldier, you are my fellow-countryman, and that is the most important thing. We are at war.)

These schematic poems insist that loyalty to the state makes a complete stranger equal to a close relative. However, it seems that personal relationships are impoverished, rather than enriched by this exemplary self-denial. On occasion the notion of the Soviet family was taken to faintly ludicrous extremes. Konstantin Simonov's poem 'Surovaia godovshchina' (Sombre Anniversary) was written for the anniversary of the 1917 Revolution in November 1941, when Moscow was under threat from the enemy. Simonov used the motif of the family as a sign of national unity, and placed Stalin at the head of the family, the figure to whom the soldier's thoughts turned first of all:

> Товарищ Сталин, слышишь ли ты нас?
> Ты должен слышать нас, мы это знаем:
> Не мать, не сына—в этот грозный час
> Тебя мы самым первым вспоминаем ...[29]

(Comrade Stalin, can you hear us? We know you must be able to hear us: in this threatening hour it is not our mothers or our sons but you whom we remember first of all.)

Poems like 'Surovaia godovshchina' were mercifully few, and, it can be assumed, were written exclusively for solemn official occasions. More commonly poets attempted to link personal and political themes through symbols such as 'Mother Russia' which carried more generalised Russian patriotic sentiment than the figure of Stalin.[30] The symbolic political interpretation of the family was soon replaced by poetry on 'real' family relationships, although once the war had moved away from Soviet territory, and the state was no longer threatened, the 'great family' and the New Soviet Man re-appeared. The 'great family' featured in hyperbolised form in a 1945 poem by Shchipachev, which casts Stalin as the father figure. A soldier stands in silence by the banks of the Elbe, thinking of home:

> ... А там сейчас, как о любимом сыне,
> Народ и Сталин думают о нем.[31]

(And there the people and Stalin are now thinking of him as of a beloved son.)

Is the reader to conclude that Stalin and The People are the soldier's parents? It can only be assumed that the status and intensity of family relationships had become diluted in the context of the Soviet family, so that the concept of the 'beloved son' has no meaning except as a formal expression of the ostensibly intimate links between the state and the individual. The return to the 'great family' was only possible as victory became certain. In 1942 victory seemed remote as a German summer offensive drove towards the Black Sea and the Caucasus. Appeals to people's concern for and responsibility towards their immediate family were more likely to provoke action than appeals to a generalised sense of community. That summer Simonov confronted his readers with their duty to defend their own mothers, wives and homes, and to uphold their fathers' honour in a lengthy tirade, 'Ubei ego' (Kill Him).[32]

In spite of some reservations, critics accepted that the 'lichnaia tema' had an important role to play in wartime poetry—that of relating private concerns with the concerns of the whole country, and of promoting a sense of optimism and continuity. Love poetry was allowed to flourish, although unlike the theme of the family, this theme lacked a pre-existing model which would relate it to wider concerns of the state. Maiakovskii, it is true, had protested against the separation of love and politics in his long poem 'Pro eto' (About That), but the predominant opinion was that love was a distraction from the important work of the state. A model for appropriate behaviour in the 1930s was given by Pavel Vasil'ev, whose hero, disconsolate at the end of a love affair, is eventually reminded by the sight of the red flag that there is work to be done which is much more important than his private unhappiness:

... И как я смел сердечную заботу
Поставить рядом со страной своей?[33]

(And how could I have dared to set the cares of my heart next to my country?)

In wartime critics proclaimed that the 'lichnaia tema' was no longer at odds with patriotism and service to the state. Most love poetry written at the time upholds this belief, demonstrating that personal and patriotic feelings could be combined harmoniously in an idealised depiction of the relationship between husband and wife. Often the husband's patriotism is confirmed by his vision of his wife as a symbol of Russia.[34] In many poems, as in Surkov's 'B'etsia v tesnoi pechurke ogon'' (A Flame Flickers in the Small Stove) the husband is so strengthened by the thought of his wife at home that the difficulties and dangers at the front are made bearable.[35] Another popular motif is that of the husband who feels his wife's continual guiding presence at the front. Home life and life at the front are made into a harmonious whole by the power of conjugal love. A typical example is this poem by Nikolai Rylenkov:

Писать всю ночь письмо. Писать, еще не зная,
Сумеешь ли послать. И все-таки писать.
Для самого себя. Поймешь ли ты, родная,
Что я хотел сказать? Нет, спутался опять!

Писать всю ночь письмо. Писать, не ожидая,
Что твой ответ придет. И все-таки писать.
Так вызывать тебя в разлуке мог всегда я,
И верю, что теперь ты явишься опять.

Незримая, войдешь в мою палатку мимо
Всех часовых. Войдешь, как входит запах трав.
Как входит лунный дым. Ты мне необходима,—
И ты пришла ко мне. Так разве я не прав?

Я навсегда тебя запомню—вот такую,
Усталую в росе. Постой, не прекословь.
За тридевять земель, узнав, как я тоскую,
Спешила ты ко мне. И это есть любовь![36]

(Writing a letter all night. Writing, without yet knowing whether you will be able to send it. And writing anyway. For yourself. Will you understand, my dear, what I wanted to say? No, I've got confused again. Writing a letter all night. Writing without expecting your answer to come. And writing anyway. When we were apart I could always summon you up this way, and I believe that you will appear again. Invisible, you will come to my tent past all the sentries. You will come in like the scent of grasses. Like smoky moonlight. You are essential to me, and you have come. How can I be wrong? I shall always remember you like this, tired, in the dew. Be quiet, don't contradict me. From many leagues away you knew how much I yearned and hurried to me. And that is what love is!)

Pavel Shubin subverts this device in a poem describing the longings of a soldier for whom constant reminders of his wife, including the contrast of blood and snow, which remind him of her mouth, serve only to intensify the painful awareness of her absence.[37] This is, however, an isolated example. In general the violence and danger of war are not thrown into stark relief by love. According to the 'dialectic of the heart', love for wife and family reinforces hatred for the enemy and provides the soldier with renewed determination to fight.[38]

A good deal of wartime love poetry was exceedingly sentimental, an understandable response in a world which offered little other comfort. It did much more than provide a new paradigm for the devotion of the Soviet soldier to the state. It explored a theme which asserted the supremacy of individual emotion and gave little consideration to any broader context. Universal human feelings were valued for themselves. Against the background of a brutal war, poetry on personal themes helped to preserve an image of life which had not been reduced to the morality of the battlefield. Love poetry, unlike the ferocious calls to revenge which were widespread in 1941, could act as a source of 'spiritual support', and, according to A. G. Kogan, 'helped to maintain spiritual life'.[39] The very existence of love poetry, regardless of quality, satisfied a real need and acted as a counterbalance to the brutalisation that war inevitably entailed.

Despite the new freedom to write about love, there were unwritten rules against offending the puritanical critics' ideas of decency. Simonov's cycle 'S toboi i bez tebia' (With You and Without You), an account of the poet's relationship with an actress, met with disapproval, as it was thought to emphasise sensuality at the expense of more spiritual aspects of love. One critic felt that Simonov's love poetry paid insufficient attention to the value of the family, which was the root of the people's unity.[40] Critics were disturbed by what they perceived as Simonov's tendency to write about personal matters while ignoring the broader context of the war. His popular poem 'Zhdi menia' (Wait for Me), perhaps the most popular poem of the whole war, does indeed celebrate the exclusive nature of the relationship between a man and a woman which surpasses the forces of rationality and death:

... Жди меня, и я вернусь
Всем смертям назло.
Кто не ждал меня, тот пусть
Скажет—повезло!
Не понять неждавшим им,
Как среди огня
Ожиданием своим
Ты спасла меня.

Как я выжил,—будем знать
Только мы с тобой,—
Просто ты умела ждать,
Как никто другой.[41]

(Wait for me, and I'll return in spite of all the deaths. Let those who did not wait say that I was lucky! Those who did not wait cannot understand how, amidst the flames, you saved me by your waiting. How I survived only you and I will know. You were simply able to wait as no-one else could.)

The lovers set themselves at odds to the rest of the world, who do not understand the mysterious power of their love. This is not an unusual sentiment in the work of British war poets, but Soviet critics found such exclusivity hard to accept.[42] In a comparison of 'Zhdi menia' with the work of Aleksandr Prokof'ev, a safely conventional poet, one critic wrote in 1944:

> All the poet's lyrical feelings are focused on the fate of one man, and on the relationship between the hero and heroine. We do not in any way wish to say that lyric poetry of such a kind is unworthy of a place in contemporary poetry. We have only indicated certain fundamental features of Prokof'ev's lyric poetry, where the 'personal' theme organically merges with a different, wider circle, and only ... in this circle does it achieve full-blooded existence.[43]

Critical disapproval of Simonov's love poetry was no obstacle to its popularity. Simonov's success, said the poet Iosif Utkin, was that of his theme, and critics who spoke out against him were, at the same time, attacking the public's preferences for something they weren't supposed to enjoy.[44]

While critics voiced anxieties about love overshadowing the theme of war, the young poet Sergei Narovchatov felt that the war threatened to dwarf the dramas of love and separation it produced:

> The war smashed, overturned, crippled so many people's existence that two young people falling out of love could hardly attract any attention. But still, the devil only knows ... A drama doesn't stop being a drama even if it is part of a tragedy.[45]

Narovchatov drew metaphors from the war to describe such emotional dramas. The loss of love is the loss of a battle, fought desperately over a deserted village which is as important as a capital city to him.[46] When Narovchatov writes of happy, untroubled love, the backdrop of war gives way to that of nature. In 'Lesnaia liubov'' (Love in the Forest), the lovers' happiness is timeless and cannot be destroyed by war:

... Пусть стороной осколки воют чаще,
Случайная погуливает смерть,
И гаубицы
Над краем древней чащи

Гремящий
Опрокидывают смерч,
Но стонов бабьих,
Томных и счастливых,
Где древность
Возникает в новизне,
Не заглушить
Ни взрывам, ни разрывам,
Самой войне.[47]

(Let the shell fragments howl past more often, random death roam free, and howitzers fling down thundering tornadoes above the edge of the ancient wood, but women's moans, languorous and happy, where antiquity arises in the new, cannot be drowned out by explosions, by shellbursts, by war itself.)

The fact that Narovchatov wrote much more of the pains of love than of its happy fulfilment sets him apart from the majority of poets who used themes of love and the family as a source of comfort and reassurance. For most poets the 'lichnaia tema' excluded any possibility of conflict; it was the one area which offered any promise of stability in war. Critics assumed that private and public interests were always identical. In fact the war confronted people with situations in which they were forced to choose between the two. Tvardovskii was one of the few poets who broached this awkward topic. His 'Ballada ob otrechenii' (Ballad about Renunciation), discussed in the previous chapter, is about the conflicting loyalties of a deserter's parents.[48] A similar conflict of love and loyalty is faced by a soldier in 'Ballada o tovarishche' (Ballad about my Comrade). After having been wounded in the retreat and harboured by a village woman until he is fit to continue his journey east, he has fallen in love with her. She suggests that he remains with her in safety, but he remains true to his duty as a soldier, though not without a struggle. When the soldier returns later to the village, now liberated, he finds the woman's house in ruins. The tragedy of the soldier's situation is heightened by the fact that the woman he mourns was not related to him in any way—belonging to the greater Soviet family is no comfort to him:

... Он плакал горестно, солдат,
О девушке своей,
Ни муж, ни брат, ни кум, ни сват
И не любовник ей.[49]

(The soldier wept bitterly about his girl, he was neither husband, nor brother, nor godfather, nor relative by marriage, nor a lover to her.)

These five negations in a row emphasise the fact that there is no word to describe the fleeting, possibly undeclared relationship between people brought together and separated by the war. In Tvardovskii's treatment of conflicting loyalties the solution he offers is not an easy one, but he does acknowledge the tragic emotional complexity of conflict at a time when conventional opinion tried to deny the very possibility of such a situation.

The fact that the critics and most poets ignored the possibility of conflict between private emotions and public obligations meant that they largely excluded one aspect of the 'lichnaia tema' which was a part of most ordinary people's experience—bereavement. The death of close relatives and friends, both at the front and in the rear, was rarely mentioned. If poets appealed to family loyalties as a model for the relations between the individual and the state, the death of family members was a disturbing reminder of people's vulnerability in wartime. In the early stages of the war, the soldier's discovery of dead relatives did appear as a common motif in poems of revenge, but towards the end of the war, revenge was said to be inspired by a whole nation's suffering and so the theme of private grief was deprived of a context which made it officially acceptable. It was considered inappropriate, at a time of triumph, to remind people of the shattered homes and families which were the price of victory. Moreover, the common man so readily invoked when the war hung in the balance was now out of favour. In demand were characters who displayed typical Soviet or socialist traits rather than the simply human, and who were supposedly better able to see the full magnitude of their victory instead of harking back to 'irrelevant' personal details.

Judging from Tvardovskii's sombre 'Otets i syn' (Father and Son) written in 1943, it was not as easy as other poets suggested to maintain a happy family life while the husband and father was away. Having been reported dead due to an error, a man returns home to a catalogue of disaster: his wife has married his best friend, and, when he was killed, gone mad with grief; his daughter has died in an air raid. His surviving son begs his father to take him back to the army.[50] In spite of the triumphant atmosphere encouraged during the last year of war, some poets did draw attention to the plight of soldiers who had lost their homes and families and had nothing to return to. In *Vasilii Terkin* Tvardovskii wrote about a soldier weeping after he visited his recently liberated home village and found out that all his family had been killed:

... На краю сухой канавы,
С гордой, детской дрожью рта,
Плакал, сидя с ложкой в правой,
С хлебом в левой,—сирота.

Плакал, может быть, о сыне,
О жене, о чем ином,
О себе, что знал: отныне
Плакать некому о нем.[51]

(On the edge of the dry ditch, with a proud, childlike tremor of the mouth, he wept, sitting with a spoon in his right hand and bread in the left—an orphan. He wept, perhaps, for his son, for his wife, for something else, for himself, as he knew that henceforward there would be nobody to weep for him.)

Confronted by the loss of his family, the soldier becomes a helpless child. In Isakovskii's 'Vragi sozhgli rodnuiu khatu...' (The Enemy Burned the Family Home), discussed in Chapter Two, grief reduces a soldier from conqueror of Budapest to a man whose world has suddenly lost its meaning.[52] The return to wife and family, to a comfortable home and 'normal' life was a theme current in the latter stages of the war. The experience of the common man was often very different from that depicted in poetry.

Death was an acceptable theme when presented in the context of the self-sacrificial hero who transcended time and the limitations of individual identity. The most usual way of commemorating the war dead in contemporary published poetry was to resort to graveside eulogies of unknown soldiers, anonymous representatives of those who had defeated fascism. While the common man is alive, he is shown to belong in the context of home and family. Dead, his status both as victor and victim is generalised. In a typical example, Mikhail Isakovskii tells his readers of the debt they owe to the dead man. Like the person they are told to honour, the addressees of the poem are anonymous, characterised only by profession. The dead man's relatives are not even mentioned:

... Кто ни был ты—рыбак, шахтер,
Ученый иль пастух,—
Навек запомни: здесь лежит
Твой самый лучший друг.

И для тебя и для меня
Он сделал все, что мог:
Себя в бою не пожалел,
А Родину сберег.[53]

(Whoever you are—fisherman, miner, scholar or shepherd—remember for ever: here lies your very best friend. For me and for you too he did all he could: he did not spare himself in battle, but saved the Motherland.)

Sergei Orlov used the conventions of the commemorative poem to assert the value of each person, no matter how ordinary, involved in the campaign. 'Ego zaryli v shar zemnoi...' (They Buried Him in the Earth's Sphere) describes the burial of a young soldier, undistinguished by high rank or medals:

Его зарыли в шар земной,
А был он лишь солдат,
Всего, друзья, солдат простой,
Без званий и наград.

Ему как мавзолей земля—
На миллион веков,
И Млечные Пути пылят
Вокруг него с боков.

На рыжих скатах тучи спят,
Метелицы метут,
Грома тяжелые гремят,
Ветра разбег бегут.

Давным-давно окончен бой...
Руками всех друзей.
Положен парень в шар земной,
Как будто в мавзолей.[54]

(They buried him in the earth's sphere, but he was just a soldier, just a simple soldier, my friends, without title or medals. The earth is like a mausoleum to him—for a million centuries, and the Milky Ways blaze around him on all sides. On reddish slopes the clouds sleep, blizzards rage, heavy thunder rumbles, the winds gather speed. Long, long ago the battle was finished ... by the hands of all his friends. The lad is laid in the sphere of earth as if in a mausoleum.)

The poem contrasts the soldier's ordinariness with the grandeur of his resting-place: the whole earth serves as his mausoleum, placing his death and burial in a cosmic context. The idea of the mausoleum—Orlov uses that specific word rather than 'grave'—contains a hint that the ordinary soldier killed in the war has achieved a status equal to, or possibly greater than that of Lenin himself. Here, it might be argued, the paradigm of heroic death and transformation is modified, made inclusive and not conditional on exceptional deeds. An ordinary man is, in himself, deserving of a memorial.

It was, of course, perfectly natural that as the end of the war approached poets began to commemorate the dead and the magnitude of their achievements. They were offered guidance on how this should be done. According to A. Egolin, writing in 1944, writers were expected to express the significance of the war in almost cosmic terms as the apotheosis of Soviet heroism:

> It is the writer's calling to record a great historical achievement—the advance of the heroic Red Army, the expulsion of the enemy from our lands, the collapse of Nazism, the liberation of the peoples groaning under the occupier's heel. The duty of the Soviet writer is to show in works of art the greatness of our Motherland and people in their historic struggle against the most evil enemy of the human race—German fascism.[55]

The point of view of the common man has vanished into insignificance.

Why should the common man have been excluded from official celebrations of victory except as an abstract representative of the Soviet people? The answer lay in his Soviet identity, or rather, lack of it. The common man had been shown to be preoccupied by his concerns for home, family and Russia, which was all very well when the country was in extreme danger. When victory was close at hand, however, this development implied an undesirable autonomy from the state, an autonomy which was underlined when poets turned towards exploring the individual experience of war, often their own, and adopted a perspective which made no reference to an external ideological framework. The authenticity of personal experience was presented as sufficient justification in itself. The revival of lyric poetry first showed itself in the re-introduction of love as an acceptable theme. This was followed by a proliferation of poems dealing with the experiences of soldiers at the front. A wealth of realistic detail revealed more about war than the usual superficial accounts of a hero's adventure; the way these details were put together gave an impression of battle seen from within.

Initial reactions to this new tendency in poetry were largely favourable. In 1942 a critic argued that personal experience actually enhanced the work of war poets:

> ... in order to inspire soldiers and workers the poet should express the thoughts and feelings of the people not in some general form, but in the light of personal experience of and reactions to the war. If this is absent, the poet is not meeting our expectations; he remains a more or less successful illustrator of events and current affairs.[56]

In 1943 the greater originality of poetry written by soldiers at the front was attributed to the fact that they were writing about things they knew at first hand:

> They all write about more or less the same themes. But it is interesting to note that the superficial monotony found in the work of 'published' poets often degenerates into cliche does not, however, deprive work which is produced in front line conditions of originality and keenness of feeling.[57]

The poet who epitomised poetry of this kind was Semen Gudzenko. In 1943 Il'ia Erenburg acclaimed his work as a new kind of war poetry written by a participant, and quoted from his best-known poem 'Pered atakoi' (Before the Attack).[58] The authenticity of Gudzenko's battle descriptions was commended in a review of his book published in 1944:

> The author knows what he is writing about, he has experienced, physically and emotionally, everything he describes. The reader believes that the hero of the poems has indeed marched along the roads at the front and knows from his own experience both the sadness of loss and the joy of victory. S.Gudzenko knows not only

> the actual authentic truth of war, he has also found a way to poetic truth in his lyrical illumination of the war theme.[59]

While young poets were at first praised for their discovery of a new, realistic view of the war, they were increasingly taken to task for the limitations inherent in this view. Later in the 1944 article on Gudzenko quoted above came the qualifying statement which became customary in many reviews written in the last year of the war: 'In order to become a major poet he must transfer his personal experience, his personal responses, intelligent and profound though they may be, to the level of broad historical generalisations, and reveal the historical meaning of events'.[60]

Gudzenko continued nevertheless to write poetry which, like 'Pered atakoi' (Before the Attack), concentrated on his personal experience of war. He describes the advance on Berlin as a time not of clarity on the eve of the final victory, but of confusion, as objects, animate and inanimate, became indistinguishable from one another. The observer in Gudzenko's poem, like Nikolai Rostov in Tolstoi's *War and Peace*, is alienated from a fragmented reality:

Горят леса от Дрездена
до самого Берлина.
Земля, как в пекле, треснута,
как в пекле, тлеет глина.

Пылают сосны, кренятся
и рушатся, как в пекле.
И все поляны в пенистом,
в сигарном сером пепле.

А дым дорогу кутает
и путает шофера.
Жара такая, будто мы
заедем в пламя скоро.

Мы, как слепые странники,
все щупаем руками.
То пни или кустарники?
То немец или камень?[61]

(The forests burn from Dresden as far as Berlin itself. The earth is cracked as if in an inferno, as if in an inferno the clay smoulders. Pine trees blaze, heel over and collapse as if in an inferno. And all the fields are covered in foamy, cigar-grey ashes. And smoke envelops the road, and confuses the driver. It is so hot that it feels as if we shall drive into the flames soon. Like blind pilgrims we feel everything with our hands. Are these tree-stumps or bushes? Is this a German or a stone?)

The contrast between a soldier on the battlefield whose vision is so obscured that he cannot distinguish between inanimate objects and the enemy, and the officially required view of events could hardly have been more pointed. The poet records his impressions from a very limited perspective, his perceptions outweigh any ideological framework, risking accusations of 'naturalism'. In actual fact the critics were in 1945 far from unanimous on this point, as is clearly shown in an article by Sergei Spasskii published early that year. He makes a vigorous defence of lyric poetry, quoting what he calls 'one of the best lyric poems of the war' in order to prove his point. Simonov's 'Ataka' (The Attack) explores the feelings of a soldier waiting to go into attack, showing his heightened perception of the immediate surroundings, the ground on which he lies:

> ... Какой уютной показалась
> Тебе холодная земля,
> Как все на ней запоминалось:
> Примерзший стебель ковыля,
>
> Едва заметные пригорки,
> Разрывов дымные следы,
> Щепоть рассыпанной махорки
> И льдинки пролитой воды.[62]

(How cosy the cold earth seemed to you as everything on it was fixed in your memory: a frozen stem of feather-grass, barely noticeable hillocks, the smoky traces of explosions, a pinch of scattered tobacco and fragments of ice from spilt water.)

The details selected by Simonov reflect the hero's perceptions and emotional state. It is precisely because the details are in themselves insignificant that they capture the hero's attention, perhaps as a distraction from what is about to happen. Unlike the birch trees in Simonov's 'Rodina', there is no specific nostalgic or emotional charge in the objects described except that they are close to the earth, imagined to be a guarantee of safety.

Spasskii sees the value of Simonov's poem in its ability to communicate the experience of war so that people who have been in the same situation will recognise their own feelings:

> Perceptions of this kind are close to everyone who has been in a similar situation. Those who have not reflected on their feelings will recognise them in the words of the author who has experienced everything on behalf of many people. And they will be grateful to him for explaining their feelings.

The poem, he continues, is only made complete when the reader associates it with his own experience. The reader is, therefore, no longer a passive recipient of 'sound' attitudes, but in collusion with the poet, sharing an experience which has no room for wider political concerns. Spasskii asserts that Simonov has found the correct solution to the question 'what should real poems about the war be like?'. Any attempt to give a broad evocation of the whole battle would, he says, result in verbosity; the cinema is better equipped for that purpose. Poetry, writes Spasskii, must deal with what the other arts cannot show, namely inner feelings: 'it is precisely the lyric poem which is capable of bearing the entire load of war. For it deals with the main thing—the person at the centre of events.'[63] It is to be noted that Spasskii does not preface the word 'person' with 'Soviet' and that he is not misled, as other critics of the time appear to have been, by lyric poetry's often apparently narrow focus. Spasskii sees emotional depth where others see a lack of perspective.

While Spasskii was defending lyric poetry as a legitimate means of portraying the war in all its fullness, other critics had already been appealing for the creation of a new, epic poetry as the best genre in which to portray events in appropriately monumental terms. There seems to have been a widespread expectation that the war would produce its own *War and Peace*, which was in fact written well after the events it described, and not from personal experience either. In 1944 Surkov looked to the future:

> With time, new, major, talented works will be written about the heroism of our people. They will be perfect in form and broad in the sweep of events portrayed. But the works created in our time will remain dear to the heart of the reader.[64]

A lengthy article in *Znamia* in late 1943 surveyed recent poetry, looking for signs of the future heroic epic. The article's basic premise is that great historical epochs such as the present day produce heroic epics. Work of a sufficiently epic stature had not yet emerged, according to the critic L. Poliak. The article displays a rather contradictory attitude towards the fusion of epic and lyric genres which Poliak notes in recent work; she discusses Antokol'skii's poem 'Syn' (The Son), in which the epic is 'warmed' by lyrical feelings, but then states that the epic is in danger of being overwhelmed by lyrical pathos. The lyrical diary, which was fragmented and constructed around heroic moods and themes, had failed to portray any genuine heroes. It was no problem to find a hero, wrote Poliak, but poets still had to 'describe him in the language of art and poetry, to reveal his essence and his historical role'.[65]

Just what was understood by the 'epic' genre is left undefined. Some comments on the epic by Mikhail Bakhtin written in 1941 are, however, revealing. The world of the epic is set at an absolute distance from the present day, complete, unchangeable, allowing for no individual perspective on events. Bakhtin points out the official nature of the genre: 'The epic world knows only one single and complete world view, which is just as obligatory for the heroes as for the author and audience'.[66] The epic hero, meanwhile, displays a 'unique beauty, wholeness, crystalline clarity and artistic perfection', but is also limited and unlifelike. The novel provides a complete contrast to Bakhtin's understanding of the epic, as it is an essentially open genre which cannot be finalised. From this brief outline it seems clear that the epic has much in common with the practices of socialist realism discussed in the previous chapter. It is also not difficult to surmise the reasons for the absence of the unadulterated epic in wartime poetry, when the dependence on formulae associated with socialist realism was reduced.

Together with increasing demands for works of epic stature came calls to depict heroes who were specifically Soviet in their outlook. The proliferation of lyric poetry had promoted themes of universal human interest, but now the possibility of universal values was questioned. In 1945 the critic Pertsov stated:

> Yes, man is the measure of all things, but that ancient truth is too vague to act as a guiding light for the contemporary artist. There is a further, new 'dimension' which did not and could not exist previously, which produced a revolution in man's entire inner world. It has appeared since it became possible to talk about the socialist man as the hero of our times. This new 'dimension' is the conscious participation of the masses in the historical process, man as the subject of history.[67]

The importance of historical perspective, frequently emphasised in critical articles, is placed here in its proper context. What was required was not a historical perspective as such, but one which would allow for the interpretation of the war as a triumph of the socialist system and of the New Soviet Man.

The renewed insistence on specifically Soviet qualities represented a return to the ideas which had governed the depiction of the soldier in the war's early months. Images used in 1941 were drawn from the immediate Soviet past, in particular from the civil war. But in his speech on 7 November 1941, however, Stalin appealed to historical associations which went back further than the creation of the New Soviet Man, as he urged the troops before him to follow the examples of Russian heroes such as Dmitrii Donskoi and Aleksandr Nevskii.[68] The romantic image of the civil war began to play a secondary role to that of medieval victories over the Tatars or the defeat of Napoleon. The Soviet soldier was increasingly removed from a specifically Soviet context and appeared as a manifestation of Russia's military glory throughout the ages. In Iakov Shvedov's 'Na Zadonshchine' (In the Land Beyond the Don), which refers in its title to a medieval poem 'Zadonshchina', written no later than 1393 about a battle against the Tatars which took place in 1380, a sentry standing by the river Volga is compared to an ancient hero.[69] Russia's past, reclaimed during the 1930s as a source of national pride, now offered a sense of stability. Soviet Man, created by the revolution, had all but vanished from the scene, and there were no eyebrows raised in 1941 when Tvardovskii described a soldier who was:

... Похож на русского солдата
Всех войн великих и времен.[70]
(Like a Russian soldier of all great wars and times.)

Such recourse to historical and national values served its purpose of mobilising patriotic emotion, but towards the end of the war historical references were said to be anachronistic. Critics now claimed that society and its members were radically different from the Russia of the past, and tried to reinforce the belief that it was the Soviet system in particular, and the people it produced, which had made victory possible. In 1945 Lev Subbotskii complained that it was impossible to equate Soviet patriotism with that previously felt by Russians, and put forward such models of the New Socialist Man as the heroes of Antokol'skii's 'Syn' (The Son) and Aliger's 'Zoia'. They were, he wrote, characters which typified the new era.[71]

The officially sponsored revival of the New Soviet Man, timed to coincide with victory, marked an attempt by the state to claim all the credit for itself. The common man was to be marginalised, as victor as well as victim of the war's suffering. It was, however, too late to suppress ordinary people's awareness of their own contribution to the victory. This trend had begun in poems like Surkov's 1941 poem 'Podoshla voina k Podmoskov'iu...' (The War has Come to the Moscow Region...) with its young lad in a grey coat, but emerged more fully in 1943, after victory at Stalingrad marked the war's turning point. As events soon showed, hopes for a new freedom were thwarted by a post-war renewal of political repression which affected the war generation, particularly those who had been in enemy captivity. The common man, who had emerged as the humble, but valued, hero during the first winter of the war had become rather too self-confident, and had to be replaced by the unequivocally loyal Socialist hero. The Soviet authorities had perhaps heeded the words of their patron poet Vladimir Maiakovskii. In December 1914, still a rebellious futurist, he wrote that war allowed the individual to gain in self-awareness, and, implicitly, to challenge the state's authority. War, he wrote, had given the Russians the opportunity to become aware of their own individuality and initiative as never before.[72] The fact that Russia's involvement in the First World War ended in revolution might seem to bear Maiakovskii's words out. When his words were referred to by Ol'ga Berggol'ts in 1945, they were, however, declared inappropriate to the 'New Soviet Man': 'The last few years have seen an unprecedented rise in even the most ordinary person's awareness of his individuality'.

There was now a new element in the process: 'It is indicative that the growth of this awareness came not through opposition of the individual to the people, but through fusion with the people, through self-sacrifice and self-denial'.[73]

By 1945 Tvardovskii's hero Vasilii Terkin was officially adopted as a model New Soviet Man, though his qualities and characteristics are more generally Russian or universally human, and the poem contains little detail belonging to a specifically Soviet context. Terkin was not, in fact, immediately identified by the critics as a Soviet Man *par excellence*. Early reactions in October 1942 were divided between describing him simply as a 'Russian man', and as a figure who combined Russian national characteristics with Soviet qualities. In 1943 Viktor Shklovskii found Terkin strongly reminiscent of figures from the civil war, while Nikolai Aseev found that there was nothing in the poem which connected Terkin with the war then in progress. In 1945 Anatolii Tarasenkov claimed that the question of Terkin's Russian or Soviet identity was irrelevant, although this claim was immediately qualified by remarks to the effect that Terkin's deep democratic feeling was obviously of Soviet origin.[74]

Evidently, by the end of the war, as the official mood turned against the representation of the patriotic but politically uncommitted common man, it was a matter of some importance that Terkin be positively identified as belonging to a specific group rather than as a figure capable of being all things to all men. In order to include 'Terkin' in the canon of war literature already being established by 1945, it was necessary to claim that his virtues were the result of the Soviet system, rather than of Russian tradition. Ol'ga Berggol'ts made these typical remarks about Terkin in May 1945:

> The most appealing feature of Terkin is his own organic and completely conscious sense of responsibility not only for his own actions and deeds, but, as it were, for the deeds and actions of the whole people, the whole state. This characteristic, produced and fostered by the Soviet, socialist system, has become stronger and developed enormously during the war years.[75]

Tvardovskii claims to have been surprised by his hero's universal appeal:

> ... Но еще не знал я, право,
> Что с печатного столбца
> Всем придешься ты по нраву,
> А иным войдешь в сердца.[76]

(But I really did not know that from the printed column you would please everyone and enter into the hearts of some.)

It is hardly surprising, though, that such an attractive figure was adopted as an exemplary product of the Soviet system. He was associated with the truth, a sense of responsibility for his country, and with high moral standards, qualities which critics suggested were not present in the ordinary Russian soldier of the past. Terkin's reputation as a Soviet paragon is not, in actual fact, supported by the text, which is singularly short on specific Soviet detail. One barrier to seeing Terkin as the Soviet man he was claimed to be is his almost complete lack of a past. He displays the air of innocence and attractive simplicity of one who is unaware of recent political upheavals. He seems unfamiliar with political rhetoric, and makes no mention of Stalin or Lenin in his conversations with his fellow-soldiers. The name of Kalinin, then president of the USSR, is mentioned when Terkin is awarded a medal by a fatherly general, the sole figure of authority he encounters, but politically neutral words outnumber specifically Soviet terminology in the description of the general's status as:

> ... Твой ЦК и твой Калинин.
> Суд. Отец. Глава. Закон.[77]

(Your Central Committee and your Kalinin. Judgement. Father. Chief. Law.)

When Terkin delivers his 'political lecture' to soldiers in retreat, the simple message is 'don't be downhearted', an implicit criticism, perhaps, of empty rhetoric and ideological messages which have no meaning to his audience.[78]

There is a much greater awareness of the Soviet context in Tvardovskii's later satirical work 'Terkin na tom svete' (Terkin in the Next World), which used the war's most popular literary hero to shed light on the bureaucratic nightmare of the Soviet present. Tvardovskii produced two versions of the poem, one in 1954, never officially published, the second in 1963, which did appear in print.[79] The poem's plot is simple: Terkin arrives in the Underworld, having been, he presumes, killed in battle. What he discovers there is a vast infernal bureaucracy, and a subterranean KGB, in a world which resembles that of the Soviet Union. Terkin learns that there are two Underworlds separated by a wall, the communist, founded on a scientific basis, and the capitalist, which offers the enticing prospect of eternal rest. An old comrade who died earlier in the war shows him round, but Terkin is ill at ease, as he still feels heat, thirst, hunger and fatigue. He is, in fact, not dead at all, being distinguished from all the others in the Underworld by the fact that he has a soul. Terkin is once more associated with the 'bitter truth', this time about the society he belongs to. His simple, uncluttered perspective harks back to that of the wartime common man, and contrasts with the views expounded by his old comrade, who feels it to be his duty to report Terkin for not being dead. Resourceful as ever, though, Terkin manages to extract himself from his predicament, and comes back to life. Of course, this poem was completed during the post-Stalin Thaw, when criticism could be voiced to some extent. However, according to G. Ulaev who worked with Tvardovskii as a journalist for the army newspaper *Krasnoarmeiskaia pravda*, Tvardovskii did read a version of what would later become the opening chapter of 'Terkin na tom svete' to his colleagues in May 1945.[80] A few lines of the earlier poem do in fact prefigure the later one. The poet includes speculation from imaginary readers on the words spoken by the dying Terkin; he asks whether the next world accepts newcomers without a certificate.[81]

The relative absence of a recognisably Soviet context in *Vasilii Terkin* reflects what Tvardovskii termed 'front-line universality'.[82] The war appears to operate as an autonomous zone where political considerations seem to be excluded. In real life, of course, the army had its quota of commissars who investigated political misdeeds, real or imaginary. What is remarkable about Tvardovskii's representation of the war is that it continually draws on non-political elements of ordinary peace-time existence even when describing specifically military actions. The terminology of war is kept to a minimum. Comparisons are drawn with objects from daily life. A shell is said to be the size of 'a pig ready for slaughter'; the earth in the trenches smells of ploughed earth; soldiers going into attack, bending down under fire, seem to be 'looking for something in the snow'.[83] War is not portrayed as something isolated from everyday civilian life, and the poem's hero more often than not is shown engaged in unwarlike activities, such as mending a clock for an old soldier.[84] All this is obviously far removed from the view of war found in poems which represented heroes in the stereotypical terms associated with socialist realism, and has little in common with the confrontational ethos that lay at the base of Soviet culture. The war is not being fought, as Tvardovskii's often-quoted words say, for glory, but out of bitter necessity:

> ... Бой идет святой и правый.
> Смертный бой не ради славы,
> Ради жизни на земле.[85]

(A sacred and just battle is being fought. A battle to the death not for the sake of glory but for the sake of life on earth.)

Of course, the lack of emphasis on a Soviet context may not show conclusively that the character in question is not, after all, a model Soviet man. The discussion of the representation of heroes has shown that no further explanations are needed if the hero is described according to socialist realist convention. The terms used to describe Terkin are, however, only tenuously linked to those used for portraying the 'positive hero', and these similarities are restricted to Tvardovskii's use of folklore elements. This is most evident in the description of Terkin's duel with a monstrous German soldier. The decisive single combat between *bogatyr'* and monster is a common motif in the traditional *bylina*, and appears in symbolic form in the socialist realist representation of heroes. In *Vasilii Terkin*, however, the hero is not transformed into a *bogatyr'*, he is simply compared to one:

... Как на древнем поле боя,
Грудь на грудь, что щит на щит,—
Вместо тысяч бьются двое,
Словно схватка все решит.[86]

(As on the ancient field of battle, breast to breast as shield to shield, instead of thousands, two men fight, as if the skirmish will solve everything.)

The description of this fight does not avoid unheroic details of blood, pain and exhaustion. The author does not glorify violence, it is only a means to an end, part of the work of war:

... Теркин ворот нараспашку,
Теркин сел, глотает снег,
Смотрит грустно, дышит тяжко,—
Поработал человек.[87]

(Terkin undoes his collar wide, sits down, swallows snow, looks forlorn, breathes heavily,—the man has been working.)

It seems as though Terkin has no part in the transcendence of ordinary reality that is available, usually posthumously, it must be admitted, to conventional heroes. Yet further on he is described by the author as follows:

... То серьезный, то потешный,
Нипочем, что дождь, что снег,—
В бой, вперед, в огонь кромешный
Он идет, святой и грешный,
Русский чудо-человек.[88]

(Now serious, now light-hearted, no matter whether it rains or snows, into battle, forward, into infernal fire he goes, holy and sinful, a Russian miracle-man.)

It is the hero's national characteristics which Tvardovskii emphasises here, his proverbially broad and resilient Russian nature. Although Terkin is the only named character in the work, apart from his namesake Ivan Terkin, and his speech is marked by lively colloquial language and proverbs, it is difficult to discern any real individuality of character. At the beginning of the poem, Terkin is 'an ordinary chap'; his status as an archetypal Russian man adds a new dimension. There is a considerable discrepancy between the critical interpretation of Terkin as a typical Soviet man and the text's insistence on the hero's Russian-ness. The Russian national character was celebrated early in the war, but by 1945 critics demanded heroes whose characteristics were attributed to socialism rather than to national influences. Tvardovskii repeatedly emphasises Terkin's Russian identity, with the implicit suggestion that the socialist system had failed to change people, and that war had allowed national characteristics to emerge with new strength. Both the absence of a Soviet context and the repeated references to Terkin as a Russian man suggest that the Soviet Man, if such a thing had existed, had simply been unequal to the demands of war.

If one thing, his nationality, is clear about Terkin's identity, then little else is. P'ianykh interprets Tvardovskii's statement that his poem is 'without a particular subject' to mean that it is not concerned with the hero's individual fate as such.[89] Indeed, Terkin is a vague figure with no past and no future that the reader can construct from the text. The eponymous hero's life mirrors Tvardovskii's description of his poem's construction:

> ... Без начала, без конца ...[90]
> (Without a beginning, without an end.)

It is known that Terkin is unmarried, a veteran of the Finnish war, and has relatives in the Smolensk district, but that is all. Terkin is first seen among a group of soldiers at the beginning of the poem, and eventually becomes lost from view as the army nears Berlin. Throughout the poem, incidents are recounted of the exploits of an anonymous soldier, eventually revealed to be none other than Terkin, a coincidence which does not surprise the reader. Terkin is repeatedly confronted by 'doubles' who reflect aspects of his own character—an old soldier and his namesake, Ivan Terkin. P'ianykh takes this to be an illustration of the nation's stability and unity, unlike the 'doubles' encountered in Dostoevskii's work, which indicate disjuncture and fragmentation.[91] As a representative of the country as a whole, Terkin is the living embodiment of national unity, a 'man-nation'.[92]

It is precisely this lack of a specific identity and personal fate which allows Terkin to be established as an ideal representation of the common man, one who embodies the true and essential characteristics of his people: 'The figure of Vasilii Terkin is realistic not because it is true to life, but because it is simply truthful. Vasilii Terkin is the embodiment of typical characteristics of many of our people.'[93] Tvardovskii had originally considered sending his hero on a mission behind enemy lines to his home region, but abandoned his plans precisely because it detracted from Terkin's universality.[94] At the same time this quality of being both universal and fundamentally elusive allies the figure of Terkin with the heroes of Russian folklore and qualifies him for the status of an epic hero. Nevertheless, in Bakhtin's terms, *Vasilii Terkin* cannot be considered an epic work because it does not have the quality of 'completedness'; open in structure, it was also open to imitation and additions from other authors.[95] Tvardovskii commented on the links between *Vasilii Terkin* and folklore:

> *Vasilii Terkin* emerged from the quasi-folkloric contemporary 'milieu' made up of satirical articles in newspapers and wall newspapers, the variety repertoire, the *chastushka*, the comic song, the *raek* etc. Now it has itself produced a lot of similar material in newspapers, pamphlets, variety, everyday talk. It has returned to its origins. And in this sense the 'Book about a soldier', as I have already mentioned, is not really my own work, but a collective one.[96]

For all this claim, however, Tvardovskii draws considerable attention to himself as the author and narrator of *Vasilii Terkin*, primarily, but not exclusively in sections entitled 'From the Author'. The collective genius of folklore may well have influenced the poem's use of language and imagery drawn from the Russian tradition of heroic epic and folk song, but *Terkin* is set apart from other wartime adaptations of folklore prototypes by the prominence given to the narrator's own voice and opinions. Terkin's 'colleagues' addressed themselves directly to their readers without the narrator as intermediary. Semen Kirsanov's 'Zavetnye slova Fomy Smyslova' (Foma Svetlov's Words of Wisdom) is a series of monologues delivered by the eponymous hero, an experienced old soldier, whose business is advising and encouraging others. Foma's advice on winter clothing is typical of the work:

> Одели тебя, товарищ, знатно. Ты в шинели и куртке ватной. Хороши и валенки—не велики, не маленькие. Чтоб ноге-то не быть потертой, много на ноги не навертывай, меж портянок клади бумажку, только чтоб не мешала шагу.[97]

(Comrade, you are splendidly dressed. You have a greatcoat and a padded jacket on. Your felt boots are good too—not too big and not too small. So that your feet don't get sore, don't wind too much cloth around them, and put paper between your footcloths, but not enough to interfere with your stride.)

The style is an imitation of the *lubok*, a written genre based on the traditions of Russian folklore, with texts accompanied by a crude illustration. The stylised traditional language used by Kirsanov was admired as an accurate imitation, but reveals nothing of the poet's attitudes and identity. The character of Terkin, on the other hand, gains in depth and variety through Tvardovskii's comments on his hero's adventures and reflections on his own experiences of the war.

The narrator's voice becomes more prominent as the poem continues; the approach of peace raises questions about the war's legacy which Terkin, concerned with more immediate matters, cannot address.

At times, Tvardovskii distinguishes himself from the voice of the archetypal and timeless Russian man by emphasising his status as author. This is particularly apparent in the last section of the poem, in which Tvardovskii considers the intentions with which he began to write:

> ... Я мечтал о сущем чуде:
> Чтоб от выдумки моей
> На войне живущим людям
> Было, может быть, теплей.[98]

(I dreamed of a real miracle: that my invention would make people living at war feel, perhaps, a little warmer.)

At other times Tvardovskii poses as someone who simply records his independent hero's adventures, following in his wake:

> Теркин—дальше. Автор—вслед.[99]

(Terkin—onwards. The author—after him.)

Tvardovskii further complicates matters by suggesting that the barriers separating himself from his hero were not necessarily as rigid as might be supposed:

> ... И скажу тебе, не скрою,—
> В этой книги, там ли, сям,
> То, что молвить бы герою,
> Говорю я лично сам.
> Я за все кругом в ответе,
> И заметь, коль не заметил,
> Что и Теркин, мой герой,
> За меня гласит порой.[100]

(And I'll tell you, I won't conceal it, that now and then in this book I myself say things the hero should say. I am fully responsible for everything, and take note, if you haven't noticed, that Terkin too, my hero, occasionally speaks for me.)

This playful variation of the relationship between author and hero is somewhat reminiscent of Pushkin's stance in *Evgenii Onegin*. And yet, like Pushkin, the narrator draws a clear line of demarcation between himself and his hero. He complements episodes concerning Terkin with his own thoughts on the war; his reflections consistently move from his hero to the larger scale of events, and increasingly to the tragedy war has brought to ordinary people. In the chapter 'Na Dnepre' (At the Dnepr), which relates the Soviet army's crossing to the west bank of the Dnepr, Tvardovskii asserts his importance as a witness which will endure even if others compose better poems about the event:

... Пусть не мне еще с задачей
Было сладить. Не беда.
В чем-то я его богаче,—
Я ступал в тот след горячий.
Я там был. Я жил тогда ...[101]

(Maybe the task was too great for me to cope with. No matter. In one thing I am richer than he,—I stepped in those burning footprints. I was there. I was alive then.)

Here Tvardovskii defends the validity of the perspective of the ordinary man on the battlefield, suggesting that no amount of historical perspective can compensate for the absence of the experience itself. He is also polemical in defence of his right to be part of his own poem, again on the grounds that it is unjust to dismiss the experience of any individual. As if to forestall potential critics, he writes:

... А читатель той порою
Скажет:
—Где же про героя?
Это больше про себя!

Про себя? Упрек уместный,
Может быть, меня пресек.
Но давайте скажем честно:
Что ж, а я не человек?

Спорить здесь нужды не вижу,
Сознавайся в чем другом.
Я ограблен и унижен,
Как и ты, одним врагом.[102]

(But the reader at times will say 'Where is there something about the hero? This is mostly about yourself!' About myself? A timely reproach has, perhaps, cut me short. But let us say honestly, am I not a person too? I see no need to argue here, you must agree on one thing. I am plundered and humiliated, like you, by the same enemy.)

The voice of the narrator becomes increasingly dominant as the poem progresses and Vasilii Terkin, with his light-hearted manner, recedes into the background. Terkin had, as it were, fulfilled his role as an inspiring national figure in times of crisis, but the war's legacy of suffering could not be approached by a figure with no past and no future. Tvardovskii, as narrator, has things to say which are relevant to post-war life, while Terkin seems to be created solely for the duration of the war, and has no prospects beyond it.

In *Vasilii Terkin*, Tvardovskii put in a convincing plea for greater consideration of the emotional damage done by war in the chapter about the orphan soldier. The human tragedy of war which surfaced in this chapter of *Vasilii Terkin* had already appeared as a theme of two poems written in 1943. 'Dve strochki' (Two Lines) and 'Za Viaz'moi' (Near Viaz'ma) consider the tragedy of the common man's involvement in a war so huge that it threatens to engulf him completely. In 'Za Viaz'moi' Tvardovskii describes a roadside scene of former retreats. Now the only corpse visible is the carcass of an abandoned army truck. The poet evokes the 'death' of the truck with pathos, implicitly comparing it to a wounded animal which tried to crawl towards a stream, but never reached it. Only then is the driver's uncertain fate considered: he may have been killed there, or found a woman in a nearby village who was willing to look after him, or have made his way back to his own regiment. The fate of the individual seems to have been drowned in the vastness and complexity of war:

... Шофер как шофер, неприметный, как все,
Угревший свое неизменное место,—
Про то неизвестно ...[103]

(An ordinary driver, inconspicuous, like everyone else, who kept to his unchanging place—which is unknown.)

The impossibility of tracing the driver is underlined through a wistful trailing-off of the last line. The driver, unlike the remains of his truck, is no longer there to testify to the events of 1941. Tvardovskii reduces the panorama of war to a single focus—the individual, whose absence is an eloquent sign of the tragedy of war.

In 'Za Viaz'moi' Tvardovskii expresses curiosity about the fate of an unknown man. In 'Dve strochki' he identifies directly with a young soldier whose dead body he saw during the war with Finland in the winter of 1939–1940. Tvardovskii's description echoes the statue imagery associated with the conventional representation of the hero, but the figure he portrays is not a titan, but almost a child:

Из записной потертой книжки
Две строчки о бойце-парнишке,
Что был в сороковом году
Убит в Финляндии на льду.
Лежало как-то неумело
По-детски маленькое тело.
Шинель ко льду мороз прижал,
Далеко шапка отлетела.

Казалось, мальчик не лежал,
А все еще бегом бежал,
Да лед за полу придержал ...

Среди большой войны жестокой,
С чего—ума не приложу,—
Мне жалко той судьбы далекой,
Как будто мертвый, одинокий,
Как будто это я лежу,
Примерзший, маленький, убитый
На той войне незнаменитой,
Забытый, маленький, лежу.[104]

(From a tattered note-book, two lines about a soldier-boy who was killed on the ice in Finland in nineteen-forty. The small, child-like body lay awkwardly somehow. Frost pinned his coat down to the ice, his hat had flown far off. It seemed as if the boy was not lying, but still running, but the ice was holding him back by his coat-flaps ... In the middle of a vast cruel war, for some reason—I can't quite work out why—I feel pity for that far-off fate, as if it was I, dead, alone, lying there, frozen, small, killed in that little known war, forgotten, small, lying there.)

Looking back at death stripped of the glorious trappings bestowed by participation in the Great Patriotic War, Tvardovskii reveals his pity both for those who died in the Finnish campaign, forgotten because that war was an embarrassment, and for all victims of war. For Tvardovskii tragedy is not diminished even when wars end in triumph. These two poems of 1943 recognise that loss of each person is, in itself, a disaster. The theme of the war dead was to continue in Tvardovskii's post-war work, reflecting an intensifying awareness of the scale of his country's loss.

The wartime prominence of the common man in poetry made for two major changes. Until the final stages of the war it was perfectly acceptable for poets to focus their attention on representative figures who were unexceptional and whose concerns centred around their homes and families rather than on ideologically-loaded heroics. The values of the ordinary man were portrayed as an expression of timeless national values, which were heavily promoted until victory began to look certain in 1943. Having fulfilled his role as a focus for national unity, the common man gradually fell from favour for being apolitical and atypical of the new man created by socialism. In a related development, poets began to write of their immediate experiences, recreating their emotional reactions to events of the war in ways which did not fit pre-existing schemes. Their work reflects a growing awareness of the importance of their contribution to the war and of the tremendous cost of victory. Above all, it demanded recognition of individual experience and placed the authentic words of a witness to war above pronouncements mediated by a rigid ideological framework.

There was a subversive element, which critics recognised, in these developments. While it would be wrong to suggest that poetic emphasis on the figure of the ordinary man implied a rejection of the Soviet state as such, there was a strong indication that the individual had been ignored for too long. In the case of *Vasilii Terkin*, Tvardovskii managed to bring together the voices of the 'ordinary hero', who is portrayed as a universal Russian man, and of the narrator, who displays a more reflective individuality. The result is balance between the universal and the particular in a work which evokes the scale and tragedy of the war without losing sight of the people caught up in events.

NOTES

1 'Vasilii Terkin', *Izbrannye proizvedeniia*, 3 vols (Moscow, 1990), II, 85.

2 Leonid Martynov, 'Mne kazhetsia, chto ia voskres ...', *Stikhotvoreniia* (Moscow, 1987), p. 67.

3 *Bodalsia telenok s dubom* (Paris, 1975), pp. 20–21.

4 'Soviet War Literature', *University of Toronto Quarterly* (April 1944), 251–257 (p. 253).

5 Hans Günther, *Die Verstaatlichung der Literatur: Entstehung und Funktionsweise des sozialistisch-realistischen Kanons der sowjetischer Literatur der dreissiger Jahre* (Stuttgart, 1984), p. 191.

6 Vasilii Lebedev-Kumach, 'Pesnia o rodine', *Izbrannoe* (Moscow, 1984), pp. 253–254.

7 'Rodina', 1940 version, quoted by M. F. P'ianykh in *Radi zhizni na zemle: poeziia perioda Velikoi Otechestvennoi voiny* (Leningrad, 1980), p. 10.

8 'Radi zhizni na zemle: sovetskaia poeziia o Velikoi Otechestvennoi voine', *Molodaia Gvardiia*, 8 (1987), 246–267.

9 'Liricheskoe otstuplenie', *Do poslednego dykhaniia: stikhi sovetskikh poetov, pavshikh v Velikoi Otechestvennoi voine* (Moscow, 1985), p. 164. These lines are among those quoted by Lazar' Lazarev in his polemical response to Kuniaev's article, '"A ikh povybilo zhelezom ...", *Znamia*, 2 (1988), 216–225.

10 See note 7 above.

11 'Rodina', 1941 version, *Sobranie sochinenii*, 12 vols (Moscow, 1979–87), I, 90.

12 'Esli zavtra voina ...', *Izbrannoe* (Moscow, 1984), p. 320.

13 'Podoshla voina k Podmoskov'iu ...', *Sobranie sochinenii*, 4 vols (Moscow, 1965–66), I, 336.

14 *Istoriia russkoi sovetskoi poezii 1941-1980*, edited by V. V. Buznik, V. A. Kovalev, V. V. Timofeeva (Leningrad, 1984), p. 29.

15 'Zashchitnik Moskvy', *Izbrannoe* (Moscow, 1989), p. 229.

16 'Prezrenie k smerti', *Krasnaia zvezda*, 24 July 1941, p. 3.

17 'Serzhant Vasilii Mysenkov', *Izbrannye proizvedeniia*, I, 217–218.

18 Ibid., p. 218.

19 'Chelovek sklonilsia nad vodoi ...', I, 310.

20 Ivan Mukha (pseud. of V. Khavchin),'Na soseda ne kivai, sam fashista ubivai', *Leningrad*, 2 (1942), p. 15.

21 'Rasskaz tankista', *Izbrannye proizvedeniia*, I, 222–223.

22 E. Sheveleva, 'Za Rodinu', *Krasnaia zvezda*, 18 January 1942, p. 3.

23 'Pisatel' i chuvstva naroda', *Literatura i iskusstvo*, 17 April 1943, p. 2.

24 'Tvorcheskii otchet na zasedanii voennoi komissii soiuza pisatelei, 12.7.43', in *Sovetskie pisateli na frontakh Velikoi Otechestvennoi voiny*, Literaturnoe nasledtstvo, 78, 2 vols (Moscow, 1966), I, 331–343 (p. 336.)

25 A. Miasnikov, 'Literatura i voina: 16 mesiatsev', *Oktiabr'*, 11 (1942), 136–144 (p. 139).

26 'Chelovek', *Russkaia sovetskaia poeziia: sbornik stikhov 1917–47* (Moscow, 1948), pp. 869–870.

27 'V gospitale', *Sobranie sochinenii*, 3 vols (Leningrad, 1988–90), II (1989), 14.

28 'Nachalo poemy', II, 11.

29 'Surovaia godovshchina', *Stikhi, p'esy, rasskazy* (Leningrad, 1949), p. 107.

30 The figure of 'Mother Russia' will be discussed in the next chapter.

31 'Soldat', *Oktiabr'*, 5–6 (1945), p. 1.

32 I, 105–107. This poem is quoted in Chapter Two.

33 'Rasstavan'e', *Stikhotvoreniia i poemy* (Leningrad, 1968), p. 150.

34 See Chapter Five on the representation of women.
35 'B'etsia v tesnoi pechurke ogon' ...', II, 347.
36 'Pis'mo', *Stikhotvoreniia i poemy* (Leningrad, 1981), p. 158.
37 'Iz serdtsa v serdtse', *Izbrannoe* (Moscow, 1988), pp. 294–295.
38 See, for example, A. Surkov, 'Vrag voshel v moi dom i razbil ...', I, 312–313; 'V smertnom oznobe pod vetrom trepeshchet osina ...', I, 332–333; N. Rylenkov, 'Volokolamskoe shosse', *Stikhotvoreniia i poemy*, 2 vols (Moscow, 1959), I, 205–206.
39 From conversations with the poet Vadim Shefner, Leningrad, November 1989, and the specialist on Soviet war literature Aleksandr Kogan, Moscow, January 1990.
40 V.Aleksandrov, 'Pis'mo v Moskvu', *Znamia*, 1 (1943), 149–160 (p. 149).
41 'Zhdi menia', I, 158–159.
42 See, for example, Alun Lewis, 'Goodbye', *Selected Poems of Alun Lewis* (London, 1981), pp. 52–53.
43 E. Dobin, 'Liricheskaia tema A.Prokof'eva', *Zvezda*, 1 (1944), 119–124 (p. 120).
44 See note 23 above.
45 Sergei Narovchatov, *My vkhodim v zhizn': kniga molodosti* (Moscow, 1980), p. 275.
46 'Predposlednee pis'mo', *Stikhotvoreniia i poemy* (Leningrad, 1985), p. 80.
47 'Lesnaia liubov'', pp. 75–76.
48 'Ballada ob otrechenii', *Sobranie sochinenii*, 6 vols (Moscow, 1976–83, II, 71–75.
49 'Ballada o tovarishche', *Izbrannye proizvedeniia*, I, 241.
50 'Otets i syn', ibid., I, 276–277.
51 'Terkin', II, 211.
52 'Vragi sozhgli rodnuiu khatu ...', *Sobranie sochinenii*, 5 vols (Moscow, 1981–82), II, 118.
53 'Zdes' pokhoronen krasnoarmeets', II, 26. See Iurii Kuznetsov's poem in the Conclusion for his rejection of memorials to the Unknown Soldier.
54 'Ego zaryli v shar zemnoi ...', *Izbrannoe* (Moscow, 1988), p. 96.
55 *Sovetskaia literatura v dni Otechestvennoi voiny* (Moscow, 1944), p. 16.
56 A. Sergeev, 'Razgovor o poezii', *Literatura i iskusstvo*, 6 June 1942, p. 2.
57 T. Gnedich, 'Poety Krasnoi Armii ob Otechestvennoi voine', *Zvezda*, 5–6 (1943), 196–199 (p. 196).
58 'V boevom poriadke', *Znamia*, 5–6 (1943), 235–238 (p. 237). See Chapter Two for the text of 'Pered atakoi'.
59 P. Gromov, 'Odnopolchane', *Zvezda*, 7–8 (1944), 192–193 (p. 192).
60 Ibid.
61 'Goriat lesa ot Drezdena ...', *Stikhi* (Moscow, 1961), pp. 113–114.
62 'Ataka', I, 97.
63 'Pis'mo o poezii', *Zvezda*, 1 (1945), 118–123 (p. 119).
64 'S narodom i dlia naroda', IV, 205–233 (p. 229).
65 'O liricheskom epose Otechestvennoi voiny', *Znamia*, 9–10 (1943), 292–299 (p. 298).
66 Mikhail Bakhtin, 'Epos i roman', in *Voprosy literatury i estetiki* (Moscow, 1975), p. 477.
67 'Podvig i geroi', *Znamia*, 9 (1945), 118–132 (p. 132).
68 Iosif Stalin, speech on Red Square, 7 November, 1941, *Novyi mir*, 9–10 (1941), 15–16.
69 'Na Zadonshchine', *Samoe zavetnoe: pesni, stikhi i poemy* (Moscow, 1976), pp. 56–57.

70 'Boitsu iuzhnogo fronta', *Izbrannye proizvedeniia*, I, 227.

71 'Oruzhie pobedy', *Znamia*, 5–6 (1945), 161–167 (p. 165).

72 V. Maiakovskii, 'Budetliane', *Sobranie sochinenii*, 13 vols (Moscow, 1955–61), I, 330–332.

73 'Put' k zrelosti', II, 356.

74 A. Tarasenkov, 'O "Vasilii Terkine" A.Tvardovskogo', *Zvezda*, 5–6 (1945), 145–147 (p. 145). See also V.Ermilov, 'Russkii voin Vasilii Terkin', *Literatura i iskusstvo*, 31 October 1942, p. 2; D. Danin, 'Obraz russkogo voina', ibid., 3 October 1942, p. 2; Z. Kedrina, 'Ispytanie ognem', *Oktiabr'*, 12 (1942), 85–93 (pp. 89–90); V. Shklovskii, 'Sovremennost' i zlobodnevnost'', *Literatura i iskusstvo*, 10 April 1943, p. 2; N. Aseev, 'O chuvstve novogo', ibid., 3 April 1943, p. 3.

75 'Put' k zrelosti', II, 356–357.

76 'Terkin', *Izbrannye proizvedeniia*, II, 88.

77 II, 147.

78 See note 76 above.

79 II, 379–431.

80 G. Ulaev, *V dni godiny gor'koi* (Voronezh, 1986), p. 133.

81 II, 193.

82 'Kak byl napisan *Vasilii Terkin*', *Sobranie sochinenii*, 6 vols (Moscow, 1976–83), V, 138.

83 II, 104; II, 137; II, 174.

84 In the chapter 'Dva soldata'.

85 II, 99.

86 II, 131.

87 II, 133.

88 II, 195.

89 P'ianykh, *Radi zhizni na zemle*, pp. 21–22.

90 II, 136.

91 P'ianykh, p. 19.

92 A. M. Abramov, *Lirika i epos Velikoi Otechestvennoi voiny*, 2nd edition (Moscow, 1975), p. 447.

93 Anatolii Tarasenkov, 'O *Vasilie Terkine* A.Tvardovskogo', p. 146.

94 G. Ulaev, *V dni godiny gor'koi*, p. 33.

95 See the contributions from readers of 'Vasilii Terkin' in *Sovetskie pisateli na frontakh Velikoi otechestvennoi voiny*, eds. I. I. Anisimov, D. D. Blagoi, A. S. Bushmin et al., Literaturnoe nasledstvo, 78, 2 vols (Moscow, 1966), I, 563–601.

96 'Kak byl napisan "Vasilii Terkin"', *Sobranie sochinenii*, V, 138.

97 'Zavetnye slova Fomy Smyslova', *Sobranie sochinenii*, 4 vols (Moscow, 1974–76), III, 188–254 (p. 205)

98 II, 227.

99 II, 155.

100 II, 154.

101 II, 205.

102 See note 100 above.

103 'Za Viaz'moi', I, 278.

104 'Dve strochki', I, 279.

CHAPTER FIVE

Women in Poetry and Women Poets

The bulk of Soviet war poetry is concerned with describing the actions and experiences of soldiers at the front. The overwhelming majority of these soldiers are men. Wartime poetry has little to say about the many women also in the armed forces, either in the medical corps or combat troops. Boris Slutskii commented that there had never been such a huge number of women at war since the mythical age of the Amazons.[1] The evidence of Soviet women soldiers' existence provided by poets both male and female is so sparse that these soldiers risk a similar relegation to the realms of legend. The work of Iuliia Drunina and Galina Nikolaeva, who were both members of the front-line medical contingent, offers some insight into the lives of these otherwise invisible women. The discrepancy between women's true involvement in the war at the front and its reflection in the poetry of the time carries the implied suggestion that the front was neither a suitable place for a woman, nor was it a suitable theme for women poets.

In actual fact, women made a substantial contribution to poetry written during wartime. Anna Akhmatova wrote a number of patriotic poems, most famous among them 'Muzhestvo' (Courage):

Мы знаем, что ныне лежит на весах,
И что совершается ныне.
Час мужества пробил на наших часах,
И мужество нас не покинет.
Не страшно под пулями мертвыми лечь,
Не страшно остаться без крова,—
И мы сохраним тебя, русская речь,
Великое русское слово.
Свободным и чистым тебя пронесем,
И внукам дадим, и от плена спасем
Навеки![2]

(We know what lies on the scales now and what is now being accomplished. The hour of courage has struck on our clocks, and courage shall not leave us. It is not terrible to fall dead beneath bullets, it is not terrible to be left without a roof,—and we shall preserve you, Russian language, the great Russian word. Free and pure we shall bear you through, and pass you on to our grandchildren, and save you from captivity for ever!)

An evacuee from Leningrad to Tashkent, Akhmatova did not forget the plight of her home city. It appears in 'Poema bez geroia' (Poem Without a Hero), both as the Petersburg of the past, and as the besieged city of the present, the backdrop to a poem spanning the distance between 1913 and 1941, marked by two world wars and a revolution. In the poem's introduction, written in Leningrad in late August 1941, Akhmatova looks across the past from the vantage point of a new war which threatens her and her city:

Из года сорокового,
Как с башни, на все гляжу.
Как будто прощаясь снова
С тем, с чем давно простилась,
Как будто перекрестилась,
И под темные своды схожу.[3]

(From the year 1940 I look at everything as if from a tower. As if once more taking leave of everything I took leave of long ago, as if I have crossed myself and am walking down beneath dark vaults.)

'Poema bez geroia' is an enigmatic work, full of allusion to the writing of other poets, but in the epilogue Akhmatova returns to the war then in progress. Against the background of Leningrad in ruins, the poet dedicates her last words to her city, now far away but still inextricably linked to her own fate:

... А не ставший моей могилой,
Ты, гранитный, кромешный, милый,
Побледнел, помертвел, затих.
Разлучение наше мнимо:
Я с тобою неразлучима,
Тень моя на стенах твоих,
Отражение мое в каналах,
Звук шагов в Эрмитажных залах,
Где со мною мой друг бродил,
И на старом Волковом поле,
Где могу я рыдать на воле
Над безмолвием братских могил.[4]

(You, who did not become my grave, granite, infernal, dear, turned pale, became lifeless, fell silent. Our separation is only an illusion: I am inseparable from you, my shadow is on your walls, my reflection is in your canals, the sound of my footsteps in the Hermitage halls, where my friend wandered with me, and on the old Volkovo field, where I can sob freely over the silence of mass graves.)

In Akhmatova's poem the war was yet another manifestation of the 'real twentieth century', a dark time of wars and revolutions. Most of the other women writing poetry at the time paid little attention to the war's broader historical context, but wrote about events of greater immediate concern, often from personal experience. Among them were Margarita Aliger, author of the poem 'Zoia', which commemorates the death of a schoolgirl partisan; Vera Inber and Zinaida Shishova, both of whom wrote major works about the Leningrad blockade, and the most prolific and effective poet on the Leningrad theme, Ol'ga Berggol'ts. The recurring theme of Leningrad in women's poetry was no coincidence. In the besieged, starving city, under regular enemy bombardments, the dividing line between soldier and civilian, which so often marginalised women's voices, was suspended. Women faced the challenge of leading a 'normal' life in conditions which tried their reserves of courage and endurance to the limit. This experience produced a new concept of heroism. Spectacular gestures of self-sacrifice were both impossible and pointless in such a situation. Survival was the highest achievement, and the hero, or, in most cases, the heroine displayed an endurance fuelled by spiritual strength. Berggol'ts was the poet who came to be closely identified with the blockade. Her work, which gave an often bleak and honest picture of conditions in the city, and her contradictory poetic persona will be examined in detail in this chapter. To begin with, however, this chapter will look at the ways in which women were commonly represented in wartime poetry, as figures of universal symbolic significance who existed outside the masculine heroic paradigms in the sphere of unruffled feminine virtues.

Apart from the annual manifestations of ritual appreciation on 8 March, International Women's Day, women's part in the war effort was neither recognised nor represented by poets in proportion to its true extent. Women did play an important role at the front, fighting, retrieving the wounded under fire, acting as wireless operators, or in support lines as surgeons, cooks, washerwomen and mechanics. The recollections of some of these officially invisible women have been recorded by the journalist Svetlana Aleksievich in her book *U voiny ne zhenskoe litso* (War Does Not Have a Woman's Face).[5] The interviews make clear that young women displayed great enthusiasm for serving at the front, which was no doubt fostered by the official rhetoric of equality, and many were unwilling to accept a safe posting well away from the fighting. It also shows that they were sometimes accepted by male soldiers only grudgingly, even though, particularly as snipers, women often performed better than men. Later Iuliia Drunina wrote of the army's initial reception of young women volunteers:

... С восторгом нас, девчонок, не встречали:
Нас гнал домой охрипший военком.
Так было в сорок первом. Медали
И прочие регалии—потом ...[6]

(They did not greet us girls with rapture: a hoarse military commissar sent us home. That was what it was like in forty-one. Medals and suchlike regalia—later.)

In fact, women were only permitted to go to the front other than as ancillary or medical personnel in 1942. The awkwardness of the idea of a woman serving at the front is transmitted in contemporary poetry, though not expressed directly, as will be shown. It is clear that these women are felt to be transgressing their proper roles, and most poets, both male and female, continually offer reminders that war is not really for women. This would seem to bear out Jean Bethke Elshtain's claim that in wartime, men and women are perceived as 'beings who have complementary needs and exemplify gender-specific virtues', so that male pacifists and female soldiers simply do not fit the accepted paradigm.[7] If the waging of war is identified as an extreme expression of masculinity, it follows that women might be expected to display virtues understood to be exclusively feminine.

More widely recognised than women's efforts at the front in poetry of the time is their 'unwarlike' contribution as wives and mothers, workers in industry and agriculture. These poems tend to take the form of a generalised and patronising eulogy of women en masse, celebrating their ability to work as hard as men and still retain their feminine charms. Although in the years of rapid industrialisation and the collectivisation of agriculture there had been a good deal of attention paid to women's achievements in the work force, during the war, from the evidence of contemporary poetry, women's efforts at work took second place to the more glamorous heroics of the male-dominated battlefield. More often than not women were represented in a domestic setting, carrying out traditional feminine roles of the wife and mother. This aura of the domestic still clung to many of the women soldiers portrayed in poetry, taking precedence over their new, aggressive role.

Any discussion of the representation of women in wartime poetry, and of their activity as poets, must be prefaced by the reminder that in the Soviet Union women were not then officially regarded as a special case in society. Women's interests were, for the Party of the 1920s, with the exclusion of figures such as Aleksandra Kollontai, held to be a distraction from the serious business of the class struggle. In the 1930s it was believed that women's legal emancipation, together with the creation of the socialist society, had automatically freed them from the restrictions imposed on them by capitalism. At the same time a renewed emphasis on the nuclear family, financial barriers to divorce and a ban on abortion emphasised the fact that women were required to maintain their traditional roles in society. While women were now officially declared equal to men, the liberation of women extended only as far as their participation in economic production.

This refusal to accept that Soviet women might be in any way disadvantaged because of their sex, or be perceived as a group with particular concerns, proved to be persistent both in the organisation of Soviet society and in attitudes towards women writers. Two poets of the war generation, Margarita Aliger and Vadim Shefner, were in 1989 both convinced that there was no validity in considering poems about or by women separately from those about or by men. Women, even those at the front line, said Shefner, experienced exactly the same things as the men, and therefore wrote in the same way.[8] These declarations of equality are not, however, widely supported by the poetry of the time. Suggestions that women are equal to men are seldom found. Instead, women are represented with special emphasis on their specifically 'feminine' qualities, and are shown to function in their roles as wives, mothers and sisters, while being excluded from the type of heroic role available to men. Conventional images of women went unchallenged by most of the women active as poets, who concentrated on themes such as home and family, considered to belong within their particular domain. Femininity evidently carried a premium during the war years, as something perceived to be under threat. In 1949 the book *Women in the Land of Socialism* looked back on the Soviet superwoman of the war years: 'Soviet women combine majestic simplicity, warmheartedness, and the indefatigability of worker and mother with, when necessary, the wrath of the valiant soldier'.[9] The women who people wartime poems are somewhat less daunting, their strength tempered with vulnerability, a sign, as it were, that their essential feminine nature survived in spite of the demands of war.

Even when it was publicly recognised that women were successfully carrying out what had been considered to be men's work, it is their specifically feminine characteristics which are singled out for special attention. In a radio broadcast on International Women's Day in 1943, Ol'ga Berggol'ts drew attention to women's involvement in industry and the armed forces: 'In Leningrad, as in the whole country, women have taken the place of all the men who have gone to the front, in absolutely every kind of work. Furthermore, women are standing alongside men, as equals, in the army and navy.' This statement was immediately qualified: 'But the main thing is that above all else, always and everywhere they are still women—mothers, sisters, daughters, friends: without a woman's care, love and affection the people could not live, let alone wage war. And we ourselves, comrades, we women know that no-one and nothing can replace us.'[10] Women appear in war poetry most often as mothers, wives, nurses, figures who exist as a source of emotional strength and moral certainty for the soldiers to whom they minister.

The women who fulfil these conventional roles are symbolically associated with nature, Russia, and are easily perceived by male writers as a manifestation of almost magical forces. Two female figures are prominent in this context: the mother and the nurse, both seen as sources of life. The mother figure often appears in a symbolic role, blessing soldiers on the way to battle, or as a memory which provides her son with strength and inspiration. The mother's role as life-giver is presented in more literal terms in a poem by Varvara Vol'tman-Spasskaia, in which a Leningrad mother tries to save a dying man with her own milk:

... И женщина, с ребенком на руках,
Остановилась и присела возле.
В ней тоже ни кровинки. На висках
Седые пряди, и ресницы смерзлись.
Привычным жестом обнажила грудь
И губы умиравшего прижала
К соску упругому. Дала глотнуть ...[11]

(And a woman with a child in her arms stopped and crouched down beside him. She was deathly pale too. On her temples were grey locks, and her eyelashes were frozen. With a habitual gesture she bared a breast and pressed the dying man's lips to her resilient nipple. She let him swallow.)

The life-giving strength of the nurse is repeatedly expressed through the symbol of her eyes, which are seen as blue flowers, and which supply strength and comfort. Sometimes the wounded soldier is comforted by a blue flower instead of a woman's eyes, the two appearing to be symbolically interchangeable, both signifying life and nature. Sel'vinskii manages to include the eyes and the flower in one poem, which begins:

Начну с того, что я нашел цветок.
Голубоглазый. Полный аромата ...

(I shall begin with my finding a flower. Blue-eyed. Full of scent.)

The poem relates how the hero, dazed after an enemy bombing raid, gazes unseeingly at a blue flower, having waved away a nurse who, undaunted, sits in front of him:

... И только тут я заприметил рядом
С ее глазами—голубой жар-цвет.
Я ухватился за его сиянье,
Чтоб избежать другого,
но глаза ...
Их близкий горизонт ... Их бирюза ...
Я зренье ощупал, как осязанье.
Не помню уж, была ль тогда весна.

Наверное была, раз это было—
Из глаз ее
мне в душу
изобильно
Блаженная
текла
голубизна.[12]

(And only then I noticed alongside her eyes a blue cornflower. I seized hold of its glow to avoid the other. But the eyes ... Their close horizon ... Their turquoise ... I sensed their gaze like a touch. I don't remember now whether it was spring. Probably it was, since that happened—from her eyes into my soul abundantly flowed a blessed blueness.)

The figure of a woman, often with a child in her arms, who represents Russia is used both as a demonstration of the country's strength and permanence, and of its suffering under enemy occupation. There is perhaps more than a slight resemblance to the image of the Mother of God of Orthodox iconography. A mother encountered on the road becomes a symbol of Russia's pain and endurance, and an appeal to the conscience of the soldier who meets her:

... Эта женщина сынишку
На руках своих несла.
Плотно были сжаты брови,
Но светились все черты.
Сколько было в ней суровой,
Русской строгой красоты!
И ни слова укоризны,
А в глазах—печаль светла ...
Воплощением Отчизны
Эта женщина была.

(This woman carried her little son in her arms. Her brows were tightly compressed, but her face shone. There was so much severe, austere Russian beauty in her! And not a word of reproach, but in her eyes sorrow was radiant ... This woman was an embodiment of the Motherland.)

This poem goes on to see a more personal significance in this unknown but familiar woman:

... Шли мы с ней горящей рожью
Под обстрелом дотемна,
Эта женщина похожей
На тебя была, жена![13]

(We walked together through burning rye, under fire, until it was dark. This woman was like you, wife!)

'Mother Russia' was a suitable symbolic figure in which to combine love of country and love of family. The image of the country personified as a woman is linked with timeless and universal values, rather than with specifically Soviet ideology. The female figure of the Motherland is an archetypal counterpart to that of

Stalin. Stalin's role in war poetry is that of father of the nation; he is presented in terms of his authority, wisdom and remoteness. His absolute power made him the centre of public adulation and private fear. He was a figure indelibly associated with the Soviet present, although references to strong leaders from Russia's past were made in order to show Stalin as their legitimate successor. The father figure, other than Stalin, rarely appears in poetry of the war, and is generally set in the context of the immediate Soviet past, as a veteran of the Civil War whose sons are now doing their duty in fighting the German invaders, as he in his time fought against foreign intervention. By contrast to the stern father figure, Mother Russia is associated with love and kindness. Her power lies not in strict control of her national family, but in her innate and enduring strength. At the same time, her status as mother gives her an aspect of weakness; her dutiful and loving sons feel duty bound to protect her. Most of all, she represents Russia's past as a symbol of continuity and tradition, and is often represented in images associated with religion. Soviet rhetoric of the 1930s had presented Stalin through the use of ecclesiastical language as a secular divinity. His much more ancient female counterpart is directly associated with Russia's Christian traditions.

Poetry written in the early stages of the war, before the victory at Stalingrad, is particularly likely to use the symbol of Mother Russia. The revival of traditional values, crystallised in Simonov's famous poem 'Ty pomnish', Alesha, dorogi Smolenshchiny...' (Do You Remember, Alesha, the Roads Near Smolensk...) is reflected in the work of many poets and particularly in the work of those who were soldiers or war correspondents, and therefore witnesses of the retreat through the Russian countryside.[14] A repeated image is that of soldiers watched by an elderly woman as they make their way to the front. In 1942, the young soldier Sergei Orlov described the autumnal Russian countryside seen from a troop train, and a woman standing at the crossing. She is at first imagined to be a soldier's mother, but on further reflection she takes on timeless qualities:

... В глазах ее—благословенье
И древняя, как мир, тоска ...
(In her eyes—a benediction and sorrow, ancient as the world.)

At the end of the poem her true identity is revealed:

... Не ты ли это, мать Россия,
Глядишь вослед твоим сынам?[15]
(Is this not you, Mother Russia, watching your sons as they go?)

Vladimir Lifshits emphasises Russia's historical continuity in a poem which uses similar terms to those just quoted. The timeless figure of a mother mediates between the past and the present, as she blesses the passing soldiers as she would have done before the battle of Kulikovo in the thirteenth century, the battle which was thought to be crucial in defeating the Tatars.[16] Although the imagery of this type of poem coincided with official rhetoric, epitomised, perhaps in the recruiting poster with the message 'The Motherland Calls You!', the tone was often subdued, expressing the sadness of the retreat and the shame of having to abandon the country, and the soldiers' own families, to enemy occupation.

Unlike men, who, as heroes in war poetry transcend ordinary temporal reality by passing through an ordeal, even death, which proves their heroic status, women are depicted as if they already had a universal, transcendent quality about them, and so do not need to pass through an ordeal to attain it. Russian folk ritual may provide at least part of the answer: it has been argued that a woman's wedding ritual had much in common with funeral customs, so that marriage represented her symbolic death. As one dead, the married woman was associated with a higher spiritual reality.[17] Whatever the origins of the assumption of women's qualities, there is an implicit message in this 'ready made' virtue: women have no choice but to obey their supposedly natural instincts. The 'natural' virtue of women is not a concept peculiar to Soviet literature, but has a long tradition in Russian literature, with its morally perfect heroines and flawed heroes. As Barbara Heldt puts it, the Russian man goes along a 'long and tortuous road to enlightenment, while she grasps the essentials of life, if not immediately, then certainly firmly and intuitively'. The moral development of the hero in the Russian nineteenth century novel is shown in detail, while 'the changes in women are mysterious givens of nature, of Womanhood'.[18] A similar idea is expressed in a wartime Soviet book: 'Russian women have always been the bearer of the best characteristics of their people—love of freedom, courage, moral strength and selfless devotion to the Motherland'.[19]

Because of the special status assigned to women, they tend to be used by wartime poets, following a long tradition, as allegorical figures such as Mother Russia or personifications of abstract ideas. Victory appears in a poem by Berggol'ts as a woman in a tattered soldier's uniform (the word for victory, 'pobeda', is feminine). Kirsanov's allegorical poem 'Boets' (The Soldier) presents the reader with a puzzling soldier who keeps apart from the other men, is very reserved—and has plaits under her helmet. The name he gives this soldier is Liubov', love, which removes her from reality to the role of a symbolic figure.[20] Although male soldiers are frequently portrayed in symbolic terms, they are rarely reduced—or elevated—to the level of personification, as they are sufficiently significant in their military, masculine role.

When women in uniform are described not as allegories but as real people, there is a marked tendency for poets to emphasise their fragility and natural feminine qualities, showing that they remain essentially domestic creatures even if they have taken on 'masculine' roles at the front. In the case of women's portrayal in war poetry, the fact that the war had disturbed family life and made women take on 'masculine' roles seems to have been compensated for by representing women as ideals of femininity. Many poems rely for effect on the assumption that women's appearance is deceptive and conceals surprising strength or skill. Vera Inber describes a girl who rescues wounded soldiers under fire reassuring one man that she may look weak, but is quite capable of carrying him.[21] According to women who did this kind of work, it was quite usual for girls to carry three times their own weight—the wounded man, and his weapons, too precious to be abandoned.[22] Another example of deceptive appearances is given in a poem about a grateful patient who wishes to thank the surgeon who operated on him, and refuses to believe that the girl at his bedside is the surgeon.[23] This paradox of strength, associated with 'masculine' activities, and 'feminine' weakness plays a major role in the way women are represented.

Women soldiers are depicted as if their tasks have absolutely nothing to do with aggression. A girl gunner at Stalingrad is shown asleep. Her stocking, darned at the knee, is presented as proof of her femininity:

... Девушка-зенитчица лежит.
Перерыв случился в канонаде,
И девчонка сладко-сладко спит.
Примостилась в холодке у стенки,
Прилегла, уснула на часок.
У нее на согнутой коленке—
Бережно заштопанный чулок.
Шелестели мины, грохотали,
Но, привычке девичьей верна,
При коптилке где-нибудь в подвале
Тот чулок заштопала она.[24]

(A girl anti-aircraft gunner is lying down. There is a break in the cannonade, and the girl is sleeping sweetly. She settled down in the draught by the wall, lay down, fell asleep for an hour or so. On her bent knee is a carefully darned stocking. Mines rumbled and crashed, but, true to girlish habit, she darned that stocking by a kerosene lamp somewhere in a cellar.)

It is not surprising that this gunner is shown asleep rather than in action. In most poets' work, women and aggression are completely incompatible. Women, it appears, are incapable of firing a shot in anger, being essentially kind creatures, the source of comfort and human companionship, softening the harsh experience of life at the front. Il'ia Sel'vinskii returns to this theme in a number of his poems, in which the unexpected presence of women in the middle of a war is a small miracle.[25]

Women's ability to be aggressive seems to belong, like strength and skill, with those qualities hidden from view by feminine appearances. Gudzenko shows a wife saying goodbye to her husband, laying her fragile, white, unblemished hands on his shoulders and saying:

... Я вот этими
задушить его,
немца,
смогу.[26]

(I could strangle a German with these.)

Georgii Suvorov seems to be alone in celebrating a woman who fights for vengeance and displays strength and fury. Her femininity here does not seem to be something which needs to be overcome, but something which gives her extra strength:

... О! Как ты крепка
На пулемете женская рука![27]

(O! How strong you are, a woman's hand on a machine gun!)

The perceived contradictions between a woman's pacific nature and the aggressive role demanded of her by the war are keenly felt in the poems of Galina Nikolaeva, who was a front-line doctor. Nikolaeva sets out her conventional pre-war thinking on the moral superiority of women over men, only to add that she is now learning to acquire those masculine qualities she would once have despised:

Я, слава богу, женщиной родилась,
Мне злой азарт и чужд, и не знаком,
Бокс не терплю. Не похваляюсь силой.
Не разрешаю споров кулаком.

Я женскую заслугу вижу в этом,
Высокое призвание мое.
Мы нежности и жертвы эстафету
Из плоти в плоть в веках передаем.

Вино, табак и прочие изъяны ...
О, право же, совсем не без причин
Одной ступенью ближе к обезьянам,
Как правило, считала я мужчин.

Пусть молодость мне будет оправданьем,
И многие разумные дела,
И то, что часто терпеливой няней
Больших детей невольно я была.

Я вот теперь учусь у них прилежно
Вести в атаку, в ураган огня.

Бить. Не прощать. Учусь тому, что прежде,
Казалось мне, унизило б меня.[28]

(I, thank God, was born a woman. Savage fervour is unknown and alien to me. I cannot bear boxing. I cannot boast of my strength. I do not solve quarrels with my fists. I see women's merit, their lofty calling in this. We pass down the baton of tenderness and sacrifice from flesh to flesh through the ages. Wine, tobacco and other failings... O, truly, it was not altogether without reason that I considered men to be one step closer to the apes. Let my youth be my justification, and many rational acts, and that I often unwillingly played nursemaid to grown up children. And now I learn diligently from them to go into the attack, into a hurricane of fire. To fight. Not to forgive. Now I learn what once, it seemed, would have degraded me.)

This adoption of attitudes previously thought alien appears in a poem contrasting the author's reactions to the deaths of her two brothers. Receiving news of the first death, she wept, but on hearing the news of the second, felt only that the gun slung on her back was her best friend. Nikolaeva is, however, equally aware that she remains vulnerable. In a poem addressed to her mother, Nikolaeva announces that although she has learned to kill, once the battle is over she longs for her and for fields unscarred by battle.[29] Yet although she is aware of the contradiction between her 'womanly' fragility and her 'manly' activities at the front, she is determined to keep going in spite of all the difficulties, because of the duty she owes to the dead:

... Я не сильна, не боец, не герой,
Но посмотрю назад:
Встал за спиной сорок второй,
Встал за спиной Сталинград.
Встал за спиной сомкнутый строй
Тех, кто костьми легли.
Женщина я, не боец, не герой,
Но я войду в Берлин.
Так приказали мне жизнь и смерть,
Память моя и кровь.
Дым на заре, дым на заре,
Ненависть, гнев, любовь.[30]

(I am not strong, no soldier, no hero, but if I look back, behind me is 1942, behind me Stalingrad. Behind me the close ranks of those who laid down their bones. I am a woman, no soldier, no hero, but I shall enter Berlin. These are my orders from life and death, from my memory and blood. Smoke at dawn, smoke at dawn, hatred, anger, love.)

It is worth noting at this point that Nikolaeva's poems on the acquisition of qualities perceived as masculine have a certain counterpart in the work of male soldier-poets such as Semen Gudzenko. His hero recounts the brutal experiences of war, but declares: 'We have nevertheless grown more tender', and devotes a significant number of poems to the theme of friendship.[31] Gudzenko does not directly identify the mutual consideration and sensitivity displayed by the soldiers in his poetry as a feminine quality, yet his poems clearly show the growth of nurturing tendencies seen by Elshtain as a typical phenomenon among male soldiers whose highest value is in self-sacrifice.[32]

It may seem from the poems written by both men and women at the front that each acquired qualities conventionally associated with the other sex, while elsewhere emphasis was placed on the gender-specific differences between them. When it comes to poetry dealing with heroes rather than personal experience, these differences are particularly underlined. The dominant concept of the heroic, circumscribed by the type of paradigms discussed in Chapter Three, had no real place for women. In poetry, at least, women were expected to fulfil their traditional roles as wife and mother. The representation of women in this respect was similar to that of ancient Russian literature. As Dmitrii Likhachev pointed out, women had no place in ancient Russia's social hierarchy except as wives or daughters. In medieval literature they were often depicted in idealised terms, transfigured as an icon of the Virgin Mary.[33] A similar idealisation of women, as has been shown, is echoed in the poetry of the war which transforms women into an embodiment of Russia, often as a mother figure, a secularised Virgin Mary.

One significant fact separates the depiction of men at war from that of women: the men are shown in terms of their actions, the women in terms of their innate qualities. Prokof'ev's admiration of a girl sniper centres on her youth and childlike appearance; the fact that she has shown considerable skill in executing her task receives little attention.[34] On the rare occasions that women are shown in action, the style of narration moves away from the heroic and focuses instead on human qualities. When the recurring tale of the signaller who dies repairing communications lines is repeated with a young girl as its central figure, attention is focused on her eyes, which are remembered as bright and shining until death extinguishes them:

... Тянулась Люба к проводу,
Собрав остаток сил.
Соединила линию.
На проводе рука ...
Погасли, не засветятся
Два теплых огонька ...[35]

(Liuba stretched out towards the wire, gathering her last reserves of strength. She connected the line. Her hand was on the wire ... The two warm lights have gone out, they will not shine again.)

Women's heroism in poetry is more likely to manifest itself in feats of endurance, such as resistance to enemy torture. Surkov describes the ordeal of a woman who witnessed the drowning of her son, an attempt to make her talk, and was shot without having said a word.[36] Another role commonly assigned to women is the preservation of certain symbolic objects, or the care of wounded soldiers, in a plot which ends with the return of the object to its rightful owners, or the soldier's return to the front. Women are entrusted with banners which they hide until the soldiers return to claim them back. Women partisans are shown to engage in suitable activities, such as darning socks, performing a motherly role rather than an active, 'masculine' one.[37]

The war did nevertheless produce its heroic women who were publicly recognised and became the subject of poetry. The most famous, Zoia Kosmodem'ianskaia, a young partisan hanged by the Germans, is the subject of Margarita Aliger's long poem 'Zoia', as well as of a number of shorter works by other poets. Zoia became the archetypal war heroine; her image overshadows another partisan, Liza Chaikina, who is commemorated in a cycle of poems by Mikhail Svetlov. Both poems take a biographical approach, charting the progress from schoolgirl to partisan; the poets accompany their heroines, talking to them, using their foreknowledge of their fate to create a sense of tragic inevitability. The girls' activity as partisans is scarcely touched upon. It is their deaths which make them into heroines and martyrs.

Svetlov's cycle is simple. Within a framework which describes the girl walking through a forest in winter, first as a schoolgirl, then as a partisan, Liza's story is briefly told. Conventional depictions of the heroic are largely absent; Liza remains an ordinary village girl, who is courageous, but undergoes no special transformation. Her heightened consciousness is suggested by the serious expression of her eyes, which remains the same from childhood. The poem written by Aliger to commemorate Zoia is constructed on a much more ambitious scale, taking in various aspects of the war, the poet's own life, reflections on the Komsomol and so on. It is laden with symbols which continually point to the tension between the feminine and the heroic in Zoia. Her consciousness is shown to have existed from childhood, indicated by her severe gaze. Her high aspirations and selfless idealism are emphasised; there is a hint of potential conflict between these qualities and her blossoming into womanhood, but war is shown to decide Zoia in favour of self-sacrifice. She readily volunteers as a partisan.

The transformation from schoolgirl to partisan and martyr is variously signalled. Torture is depicted as a rite of passage. Zoia's transformation through her ordeal is confirmed by the fact that she refuses to reveal her real name, telling her interrogators only that she is called Tat'iana. After the ordeal of interrogation has been honourably withstood, Zoia passes into a new state of being, beyond the possibility of pain:

> ... Стала ты под пыткою Татьяной,
> онемела, замерла без слез.[38]

(Under torture you became Tat'iana, grew numb, fell silent, without tears.)

Aliger emphasises Zoia's ethereal quality as she goes to her death, already not quite of this world:

> ... И уже почти что над снегами,
> легким телом устремясь вперед,
> девочка
> последними шагами
> босиком в бессмертие идет.[39]

(And now almost above the snows, forging ahead with her light body, the girl walks her last steps barefoot into eternity.)

Parallels between Zoia as heroine and as bride suggest Aliger's solution to the paradox of heroism and femininity, as well as harking back to traditional similarities to women's funeral and marriage customs.[40] The woman who helps her dress for execution suddenly remembers dressing her own daughter for her wedding.[41] Aliger devotes a section of the poem to a contemplation of the photograph of Zoia's body, fusing the heroic image of a statue and the image of the girl as a bride:

> ... Это девичье тело,
> не мертвое
> и не живое.
> Это Зоя из мрамора
> тихо лежит на снегу.
> Беспощадной петлей перерезана тонкая шея.
> Незнакомая власть в запрокинутом лице твоем.
> Так любимого ждут,
> сокровенной красой хорошея,
> изнутри озаряясь таинственным женским огнем.
> Только ты не дождалась его, снеговая невеста.
> Он—в солдатской шинели,
> на запад лежит его путь,
> может быть, недалеко от страшного места,
> где ложились снежинки на строгую девичью грудь
> Вечной силы и слабости неповторимо единство.[42]

(This is a girlish body, not dead and not alive. It is Zoia made of marble, lying quietly on the snow. The slender neck is cut by a merciless noose. There is an unfamiliar power in your flung-back face. This is how women wait for the man they love, grown more beautiful with a secret charm, glowing from within from a mysterious womanly flame. But you could not wait for him, bride of the snow. He is in a soldier's greatcoat, his path points to the west, perhaps not far from this terrible place, where snowflakes have settled on your severe maidenly breast, a unique unity of weakness and strength.)

The paradoxical feminine combination of weakness and strength is clearly expressed here by Aliger. Death appears to be a consummation of Zoia's heroic destiny, and a denial of her destiny as an ordinary woman, assumed here to be marriage and motherhood. Aliger, however, compensates for what Zoia has not lived to experience by depicting her dead body as a that of a bride. She dies as martyr and virgin, her symbolic purity untouched by the blemish of the rope around her neck. Her physical substance is transformed into marble, taking on the whiteness of snow to show that she is essentially untouched by her ordeal, which has only served to emphasise her virtues. Svetlov, like Aliger, refers to the fact that Liza dies without having experienced a man's love, but treats this as the destruction of two people's happiness and grounds for revenge, rather than the thwarting of female destiny:

... И не только за поселок каждый,
За свое сожженное село,—
Месть и месть за двух прекрасных граждан,
До которых счастье не дошло![43]

(And not just for each hamlet, for your own burned village, revenge and revenge for two fine citizens whom happiness failed to reach!)

In general, the poetic celebration of female heroism was rare. The great majority of poems depicted women who were felt to be fulfilling their 'natural' role. Women like the soldiers and heroines discussed above were shown to have transgressed this role, but only in the course of duty, and so retained their feminine identity. Those who transgressed woman's 'natural' role for purely selfish ends were dealt with more severely. The widespread celebration of faithful wives had its counterpart in a few poems like Simonov's 'Otkrytoe pis'mo' (Open Letter). The poem is addressed to a woman whose letter to her husband, saying that she has found another man, arrives at the front shortly after his death in battle. Her worst crime, says the poet, is that she has made other men anxious about their own wives' integrity:

... Вы попытались запятнать
Своими строками пустыми
Тот образ женщины, что знать
Хотим мы только как святыню.

(You tried to besmirch with your meaningless lines the image of woman which we want to know only as sacred.)

By her actions she is exposed as a counterfeit:

... Пускай поставят вам в вину
Что душу птичью вы скрывали,
Что вы за женщину, жену,
Себя так долго выдавали.[44]

(May you be charged with the crime of having concealed your bird's soul and masqueraded for so long as a woman and a wife.)

In conclusion the poet, having earlier claimed that he has no wish to judge her, announces that copies of this poem are to be sent all over the country, so that she will be recognised wherever she goes. The warning to other potential traitors to their sex is blunt; for women to transgress against their nature is a hideous crime indeed. As Barbara Heldt points out, the virtues of women were the yardstick against which men in literature measured themselves.[45] If that measure turns out to be flawed, an entire system of values is threatened.

This conviction that women are morally superior to men holds, to a certain extent, for women on the side of the enemy too. Margarita Aliger, widowed in the early months of the war, addresses a poem to her newly-widowed German counterpart. The woman she imagines is no fervent supporter of National Socialism, but a 'soft-hearted human being', to whom the poet wishes to speak as one woman to another, suppressing her hatred, and suggesting that she has the potential to start a rebellion against the regime and the war:

... А вдруг такой великий миг настанет,
когда, от новой силы побледнев,
она расправит плечи, твердо встанет
и в ней проснется грозный женский гнев.
Она сорвет свою косынку вдовью
и развернет ее над головой,
окрашенную человечьей кровью,
горячей, несмываемой, живой.
И сколько не дождавшихся ответа
живых людей пойдет за ней вослед,
за знаменем того святого света.
У правоты другого света нет.[46]

(And suddenly a great moment shall arrive, when, pale from a sense of new strength, she shall straighten her shoulders, stand up firmly, and in her shall awake a terrible woman's anger. She shall tear off her widow's headscarf and unfurl it, dyed in human blood, hot, indelible, alive, above her head. And many living people who have received no answer shall follow her, under a banner of that sacred colour. Truth has no other colour.)

It is very rare in the whole of Soviet war poetry to find an evocation of the enemy which does, like Aliger's poem, recognise the humanity of those on the opposing side. The Russian widow knows exactly what the German widow is going through. Enemy women, it seems, might just by virtue of their shared feminine experience be seen as potential allies, although Aliger's poem is not altogether optimistic on that score.

Women in war poetry, then, are assigned the role of society's moral guardian. Their fulfilment of this role depends on their adherence to what are presented as 'natural' 'feminine' virtues. At the same time, the circumstances of war required them to take on roles as workers and soldiers which were felt to be at odds with their female identity. The poems discussed above give a view of women which is full of internal contradictions. Men, on the other hand, are almost invariably portrayed from a single perspective, either as anonymous hero or as an ordinary man. If the ordinary and heroic are combined, moreover, there is no sense of contradiction. Defence of the country is simply an extension of the defence of home and family. Women, however, are shown to be weak, yet strong, doing men's work, yet retaining their femininity, to be individually responsible for the well-being of husbands and children while acting as symbolic guarantees for the survival of the nation. On one hand women are shown to be more limited than men in their interests and actions, while on the other hand their consistent representation as symbolic or allegorical figures allows them to mediate between the personal and the universal.

Women portrayed in Soviet war poetry are paradoxical creatures whose spiritual determination belies their supposed physical frailty. The same sense of paradox emerges in discussions of one of the most prominent and popular women poets of the war, Ol'ga Berggol'ts, who spent the nine hundred days of the blockade in Leningrad. Berggol'ts was unusual because she was both a woman and a civilian in a war which was presented as an almost exclusively masculine and military enterprise. Her assumption of a 'masculine' role is seen by the critic Pavlovskii as something of an anomaly:

> How can one not be surprised by the fact that the voice of the Great Soldier which was Leningrad at that time belonged to a woman, a very young poetess, who so courageously took upon herself the role of soldier-poet, a role which was so difficult and, it might have seemed, essentially masculine.[47]

In reply to Pavlovskii's perplexity it must be argued that Berggol'ts's success did depend, to a certain extent, on the fact that she was a woman. The persona she adopted as poet of the Leningrad siege corresponds to expectations that women should show strength of a spiritual kind and take on universal, impersonal roles, of a mother, or even Mother Russia, while still remaining approachable and capable of intimate relationships. In other words, this ideal persona was simultaneously a real human being and a symbolic embodiment of moral and patriotic values, a figure who could mediate between the personal and the universal. The poetic persona adopted by Berggol'ts draws on these apparently contradictory qualities, giving expression to the perceived paradoxical nature of a woman's role in the war.

Her poems addressed contemporary readers with unprecedented candour; they are also marked by striking disruptions of style and language as the poet veers between her authoritative 'public' role and her intimate 'private' role. For the majority of Soviet writers this disunity of the private and public self was an inevitable result of contemporary censorship. Berggol'ts was particularly aware of the discrepancies between proclaimed realities and her personal experience following her arrest in 1938. A devoted Party member, she responded to the persecution leading up to her arrest with bewilderment, and then with renewed declarations of loyalty. Her experience of imprisonment, which lasted slightly over six months, gave Berggol'ts an indelible insight into the divisions between the official truth and the actual truth. In her diary, on the day that Kiev was occupied by the Germans in September 1941, she wrote that this division had contributed to the disastrous Soviet retreat:

> Perhaps all that people were doing was keeping up appearances? Over the last few years we've been concerned above all with keeping up appearances ... Oh, this is just what I was afraid might happen! The savage falsehood which suffocated me as a writer was terrible to me not just because it stifled my own soul, but because I saw what it was leading to, that the gulf between the people and the state was growing, that two lives—the real and the official—were moving ever further apart.[48]

Her awareness of this breach is answered in Berggol'ts's poetry by frequent attempts to reconcile the irreconcilable. Sometimes this results in paradox, as in a poem of 1945, 'Stikhi o sebe' (Verses about Myself). Here she attempts to describe her contradictory sensations at the end of the war:

... Какое сердце стало у меня,
сама не знаю, лучше или хуже:
не отогреть у мирного огня,
не остудить на самой лютой стуже.

(What has become of my heart I do not know myself, whether it is better or worse: I cannot warm it by a peaceful fire or chill it in the fiercest frost.)

Like Nikolaeva, who perceives the tensions between her femininity and her wartime activities, Berggol'ts feels that her sense of identity as a woman has been put in question by her role as a war poet, which has invested her with the sombre and irrevocable duty of preserving the memory of the dead:

... И в черный час сожженные войною
затем, чтобы не гаснуть, не стихать,
неженские созвездья надо мною,

неженский ямб в черствеющих стихах ...

... И даже тем, кто всё хотел бы сгладить
в зеркальной, робкой памяти людей,
не дам забыть, как падал ленинградец
на желтый снег пустынных площадей.[49]

(And, kindled by war in a dark hour, never to go out or die down again, is the unwomanly constellation above me, the unwomanly iambus of my bristling verses. And even those who would like to smooth everything over in people's timid, mirror-like memories I shall not allow to forget how the Leningraders fell on the yellow snow of deserted squares.)

To express her paradoxical feelings of joy and sorrow, Berggol'ts uses in this poem the image of two trees, with intertwining roots and branches, which grow up from the suffering of Leningrad into the future. As long as the conflict in the poet's emotional world is acknowledged and openly expressed, Berggol'ts can create the illusion of wholeness, yet when she presents contradictory elements as if there were no conflict, the conflict still emerges on the level of style.

The persona she adopts in much of her wartime work has, as it were, two distinctive voices. During the war Berggol'ts read much of her poetry on Leningrad radio, which gave her the extra-personal identity of the 'voice' of Leningrad, an ideal public persona. As the situation in the city deteriorated, she gradually introduced a more intimate approach into her poetry, and so was able to use the very public, official context of radio to suggest the atmosphere of a private conversation. In October 1941, Berggol'ts began a poem addressed to an unspecified, anonymous fellow-citizen:

... Я буду сегодня с тобой говорить,
товарищ и друг ленинградец,
о свете, который над нами горит,
о нашей последней отраде.

(I shall talk to you today, comrade and friend, citizen of Leningrad, about the light which shines above us, about our last joy.)

Here the identity of the speaker is as generalised as that of her presumed interlocutor, and the supposed conversation is in fact an occasion for the issuing of authoritative instructions:

... Товарищ, прислушайся, встань, улыбнись
и с вызовом миру поведай:
«За город сражаемся мы не одни—
и это уже победа».[50]

(Comrade, listen, stand up, smile, and challenge the world with your words: 'We are not fighting alone for the city—and that is already a victory'.)

These rather impersonal 'conversations' were gradually supplanted by poems with a more intimate approach. The motif of the family, an established image of the unity between private and public existence, first entered Berggol'ts's wartime poetry in its conventional, schematic form, but took on increasingly personal overtones. 'Sestre' (To My Sister), written in September 1941 to be broadcast outside the city, is ostensibly addressed to her sister Mariia in Moscow, but the relationship between the poet and her sister is widened to include the 'great family', and the rapid shift of focus from exclusive, personal details to generalisations make the poem's opening seem awkward and artificial. Berggol'ts speaks as the voice of Leningrad, and as a sister simultaneously:

> Машенька, сестра моя, москвичка!
> Ленинградцы говорят с тобой.
> На военной грозной перекличке
> слышишь ли далекий голос мой?[51]

(Mashen'ka, my sister, Moscow dweller! The Leningraders are talking to you. In the grim wartime roll-call can you hear my distant voice?)

One poem, which Berggol'ts begins as a letter to her mother, is later explicitly addressed to a wider audience, turning into a didactic demonstration of how to write to relatives. 'Pis'mo na Kamu' (Letter to the River Kama) ends:

> ... И я кричу знакомым людям:
> Пишите правду матерям.
> Пишите им о том, что будет.
> Не жалуйтесь, что трудно нам...

(And I shout to people I know: write the truth to your mothers. Write to them about what will be. Do not complain that things are hard for us.)

While Berggol'ts speaks here as if from a tribune, the voice she uses earlier in the same poem is quieter and tells the bleak truth about life in the city. In a reversal of our expectations, this restrained voice does not appear in the quoted letter to her mother. The daughter speaks to her mother using the language of public rhetoric, protesting her readiness to face death rather than dishonour. Following this ostensibly personal interlude, Berggol'ts confides to her readers what she is not going to tell her mother:

> ... Я не пишу—и так вернее—
> что старый дом разрушен наш,
> что ранен брат, что я старею,
> что мало хлеба, мало сна.[52]

(I shall not write—and it is more truthful this way—that our old house has been destroyed, that my brother is wounded, that I am growing old, that we have little bread or sleep.)

From this example we can see that Berggol'ts's use of language identifying her either as a public orator or a confiding and honest individual is not necessarily determined by her use of forms such as a private conversation or a letter, and that she moves from one voice to another in defiance of the reader's expectations. Her 'public voice' was increasingly supplanted by her 'private voice' as conditions in Leningrad worsened. In late August 1941, before the city was completely surrounded, she was still making conspicuous attempts to give her poetry a universal significance by addressing the whole of Russia on behalf of Leningrad:

...Мы будем драться с беззаветной силой,
мы одолеем бешеных зверей,
мы победим, клянусь тебе, Россия,
от имени российских матерей.[53]

(We shall fight with selfless strength, we shall defeat the savage beasts, we shall be victorious, I swear to you, Russia, in the name of Russian mothers.)

By early December, when deaths from cold and starvation were mounting and the bread ration was 125 grammes a day for non-manual workers, Berggol'ts no longer declaimed. Instead, she sat down with her neighbour for a chat as one Leningrad housewife to another:

Дарья Власьевна, соседка по квартире,
сядем, поговорим вдвоем.
Знаешь, будем говорить о мире,
о желанном мире, о своем.

Вот мы прожили почти полгода,
полтораста суток длится бой.
Тяжелы страдания народа—
наши, Дарья Власьевна, с тобой.

О, ночное воющее небо,
дрожь земли, обвал невдалеке,
бедный ленинградский ломтик хлеба—
он почти не весит на руке.

(Dar'ia Vlas'evna, my neighbour, let us sit down and have a chat together. You know, we'll talk about peace, the peace that we long for, our peace. We have lived through almost half a year, the battle has been going on for a hundred and fifty days. The people's sufferings are great, your suffering, Dar'ia Vlas'evna, and mine. O, the howling night sky, the tremor of the earth, a ruin nearby, the poor Leningrad crust of bread—you can hardly feel its weight in your hand.)

The poem ends with a triumphant celebration of her neighbour's endurance, moving from the personal level to the universal, to the symbol of Mother Russia:

... Дарья Власьевна, твоею силой
будет вся земля обновлена.
Этой силе имя есть—Россия.
Стой же и мужайся, как она![54]

(Dar'ia Vlas'evna, it is your strength that will renew the whole earth. The name of that strength is Russia. Stand firm and be courageous, just like her.)

Other 'private conversations' of this kind follow a similar pattern, beginning with an admission of the shared ordeal of the blockade, and ending with an exhortation. The effect of this is twofold: Berggol'ts preserves her authoritative public persona, while giving an enhanced impression of integrity by her honest descriptions of the situation shared by herself and her audience. She is also protected by her status as trusted adviser from making painful admissions about her private experiences of the blockade.

Berggol'ts's public persona allowed her to live up to the standards she herself saw as typical of Leningrad women: 'And so the everlasting, irreplaceable womanly qualities—endurance, self-sacrifice, love—shone with particular brightness in the women of Leningrad, the city which has been fated to bear so much grief'.[55] In actual fact, while Berggol'ts was composing her encouraging words to her fictitious neighbour Dar'ia Vlas'evna in December 1941, her second husband Nikolai Molchanov was dying of epilepsy and starvation combined. His death, in January 1942, is marked by a poem of bleak desperation:

Отчаяния мало. Скорби мало.
О, поскорей отбыть проклятый срок!
А ты своей любовью небывалой
меня на жизнь и мужество обрек.

Зачем, зачем?
Мне даже не баюкать,
не пеленать ребенка твоего.
Мне на земле всего желанней мука
и немота понятнее всего.

Ничьих забот, ничьей любви не надо.
Теперь одно всего нужнее мне:
над братскою могилой Ленинграда
в молчании стоять, оцепенев.

И разве для меня победы будут?
В чем утешение себе найду?!
Пускай меня оставят и забудут.
Я буду жить одна—везде и всюду
в твоем последнем пасмурном бреду.

Но ты хотел, чтоб я живых любила,
Но ты хотел, чтоб я жила. Жила
всей человеческой и женской силой.
Чтоб всю ее истратила дотла.
На песни. На пустячные желанья.
На страсть и ревность—пусть придет другой.
На радость. На тягчайшие страданья
с единственною русскою землей.

Ну что ж, пусть будет так ...[56]

(Little despair, little grief. O, if only I could serve the cursed sentence as fast as possible! But you, by your amazing love, have condemned me to life and courage. Why, why? I cannot even cradle or swaddle your child. Anguish is what I desire most of all in this world, and silence is what I understand best. I need no-one's care, no-one's love. Now I need one thing above all, to stand in silence, fixed to the spot, over the mass grave of Leningrad. And how can there be any victories for me? Where shall I find comfort?! Let me be abandoned and forgotten. I shall live alone, everywhere in your final gloomy delirium. But you wanted me to love the living. But you wanted me to live. To live with all my human and womanly strength. To squander it on songs, on petty wishes. On passion and jealousy—let there be another man. On joy. On the deepest suffering with the one and only Russian land. Oh well, so let it be ...)

Her evocation of strained silence and sense of isolation is reminiscent of that in earlier poems about her imprisonment of 1938 and 1939. Both events brought considerable suffering, but circumstances in the late 1930s made it impossible for Berggol'ts to express her feelings in public. The experience of arrest or bereavement was shared by many, but while the war made it possible to speak about the death of loved ones, within certain limits, political imprisonment remained a taboo subject in literature until the thaw under Khrushchev. It was only in 1965 that Berggol'ts published a selection of her prison poetry written a quarter of a century earlier.[57] It portrayed the purges as a personal test of loyalty imposed by her country, though some poems are dedicated to friends in prison, or, later, to those returning from exile. The broadest evocation of the arrests of the 1930s as a national tragedy is given in 'Net, ne iz knizhek nashikh skudnykh...' (No, not from our sparse books...) written in 1940 and first published in the Soviet Union in 1987.[58]

Two recurring themes of her pre-war poetry are the impossibility of speaking of her prison experiences to a wider audience and the burden placed upon her by the painfully ineradicable memory of her recent past. The second poem of the cycle 'Vozvrashchenie' (The Return), describing the poet's release from prison, is a useful key to the understanding of her position during the war, when, although many of her poems could reach the public, and did address the city's suffering, there were still some things about which she could not, or would not speak. The poem begins:

Мне надо было, покидая
Угрюмый дом, упасть в слезах
и на камнях лежать, рыдая,
у всех прохожих на глазах.

(On leaving that grim house I should have fallen down in tears and lain on the stones sobbing in the sight of all the passers-by.)

Such a public display of emotion was, of course, unthinkable at the time, even though the poet states that her pain was shared by all.

Berggol'ts goes on to speak of what her friends admired as her courage, but what she experiences as an enforced and artificial silence:

... Но злая гордость помешала.
И, стиснув зубы добела,
стыдясь, презрев людскую жалость,
я усмехнулась и ушла.
И мне друзья потом твердили
о некоем мужестве моем
и как победою, гордились
удушливо бесслезным днем.

Им не понять, что черной платой
за это мужество плачу:
мне петь бы вам—и плакать, плакать ...
Но слезы отняты. Молчу.[59]

(But wicked pride got in the way. And, gritting my teeth firmly, ashamed, scorning people's pity, I laughed and walked away. And then my friends told me about my courage, and, as if in a victory, took pride in the suffocatingly tearless day. They are not to know that it is a black penalty I pay for that courage. I should sing to you, and weep, weep ... But my tears have been taken away. I am silent.)

The poet feels an inner need for a cathartic confession, but cannot allow herself to satisfy it. This painful silence was broken by the onset of war, which made it possible for Berggol'ts to write once more of her personal experience as part of the experience of the whole nation. Berggol'ts wrote in her diary in 1942 that the bitterness she felt over her imprisonment had vanished with the outbreak of war.[60] In July 1941 she declared her renewed love and loyalty to her country:

... Я и в этот день не позабыла
горьких лет гонения и зла,
но в слепящей вспышке поняла:
это не со мной—с Тобою было,
это Ты мужалась и ждала.

Нет, я ничего не позабыла!
Но была бы мертва, осуждена—
встала бы на зов Твой из могилы,
все б мы встали, а не я одна.[61]

(I had not forgotten, even on that day, the bitter years of persecution and evil, but in a blinding flash I realised: it wasn't happening to me, but to You, it was You who found courage and waited. No, I have forgotten nothing! But even if I were dead, condemned, I would rise up from the grave at your summons, we would all rise up, not I alone.)

Self-denial and the acceptance of an ordeal, themes shared by her prison poetry and her war poetry, emerged into the public arena. Suffering, which in her prison poetry was a matter of individual shame and secrecy, could now be admitted as a shared burden and therefore a source of strength. Even so, in most of her poems Berggol'ts appears to be trying to subsume her private grief in an evocation of the whole mourning city. Other poems, unpublished at the time, show that these attempts failed to diminish her pain.

The death of her second husband was by no means Berggol'ts's first experience of bereavement; earlier poems commemorate the deaths of her two daughters Maia and Irina, the loss of her unborn child while in prison, and the execution of her former husband, the poet Boris Kornilov, in 1938. Although these poems remained private for some time, Berggol'ts had already begun to interpret her own loss as a source of understanding for the feelings of others in the same situation, putting her private life into some kind of public context. From her earliest poems, dating back to the second half of the 1920s, the unity of her private and public existence is a central theme, though at first it is generally unproblematic. A short poem of 1939 prefigures the beginning of 'Fevral'skii dnevnik' (February Diary) written three years later. The later poem recounts how Berggol'ts, recently widowed, receives a friend whose own husband has just died; the earlier poem concerns a friend's grief at the loss of a child. In 1940 Berggol'ts discovers the role of a comforter which she was to adopt fully in wartime:

> ... Я с подругой всю ночь говорила,
> я утешила сердце ее ...
> ... Вот и горе мое пригодилось,
> безутешное горе мое ...[62]

(I talked to my friend all night, I comforted her heart ... So my grief too has found a use, my inconsolable grief.)

The depth of suffering in the Leningrad blockade, where bereavement became part of everyday life, made it harder to find comforting words; they are replaced by silent understanding:

> Был день как день.
> Ко мне пришла подруга,
> не плача, рассказала, что вчера
> единственного схоронила друга,
> и мы молчали с нею до утра.
>
> Какие же я могла найти слова,
> я тоже—ленинградская вдова.[63]

(It was a day like any other. My friend came to see me, and, dry-eyed, said that yesterday she had buried the only man she loved, and we sat in silence until morning. What kind of words could I find, I am a Leningrad widow too.)

The difference between Berggol'ts's position here and in 'Ia budu segodnia s toboi govorit'...', quoted above as an example of the poet's public, authoritative role, is that while in the earlier poem she speaks from a position of superior, ideologically determined insight, here she speaks by the right of shared suffering. When Berggol'ts attempts to amalgamate these two positions, citing her shared fate with the rest of the city as grounds to deliver an 'improving' lecture, silence and restraint give way to verbosity. In 'Fevral'skii dnevnik', following a bleak evocation of the two widows' mute vigil, Berggol'ts declares herself impelled to speak in what is presented as a private conversation. The rhetorical use of repetition and the elevated vocabulary, however, contrasts with the direct and apparently unemotional style of the poem's opening. This conversation is clearly intended for a wider audience:

> ... Как мы в ту ночь молчали, как молчали ...
> Но я должна, мне надо говорить
> с тобой, сестра по гневу и печали:
> прозрачны мысли и душа горит.
>
> Уже страданиям нашим не найти
> Ни меры, ни названья, ни сравненья.
> Но мы в конце тернистого пути
> и знаем—близок день освобожденья.[64]

(How silent we were that night, how silent ... But I must, I have to speak to you, sister in anger and sadness: my thoughts are crystal clear and my soul burns. Now for our suffering there can be found no measure, name or comparison. But we are at the end of a thorny path and we know that the day of liberation is at hand.)

Throughout the rest of the poem the dominant tone is similarly rhetorical, with only occasional glimpses of earlier verbal and emotional restraint, which provide a disruptive contrast to the general tone. It seems that Berggol'ts reverts to her authoritative and optimistic voice as a counter-argument to the strikingly grim initial picture of Leningrad life. This transition is marked by a jarring change of key, which is particularly obvious in the second section of 'Fevral'skii dnevnik'. Berggol'ts gives a restrained and striking description of the scene on Nevskii Prospekt, with its grim traffic of corpses being taken for burial:

> ... А город был в дремучий убран иней.
> Уездные сугробы, тишина ...
> Не отыскать в снегу трамвайных линий,
> одних полозьев жалоба слышна ...
>
> А девушка с лицом заинведелым,
> упрямо стиснув почерневший рот,
> завернутое в одеяло тело
> на Охтинское кладбище везет.

(The city was decked in a thick hoar frost. Provincial snowdrifts, silence ... The tramlines hidden under the snow, the only sound the squeal of sledge runners ... And a girl with a frost-covered face, stubbornly clenching her blackened lips, takes a body wrapped in a blanket on a sledge to the Okhta cemetery.)

The next stanza begins in similar tones, but the exclamation in the third line ushers in a passage of rhetorical exhortation, as the poet steps out of her role as observer to instruct her readers:

... Везет, качаясь,—к вечеру добраться б ...
Глаза бесстрастно смотрят в темноту.
Скинь шапку, гражданин!
                                        Провозят ленинградца,
погибшего на боевом посту.

Скрипят полозья в городе, скрипят ...
Как многих нам уже недосчитаться!
Но мы не плачем: правду говорят,
что слезы вымерзли у ленинградцев.

Нет, мы не плачем. Слез для сердца мало.
Нам ненависть заплакать не дает.
Нам ненависть залогом жизни стала:
объединяет, греет и ведет.[65]

(She pulls the sledge, swaying,—if she can only get there by nightfall ... Her eyes look dispassionately into the darkness. Take your hat off, citizen! A Leningrader who died at his post is passing on his way. The sledge runners squeak and squeal in the city ... How many people we have lost already! But we do not weep: they tell the truth who say that the Leningraders' tears are frozen. No, we do not weep. Tears are not enough for the heart. Hatred does not allow us to weep. Our hatred has become a pledge of life: it unites, warms and leads us.)

Most critics have so far tended to gloss over the question of the strongly contrasting styles in Berggol'ts's blockade poetry. An exception is Carin Tschöpl, who points out that it is either the poems' honest representation of life under siege, or the repeated statements of determination and belief in victory that is singled out as their basic message.[66] The unevenness of style is, however, too obvious to overlook; it plainly echoes Berggol'ts's diary entry on the double reality of Soviet life, and the motif of the double life that appears again in 'Fevral'skii dnevnik'.[67] Tschöpl argues convincingly that the aesthetic flaw in these poems can be seen as a sign of their authenticity, an open acknowledgement of the gap between official rhetoric and reality. In Tschöpl's view, Berggol'ts presents her readers with the truth of personal experience in order to express her understanding of their shared predicament, but then counters it with exhortations and exclamations which would seem to deny the force of real circumstances. This counter-argument is aimed at convincing both poet and audience that they will live to see victory.

In her role as a source of public comfort and encouragement, Berggol'ts speaks fluently and at length; when approaching her private pain, she can hardly find any words to express her feelings. But in 'Leningradskaia poema' (Leningrad Poem) her grief surfaces in the course of a triumphant celebration of her fellow-citizens' physical and spiritual resilience, even though it is followed by an affirmation of her own strength:

... И я утрату понесла.
К ней не притронусь даже словом—
такая боль ... И я смогла,
как вы, подняться к жизни снова.
Затем, чтоб вновь и вновь сражаться
за жизнь.[68]

(I too suffered a loss. I do not touch on it even with a word—it is so painful. And I managed, like you, to raise myself up again to life. Thereafter to fight for life again and again.)

Berggol'ts repeatedly sets aside her own experience of the blockade in favour of a more universal approach. In 'Leningradskaia poema' she tells her sister:

... Ты знала—я теперь одна,
мой муж погиб, я голодаю.
Но то же, то же, что со мной,
со всеми сделала блокада.[69]

(You knew that I was alone now, my husband was dead, I was starving. But the blockade has done to me exactly what it has done to all.)

This could be interpreted as heroic self-denial, but the dismissal of exclusive experience hints at an attempt to exclude an area of her life which Berggol'ts found too painful to contemplate at length. This repression of private grief was part of an ethos which emphasised the importance of the collective, rather than the individual. But, to judge from the poetry of the time, it seems as though women were assigned the role of an emotional safety-valve, as they were believed to be more vulnerable and sensitive than men by nature. Women were tacitly allowed to express their feelings of suffering and fear, not just as individuals, but on behalf of society. Men, of course, were required to exclude signs of emotional weakness from their poetry, but Iuliia Drunina, who served at the front as a nurse, was able to make an admission which would not have been acceptable if made by a man:

Я только раз видала рукопашный,
Раз—наяву. И тысячу—во сне.
Кто говорит, что на войне не страшно,
Тот ничего не знает о войне.[70]

(I only saw hand-to-hand fighting once. Once—for real. And a thousand times in my dreams. Anyone who says war isn't frightening knows nothing at all about war.)

While it was permissible for women to admit their fears, it was still expected that they did so without excessive displays of emotion. Hysteria was considered the ultimate female weakness, and critics were vigilant in their search for poetry which was felt to over-emphasise suffering. In Berggol'ts's case, the pressure of critical opinion combined with internal pressures to maintain her public role as the 'voice of Leningrad', so that her public expression of her own grief was restrained. It may well also be true to say that the war effort demanded that excessive private emotion be set aside for the duration. The women who symbolised Mother Russia in other poets' work were indeed shown to bear their grief with fortitude.

One long poem written towards the end of the war attempts to turn the isolation of those in mourning, the poet included, into a community of shared grief. 'Pamiati zashchitnikov' (In Memory of the Defenders) was written in 1944 at the request of a young girl who wanted her brother, killed in the final attack which broke through the blockade, to be commemorated. Her words, as recorded by the poet, set the poem's task:

> ... Она просила только: «Напишите
> не для того, чтобы его прославить,
> но чтоб над ним могли другие плакать
> со мной и мамой—точно о родном ...»[71]

(She asked only: "Write not so as to glorify him, but so that others can weep for him with mother and me as if for one of their own family.)

Berggol'ts's acceptance of the commission has a personal motive. She describes her feelings of surprise when shown a photograph of the girl's dead brother; he bears a striking resemblance to her late husband as he was before hunger and illness changed him. This reminds the poet that she has yet to commemorate him in her work; her lament for the 'universal son and brother', as the anonymous subject of the piece is called, is offered as a sufficient substitute for the unwritten requiem. In 'Pamiati zashchitnikov' Berggol'ts emphasises the unity of public and private emotion. An earlier poem, written in 1942, shows the complete breakdown of links between the poet's public and private self brought about by grief. In 'Otryvok' (Fragment) the scene is set on a dismal rainy evening, as the poet is stopped on the street and her pass examined:

> Октябрьский дождь стучит в квадрат оконный,
> глухие залпы слышатся вдали.
> На улицах, сырых и очень темных,
> одни сторожевые патрули.
>
> Мерцает желтый слепенький фонарик,
> и сердце вдруг сжимается тоской,
> когда услышишь:—Пропуск ваш, товарищ ...—
> Как будто ты нездешний и чужой.
>
> «Вот пропуск мой. Пожалуйста, проверьте.
> Я здешняя, и этот город—мой.

У нас одно дыхание, дума, сердце ...
Я здешняя, товарищ постовой».

(The October rain beats against the square of the window, far off muffled salvos can be heard. On the streets, damp and very dark, there are only sentry patrols. A yellow, dim torch gleams, and your heart suddenly constricts with melancholy when you hear: 'Your pass, comrade'. As if you are not local, an outsider. 'Here is my pass. Do check it, please. I am local, and this is my city. We share one breath, one thought, one heart. I am local, comrade sentry.')

The repeated assertions to the sentry, her audience, of her identity as a Leningrader, together with the sense of dismay at being challenged, suggest, perhaps, that the speaker has to confirm her identity to herself as well. And, indeed, immediately after the confident announcement to the sentry come the words she confides to the reader alone, a continuation and questioning of her public statement. Now fragmentary speech contrasts with her previous fluency and underlines the poet's uncertainty:

... Но я живу в квартире, где зимою
чужая чья-то вымерла семья.
Всё, что кругом,—накоплено не мною.
Всё—не мое, как будто б я—не я.

(But I live in a flat where last winter someone else's family died out. Everything around me was collected not by me. Everything is not mine, as if I were not myself.)

Although the poet, in her role as a public figure, identifies herself completely with her city, in her private life she feels a lack of identity, having lost in succession her children, husband and home. She describes the piercing, inexpressible sadness she feels when she visits her former home, made uninhabitable by the first blockade winter. It is a place which is full of memories of her dead husband and children, yet now these memories seem alien to her, except for a brief moment when she succeeds in remembering how she used to return home to find her husband waiting there. Now, in his absence, it is as if her senses have betrayed her:

... Как будто я ослепла и оглохла:
не услышать тебя, не увидать.
Я слышу только дождь: он бьется в стекла,
и только дождь такой же, как тогда ...[72]

(It is as if I have gone blind and deaf: I cannot hear or see you. I can only hear the rain: it is beating against the glass. And only the rain is the same as it was then.)

The return to the motif of the rain beating against the window completes the poem, and leaves no hope of escape, an uncharacteristic end for Berggol'ts, whose war poems almost invariably end on a note of optimism. In 'Otryvok', at least, Berggol'ts refrains from forcing a change of mood, but returns to the poem's opening image, the rain at the window. Between the repetitions of this image comes the realisation that the past cannot be brought back, giving the conclusion a sense of hopeless circularity and enclosure.

In 'Tvoi put'' (Your Road), written in 1945, Berggol'ts appears to have found a solution to the conflict between her public and private self. She describes how her role as the city's poet, charged with the task of mourning the dead, made the pain of her own bereavement easier to bear. Her vocation does not, however, release her from suffering. By taking on the suffering of the whole city, she is released from the confines of private, inexpressible grief:

... там я приказ гордый выполняла ...
Неся избранье трудное свое,
из недр души
я стих свой выдирала,
не пощадив живую ткань ее ...[73]

(There I carried out a proud order ... Bearing my difficult vocation, from the depths of my soul I ripped out my poem, not sparing its living tissue ...)

The acceptance of suffering on behalf of all the dead sublimates and transforms her grief into a source of hope. The memory of her second husband loses its painful intensity, and his image is:

... слит во всем, что больше жизни было—
мечта,
душа,
отчизна,
бытие ...[74]

(Fused with all that was more than life—dream, spirit, fatherland, being ...)

In spite of these words, other poems suggest that her husband's memory remained deeply painful. There is considerable irony in the fact that Berggol'ts was able to commemorate those she had never known, while failing to mourn her husband fittingly:

... Мне легче незнакомых, неизвестных,
мне легче мир оплакать, чем тебя.

И всё, что говорю,—одни подобья,
над песней неродившейся надгробье ...[75]

(Unknown, unfamiliar people are easier for me to mourn than you. And everything I say is all the same, the gravestone over an unborn song.)

The mixture of repressed grief and guilt later found expression in poems about the return of her dead husband to find her re-married, a vivid illustration of the return of the repressed.[76] Denial of her own grief was essential to the functioning of Berggol'ts's public persona, as was the recognition of the suffering of others. When, in 1944, the theme of victory was beginning to gather triumphant momentum, Berggol'ts did not hesitate to recognise other people's psychological wounds:

... I saw people who had been very severely affected by two years of German slavery. They are broken. They must be helped to stand on their feet again. And we have so many widows and inconsolable mothers. Writers must play an enormous role in helping people find their place in life and heal the many, many spiritual wounds.[77]

But who was to provide comfort for the sorrowing writer? That question did not arise for Berggol'ts, who saw the writer's role in sacrificial terms.

In May 1945 she made a plea for the place of tragedy in war literature, saying that while tragedy did not comfort, its cathartic effect was now greatly needed. The poet's role, as she saw it, was to reveal the most painful emotions through confession:

Confession has nothing in common with the revelation of trivial, unimportant details about one's own life and one's relatives, and only pure, restrained souls have the right to confess. This is because confession comes from the most fundamental, profound and searing movements of the human soul. The more pitiless towards oneself, the more openly the engineer of human souls, who has accumulated the feelings of hundreds and thousands of people, will write, and the effect of his work on the reader, on the people, will be the stronger.[78]

A poem written by Berggol'ts in August 1946 as part of the cycle 'Piat' obrashchenii k tragedii' (Five Addresses to Tragedy) contains a definition of her poetic persona, one who speaks for all, both the living and the dead, and whose assumed universal identity cannot conceal personal tragedy. The relevance of these words to her wartime poetry is clear:

... И вот я становлюсь многоликой,
и многодушной, и многоязыкой.
Но мне же суждено самой собой
остаться в разных обликах и душах,
и в чьем-то горе, в радости чужой
свой тайный стон и тайный шепот слушать
и знать, что ничего не утаишь ...
Все слышат всё, до скрытого рыданья ...
И друг придет с ненужным состраданьем,
И посмеются недруги мои.[79]

(And now I assume many faces, many souls and many tongues. But I am fated to remain myself in different forms and souls, and in someone else's grief, someone else's joy, to hear my secret moan and secret whisper and to know that nothing can be concealed ... Everyone hears it all, even the hidden sobs ... And a friend will come with unnecessary sympathy, and my enemies will laugh.)

It was common practice in Soviet wartime literature to depict women as a meeting point of the individual and the universal, and to find in this portrayal a source of comforting profundity. When Berggol'ts explored her position as a mediator between these two levels, using tragedy as the unifying force, the result was a rejection of glib comfort. She refused to dismiss suffering, and was criticised for what Prokof'ev called in 1945 'the celebration of suffering', but the concept of spiritual purification through suffering lay at the heart of her portrayal of the heroism of Leningraders under siege.[80] In 1943 Vera Inber complained of Berggol'ts's inability to leave behind the theme of the first blockade winter and move on to subjects more in keeping with the times. Aleksandr Prokof'ev, commenting on Berggol'ts's Leningrad poetry at the tenth plenum of the Writers' Union in May 1945, welcomed the sincerity and inspired tone of much of her work. But, like Inber, he found Berggol'ts too preoccupied with suffering: 'Berggol'ts, like some other poets, concentrates on the subject of the sufferings of the people in the besieged city'.[81]

In answer to those who accused her of a preoccupation with suffering, Berggol'ts said that to deny suffering was to deny the real extent of the people's achievement in war:

> There is a tendency, supporters of which protest in every way possible against the depiction and portrayal of the great ordeals endured by our people as a whole and by each person individually on the way towards their dazzling victory. But why make the people's achievement less valuable? ... if poets, novelists and dramatists show how the people overcame the most terrible events and emerged from them not broken, but enriched, mature, even if less joyful and carefree than before,—how can you accuse these writers of 'celebrating suffering'? And how, then, if we aspire to record the courage of the victorious Soviet people can we manage without depicting the circumstances in which this courage manifested itself?[82]

Berggol'ts was in fact concerned more with portraying the degree of spiritual strength shown by the Leningraders in overcoming physical suffering than with the horrors of death and starvation. This was recognised in 1943 by the critic Iurii Danilin, who wrote: 'Ol'ga Berggol'ts's realism is as courageous as the struggle of Leningrad's defenders. The poetess is not afraid to touch upon the most extreme situations, for she does not produce a naturalistic photograph, but an artistic canvas which is purposeful and forward-looking.'[83] There is nothing naturalistic in the way Berggol'ts describes her heroines. Every detail contributes to an understanding of her concept of the heroic.

If the poetic persona adopted by Berggol'ts in her war poetry accentuated the disunity it was meant, perhaps, to conceal, her representation of heroism, particularly as it related to women, was much more successful. Berggol'ts did not follow the usual paradigms of action leading to transformation, which was in any case unsuitable for the largely static circumstances of the blockade. Instead, transformation came through the attainment of a new state of being in which physical suffering was transcended through spiritual strength. Berggol'ts's use of religious imagery is most important in this context. Few contemporary critics, as we have seen, noted her adaptation of existing heroic paradigms, being too preoccupied by her honest evocation of conditions in Leningrad to examine the way Berggol'ts actually dealt with the theme of suffering.

The heroines Berggol'ts portrayed were rather different from those preferred by most poets, being both women and civilians. Berggol'ts equated the work of Leningrad housewives with that of soldiers. In a broadcast on 8 March 1943, she said:

> The people's grateful memory shall always preserve, together with the image of the Komsomol member Vera Chertilova, who led a company of marines into an attack, the image of any anonymous Leningrad woman leading an enfeebled man by the hand along the wintry streets of Leningrad. That woman went into the attack as well. Leningrad women were soldiers everywhere—in icy rooms, cooking lunch at a temporary stove, and on the allotments and rooftops of their city. Everything Leningrad women did and does is part of a battle, such as the world never witnessed before, for the very basis of human life.[84]

Berggol'ts concluded her broadcast with a poem which examines women's heroism from two angles. An artist defends his idealised portrayal of a Leningrad housewife by appealing to her symbolic status as 'Love and Life itself, Leningrad's Fearlessness and Glory!'. Although he is allowed to have the last word, the woman's own words take up most of the poem. She protests her lack of resemblance to this smiling, beautiful creature:

> ... Не похоже.
> Я проще, я угрюмее была.

(It's not like me. I was more simple, more sombre.)

The woman confesses her fears, her exhaustion and hunger, tells how her appearance has changed, but, at the same time, how she has gained new skills and strength:

> ...И день за днем лицо мое темнело,
> седины появились на висках,
> Зато, привычная уже к любому делу,
> почти железной сделалась рука.
>
> Смотри—как цепки пальцы и грубы!
> Я рвы на ближних подступах копала,
> сколачивала жесткие гробы
> и малым детям раны бинтовала.[85]

(And day by day my face grew darker, grey hairs appeared on my temples, nevertheless, accustomed to any work, my hand has become almost like iron. Look how tough and coarse my fingers are! I dug ditches close to the city, hammered together rough coffins and bandaged small children's wounds.)

As will be shown later, religious imagery plays a major role in Berggol'ts's concept of heroism. Therefore it is justifiable to say that this Leningrad housewife displays the stigmata of blockade life, signs which, unlike the statuesque poses and determined expressions of conventional heroes, reveal the suffering she has undergone. For Berggol'ts, heroism inevitably entails suffering. Few contemporary critics understood this connection.

Berggol'ts reverses the accepted hierarchy of heroism both by her choice of hero-figure, and by the acts which he, or more usually she, performs. Most of her heroes are women civilians going about their everyday domestic tasks. Berggol'ts makes no apologies for her choice; she repeatedly insists that each citizen of Leningrad is:

> ... не просто горожанин, а солдат,
> по мужеству подобный ветерану.[86]

(Not just a city-dweller, but a soldier, equal in courage to a veteran.)

Berggol'ts perceives the presence of the heroic where few other poets would even have looked for it. She violates convention still further by using the image of the statue associated with soldiers performing acts of exceptional courage to describe the fire-watchers on Leningrad rooftops. This is no instant transformation of the type achieved by the textbook hero, but a vision of the marble statues which will replace the fire-watchers in future years:

> ... Но мы стояли на высоких крышах
> с закинутою к небу головой,
> не покидали хрупких наших вышек,
> лопату сжав немеющей рукой.
>
> И вот тогда на самом стройном зданье,
> лицом к восходу солнца самого
> поставим мраморное изваянье
> простого труженика ПВО.
>
> Пускай стоит, всегда зарей объятый,
> так, как стоял, держа неравный бой:
> с закинутою к небу головой,
> с единственным оружием—лопатой.[87]

(But we stood on high rooftops, our heads flung back towards the sky, we did not leave our fragile perches, clasping a spade in our numb hands. And then, on the most shapely building, face pointing towards the rising sun, we shall set up a marble statue of a simple air raid warden. Let him stand there, forever embraced by the dawn, just as he stood, fighting an unequal battle, his head flung back towards the sky, with his sole weapon—a spade.)

The emphasis given to the fact that the fire-watcher is armed only with a spade is at odds with the elevated quality, both literally and figuratively, assigned to the statue. Berggol'ts plays on the conventional attributes of heroism, stressing the discrepancies between them and her apparently incongruous hero figures in order to heighten the sense of extraordinary achievement. The poet imagines her neighbour Dar'ia Vlas'evna, immortalised as a statue, complete with purse and headscarf, icons of domesticity:

> ... Вот такой же: исхудавшей, смелой,
> в наскоро повязанном платке,
> вот такой, когда под артобстрелом
> ты идешь с кошелкою в руке.[88]

(Just like this: gaunt, brave, in a hurriedly tied headscarf, as you are when you walk, shopping bag in hand, under artillery fire.)

The statue imagined by Berggol'ts was not taken up as a suggestion by the creators of Soviet war memorials, for whose subjects the machine-gun and the banner are essential accessories. There is a definite sense of disenchantment at the lack of appropriate official recognition of the Leningrad women's vital role in 'Vtoroi razgovor s sosedkoi' (Second Conversation with a Neighbour), the 1944 sequel to the poem addressed to her neighbour in 1941:

> ... Мы с тобою танков не взрывали.
> Мы в чаду обыденных забот
> безымянные высоты брали—
> но на карте нет таких высот.
>
> Где помечена твоя крутая
> лестница, ведущая домой,
> по которой, с голоду шатаясь,
> ты ходила с ведрами зимой?
>
> Где помечена твоя дорога,
> по которой десять раз прошла
> и сама—в пургу, в мороз, в тревогу—
> пятерых на кладбище свезла?
>
> Только мы с тобою, мы, соседка,
> помним наши тяжкие пути.
> Сами знаем, в картах или в сводках
> их не перечислить, не найти.[89]

(You and I didn't blow up any tanks. In the welter of everyday cares we took unnamed heights—but there are no such heights on any map. Where is there marked your steep staircase, leading home, up which, swaying with hunger, you walked, carrying buckets, in winter? Where is there marked that road you walked ten times yourself—in blizzard, frost and air raid—taking five to the cemetery? Only you and I, we, neighbour, remember our dreadful journeys. We know that in maps and despatches they are not numbered and cannot be found.)

Now it seems that these women's heroism can only be perceived by those who have experienced life in the blockade for themselves. That, to a certain extent, is true of all her heroines, in that Berggol'ts shows us women whose actions are not outwardly dramatic or likely to call attention to themselves. Their heroism is essentially a private, internal phenomenon based less on action and more on moral and spiritual qualities. In effect, heroism and life are one and the same:

... Я никогда героем не была,
Не жаждала ни славы, ни награды.
Дыша одним дыханьем с Ленинградом,
я не геройствовала, а жила.[90]

(I was never a hero, I did not long for glory or reward. I breathed with the same breath as Leningrad, I did not play the hero, I simply lived.)

Berggol'ts sees true heroism in the ability to retain human moral values in blockaded Leningrad, under constant threat of starvation or enemy shells:

... Но тот, кто не жил с нами,—не поверит,
что в сотни раз почетней и трудней
в блокаде, в окруженье палачей
не превратиться в оборотня, в зверя ...[91]

(But those who did not live with us will not believe that it is a hundred times more difficult and worthier, under siege, surrounded by hangmen, not to turn into a werewolf, an animal.)

It should be noted that this unspectacular heroism, which might be expected to come naturally from women, on account of their assumed moral superiority, is shown by Berggol'ts to be far from effortless.

When Berggol'ts attempts to depict heroism of a more conventional type, such as the self-sacrificial death of a soldier in battle, her work appears stilted and uninspired. Critics, even during the war, noticed that Berggol'ts's poetry was more successful when it was dealing with the theme she had made her own—the human capacity to transcend suffering—than when it tried to bring more standard heroic details into the picture. Set pieces, often subjects which Berggol'ts had not herself witnessed, such as the driver who, crossing Lake Ladoga, has frostbitten hands which he must set alight in order to move them and repair his truck, or the commander who dies leading an attack, were found unconvincing by E. Dobin.[92] 'Leningradskaia poema' is an attempt to depict the blockade through a broad panorama of detail. The heroic death of the commander portrayed in the poem's fifth section contains a rather laboured treatment of the conventional symbolism of blood as a banner:

... А он лежал в крови густой,
ничком, с простертыми руками,
как будто прикрывал собой
под ним распластанное знамя.
И что же—верно: кровь свою
он, точно стяг, легко и гордо
пронес в решающем бою
за жизнь твою, любимый город.[93]

(But he lay in thick blood, face down, his hands outspread, as if covering with his body a banner spread out beneath him. And, well—it was true: his blood he, like a standard, lightly and proudly bore into the decisive battle for your life, beloved city.)

The women seen by Berggol'ts on the streets of Leningrad are associated with a different repertoire of imagery drawn from the immediate reality of their existence. In 'Leningradskaia osen'' (Leningrad Autumn) one woman carries firewood home; in 'Fevral'skii dnevnik' (February Diary) a girl drags a sledge bearing a corpse, while in 'Leningradskaia poema' (Leningrad Poem) the poet is faced with a neighbour begging for a piece of bread, the price of a coffin for her daughter. These details are not supplied with the banner's ready-made significance, but Berggol'ts endows them with a new meaning far beyond their everyday origins. The old, everyday meaning of firewood and bread has been lost in the blockade, as the context of normal, peaceful existence has vanished. Everyday existence, encapsulated in the word 'byt' with its connotations of the humdrum, becomes transformed in Berggol'ts's perceptions into something qualitatively different:

... В те дни исчез, отхлынул быт. И смело
в права свои вступило бытие.[94]

(In those days everyday life vanished, suddenly fell away. And, boldly, being came into its own.)

Life is pared down to the essentials by this transforming vision. In one sense Berggol'ts is very close to the conventions of socialist realism by her references to a higher reality beyond ordinary material existence. Her sense of time, like that of myth, does not acknowledge the merely chronological. In her book of autobiographical prose, *Dnevnye zvezdy* (Daytime Stars), Berggol'ts recalls her feelings in October 1941:

> It was once said that time would cease to exist. You may not believe this, but I know what it is like when time stops: time stopped that day,—it was all compressed into a bundle of light inside me, all of time, all of existence. And the barriers between life and death, between the past, present and future came merrily crashing down. O, how fragile they turned out to be, how contingent; it was so easy for me to enjoy the whole of life at once, all its poetry and tragedy at life's very limits ... in one moment when the artillery bombardment fell silent.[95]

In several of her poems Berggol'ts observes the present from the perspective of the future; this is most obvious in 'Leningradskaia osen'', in which she pictures a museum of the distant future, where ash from the stoves of the besieged city is preserved as a sacred relic. In 'Fevral'skii dnevnik', which she wrote in January and February

1942, the most terrible phase of the blockade, Berggol'ts again speaks of the present and the future existing simultaneously:

... Двойною жизнью мы сейчас живем:
в кольце, во мраке, в голоде, в печали
мы дышим завтрашним, свободным, щедрым днем,
мы этот день уже завоевали.[96]

(We are now living a double life: in encirclement, darkness, hunger, sorrow we breathe tomorrow's free and generous air, we have already conquered that day.)

This concept has strong echoes of the christian idea that the trials of earthly life are as nothing if one has faith in the heavenly bliss to come. The neo-religious ideas inherent in the conventions of socialist realism emerge with considerable clarity in Berggol'ts's work. What really distinguishes her concept of heroism from that used by most other contemporary poets is that while the conventional hero is not shown to suffer, and his ordeal is soon complete, Berggol'ts's women are clearly marked by prolonged suffering and can see no end to it. Berggol'ts promotes a view of heroism which is close to the basic christian belief that salvation was gained through the suffering and crucifixion of Christ. In her poetry the role of Christ is played by the women of Leningrad themselves.

In 'Leningradskaia osen'' (Leningrad Autumn) Berggol'ts describes a woman carrying firewood, an important but mundane task in the city preparing for another winter under siege. Through the whole poem, however, runs a thread of imagery connected with the crucifixion and redemption through suffering, which transforms the woman into a Christ figure silently bearing her cross on the road to Calvary:

... Вот женщина стоит с доской в объятьях;
угрюмо сомкнуты ее уста,
доска в гвоздях—как будто часть распятья,
большой обломок русского креста.

(There is a woman standing clasping a plank in her arms; her lips are grimly pressed together, there are nails in the plank—like part of a crucifix, a large chunk from a Russian cross.)

In the museum of the future, the remains of the woman's burden, a heap of ashes mixed with nails, can be identified as the equivalent of a fragment of the True Cross, their humble appearance disguising their elevated significance:

... И с трепетом, почти смешным для нас,
снесут в музей, пронизанный огнями,
и под стекло положат, как алмаз,
невзрачный пепел, смешанный с гвоздями![97]

(And with a tremor, almost funny to us, they shall take it to a museum, full of light, and place it under glass, like a diamond, unsightly ashes mixed with nails!)

In the same way as the wood has both a practical and a spiritual significance, the fire which has reduced it to ashes can be interpreted on two levels. First, it is essential to physical survival, but it is also a religious symbol of spiritual transformation, associated with the festival of Pentecost. Fire burns, but it also alters and purifies that which it burns. Berggol'ts imagines the museum curator of the distant future extolling the Leningraders' spiritual triumph as inventors of 'new laws of human happiness and love', and casting them in the role of a new religion's early martyrs.[98]

Another symbol used by Berggol'ts which is directly related both to the details of blockade life and to the christian religion is bread. Bread was literally of vital importance to Leningraders; in Berggol'ts's poetry it is given a high symbolic value because it is sanctified by the human suffering and loss of life involved in bringing flour to the besieged city, concepts which echo religious symbolism of bread as the broken body of Christ:

> ... О, мы познали в декабре—
> не зря «священным даром» назван
> обычный хлеб, и тяжкий грех—
> хотя бы крошку бросить наземь:
> таким людским страданьем он,
> такой большой любовью братской
> для нас он ныне освящен,
> наш хлеб насущный, ленинградский.[99]

(O, in December we learned that it is not for nothing ordinary bread is called a "holy gift", and that it is a great sin to drop even a crumb on the ground: so much human suffering, so great a brotherly love sanctifies it for us now, our Leningrad daily bread.)

Bread and wine appear together, a suggestion of the Eucharist, in 'Razgovor s sosedkoi' (Conversation with a Neighbour). The poet looks forward to peace and plenty:

> ... Будем свежий хлеб ломать руками,
> темно-золотистый и ржаной.
> Медленными, крупными глотками
> будем пить румяное вино.[100]

(We shall break fresh bread with our hands, dark golden, made of rye. We shall drink slow, large mouthfuls of rosy wine.)

The opening section of 'Leningradskaia poema' (Leningrad Poem) depicts a highly dramatic situation. The poet is asked to give a neighbour bread so that she may buy her daughter a coffin. Perhaps the parallel of the temptation of Christ in the wilderness is not too far-fetched; the neighbour is persistent, and appeals to the poet's weak spot as a mother who has lost a child of her own. Berggol'ts makes it clear that a fierce moral struggle is in progress, a struggle which she wins with magnanimity:

... Как будто на краю земли,
одни, во мгле, в жестокой схватке,
две женщины, мы рядом шли,
две матери, две ленинградки.
И, одержимая, она
молила долго, горько, робко.
И сил хватило у меня
не уступить мой хлеб на гробик.
И сил хватило—привести
ее к себе, шепнув угрюмо:
«На, съешь кусочек, съешь... прости!
Мне для живых не жаль—не думай!»[101]

(As if at the edge of the earth, alone, in darkness, in a bitter skirmish, two women, we walked side by side, two mothers, two Leningrad women. And as one possessed, she begged at length, bitterly, timidly. And I found the strength not to let her have my bread for a coffin. And I found the strength to bring her home, and grimly whisper: 'There, eat that piece, eat it ... forgive me! I don't begrudge the living, don't think I do!')

This is just one episode in the poet's own 'rite of passage' through the blockade. Unlike conventional heroes whose transformation is instantaneous, almost effortless, Berggol'ts shows herself undergoing a painful process of enlightenment which is more reminiscent of a spiritual journey rather than of an allegory of Marxism-Leninism. This is particularly evident in Berggol'ts's last long work written in wartime, 'Tvoi put'' (Your Road). The first winter of the war appears as a point of reference, a source of contact with truth and reality marking a turning point in her life. The memory of that time is endowed with a reality which makes it, as she repeatedly asserts, 'more than just a memory'.[102] It acquires the status of a personal 'heroic age' which transforms the poet both physically and spiritually. Her pre-war self bears the outward attributes of the heroic, remembered high up on a mountain pass in the Caucasus, full of confidence and thirst for life. This former self is someone Berggol'ts now fears, as the ordeal of war proved it false, without substance. The new self created by the experience of the blockade is outwardly much reduced but spiritually enriched, reversing the conventional association of transcendence with a calm and beautiful appearance. She remembers herself as:

... Вот этой серой, беспощадной, страшной,
глядящей из блокадного угла.[103]

(This grey, merciless, terrible woman, looking out of a blockade corner.)

Her account of this spiritual journey is full of religious imagery. Berggol'ts traces her symbolic death and resurrection, and takes on Christ's role by accepting suffering and crucifixion. In imitation of the parable of the Good Samaritan, 'as in sacred and holy parables', the poet is brought home by a stranger from where she had fallen on the street, too weak to get up.[104] The progress from high to low, symbolic of fall and subsequent redemption, is reflected at many points throughout the work. The poem charts a return to life. The coming of spring, the opening of a window to let in the air, is a moment of rebirth, compared to the wonder of someone born blind, to whom sight has been miraculously restored.[105] The poet and her new husband are implicitly compared to Adam and Eve, seeing everything on earth for the first time.

Imagery of a new creation, of paradise regained, links 'Tvoi put'' with the end of Maiakovskii's 'Voina i mir' (War and the Universe) which pictures a world forever redeemed from war. Like Maiakovskii, Berggol'ts depicts herself as a crucified Christ figure. But Maiakovskii is resurrected to enjoy the new perfect world he has redeemed, while Berggol'ts remains in the thrall of Leningrad's icy past:

> ... я к твоему пригвождена виденью,
> я вмерзла
> в твой неповторимый лед.[106]

(I am nailed to your vision, I am frozen in your unique ice.)

Ice, the antithesis of fire, symbolises the power of memory. While fire is associated with spiritual transformation, ice only preserves and does not transfigure. Berggol'ts cannot transform the suffering of Leningrad through her own ordeal, but she can bear witness to it, preserving it from oblivion in her memory as ice preserves from decay. In 'Tvoi put'' (Your Road) Berggol'ts describes the body of a man, frozen on the street by the water from a burst water main, and left there, visible to all, until the thaw, while people come to draw water from close by. Like the poet he is imprisoned as a timeless witness:

> ... Я знаю все. Я тоже там была,
> я ту же воду жгучую брала
> на улице, меж темными домами,
> где человек, судьбы моей собрат,
> как мамонт, павший сто веков назад,
> лежал, затертый городскими льдами.[107]

(I know everything. I was there too, I took that burning water on the street, between dark houses, where a man, my brother in fate, like a mammoth that fell a hundred centuries ago, lay covered in the city's ice.)

The system of imagery Berggol'ts uses in 'Tvoi put'' leads to the inexorable conclusion that although the poet found spiritual renewal in the Leningrad siege, there can be no final redemption, no escape from memory, or from painful personal experience.

The transition from war to peace proved difficult for Berggol'ts, who, by the end of the war, had come to see her role as a poet to be that of preserving the memory of Leningrad's suffering. In her public role as dispenser of advice, however, she looked to the future and to the part women would have to play in bringing the city back to normal. Appealing to her neighbour Dar'ia Vlas'evna's maternal feelings, Berggol'ts made it clear that the end of the blockade did not mean that the women of Leningrad could consider their duty done:

... Дарья Власьевна, не мы, так кто же
отчий дом к победе приберет?
Кто ребятам-сиротам поможет,
юным вдовам слезы оботрет?

Это нам с тобой, хлебнувшим горя,
чьи-то души греть и утешать.
Нам, отдавшим все за этот город,—
поднимать его и украшать.

Нам, не позабыв о старых бедах,
сотни новых вынести забот,
чтоб сынов, когда придут с победой,
хлебом-солью встретить у ворот.[108]

(Dar'ia Vlas'evna, if not us, then who will prepare our fathers' house for victory? Who will help the orphan children, and dry the young widows' tears? It is for us, who have tasted grief, to warm and comfort others' souls. For us, who gave everything for this city, to raise it up again and decorate it. It is for us, who have not forgotten old misfortunes, to bear hundreds of new cares, so as to meet our sons, returning victorious, with bread and salt at the gates.)

Almost immediately after the end of the war the theme of reconstruction was introduced from above, and the poems on the subject were almost invariably about men returning from the front to rebuild industry or agriculture. Women's part in the process was considerable—in some villages there were no men left to return home—but barely acknowledged. Perhaps, as with the under-representation of women's contribution to the war itself, it was desirable to underplay the disasters which had made women's involvement necessary on such a large scale.

Of all the male poets, Aleksandr Tvardovskii showed himself to be the most aware of the need to recognise women's part in the war. On the one hand, he follows tradition by depicting women as creatures of intuition, grasping immediately the scale of the catastrophe of war, and bearing the memory of tragedy even when the war is over.[109] On the other hand, he depicts women in a more mundane guise, uprooted by war, struggling to look after their children and not lose hope. 'V puti' (On the Road) of 1943 describes a wayside meeting between a soldier and an exhausted mother with two children. It is a meeting of equals who offer each other mutual support. The fact that the woman feels immediately certain that the soldier will be able to understand her problems suggests that both face similar demands on their endurance:

... И так ей показалось,
Когда взглянула мать,
Что всю ее усталость,
Всю боль он мог понять.

(So it seemed to the mother when she looked at him, that he could understand all her tiredness and pain.)

Each tries to dispel the other's anxiety about their respective spouses. Women, she tells him, are coping well with the war:

... Черна на небе туча,
Страшна беда война.
Да бабья мощь живуча,
Тягуча, брат, она.
Не в шутку говорится—
На бабах все сейчас.
Осталось научиться
Рожать одним без вас.[110]

(The clouds in the sky are black, the war is a terrible misfortune. But women's strength is mighty and steadfast, brother. It's no joke when they say that everything depends on women now. We just have to learn how to produce babies without you.)

In a more serious vein, 'Dom u dorogi' (The House by the Roadside), begun in 1942 and completed in 1946, tells the story of a Russian woman who gives birth to a son in German captivity, conceived at a last meeting with her husband. Tvardovskii recognised that this war had touched many civilians just as much as the soldiers:

... Куда там было в старину,—
Все ныне по-иному:
Ушел хозяин на войну,
Война подходит к дому.[111]

(Whatever it was like in the old days, everything is different now: the man of the house has gone to war, war has come to his home.)

'Dom u dorogi' catalogues the suffering war brought to women who saw their husbands paraded as prisoners of war and their homes taken over by enemy soldiers. When poets did write on civilian life under enemy occupation, which was seldom, they show women joining the partisans, undergoing the ordeal of interrogation. The fate of Tvardovskii's heroine is more representative and less spectacular. His poem closes with a reversal of the usual end-of-war situation by showing a soldier waiting at home for his wife and children to return.

If the return of peace brought some, although slight, recognition of the ordeals and achievements of women civilians, the position of women who had served at the front was hardly spoken of at all.

Their homecomings are not recorded in verse. A recurring theme in the reminiscences of the female war veterans interviewed by Svetlana Aleksievich is the difficulties they faced returning to civilian life. Beyond the problems which faced men, such as their wounds and psychological traumas, there were those specifically linked to their position in society as women. Some found it difficult to revert to 'feminine' modes of dress and behaviour. Most commonly, however, these women concealed their past; rumours of front-line promiscuity threatened reputations which, as prospective wives, they could not afford to lose. There was little official recognition of their work, while former male soldiers found themselves honoured. War had not, as it turned out, been a liberation for most of these women. It had given them, for a while, considerable status in the eyes of the soldiers at the front, as they overcame prejudice and demonstrated their skill and endurance. In a wartime poem by Iuliia Drunina, a nurse whose work involved retrieving the wounded under fire, the differences between men and women seem to have vanished:

... Кажется рожь несжатая.
Шагают бойцы по ней.
Шагаем и мы, девчата,
Похожие на парней.[112]

(It seems that the rye is unharvested. Across it soldiers stride. We girls stride along too, looking like the lads.)

Drunina's war record was exemplary. Born in 1924, in 1941 she became an army nurse, was severely wounded, but returned to the army as a medical officer. Her experiences form a large part of her poetic repertoire. After the war, pride at her achievements mingled with their denial. The 'womanly' weaknesses were once more in demand:

... Я не привыкла, чтоб меня жалели,
Я тем гордилась, что среди огня
Мужчины в окровавленных шинелях
На помощь звали девушку—меня.

Но в этот вечер, мирный, зимний, белый,
Припоминать былое не хочу,
И женщиной, растерянной, несмелой,
Я припадаю к твоему плечу.[113]

(I am not used to being pitied, I was proud that, under fire, men in bloodied greatcoats called to me—a girl—for help. But on this peaceful white winter evening I do not want to remember the past, and like a distraught and timid woman I lean against your shoulder.)

Drunina partially echoes, then questions the words of Semen Gudzenko, which she quotes in a later poem in his memory:

Нас не нужно жалеть, ведь и мы никого б не жалели ...[114]

(There is no need to pity us, we wouldn't have pitied anyone.)

In Drunina's work the theme of war has persisted strongly; in many poems the memory of her youth at the front obliterates the present. This constant theme is linked with apologies:

> ... Я родом не из детства—из войны.
> Прости меня, в том нет моей вины.[115]

(My origins are not in childhood, but in war. Forgive me, it is not my fault.)

She writes of women of her generation who bear the burden, invisible to others, of their memories:

> ... Я опять о своем, невеселом—
> Едем с ярмарка, черт побери!..
> Привыкают ходить с валидолом
> Фронтовые подружки мои.
>
> А ведь это же, честное слово,
> Тяжелей, чем таскать автомат ...
> Мы не носим шинелей пудовых,
> Мы не носим военных наград.
>
> Но повсюду клубится за нами,
> Поколеньям другим не видна,
> Как мираж, как проклятье, как знамя,
> Мировая вторая война ...[116]

(I'm on about the same old dreary thing—to hell with the fair, let's go home!.. We are getting used to carrying tranquilisers, my friends from the front and I. And, to be honest, that is harder than dragging a heavy machine gun... We don't wear weighty greatcoats, we don't wear our military medals. But everywhere behind us swirls, invisible to other generations, like a mirage, a curse, a banner, the Second World War...)

Women's experience of the war, unrecognised by society, became a mirage, real only to those who knew it at first hand. Women war poets like Drunina and Berggol'ts have been haunted by the theme perhaps more than their male contemporaries because they witnessed a side of the war which has been ignored. The statue of the Leningrad housewife envisioned by Berggol'ts does not yet exist. The official Soviet memory of war has excluded women, so that while soldiers may still remember with gratitude the women who rescued them from the battlefield, Drunina asks: 'Where is the tomb of the Unknown Nurse?...'[117] Women war poets adopted the theme of memory in order to preserve their experience which is not acknowledged or commemorated elsewhere. Preserving the memory of the war and of the dead is a burden, but also a sacred duty taken on, it seems, very much in the spirit of self-sacrificial virtue identified with the feminine ideal.

NOTES

1 'Sred' ognia', foreword to Iuliia Drunina, *Ne byvaet liubvi neschastlivoi* (Moscow, 1977), p. 3. For an account of Soviet women's involvement in the armed forces, see John Erickson, 'Soviet Women at War', in *World War Two and the Soviet People*, edited by John and Carol Garrard (London, 1993), pp. 50–76.

2 'Muzhestvo', *Sochineniia*, 2 vols (Moscow, 1986), I, 199.

3 'Poema bez geroia', I, 276.

4 I, 297.

5 *U voiny ne zhenskoe litso* (Moscow, 1989).

6 Iuliia Drunina, 'Net, eto ne zasluga, a udacha ...', *Izbrannoe*, 2 vols (Moscow, 1989), I, 375.

7 Jean Bethke Elshtain, *Women and War* (Brighton, 1987), p. 4.

8 From conversations with Vadim Shefner, Leningrad, November 1989, and Margarita Aliger, Moscow, December 1989.

9 N. Popova, *Women in the Land of Socialism* (Moscow, 1949), p. 141.

10 'Khoziaika Leningrada', *Sobranie sochinenii*, 3 vols (Leningrad, 1988-90), II, 218–223 (p. 221).

11 'Mat'', *Pobeda: poety o podvige Leningrada v Velikoi Otechestvennoi voine* (Leningrad, 1970), p. 118.

12 'Lazur' tsvetok', *Sobranie sochinenii*, 6 vols (Moscow, 1971–74), I, 403–404. For poems on similar themes, see Georgii Suvorov, 'M.Romanovoi', *Zvezda*, 2 (1943), p. 21; Sergei Narovchatov, 'O golubom tsvetke', *Stikhotvoreniia i poemy* (Leningrad, 1985), p. 118; Iosif Utkin, 'Sestra', *Izbrannoe* (Moscow, 1975), p. 290.

13 Iakov Shvedov, 'Tvoe pis'mo', *Samoe zavetnoe: pesni, stikhi, poemy* (Moscow, 1976), p. 54.

14 'Ty pomnish', Alesha, dorogi Smolenshchiny ...', *Sobranie sochinenii*, 12 vols (Moscow, 1979–87), I, 88–89.

15 'Osen'', *Izbrannoe* (Moscow, 1988), p. 32.

16 'Mat'', *Leningrad*, 3 (1942), p. 7.

17 See Natalie Kononenko, 'Women as Performers of Oral Literature: a Re-examination of Epic and Lament', in *Women Writers in Russian Literature*, edited by Toby Clyman, Diana Greene (Westport, CT, 1994), pp. 17–28.

18 *Terrible Perfection: Women and Russian Literature* (Bloomington, Indiana, 1987), p. 2.

19 N. Prianishnikov, *Obraz russkoi patriotki v khudozhestvennoi literature* (Chkalov, 1943), p. 3.

20 O. Berggol'ts, 'Zapomini eti dni ...', II, 295; S. Kirsanov, 'Boets', *Sobranie sochinenii*, 4 vols (Moscow, 1974–76), I, 186–187.

21 'Devushka rodnaia', *Leningrad*, 5 (1942), inside front cover.

22 *U voiny ne zhenskoe litso*, p. 60.

23 E. Sheveleva, 'Nasha devushka', *Krasnaia zvezda*, 7 March 1943, p. 3.

24 Boris Paliichuk, 'Na bul'vare pyl'nom v Stalingrade ...', *Radi zhizni na zemle: Stikhotvoreniia o Velikoi Otechestvennoi voine* (Moscow, 1975), p. 240.

25 'Chelovecheskoe', I, 381; 'Epizod', I, 380—the latter was listed along with 'Rossii' and 'Kogo baiukala Rossiia' as evidence of his ideological mistakes in Central Committee documents (see Ch. 2).

26 'Stikhi o rodnykh', *Stikhi slagalis' na khodu* (Moscow, 1990), p. 56.

27 'Keta Braun', *Zvezda*, 2 (1943), p. 22.

28 'O zhenshchine', *Sobranie sochinenii*, 3 vols (Moscow, 1987–88), III, 307.

29 'O dvukh brat'iakh', III, 306; 'Dai ruku, mama ...', III, 335.

30 'Dym na zare', III, 321.

31 Semen Gudzenko, 'Prozhili dvadtsat' let ...', *Stikhi slagalis' na khodu*, p. 46. On friendship, see 'Ballada o druzhbe', pp. 78–81; 'Pervaia smert'', pp. 47–48; 'Tishina', pp. 61–62.

32 Jean Bethke Elshtain, *Women and War*, pp. 206–210.

33 D. S. Likhachev, *Chelovek v literature drevnei Rusi* (Moscow-Leningrad, 1958), pp. 75–79.

34 'Ol'ga', *Zvezda*, 1 (1943), p. 5.

35 Iurii Petrov, 'Pesnia o Lize Kozlovoi', *Lirika 40-kh godov* (Frunze, 1977), p. 484.

36 'Praskov'ia', *Sobranie sochinenii*, 4 vols (Moscow, 1965–66), I, 533.

37 See, for example: Aleksandr Tvardovskii, 'Nagrada', *Izbrannye proizvedeniia*, 3 vols (Moscow, 1990), I, 281; Nikolai Rylenkov, 'Soldatka', *Stikhotvoreniia i poemy*, 2 vols (Moscow, 1959), I, 336–346; also Mikhail Isakovskii, 'Partizanka', *Sobranie sochinenii*, 5 vols (Moscow, 1981–82), II, 58–61.

38 'Zoia', *Sobranie sochinenii*, 3 vols (Moscow, 1984–85), I, 309.

39 I, 311.

40 See note 17 above.

41 I, 312.

42 I, 318.

43 'Iz stikhov o Lize Chaikinoi', *Sobranie sochinenii*, 3 vols (Moscow, 1974–75), I, 422.

44 'Otkrytoe pis'mo', *Stikhi, p'esy, rasskazy* (Leningrad, 1949), pp. 140–144. The version in *Sobranie sochinenii*, I, 129–133, omits these two stanzas.

45 See note 18 above.

46 'Nemetskoi zhenshchine', I, 201.

47 A. I. Pavlovskii, *Stikh i serdtse* (Leningrad, 1962), p. 34.

48 'Blokadnyi dnevnik', *Aprel'*, 4 (1991), p. 135.

49 'Stikhi o sebe', II, 88–89.

50 'Ia budu segodnia s toboi govorit' ...', II, 21–22.

51 'Sestre', II, 14.

52 'Pervoe pis'mo na Kamu', II, 182.

53 'Ia govoriu s toboi pod svist snariadov ...', II, 13.

54 'Razgovor s sosedkoi', II, 30–31.

55 See note 10 above.

56 '29 ianvaria 1942', II, 33.

57 *Uzel* (Moscow–Leningrad, 1965).

58 'Net, ne iz knizhek nashikh skudnykh ...', I, 169–170.

59 'Vozvrashchenie', I, 166–167.

60 'Iz dnevnikov Ol'gi Berggol'ts', *Vremia i my*, 6, no.57 (1980), p. 300.

61 'My predchuvstvovali polykhan'e ...', II, 7.

62 'Pozdnei noch'iu, fevral'skoi, unyloi ...', I, 179.

63 'Fevral'skii dnevnik', II, 34.

64 II, 35–36.

65 II, 35.

66 Carin Tschöpl, *Die sowjetische Lyrik-Diskussion: Ol'ga Berggol'c' Leningrader Blockadedichtung als Paradigma* (München, 1988), p. 190.

67 See note 48 above for Berggol'ts's diary. The double life motif in appears twice in 'Fevral'skii dnevnik', II, 36; 39.

68 'Leningradskaia poema', II, 47.

69 Ibid.

70 'Ia nikogda ne vidala rukopashnyi ...', *Izbrannoe*, I, 17.

71 'Pamiati zashchitnikov', II, 69.

72 'Otryvok', II, 53–54.
73 'Tvoi put'', II, 84.
74 Ibid.
75 'Mne ne povedat' o moei utrate ...', II, 87.
76 See 'Izmena', II, 91; 'O, ne ogliadyvaites' nazad ...', II, 96.
77 'Velikie temy sovremennosti', II, 341.
78 'Put' k zrelosti', II, 357.
79 'Ot serdtsa k serdtsu. Tol'ko etot put' ...', II, 109.
80 'Preniia po dokladu N.Tikhonova', *Literaturnaia gazeta*, 26 May 1945, p. 2.
81 Inber, 'Razgovor o poezii', *Literatura i iskusstvo*, 28 August 1943, p. 2; Prokof'ev—see note 80 above.
82 'Put' k zrelosti', II, 357—358.
83 'Poemy Ol'gi Berggol'ts', *Oktiabr'*, 2 (1943), 111–113 (p. 112).
84 'Khoziaika Leningrada', II, 218–219.
85 'Leningradke', II, 222–223.
86 'Fevral'skii dnevnik', II, 37.
87 II, 36–37.
88 'Razgovor s sosedkoi', II, 31.
89 'Vtoroi razgovor s sosedkoi', II, 66–67.
90 'Fevral'skii dnevnik', II, 38.
91 See note 86 above.
92 'Pereklichka serdets', *Zvezda*, 5–6 (1945), 146–152 (p. 149).
93 'Leningradskaia poema', II, 45.
94 'Tvoi put'', II, 77.
95 *Dnevnye zvezdy* (Leningrad, 1960), p. 151.
96 'Fevral'skii dnevnik', II, 36.
97 'Leningradskaia osen'', II, 51–52.
98 II, 52.
99 'Leningradskaia poema', II, 43.
100 See note 88 above.
101 'Leningradskaia poema', II, 41.
102 'Tvoi put'', II, 75.
103 Ibid.
104 II, 74.
105 II, 80.
106 II, 84.
107 II, 77.
108 'Vtoroi razgovor s sosedkoi', II, 67.
109 See 'Voina, voina. Liuboi iz nas ...', I, 246; 'Pod vrazh'im tiazhkim kolesom ...', I, 247.
110 'V puti', I, 270–271.
111 'Dom u dorogi', II, 240.
112 'Kazhestsia, rozh' neszhataia ...', I, 15.
113 'Ia ne privykla, chtob menia zhaleli ...', I, 164.
114 'Moe pokolenie', *Stikhi slagalis' na khodu*, p. 128. This poem is discussed in Chapter Two. Drunina quotes Gudzenko's words in 'Na vechere pamiati Semena Gudzenko', I, 480.
115 'Ia rodom ne iz detstva, iz voiny ...', I, 376.
116 'Ia opiat' o svoem, neveselom ...', I, 305.
117 'I opiat' my podnimaem charki ...', I, 368.

CHAPTER SIX

'No-one is Forgotten and Nothing is Forgotten': The War in Post-war Poetry

Boris Slutskii pointed out that there was one section of Soviet society which had gained something from the war. While others had lost limbs, writers had acquired an assortment of things:

> ... Кто—память, кто—воспоминания.
> Кто—нервный смех, кто чуткий сон.
> Кто—просто список поминаний
> На сто, на пятьдесят персон.
> Кто—фабулы.
> Кто—просто темы.
> Кто—чувство долга и вины
> пред рано умершими,
>   теми
> невозвращенцами с войны.[1]

(Some—memory. Some—recollections. Some—nervous laughter, some light sleep. Some—just a list of the dead, fifty or a hundred persons. Some—plots. Some—just themes. Some—a sense of duty and guilt before those who died early, those who did not return from the war.)

Of this list, it is the final item, the awareness of the debt owed by the living to the dead, which receives most of Slutskii's attention in this poem. The memory of the war dead and the commemoration of the victory they had died to bring about is a constant theme in post-war poetry, one shared by the literary establishment and those on its margins, though each group naturally had its own interpretation of the theme. The war as a literary theme should not be considered as being the exclusive property either of conformist writers or of writers critical of the state. That the defeat of fascism had been a tremendous achievement, and that the people of the Soviet Union had undergone terrible suffering was beyond debate. Where differences of opinion might begin, however, was on questions such as whether the war had been won because of the Stalinist system, or in spite of it, what the implications of the war for the future might be, and what the place of individual memory was in relation to official large-scale commemoration.

The commemoration of the victory over fascism, and of the war dead, became an important part of Soviet official culture. The war was presented as a time when the people and the state were united in the unambiguously virtuous fight against Hitler's Germany. This wartime unity, it was implied, survived into the present as the people's vote of confidence in communist rule. From the mid-1960s onwards, war memorials were constructed on a massive scale. The construction of the last of these giant projects, the museum at Poklonnaia Gora in Moscow, took place in the early 1990s. By the time designs were being finalised for this project, however, the cultural monolith which had produced so many memorials was under attack in the name of *glasnost'*.[2]

Once the Soviet Union began to collapse, the commemoration of the war dead, whose sacrifice was, after all, presented as the system's justification, began to be questioned, particularly by those too young to have any memory of the war. During the Gorbachev years and in the initial post-Soviet period there was more concern with providing memorials to those who lost their lives in Stalin's prisons and labour camps. These could be seen as the innocent, forgotten victims of tyranny; the war dead, so heavily commemorated by the state, risked being identified with the state and rejected with it. Their historical achievement, the defeat of fascism, became less prominent than the fact that they had helped to establish Soviet domination of Eastern Europe. In the late 1980s people in the countries of Eastern Europe showed their discontent with communist rule by vandalising memorials to the Soviet soldiers who had liberated them from Nazi rule at the end of World War Two, while in Russia doubts were expressed about the necessity of taking the war beyond Soviet borders; the implication was that many had lost their lives to no purpose, or while serving the imperialistic aims of a totalitarian state. The aspirations of many who fought against Hitler, but also for greater freedom at home, were effectively blotted out by the passage of time, by the state-sponsored cult of the war dead, and by the decades of oppression which had in fact followed the victory. Questions raised about the nature and purpose of Soviet involvement in Afghanistan, proclaimed as the fulfilment of the Soviet army's international duty when it began in late 1979, also helped undermine the status of the victory of 1945. As it became public knowledge that the war in Afghanistan was marked by high casualties and little military success, the belief in war justified by a purpose other than self-defence began to be questioned.

This chapter will explore how poets dealt with the war after 1945, and also look at some of the poetry written about the war in Afghanistan. The three main topics that will be dealt with are the poetry of the immediate post-war period, the work that emerged after Stalin's death, and the poetry written by those who were children during the war years. The poetry already written during the war years shows that many poets used the war theme to extend the boundaries of what had previously been permissible. Although the theme was subsequently claimed for 'official', commemorative poetry, it still played a significant role in the work of poets who used their own wartime memories to make critical observations both about the war and contemporary reality, and to counteract the effect of the creation of mythologised, unrealistic portrayals of the war. While the state implied that the sacrifice of the dead somehow legitimised its oppressive authority, former soldiers tended to suggest that they owed it to the dead to maintain the values of honesty, independence and courage their generation had shown. Individual memory is offered as a counterweight to mass, anonymous commemoration.

While the war theme had already shown a potential for controversy in 1945 which emerged more strongly as a result of the post-Stalin Thaw, it enjoyed steady popularity in the work of mainstream poets who continued to celebrate its conventionally heroic and patriotic aspects through cultural Thaws, renewed oppression and *glasnost'*. The fortieth anniversary of the victory in 1985 was marked by a renewed wave of patriotic poetry, most of it showing an undimmed enthusiasm for things military in spite of the embarrassing and inconclusive campaign in Afghanistan, then in its sixth year. It was, of course, more palatable to contemplate victory in a war universally acknowledged as 'good' and necessary, than failure in Afghanistan. Until *glasnost'* came into effect, that war was surrounded by silence which has been compared to the silence surrounding the disasters of the winter war against Finland in 1939–40.

The dominant concerns of poetry in the immediate post-war poetry years are memory and commemoration, concepts that did not necessarily coincide. Broadly speaking, the remembrance of any war involves celebration of victory and mourning for the dead. Nevertheless, in the early post-war years, it seemed that even poems about the victory were not in great demand, and it was made clear that the latter theme was not acceptable. In view of the cult of commemoration that did come into being in later years, it is rather surprising that in 1945 Ol'ga Berggol'ts evidently felt that the tragedy of the Leningrad blockade might be in danger of being forgotten:

... И даже тем, кто всё хотел бы сгладить
в зеркальной, робкой памяти людей,

не дам забыть, как падал ленинградец
на желтый снег пустынных площадей ...[3]

(And even those who would like to smooth everything over in people's timid, mirror-like memories I shall not allow to forget how the Leningraders fell on the yellow snow of deserted squares.)

In the immediate aftermath of the war, poets, particularly those of the younger generation, most of whom were war veterans, were urged to leave behind the war theme and write about post-war reconstruction. This was a subject fraught with difficulties. The war had left the country drained of resources, devastated. There were countless widows, orphans, and invalids. Circumstances demanded that the true state of affairs could not be revealed, so that writing about post-war developments was, at best, a compromise, at worst a complete fabrication. The theme of reconstruction had been put forward by the authorities as a suitable theme for young poets, who were expected to set aside 'inappropriate' memories of war and look to the future. The young poets returning from the front seemed about to become established as successful Soviet writers. Some had already had work published in major literary journals. Aleksandr Mezhirov's long poem about life on the Leningrad front, 'Na rubezhakh' (On the Front Lines), appeared in *Znamia*, as did the poetry of Iuliia Drunina and Semen Gudzenko, in publication terms the most senior of his generation. They had a ready audience among their contemporaries, and were recognised as the generation who would guarantee Soviet poetry a flourishing future.[4]

Three of the young poets who had written about their experiences at the front, Aleksandr Iashin, Aleksei Nedogonov and Nikolai Gribachev, did contribute large-scale works which celebrated the renewal of collective farms, something which in actual fact was hardly a cause for celebration among the peasants, who had been allowed a little more latitude during the war as far as the use of land for private cultivation was concerned.[5] Others, like Semen Gudzenko, made efforts to adapt to post-war demands, yet the war theme kept returning in their work. There were tones in the poetry of returning front-line soldiers which ran counter to official triumphalism. They were equally aware of the war as a tragedy and as proof of their own worth. In 1945 they expressed hopes for, even demanded a future worthy of their achievements. The fact that the war theme harboured potential for controversy had been tacitly recognised by attempts late in the war to attribute the victory to the virtues of Soviet Man and the state which had produced him.

The war was a theme which the younger generation clearly associated with honesty and integrity, an implicit contrast with the present day. Other representatives of the same generation, those who had not survived to question what had been made of the victory they had fought for, were more acceptable to official opinion. Before Stalin's death, certain of the young poets who had died in the war began to be published posthumously. They were presented as an idealistic generation of Soviet citizens who had sacrificed themselves for their country. These, figures like Mikhail Kul'chitskii, Nikolai Maiorov and Pavel Kogan, could no longer cause the literary establishment any embarrassment by addressing awkward aspects of the war, and any unsuitable poems could be suppressed.

The literary establishment found it a little less simple to deal with the survivors. In spite of initial enthusiasm from readers and critics, the young poets were soon deprived of the metaphorical halo bestowed on them by their status as war veterans. Reservations had already been expressed in 1945 about their tendency to write on themes of grief for lost friends.[6] Discussion turned to virulent attack after the Central Committee resolution in August 1946 condemning the journals *Leningrad* and *Zvezda*, particularly for their publication of 'ideologically harmful' work by Zoshchenko and Akhmatova. This was a clear signal that the wartime relaxation of literary controls was finally over. The younger poets who had begun their careers in the less oppressive war years were attacked in a number of articles which had little to do with literary criticism, except, of course, in the socialist realist understanding of the term, which casts the critic as an ideological policeman. An article published in October 1946 denounced the younger generation of poets for writing about the war in tones of 'unrelieved sadness, occasionally turning into whining'. Lukonin and Gudzenko replied promptly with a defence of their generation's poetry, stating that to remember the dead was to remember the sacrifice they had made for the living. Older writers came to their defence, such as the dramatist Vsevolod Vishnevskii and the critic Anatolii Tarasenkov, who stated that the reader would not believe poets if they began to 'skip and tap their heels and pretend nothing had happened'. Simonov too joined the debate on the side of the younger generation.[7]

Even a brief acquaintance with the work of the young poets accused of being dolefully preoccupied with mourning for their dead friends shows this claim to lack foundation. It is much more likely that what had offended was their proclaimed sense of identity as the generation that had withstood a great trial and emerged with their values of wartime comradeship intact. Aleksandr Mezhirov's poem 'Druz'iam' (To my Friends) is dedicated to the memory of dead friends, but is a declaration of solidarity with them, rather than a simple expression of grief:

На утрату нижется утрата,
Но такого позабыть нельзя.
Вечно живы в памяти ребята,
Фронтовые, кровные друзья.
К одному один. И каждый—лучше,
Каждый заправила и вожак.
Прикажи—поразгоняют тучи,
Прикажи—грозою освежат.
Я люблю их больше всех на свете,
Потому что вместе нас прожег
Самый горький и суровый ветер—
Ветер отступающих дорог.

И еще за то, что наши роты
В петлях окружений, взаперти
Верили в крутые повороты,
Верили в обратные пути.[8]

(One loss follows another, but it is impossible to forget such things. In memory the boys are eternally alive, my closest friends-in-arms. One as good as another. And each one—better than the last, each one a boss and a leader. If you order them, they'll chase away the clouds, if you order them, they'll refresh the air with a storm. I love them more than anyone on earth, because together we were seared by the most bitter and severe wind, the wind of retreating roads. And also because our companies, trapped in the noose of encirclements, believed in sudden changes, believed in the way back.)

While on the one hand young poets were being accused of manifesting excessive sadness, it was also claimed that the war had not produced a 'lost generation' of writers such as the one created in Europe by the First World War. In actual fact there were signs that returning front-line soldiers did potentially constitute precisely such a group of outsiders, trying to cope with the trauma of war, with memories and experiences which had catapulted them from childhood to maturity, and at the same time beginning to realise that the hopes for greater freedom they had pinned on victory were not to be fulfilled. Mezhirov's 'Proshchai, oruzhie!' (Farewell to Arms!) is a bleak statement of the predicament of a former soldier who looks at himself from the outside, and sees someone who is neither dead nor alive, alienated from the world of nature, exhausted by war:

... Вот по берегу я иду.
В небе пасмурном, невысоком
Десять туч. Утопают в пруду,
Наливаясь тяжелым соком,
Сотни лилий. Красно. Закат.
Вот мужчина стоит без движенья
Или мальчик. Он из блокад,
Из окопов, из окружений.

Ты пришла на него смотреть.
А такого нету в помине.
Не от пули он принял смерть,
Не от голода, не на мине
Подорвался. А просто так.
Что ему красивые песни
О размахе лихих атак,—
Он от этого не воскреснет...

Он от голода умирал.
На подбитом танке сгорал.
Спал в болотной воде. И вот
Он не умер. Но не живет.

Он стоит посередине Века.
Одинешенек на земле.
Можно выстроить на золе
Новый дом. Но не человека.

Он дотла растрачен в бою.
Он не видит, не слышит, как
Тонут лилии и поют
Птицы, скрытые в ивняках.[9]

(Now I am walking along the bank. In the gloomy, lowering sky are ten clouds. Floating in the pond, swelling with heavy juices are hundreds of lilies. Redness. Sunset. There's a man standing motionless. Or a boy. He's from the blockades, from the trenches, from encirclements. You have come to look at him. But there is no such person. It was not from a bullet that he met his death, not from hunger, nor was he blown up on a mine. But simply because. What use to him are pretty songs about the grandeur of spirited attacks,—that won't bring him back from the dead. He was dying from hunger. He burned in a tank which was put out of action. He slept in marsh water. And, look, he did not die. But he is not alive. He stands in the middle of the Century. Completely alone on the earth. You can build a new house on ashes. But not a man. He was totally spent in battle. He does not see or hear the lilies floating in the pond or the singing birds hidden in the willow-beds.)

The conspicuous lack of reference in the poem to any victories suggests a polemical response to official demands for celebration and a positive attitude towards the future. Mezhirov's poem confronts criticism of 'depressing' poetry with a refusal to indulge in false optimism, and a call for the problems of adapting to post-war life to be recognised, not suppressed.

Unlike Mezhirov, Semen Gudzenko did make obvious attempts to meet official demands for new themes. In the late forties he travelled extensively across the country in search of new material, spending time with the army in its peacetime garrisons. But his memories of the war remained powerful. In 1947 Gudzenko said:

> I cannot switch automatically from one theme to another, especially from the theme which brought me to full-blooded artistic life. It is easier to switch from the production of tires or gas burners, but that cannot be a point of departure for taking on a

> different artistic theme. The life a poet leads, his environment and world view will inevitably colour work which will be written about an earlier phase of his existence. The difficult and magnificent past will find expression in a new theme, if the poet approaches one.[10]

If Gudzenko was, on the surface, loyal to post-war demands for thematic diversification, memories of war were never far away. Old wounds had undermined his health, and images of the war emerge with new strength in poems recounting long spells in hospital before his death in February 1953. Illness is another enemy to be overcome, while his wife once more waits for news of him, as for news of a missing soldier.[11]

In 1946 he made a programmatic statement which placed the war at the very centre of his identity as a poet. He recalls the reactions of an audience of peace-time soldiers in the Carpathians as he recited his poetry to them, and notes that their response rekindled the sense of comradeship he experienced at the front:

> Я в гарнизонном клубе за Карпатами
> читал об отступлении, читал
> о том, как над убитыми солдатами
> не ангел смерти, а комбат рыдал.
>
> И слушали меня, как только слушают
> друг друга люди взвода одного.
> И я почувствовал, как между душами
> сверкнула искра слова моего.
>
> У каждого поэта есть провинция.
> Она ему ошибки и грехи,
> все мелкие обиды и провинности
> прощает за правдивые стихи.
>
> И у меня есть тоже неизменная,
> на карту не внесенная, одна,
> суровая моя и откровенная,
> далекая провинция—
> Война ...[12]

(In a garrison club beyond the Carpathians I read poems about the retreat, read of how, over the bodies of dead soldiers sobbed not the angel of death, but the battalion commander. And they listened to me as only men of the same platoon listen to one another. And I sensed that the spark of my word flashed between our souls. Each poet has his province. It forgives his mistakes and sins, all petty insults and wrongdoings for truthful poems. I too have an unchanging one, not marked in the map, one, austere and honest, a distant province—War.)

In another poem of 1946 Gudzenko expresses his enthusiasm about facing the new challenges of post-war life. Yet even while he declares his intention to turn from 'war' to 'life' (a division Aleksandr Mezhirov refused to accept), his picture of the peaceful future is shaped by metaphors drawn from battle:

... Я лишь вспоминаю иногда
о фронтовых мытарствах,
о том, как брали города
в далеких государствах.

Да,
память—это хорошо,
но в двери жизнь стучится.
И для меня вопрос решен:
я к ней иду учиться!

Нам снова отступать нельзя,
в чехол не прячьте знамя,—
ведь с нами мертвые друзья
и раненые с нами.

И, как весенний громобой,
кровь громыхает в теле.
Мы снова в схватке лобовой,
опять в нелегком деле.[13]

(I do sometimes remember the hardships at the front, and how we took cities in far-off states. Yes, memory is a fine thing, but life is knocking at the door. And for me the problem is solved, and I go to life in order to learn! We must not retreat again, don't hide the banner in its case,—you know our dead friends are with us, and the wounded are with us. And, like a roll of thunder in spring, blood pulses in the body. We are once more in a frontal attack, once more in a difficult situation.)

Gudzenko's reference to battle here is ambiguous. Once the war is over, and the enemy defeated, who could there possibly be to fight against? The vast army of the living and the dead evoked by Gudzenko is the army which liberated the country from enemy occupation, men who fought for freedom and now seek a suitable reward. Other poems by Gudzenko of the period also speak of the present in terms of battle. One ends:

... Ничего, что нам из-под обстрела,
может, никогда не уходить.
Мы с тобой без подвига, без дела,
без тревоги не можем жить!

Будет всякое!
Конечно, будет всякое.
Наша жизнь—
всегда перед атакою![14]

(No matter that we might never escape from under fire. We cannot live without heroic feats, without action, without disturbances. There will be all sorts of things! Of course, there will be all sorts of things. Our life is always facing an attack!)

The last line echoes the title of Gudzenko's most famous wartime poem 'Pered atakoi' (Before the Attack)—this is not, we can assume, pure coincidence. Aleksandr Mezhirov, like Gudzenko, uses military metaphor to describe post-war existence, making it clear that it can be just as hostile and dangerous as the war. He protests against the separation of 'war' and 'life':

> О войне ни единого слова
> Не сказал, потому что она—
> Тот же мир, и едина основа
> И природа явлений одна.
>
> Пусть сочтут эти строки изменой
> И к моей приплюсуют вине:
> Стихотворцы обоймы военной
> Не писали стихов о войне.
>
> Всех в обойму военную втисни,
> Остриги под гребенку одну!
> Мы писали о жизни ...
> о жизни,
> Не делимой на мир и войну.
>
> И особых вопросов не стоим:
> Были мины в ничьей полосе
> И разведки, которые боем,
> Из которых вернулись не все.
>
> В мирной жизни такое же было:
> Тот же холод ничейной земли,
> По своим артиллерия била,
> Из разведки саперы ползли.[15]

(About war I said not a single word, because it is the same world, the foundation is the same and the nature of phenomena is the same. Let them consider these lines a betrayal and add them to my faults: the poets of the wartime brigade didn't write poems about the war. Squeeze everyone into the wartime brigade, trim them all by the same measure! We wrote about life ... about life, which is indivisible into peace and war. And there's no need of particular questions: there were mines in no man's land and reconnaissance parties, some in force, from which not all returned. In peaceful life it was just the same: the same cold of no man's land, the artillery fired on its own men, sappers crawled back from reconnaissance.)

Two further poems by Mezhirov reflect this programmatic statement. One is written from the perspective of a soldier under fire, the other from the point of view of a former soldier listening to the sounds of other people getting up for work. Both look to their memories of peace or war to maintain their spiritual balance. The soldier thinks of an unknown person going about his ordinary business somewhere else:

> Человек живет на белом свете.
> Где—не знаю. Суть совсем не в том.
> Я—лежу в пристрелянном кювете,
> Он—с мороза входит в теплый дом.[16]

(A man lives in the wide world. Where—I don't know. That isn't the point at all. I am lying under fire in a ditch, he is going in from the frost to a warm house.)

This image of life beyond the war helps the soldier withstand the cold and the fear which precede an attack. He does not envy the distant stranger, but calls him 'My distant reflection! My double!'. In the later poem, the former soldier remembers these comforting thoughts about his double:

> ... Мне вспоминалась песенка о том,
> Как человек живет на белом свете,
> Как он с мороза входит в теплый дом,
> А я лежу в пристрелянном кювете.
>
> Воспоминанье двигалось, виясь,
> Во тьме кромешной и при свете белом,
> Между Войной и Миром—грубо, в целом—
> Духовную налаживая связь.[17]

(I remembered a song about a man living in the wide world, going in from the frost to a warm house, and me, lying in a ditch under fire. The recollection moved, unfurling, in infernal darkness and white light, between War and Peace, roughly, on the whole, establishing a spiritual connection.)

The most tenacious connection between past and present, war and peace is, in the poetry Aleksandr Tvardovskii wrote between 1948 and 1951, the memory of those who lost their lives in the war. Tvardovskii, unlike the two poets discussed above, was already a fixture in the literary establishment who had won two Stalin prizes by the end of the war. His poetry on the war dead is not merely a ceremonial gesture of acknowledgement, however, but painful, personal and immediate. Tvardovskii retains a strong sense of the dead soldiers' presence and of his duty towards them. He cannot deny the memory of the suffering war had brought to the country either by looking ahead to a bright new future or back at the victory of 1945:

> ... Окаменела память,
> Крепка сама собой.
>
> Да будет камнем камень,
> Да будет болью боль.[18]

(Memory has turned to stone, it is strong in itself. Let stone be stone, let pain be pain.)

The tragedy of war had come increasingly to the fore in his wartime poetry, bringing new tones into *Vasilii Terkin*, replacing humour with serious contemplation of the destruction the war had left behind. The theme of tragedy sounded still more clearly in his narrative poem 'Dom u dorogi' (The House by the Roadside) begun in 1942 and completed in 1946, which deals with the rare theme of the plight of civilian families caught up in war. Tvardovskii linked victory and tragedy in the poem's first chapter:

> ... Так память горя велика,
> Глухая память боли.

Она не стишится, пока
Не выскажется вволю.

И в самый полдень торжества,
На праздник возрожденья
Она приходит, как вдова
Бойца, что пал в сраженье.

Как мать, что сына день за днем
Ждала с войны напрасно,
И позабыть еще о нем,
И не скорбеть всечасно
Не властна.

Пусть меня простят,
Что снова и до срока
Вернусь, товарищи, назад,
К той памяти жестокой.[19]

(So great is the memory of grief, the dull memory of pain. It will not ebb away until it has been expressed fully. And at the very zenith of triumph, at the festival of renaissance it arrives, like the widow of a soldier who fell in battle. Like a mother, who day after day waited in vain for her son to come back from the war, and who has as yet no power to forget him and not to grieve each hour. May I be forgiven, that once more and prematurely I return, comrades, to that cruel memory.)

'Dom u dorogi' won general official acceptance, and, indeed, brought Tvardovskii a third Stalin prize, the previous two being for his poem on collectivisation, 'Strana Murav'ia' (The Land of Murav'ia) and *Vasilii Terkin*. As an established figure Tvardovskii was not such an easy target for attacks as his younger colleagues. However, at a meeting of the Writers' Union presidium in 1946 some critics did express regret that 'Dom u dorogi' devoted much less space to rejoicing at victory than to remembering the people's suffering. Tvardovskii replied by reciting a new poem, 'Ia ubit podo Rzhevom...' (I was killed near Rzhev), in which one of the victims of the war spoke directly of his fate.[20] Semen Kirsanov uses the same device in his long poem 'Aleksandr Matrosov', written between 1944 and 1949, allowing the eponymous hero to speak from beyond the grave of his last moments before he threw himself onto an enemy machine-gun in an act of 'conscious' self-sacrifice. This poem will be discussed later as an example of the 'appropriation' of the war theme for official ends. Matrosov, presented as a rather one-dimensional character, realises that victory has been achieved, as his resuscitation coincides with the victory celebrations in Moscow.[21] Tvardovskii's unnamed soldier does not; his knowledge ends with his sudden death:

Я убит подо Ржевом
В безыменной болоте,
В пятой роте,

На левой,
При жестоком налете.

Я не слышал разрыва,
Я не видел той вспышки,—
Точно в пропасть с обрыва—
И ни дна, ни покрышки.

И во всем этом мире,
До конца его дней,
Ни петлички, ни лычки
С гимнастерки моей...

(I was killed near Rzhev in a nameless marsh, in company five, on the left, in a savage attack. I did not hear the explosion, I did not see the flash, as though falling from a precipice into an abyss—my luck ran out. And in the whole of this world, to the end of its days, there's not a loop or a fragment of my tunic left.)

The dead, says Tvardovskii's unnamed soldier, wish to know that their deaths in the name of victory have not been in vain. They too have their part in the happiness of the living:

... В нем, том счастье, бесспорная
Наша кровная часть,
Наша, смертью оборванная,
Вера, ненависть, страсть.

Наше все! Не слукавили
Мы в суровой борьбе,
Все отдав, не оставили
Ничего при себе...[22]

(Our vital part in that happiness is unquestioned, our belief, hatred, passion, cut short in death. Our all! We used no guile in the fierce fight, gave everything away, leaving nothing for ourselves.)

The dead soldier enjoins the living to continue serving their country with honour, and to mourn and rejoice within measure:

... Горевать—горделиво,
Не клонясь головой,
Ликовать—не хвастливо
В час победы самой.

И беречь ее свято,
Братья, счастье свое—
В память воина-брата,
Что погиб за нее.[23]

(To mourn—proudly, without bowing your head, to rejoice—not boastfully, in the hour of victory itself. And to preserve it sacredly, brothers, your happiness—in memory of your brother-soldier who died for it.)

Although the speaker here assures his listeners that he does not reproach the living or consider them in his debt, it is clear from a poem of 1948 that Tvardovskii did feel a strong obligation to the dead. He declares that all his words are written with them in mind.

Even though they cannot hear his poems, he reasons, they knew his work and took part of him with them when they died:

> ... Я ваш, друзья,—и я у вас в долгу,
> Как у живых,—я так же вам обязан.
> И если я, по слабости, солгу,
> Вступлю в тот след, который мне заказан,
>
> Скажу слова без прежней веры в них,
> То, не успев их выдать повсеместно,
> Еще не зная отклика живых,
> Я ваш укор услышу бессловесный.[24]

(I am yours, my friends, and I am in your debt as to the living, I am just as obliged to you. And if, out of weakness, I tell a lie, step onto the path which is forbidden to me, say words without my former belief in them, then, before I have had time to broadcast them far and wide, without knowing the response of the living, I shall hear your wordless reproach.)

The dead are cast by the poet in the role of his conscience, having precedence over the judgement of the living, by whom he presumably means the over-vigilant critics concerned with political orthodoxy more than with the truth. Tvardovskii's appointment as editor of *Novyi mir* in 1950 presented him with the opportunity to attempt to follow his conscience rather than other authorities; although he was removed in 1954, he returned four years later to make the journal a centre for permitted literary dissent.

In 1966 the theme of the war dead resurfaced yet again in a short poem by Tvardovskii, evoking tenacious feelings of guilt and responsibility:

> Я знаю, никакой моей вины
> В том, что другие не пришли с войны,
> В том, что они—кто старше, кто моложе—
> Остались там, и не о том же речь,
> Что я их мог, но не сумел сберечь,—
> Речь не о том, но все же, все же, все же ...[25]

(I know I am not at all to blame that others did not come back from the war, that they, some older, some younger, remained there, and there is no suggestion that I could have, but failed to save them,—no suggestion of that, but still, but still, but still...)

Tvardovskii's treatment of the theme of the war dead, with its concomitant appeals to conscience and a certain set of moral values, was unwelcome in the years of post-war repression, as it implied a contrast between the virtuous past and the corrupt present. This contrast lies at the centre of a later poem by Aleksandr Galich, in which the dead of 1943, hearing the sound of bugles and gunfire, believe that Russia is summoning them to serve her once more. In reality, what they hear is the sound of the Kremlin elite on a hunting expedition.[26] Writing about the war dead of former allies, now Cold

War enemies, was a much safer bet, as criticism was clearly directed elsewhere. Poems relating to the anti-Western campaign which followed the war, made a contrast between the Soviet Union, which had supposedly remained true to its wartime ideals, and the West which had betrayed them. The theme of the dead soldier in judgement on the society he had died to protect was transferred to the United States, as in Narovchatov's poem about an unknown American soldier rising from the grave to protest at his country's belligerent behaviour. Other variations of the Cold War theme appeared in appeals to American soldiers encountered on the Elbe not to let their government betray that moment of friendship, and in a poignant evocation of a homeless ex-soldier, veteran of Dunkirk and El-Alamein, whose family had perished in the Blitz, who was reduced to busking on the street while people in warm ministerial offices made plans for a new war.[27] All these themes, of course, could have applied just as well in the Soviet context, but that would have been unthinkable.

In a gesture recalling the recurring motif of death and resurrection in Maiakovskii's work, Semen Kirsanov's poem *Aleksandr Matrosov* brought back to life one of the celebrated heroes of the war, a young soldier who had reportedly thrown himself on an enemy machine gun. His act of self-sacrifice interrupted fire for long enough to allow his comrades to advance. The resurrected Matrosov in Kirsanov's poem is no baleful, reproachful presence, but a socialist realist hero, offering the readers his 'autohagiography', the background leading up to his final actions, then exhorting them to work towards the perfection of society. The poem shows some formal variety, marking the boundaries between the hero's present immortal state and the recreation of his inner state during his last moments alive. Matrosov's posthumous generalisations on the meaning of his life and death for his country, which contain direct political comment, are conveyed in iambic pentameter quatrains with regular rhyme. His more emotionally charged, immediate impressions are conveyed in short, broken lines, with internal rhyme and heavy emphasis on the end of the line. The contrast between the two is shown clearly at the point when, having pondered the reasons behind his deed, the hero relives the moments preceding his decision to sacrifice himself:

> ... Хочу, чтоб люди распознать сумели,
> встречая в мире светлую зарю,
> какой Матросов добивался цели!
> Добился ли?
> Добился!—говорю.
>
> И—недоволен я такой судьбою,

Что свел всю жизнь в один минутный бой?
Нет! Я хотел прикрыть народ собою—
и вот могу прикрыть народ собой.

Очень
        белый снег,
в очи—
        белый свет,
снег—
        с бровей и с век,
сзади—
        белый след.
Разве
        я не могу
лечь,
        застыть на снегу,
разве
        не право мое—
яма—
        врыться в нее?
Трудно
        к пулям ползти,
но я не сойду
        с полпути,
не оброню слезу,
в сторону
        не отползу.[28]

(I want people to be able to see, as they greet the bright dawn in the world, what a great aim Matrosov pursued! Did he achieve it? He did!—I say. And am I dissatisfied with the fate that reduced a whole life to a minute-long fight? No! I wanted to shield the people with my body—and now I can shield them with my body. Very white snow, in my eyes—white light, snow off my brows and eyelids, behind—a white track. Surely I can lie down, lie still in the snow, surely I have that right—a hole—to dig myself in? It is hard to crawl towards bullets, but I won't change course half-way, won't shed a tear, won't crawl off to one side.)

The text is interspersed with passages in prose that recall Kirsanov's rhyming prose in his 'Zavetnye slova Fomy Smyslova' (Foma Smyslov's Words of Wisdom); the language is colloquial, the tone down-to-earth. Matrosov emerges as a figure who combines simplicity, patriotic enthusiasm and wisdom, a socialist realist hero who has gained the superior insight available through the transforming ordeal of heroic self-sacrifice. During the war there were hundreds of cases of direct emulations of Matrosov's act. It was part of the myth built up round Matrosov that he had been an orphan brought up in a children's home; true to the conventions of the day, the poem emphasises that he found a family in the state that brought him up. Matrosov is confident that other nations will find their home in the Soviet family, just as he did. The fact that he served in a penal battalion after a spell in a corrective labour colony was merely hinted at by Kirsanov.[29] Towards the end of the poem, Matrosov appears as a colossal figure, a sentry on the frontier warning of foreign plots to start a new war and proclaiming the Soviet people's strength and determination to build a better future. The posthumous appearance of Kirsanov's war hero has none of the appeals to conscience made by Tvardovskii's soldier who died at the battle for Rzhev. Instead, he is recruited as a spokesman for the vision of the post-war world which moves relentlessly towards perfection.

While the dead of the younger generation were liable to be represented as heroic idealists loyal to the Soviet state, some of their surviving contemporaries chose to address awkward questions about the war and its aftermath. For many of them, however, the war remained a touchstone of genuine values, a contrast to the present. Boris Slutskii, a close friend of the poet Mikhail Kul'chitskii who died at the front, was unable to publish his work during the post-war phase of compulsory optimism. Slutskii describes the grim realities of life in the post-war Soviet Union in characteristically terse, unadorned language. In one poem he questions promises of freedom and plenty, remembering early post-war years when:

> ... легче было
> победить, чем пообедать.

(It was easier to win the war than to find something to eat.)

The Criminal Code proved a fierce instrument of social control:

> ... На его страницах смерть встречалась
> много чаще, чем в балладах.

(On its pages you encountered death much more often than in ballads.)

Having fought for a better future, returning soldiers found that the oppressive state had been reinforced by the victory they themselves had won; many of their contemporaries had been welcomed home from German prisoner of war camps by being sent to the Gulag. The ironic predicament of the oppressed liberators did not escape Slutskii's attention:

> ... Странная была свобода!
> взламывали тюрьмы за границей
> и взрывали. Из обломков
> строили отечественные тюрьмы.[30]

(It was a strange freedom! We smashed prisons abroad and blew them up. From the fragments we built prisons back home.)

The generation who had been hailed as the liberators of Europe came home to a society no longer united by the need to devote all energies to the war effort. Certain tensions had been created by the fact that while the majority of men had served at the front, in danger, others had found safe posts for themselves at home, and were now unwilling to give up their jobs to outsiders. Slutskii wrote, with typical conciseness:

Когда мы вернулись с войны,
я понял, что мы не нужны.

Захлебываясь от ностальгии,
от несовершенной вины,
я понял: иные, другие,
совсем не такие нужны.

Господствовала прямота,
и вскользь сообщалось людям,
что заняты ваши места
и освобождать их не будем,

а звания ваши, и чин,
и все ордена, и медали,
конечно, за дело вам дали ...[31]

(When we came back from the war, I realised that we weren't needed. Choking from nostalgia, from a guilt complex, I realised that other men, different ones, men completely unlike us were needed. Directness reigned, and in passing people were informed that your places are occupied, and we are not going to give them up, though your titles and ranks, and all your decorations and medals were, of course, given you for your actions ...)

Elsewhere, however, he admitted that those who had stayed in the rear had not enjoyed an easy life either. In 'Skandal sorok shestogo goda' (Scandal of Nineteen Forty-six) an angry ex-soldier confronts a civilian factory worker:

—Где же вы были в годы войны?
Что же вы делали в эти годы?
Как вы использовали бронь и льготы,
ах, вы, сукины сыны!

В годы войны, когда в деревнях
ни одного мужика не осталось,
как вам елось, пилось, питалось?
Как вы использовали свой верняк?

В годы войны, когда отпусков
фронтовикам не полагалось,
вы входили без пропусков
в женскую жалость, боль и усталость.

В годы войны, а тех годов
было, без небольшого, четыре,
что же вы делали в теплой квартире?
Всех вас передушить готов!

—Наша квартира была холодна.
Правда, мы там никогда не бывали.
Мы по цехам у станков ночевали.
Дорого нам доставалась война.[32]

(Where were you in the war years? What did you do in those years? How you used your exemption and your privileges, you sons of bitches! In the war years, when there wasn't a single man left in the villages, how did you eat, drink, feed yourselves? How did you use your safe bet? In the war years when leave was not allowed for front-line soldiers, you entered without passes into women's pity, pain and fatigue. In the war years, and there were very nearly four of them, what did you do in your warm flat? I could strangle the lot of you!—Our flat was cold. Actually, we were never there. We spent the nights in the factories by our machines. The war cost us dear.)

There are distinct notes of post-war disillusion in Margarita Aliger's poem of 1946, 'Bol'shie ozhidania' (Great Expectations). The poet recalls reading Dickens' novel in late 1941, while Moscow was under threat and Leningrad besieged. Then she dreamed of a better future, but victory has turned out to be less thrilling in reality than in anticipation:

... Отрадны борьбы и лишенья
пути, устремленного к ней.
И даже большие свершенья
больших ожиданий бледней.[33]

(Joyful are the roads of struggle and privation which lead to victory. And even great achievements are paler than great expectations.)

There are no reasons given for Aliger's disillusion, but it is clear that sentiments of this kind, seeing the war as a time of great potential which has gone to waste, rather than as a triumphant prelude to the still greater triumphs of post-war reconstruction, gave the literary establishment a cue to encourage a move away from the war theme. Even in 1970, however, looking back at the war, Sergei Narovchatov displays a similar veiled disillusion with the events which followed the great expectations created by the victory. Narovchatov remembers himself in 1945, standing in a muddy trench, and realises with hindsight that this was the high point of his life. His extravagant hopes for life after the victory have turned out to be mistaken:

... Ведь как-никак мы в сорок пятом,
Победа—вот она! Видна!
Выходит срок служить солдатам,
А лишь окончится война,

Тогда—то, главное, случится!..
И мне, мальчишке, невдомек,
Что ничего не приключится,
Чего я б лучше делать смог.

Что ни главнее, ни важнее
Я не увижу в сотни лет,
Чем эта мокрая траншея,
Чем этот серенький рассвет.[34]

(So here we are in forty-five, victory—there it is! In sight! The soldier's tour of duty almost over, as soon as the war ends, and then the most important things will happen!.. And I, a boy, did not know that nothing would occur that I could do better. That I would see nothing more important or significant for hundreds of years than this damp trench, this grey dawn.)

Ol'ga Berggol'ts, who, like Gudzenko, achieved a peak of creativity in the war years, had her own 'distant province' in the Leningrad blockade. Her memories of the war form a zone of absolute truth and integrity, a measure which reveals the shortcomings of the present. Writing in 1946, Berggol'ts describes how her poetry came to her during the war 'in naked and incorruptible purity', but how the genuine glories of the past are now defaced by 'the heroes of residence permits and standard references'.[35] Berggol'ts was among those who, in the post-Stalin Thaw of 1954, spoke out for greater honesty in literature; her association of blockade memories with the truth persisted after the end of the Khrushchev Thaw in 1963. In a poem of 1964, Berggol'ts retraces her steps through the scenes of her blockade existence, searching for a sense of integrity to counter the falseness of the present:

... В том году,
в том бреду,
в том чаду,
в том, уже первобытном, льду
я тебя, мое сердце, найду,
может быть, себе на беду.
Но такое,
в том льду,
в том огне,
ты всего мне сейчас нужней.
Чтоб сгорала мгновенно ложь—
вдруг осмелится подойти,—
чтобы трусость бросало в дрожь,
в леденящую—не пройдешь!—
если встанет на пути.[36]

(In that year, in that delirium, in that miasma, in that already primeval ice I shall find you, my heart, perhaps to my cost. But there is something in that ice, in that fire, I need you most of all now. To make lies burn up instantly—should they dare to come near,—to make cowardice tremble with icy shudders—you shall not pass!—if you stand in the way.)

The contrast between official hypocrisy of the post-war world and the genuine values of wartime is also made by Berggol'ts in a poem written in 1948–49, but first published in the Soviet Union in 1987. Here Berggol'ts describes her feelings of shame and sorrow at her own behaviour in official meetings, and her relief in honest conversation with two war invalids over a glass of vodka. The war provides them with a metaphor for the state's unjust treatment of its people:

... Мы припомнили между собою,
старый пепел в сердце шевеля:
штрафники идут в разведку боем—
прямо через минные поля!..
Кто-нибудь вернется награжденный,
остальные лягут здесь—тихи,
искупая кровью забубенной
все свои небывшие грехи!
И соображая еле-еле,
я сказала в гневе, во хмелю:
«Как мне наши праведники надоели,
как я наших грешников люблю!»[37]

(We remembered amongst ourselves, stirring the old ashes in our hearts: men in punishment battalions go out on reconnaissance straight across mine fields!.. Some will return with a medal, the rest will fall here—quiet, atoning with their reckless blood for all their nonexistent sins! And, barely knowing what I was saying, I spoke in anger, in drunkenness: "How fed up I am of our righteous men, how I love our sinners!")

Like Berggol'ts, Aleksandr Mezhirov used metaphors drawn from battle to describe the state's war against its own people. A supposedly real incident of soldiers being fired on by their own artillery can be read as a thinly disguised reference to the purges of the thirties and forties, as well the result of the inevitable confusion of warfare.[38]

The destruction of old certainties after Khrushchev's 1956 Secret Speech was unsettling for many who had fought under the slogan 'For the Motherland, for Stalin!'. Aleksandr Mezhirov, author of the super-patriotic 'Kommunisty, vpered!' (Communists, Forward!) written some time in the 1940s—Mezhirov makes a point of publishing his poems without dates—later looked back on his generation's former beliefs with some irony:

Что ты плачешь, старая развалина,—
Где она, священная твоя
Вера в революцию и в Сталина,
В классовую сущность бытия...

Вдохновлялись сталинскими планами,
Устремлялись в сталинскую высь,
Были мы с тобой однополчанами,
Сталинскому знамени клялись.

Шли, сопровождаемые взрывами,
По своей и по чужой вине.
О, какими были б мы счастливыми,
Если б нас убили на войне.[39]

(What are you crying for, you old ruin,—where is it, your sacred faith in the revolution and in Stalin, in the class essence of existence ... We were inspired by Stalin's plans, we strove upwards towards Stalin's heights, we were both in the same regiment, we swore an oath to Stalin's banner. We went, accompanied by explosions, the fault of ourselves and others. O, how happy we would have been if we had been killed in the war!)

During the Thaw which followed the Twentieth Party Congress of 1956, it became possible to discuss more openly those aspects of the war which linked it indelibly with Stalinist oppression. Mikhail Dudin wrote in 1957 of the soldiers' blindness to what was happening at home:

... Я видел впереди Берлин
Через блокадный хлеб.
Как многие,—не я один—
Был на затылок слеп.[40]

(I saw Berlin ahead, through blockade bread. Like many, not I alone, I was blind at the back of my head.)

While there was, from the early 1950s, a body of published poetry on themes of resistance and integrity written in German concentration camps by Soviet prisoners, the literature and culture of domestic labour camps was still unknown. While the war theme was acceptable in the work of Soviet prisoners of war—their 'crime' of being taken prisoner was, apparently, redeemed by their martyrdom in German hands—it did not yet, in the early 1950s, redeem the work of poets such as Boris Ruch'ev, whose patriotism was impeccable, but who had written his war poetry in a Soviet camp.[41] It is more understandable that Solzhenitsyn's 'Prusskie nochi' (Prussian Nights), a narrative poem composed, not written, in a labour camp in 1950, had even less chance of becoming known to the outside world, describing as it does the ferocious advance of Soviet hordes through East Prussia in 1944, indulging in wanton murder, rape, looting and senseless destruction.[42]

The army's unjust treatment of its own soldiers is dealt with in Boris Slutskii's poetry. As a political officer, one aspect of whose job it was to send people to the camps or punishment battalions for their misdemeanours, he was well aware of his part in the machine of persecution. Slutskii considers the dilemmas he confronted, as in a poem about an encounter with a soldier who had wounded himself to escape combat.[43] The burden of judging others is something Slutskii found distasteful in the extreme:

Я судил людей и знаю точно,
что судить людей совсем не сложно,—
только погодя бывает тошно,
если вспомнишь как-нибудь оплошно.
Кто они, мои четыре пуда
мяса, чтоб судить чужое мясо?
Больше никого судить не буду.
Хорошо быть не вождем, а массой.[44]

(I judged people and know perfectly well that it is not at all complicated to judge people,—only you feel wretched afterwards, if you remember it somehow by mistake. What are they, my four poods of meat, to judge another's meat? I shall not judge people any more. It is good to be not the leader, but the masses.)

Here and elsewhere Slutskii echoes the futurist Velimir Khlebnikov's words:

> Мне гораздо приятнее
> Смотреть на звезды,
> Чем подписывать
> Смертный приговор ...
> Вот почему я никогда,
> Нет, никогда не буду Правителем![45]

(I find it much more pleasant to look at the stars than to sign a death sentence ... That is why I shall never, never be a Ruler!)

In a poem of the late 1960s or early 1970s Slutskii recalls the execution of a soldier who, as sole survivor of a German attack, was suspected of the intention to betray his country.[46] In another poem, 'Govorit Foma' (Foma Speaks), a Soviet soldier equates Stalinism with fascism. German prisoners of war declared they did not believe in Hitler or in Goebbels, that the whole world was propaganda. Foma agrees with them. Books tell him that horses eat hay and oats, but he remembers that in the Ukraine in 1933 horses ate straw, thatch from roofs, and then died.[47] The association of truth and war poetry, which began with poets giving a truthful picture of the war itself, extends to the truth about other areas of the Soviet past.

Among the poems Bulat Okudzhava wrote in the late 1950s, many of which he set to music and performed, the war is a recurring theme, and one on which Okudzhava wrote from personal experience, having volunteered for army service in 1942. His poems emphasise the fragility of human beings caught up in war, from the young recruit on his first day at the front, who is worried about how he will cope with battle, to the experienced soldier who has learned not to be over-confident.[48] In other poems of this period Okudzhava writes elegiacally of those who did not return from the front.[49] Although he refrains from overt political comment in his poetry, there are satirical overtones in his song of the paper soldier who strides bravely into the flames.[50] In elegiac tones Okudzhava writes of the young men who leave for the front and an uncertain future:

> Вы слышите: грохочут сапоги,
> и птицы ошалелые летят,
> и женщины глядят из-под руки?
> Вы поняли, куда они глядят?
>
> Вы слышите: грохочет барабан?
> Солдат, прощайся с ней, прощайся с ней ...
> Уходит взвод в туман-туман-туман ...
> А прошлое ясней-ясней-ясней.

А где же наше мужество, солдат,
когда мы возвращаемся назад?
Его, наверно, женщины крадут
и, как птенца, за пазуху кладут.

А где же наши женщины, дружок,
когда вступаем мы на свой порог?
Они встречают нас и вводят в дом,
но в нашем доме пахнет воровством.

А мы рукой на прошлое: вранье!
А мы с надеждой в будущее: свет!
А по полям жиреет воронье,
а по пятам война грохочет вслед.

И снова переулком—сапоги,
и птицы ошалелые летят,
и женщины глядят из-под руки...
В затылки наши круглые глядят.[51]

(Do you hear: boots are clattering, crazy birds are flying, and women are looking from beneath their hands? Have you realised what they are looking at? Do you hear: the drums are beating? Soldier, say goodbye to her, goodbye to her... The platoon goes off into the mist, the mist, the mist ... But the past is clearer, clearer, clearer. And where is our courage, soldier, when we come back? Probably the women will steal it and, like a fledgling, hide it in their bosom. But where are our women, my friend, when we cross over the threshold? They greet us and lead us into the house, but the house smells of theft. We wave a hand at the past—lies! And with hope we look to the future—light! But on the fields the carrion crows grow fat, and at our heels the war rumbles behind us. And once more along the lane—boots, and crazy birds are flying, and women are looking from beneath their hands ... They are looking at the round backs of our heads.)

While poets who, like Tvardovskii, were closely associated with the Khrushchev Thaw, questioned past and present in their work associated with the war theme, other writers, memoirists, and historians persisted in giving an edited version of the war as an undiluted national triumph. Slutskii's response to official falsifications of this kind can be found in his poem 'Shestoe nebo' (The Sixth Heaven):

... Седьмое небо—хоры совершенств.
Шестое небо—это то, что надо.
И если то, что надо, совершил,
То большего вершить тебе не надо ...

Шестое небо—это взят Берлин.
Конец войне, томительной и длинной.
Седьмое небо—это свод былин
Официальных
о взятии Берлина.[52]

(The Seventh Heaven is choirs of perfection. The sixth heaven is just what is required. And if you have done all that is required, then there is no need for you to achieve anything more ... The Sixth Heaven—Berlin is taken. The end of war, long and wearisome. The Seventh Heaven—a cycle of official legends about the taking of Berlin.)

Official 'legends' of the war have been challenged repeatedly in the work of poets who have described aspects of the war not normally included in the canon. The fact that the Jews were the first, and most numerous, victims of Nazi occupiers' persecution received minimal attention in a post-war state which was planning its own anti-semitic excesses. Although it was acceptable in 1945, and perhaps unavoidable, bearing in mind the numbers of Soviet witnesses, to report the horrors of the Holocaust, in the following year Pavel Antokol'skii's poem 'Ne vechnaia pamiat'' (Not Eternal Memory) on the same theme provoked official wrath. Semen Gudzenko's 'Ballada o rvakh' (Ballad about the Ditches) of 1948 speaks of racial theories, and imagines himself among those buried in ditches. Evgenii Evtushenko's poem 'Babii Iar' of 1961 revived the theme with a fervent attack on anti-semitism, and a condemnation of the fact that the massacre of the Jews of Kiev had not been properly commemorated.[53] Even now, the memorials to the Jewish victims of the war are few in number and extremely modest compared with those to Soviet soldiers.

The plight of the war widows is another theme which has appeared rarely in poetry, unlike the theme of the soldier who died in battle. Boris Slutskii's poem 'Vot vam selo obyknovennoe' (Here's an Ordinary Village) evokes the 'bitter cheerfulness' of the women who restored the village to normality after the war, but never regained their own happiness:

> ... Она войну такую выиграла!
> Поставила хозяйство на ноги!
> Но как трава на солнце,
> выгорело
> То счастье, что не встанет наново.[54]

(She won such a war! She put the household back on its feet! But like grass in the sun, happiness burned up, never to rise again.)

These and other 'awkward' themes have been dealt with most fully in works of prose. War novels proliferated throughout the 1960s, 1970s and 1980s, and cover the entire spectrum of ideology and subject matter, from the unconditionally loyalist to the uncompromisingly critical. The epics telling the story of a glorious campaign which critics had predicted in 1945 did not appear in the form of poetry, but in prose and subsequently in film. War novels have provided writers with a theme which was officially acceptable, within certain limits, and which allowed more scope for moral discussion against the background of life and death than descriptions of present-day life. Poetry has been more successful in capturing specific memories and moments of the war, rather than with creating a panoramic view of the war as a whole. Attempts at poetic evocations of the war on a grand scale, like Evgenii Dolmatovskii's 'Dobrovol'tsy' (The Volunteers), which relates the life-story of several young volunteers who built the Moscow metro and fought for their country, cannot be described as a modern *Iliad*, as it lacks depth and is stylistically monotonous, a recitation of standard motifs.[55]

As the official legends of the war became fixed in Soviet culture, Iurii Belash, a war veteran, started to write his poems which show a different kind of war, at times horrific, chaotic, anything but heroic. Belash had been trained as a literary critic, but began writing poetry in 1967. He shows life at the front in all its most unappealing aspects, making no attempt to poeticise the soldier's job of killing, and criticising the squander of human life by incompetent commanders.[56] His poems are an often polemical demand for honesty in the depiction of the war, for example, 'Naturalizm' (Naturalism):

> Ему живот осколком распороло ...
> И бледный, с крупным потом на лице,
> он грязными, дрожавшими руками
> сгребал с землею рваные кишки.
>
> Я помогал ему,—хотя из состраданья
> его мне нужно было застрелить,—
> и лишь просил: «С землею-то, с землею,
> зачем же ты с землею их гребешь?..»
>
> И не было ни жутко, ни противно.
> И не кривил я оскорблено губ:
> товарищ мой был безнадежно ранен,—
> и я обязан был ему помочь ...
>
> Не ведал только я, что через годы,
> когда об этом честно напишу,—
> мне скажут те, кто пороху не нюхал:
> «Но это же прямой натурализм!..»
>
> И станут—утомительно и нудно—
> учить меня, как должен я писать,—
> а у меня всё будет пред глазами
> товарищ мой кишки свои сгребать.[57]

(His belly had been ripped apart by a shell fragment ... And, pale, with large beads of sweat on his face, with dirty, trembling hands he scraped his torn guts off the ground. I helped him—though I should have shot him out of mercy,—and I only asked: 'Why are you scraping them up with earth, with earth on them?..' And it was neither frightening nor disgusting. And I did not curl my lip disdainfully: my comrade was hopelessly wounded,—and I was obliged to help him ... But I did not know that years later, when I would write about this honestly,—I would be told by men who had never smelt gunpowder: 'But that's pure naturalism!..' And they would start—tiresomely and tediously—to teach me how to write,—but before my eyes my comrade would still be scraping up his guts.)

A different angle on the war theme is evident in the work of poets who experienced the war as children, whose impressions were, naturally, limited but intense. Evgenii Evtushenko describes his feelings of fatalism when dancing at weddings which immediately preceded the new husband's departure for the front:

... Невесте горько плачется,
стоят в слезах друзья.
Мне страшно.
Мне не пляшется,
Но не плясать—
нельзя.[58]

(The bride is weeping bitterly, the friends stand in tears. I'm afraid. I don't feel like dancing, but dance I must.)

Childhood memories of the end of the war are concentrated in a poem by Iunna Morits, recreating the impressions of her eight-year-old self returning from the bath-house with her mother:

В развалинах мерцает огонек,
Там кто-то жив, зажав огонь зубами.
И нет войны, и мы идем из бани,
И мир пригож, и путь мой так далек!..
И пахнет от меня на три версты
Живым куском хозяйственного мыла,
И чистая над нами реет сила—
Фланель чиста, и волосы чисты.
И я одета в чистый балахон
И рядом с чистой матерью ступаю.
И на ходу почти что засыпаю,
И звон трамвая серебрит мой сон.
И серебрится банный узелок
С тряпьем. И серебрится мирозданье.
И нет войны, и мы идем из бани,
Мне восемь лет, и путь мой так далек!
И мы в трамвай не сядем ни за что—
Ведь после бани мы опять не вшивы!
И мир пригож, и все на свете живы,
И проживут теперь уж лет по сто!
И мир пригож, и путь мой так далек,
И бедным быть—для жизни не опасно,
И, господи, как страшно и прекрасно
В развалинах мерцает огонек.[59]

(In the ruins a small light flickers, there is someone alive there, a fire clenched between his teeth. And there is no war, and we are coming back from the bath-house, and the world is fine, and my journey is so long!.. And you can smell the scent of a real piece of laundry soap on me from miles away, and a clean force wreathes above us—the flannel is clean and our hair is clean. And I am wearing a clean overall, and am walking beside my clean mother. And I am almost falling asleep as I walk, and the tram's ringing bell sprinkles silver in my dream. And the bath-house bundle of clothes sparkles silver. And the universe sparkles silver. And there is no war, and we are coming back from the bath-house, I am eight years old, and my journey is so long! And we won't get into the tram for anything—after the bath we have no lice again! And the world is fine, and everyone in the world is alive, and will live now for a hundred years! And the world is fine, and my journey is so long, and being poor is not a threat to life, and, Lord, how terribly and beautifully the small light in the ruins flickers.)

The repetition of certain words and phrases, the simplicity of the language and the repeated 'and ... and ...' at the beginning of lines all convey the point of view of a small, sleepy child for whom the end of the war and the visit to the bath-house are fused. The world is cleansed of war as she is of lice. With the exclamation at the end of the poem, however, an adult perspective is introduced, putting into words the contradictory feelings evoked by the light shining from within the ruins.

Evocations of childish naivety are rare in the work of Iurii Voronov, who began writing poetry as a child in the Leningrad blockade. His work describes the effect of the blockade on those who were made prematurely old by experiences which do not belong to the conventional image of childhood:

... В блокадных днях
Мы так и не узнали:
Меж юностью и детством
Где черта?..
Нам в сорок третьем
Выдали медали.
И только в сорок пятом—
Паспорта.

И в этом нет беды...
Но взрослым людям,
Уже прожившим многие года,
Вдруг страшно оттого,
Что мы не будем
Ни старше, ни взрослее,
Чем тогда ...[60]

(In the blockade days we never did find out where the line was between youth and childhood ... In forty-three we were given medals. And only in forty-five—passports. And there is nothing wrong with that ... But grown ups, who had already lived for many years, were suddenly afraid that we would never be older or more grown up than we were then ...)

The war found its way into the work of poets too young to have much of a recollection of its events. However, the trauma to which the whole country was subjected left its traces. For Iurii Kuznetsov, born in February 1941, the war meant the death of his father, and this personal tragedy provided him with an insight into a national tragedy. Many of Kuznetsov's poems are concerned with the father he could not remember except as an absent figure, a void. In one poem he accuses his father of having failed to provide happiness by leaving his wife and child to cope with life alone.[61] In later poems there are visions of his father's return, summoned either by his widow's yearning, or by his son in a quest reminiscent of a fairy tale in which his father returns as a presence weighing down his son's shadow, along with the four hundred others who were buried with him. In 'Vozvrashchenie' (The Return), written in 1972, his father's return is perceived as uncanny, possibly threatening:

> Шел отец, шел отец невредим
> Через минное поле.
> Превратился в клубящийся дым—
> Ни могилы, ни боли.
>
> Мама, мама, война не вернет ...
> Не гляди на дорогу.
> Столб крутящейся пыли идет
> Через поле к порогу.
>
> Словно машет из пыли рука,
> Светят очи живые.
> Шевелятся открытки на дне сундука—
> Фронтовые.
>
> Всякий раз, когда мать его ждет,—
> Через поле и пашню
> Столб клубящейся пыли бредет,
> Одинокий и страшный.[62]

(My father walked, my father walked unscathed across a minefield. He changed into swirling smoke—no grave, no pain. Mother, mother, war won't send him back ... Don't look at the road. A column of whirling dust is going through the field to our door. As though a hand waves from the dust, living eyes shine. At the bottom of the trunk move postcards—from the front. Each time my mother waits for him,—across the field and ploughed land a column of swirling dust wanders, lonely and terrible.)

Vladimir Vysotskii, actor, poet, singer, was born three years earlier than Kuznetsov. His father survived the war, and Vysotskii's treatment of the war theme in his work does not appear to have the same personal roots as in Kuznetsov's. The war he portrays in his poems and songs is not necessarily identifiable as the Second World War—Vysotskii reportedly used the war theme because it allowed him to portray people in extreme situations, risking their lives.[63] In a discussion of the war theme in poetry and song over the last twenty years or so, Ksenia Mialo characterised Vysotskii's view of the war as a clash of absolutes, Good and Evil, with key words being 'sunrise', 'light', 'the east'. Underlying the songs is the idea of a self-sacrificial death for the sake of others.[64] All these elements are, of course, present in the tradition of Soviet war poetry. Vysotskii's work, however, has little in the way of detail that fixes it specifically in the Second World War; the idea of war as an ordeal, a proof of character, is uppermost. His 'Pesnia o novom vremeni' (Song of New Times) is representative:

Как призывный набат прозвучали в ночи тяжело шаги.
Значит, скоро и нам уходить и прощаться без слов.
По нехоженым тропам протоптали лошади, лошади,
Неизвестно, к какому концу унося седоков.

Значит, время иное, лихое, но счастье как встарь ищи,
И в погоню летим мы за ним, убегающим, вслед.
Только вот, в этой скачке теряем мы лучших товарищей,
На скаку не заметив, что рядом товарища нет.

И еще будем долго огни принимать за пожары мы,
Будет долго зловещим казаться нам скрип сапогов,
Про войну будут детские игры с названьями старыми,
И людей будем долго делить на своих и врагов.

А когда отгрохочет, когда отгорит и отплачется,
И когда наши кони устанут под нами скакать,
И когда наши девушки сменят шинели на платьица,—
Не забыть бы тогда, не простить бы и не потерять.[65]

(Like a call to arms footsteps rang out heavily in the night. So soon we shall have to leave and part without words. Horses, horses trampled over untrodden paths, no knowing what has become of their riders. So it is a different time, wild, but search for happiness as of old, and we fly in pursuit after it as it runs away. But in this race we lose the best comrades, in the race not noticing that our comrade is not beside us. And for a long time yet we shall still mistake lights for fires, the creak of boots shall seem ominous to us for a long time yet, there will be children's games about war with old names, and we shall for a long time divide people into us and the enemy. And when the rumbling dies down, the fires go out and people have finished weeping, and when our horses are tired of racing beneath us, and when our girls exchange their greatcoats for dresses,—we must not forget then, not forgive and not lose.)

Here, as in other of Vysotskii's songs on similar themes, the absence of specific historical reference seems to invite a metaphorical interpretation of the battles he describes. Like Gudzenko and Mezhirov, Vysotskii could well have been drawing comparisons between the present day and a state of war. In another song, the comparison is made explicit:

Давно смолкли залпы орудий,
Над нами лишь солнечный свет.
На чем проверяются люди,
Если войны уже нет?..

... Покой только снится, я знаю,
Готовься, держись и дерись.
Есть мирная передовая,
Беда, и опасность, и риск ...[66]

(The guns' salvoes fell silent long ago, above us is just the sunlight. What are people tested by if there is no war? ... I know peace is only an illusion, be prepared, stand firm and fight. There is a peaceful front, misfortune, danger and risk.)

It may not be too much of an overstatement to suggest that Vysotskii's influence in the many songs composed by Soviet soldiers in Afghanistan was considerable. But instead of a metaphorical battle, this was a real, at times desperate war. The true nature of this war was not immediately evident from poetry published in the late 1970s and early 1980s when, according to one critical account, it was the theme of duty rather than adventure which was prominent in patriotic poetry:

> In heroic-patriotic poetry by young writers in the seventies and early eighties there are frequent reflections on military duty. Most of all these reflections have a general, universal character: if the Motherland calls, we shall join the ranks and fulfil our duty to the Motherland.[67]

The notion of duty was, for obvious reasons, heavily propagandised. Duty to friends and to the memory of the dead is in fact a much more prominent theme in poetry written by combatants in Afghanistan than international duty or devotion to the Motherland.

The subject of the Afghan war may be prefigured in a 1979 poem celebrating the vigilance of Soviet border guards:

... В песках азиатской пустыни,
Где шквал набежавший колюч,
Где горы задумчиво сини,
Афганец свиреп и могуч ...[68]

(In the sands of the Asiatic desert, where the approaching squall is fierce, where the mountains are pensively blue, the Afghan is savage and mighty.)

There are hints in 1987 of an attempt at justification:

Дается дорого
свобода.
Мы посылаем
сыновей
По зову близкого
народа,
По долгу совести
своей ...[69]

(Freedom is given dearly. We send our sons, at the summons of a close people, at the prompting of our conscience.)

The author continues with a reference to Mikhail Svetlov's poem of the 1920s 'Grenada' (Granada), with its appeal to internationalist sentiments. Two years later, when the troops were finally brought back to the Soviet Union in 1989, *glasnost'* made it possible for Pavel Bulushev's 'Afganskii rekviem' (Afghan Requiem) to appear, condemning the false marshals who had deceived the people and brought so much suffering upon them.[70] Since then, songs and poems written by the soldiers who fought in Afghanistan have appeared; the last war fought by the Soviet Union, like its predecessors, produced its own poets. For a generation brought up to venerate the soldiers of the Soviet Army who fought to drive German invaders from their country, and to read the poetry of that war, Afghanistan was different, unsettling in its partial familiarity:

> Идут в атаку молча, стиснув зубы.
> Призыва нет: «За Родину, вперед!»
> Лишь матернут запекшиеся губы
> С горы в упор хлестнувший пулемет.
> Здесь все другое, не Москва за нами,
> Не топчет враг родимые поля,
> Пылит земля чужая под ногами
> И все же дорогая, как своя.[71]

(They go into attack in silence, gritting their teeth. There is no rallying cry: 'Forward, for the Motherland!' Only parched lips curse the machine gun lashing out from the mountainside. Here everything is different, it's not Moscow behind us, no enemy tramples the dear fields, an alien soil raises dust beneath our feet, and still it is as dear to us as our own.)

Some of the poems written about Afghanistan do compare the war there with World War Two. Iuliia Drunina feels that she understands the young veterans' nostalgia for front-line camaraderie; one soldier dedicates a poem to Aleksandr Matrosov, while another echoes a poem by Evgenii Vinokurov, remembering two Moscow friends, Serezhka from Malaia Bronnaia and Vit'ka from Mokhovaia Street, who failed to return.[72] Viktor Verstakov's 'Mir prekrasen' (The World is Beautiful) draws a parallel between the soldiers in Afghanistan and their grandfathers in World War Two; it is, moreover, strongly reminiscent of Vysotskii's 'K vershine' (To the Summit) in both imagery and rhythm. Vysotksii's song is not about war, but about the difficult ascent to unspecified metaphorical heights.[73] The mountains here are, however, real:

> ... Обернешься назад—выше нет высоты,
> Мир прекрасен, солдат, да подъемы круты.
> Ни тропы, ни следа—льды и скалы внавал.
> Здесь никто до тебя никогда не бывал.
>
> Птицы ниже летят, тучи ниже плывут,
> Мир прекрасен, солдат, да нелегок твой труд.
> Отступился—держись, обессилел—не верь.
> Начинается жизнь выше прежней теперь.
>
> Ты стоишь наверху, ты приблизил рассвет,
> Как отец твой в цеху, как на фронте твой дед.
> Пусть он холодноват—первый луч над горой,
> Мир прекрасен, солдат, хоть немирен порой.
> Путь пройдешь до конца, свет над миром спасешь.
> Ты похож на отца, ты на деда похож.[74]

(If you turn back—there is no peak higher, the world is beautiful, soldier, and the inclines are steep. No paths, no tracks—ice and cliffs piled high. No one has ever been here before you. Lower down birds fly, clouds float by, the world is beautiful, soldier, and your work is not easy. If you've missed your footing, stand firm, if you have no more strength, don't believe it. Now a life is beginning which is higher than the past one. You stand up above, you have brought the dawn closer, like your father in the factory, like your grandfather at the front. It may be cold—the first rays are above the mountain, the world is beautiful, soldier, though sometimes not peaceful. If you follow the path to the end you will save the light above the world. You are like your father, you are like your grandfather.)

To judge from what is admittedly a small sample of two anthologies, the general impression is that those involved in the war were less concerned with the reasons behind their involvement than with survival, courage and friendship. The tone is realistic, with few attempts at romanticising warfare. The dominant mood is one of resignation—there is no point questioning the purpose of the war—and a touch of defiance:

Какие здесь законы?—
Спросите у судьбы.
Хватило бы патронов
Да цинка на гробы.
Ошибка—не ошибка,
Вина иль не вина—
С беззубою улыбкой
На нас глядит Война.
Кривляется, смеется,
Как ведьма на огонь,
И кровь людская льется
В костлявую ладонь.
У пули снисхожденья
Напрасно не проси—
Хватило бы везенья,
Да выдержки, да сил.
Налей в пустую флягу
Воды из миража,
И топай шаг за шагом
По скалам не спеша.
Шагай, солдат, шагай,
Лицо подставив ветру,
И жизнь свою считай
На тонно-километры.
Такой он есть, Восток,
И злобный и печальный,
А кто-то все про долг
Интернациональный.
Кому и что должны
Усталые солдаты?
Хватило б тишины,
А большего не надо.[75]

(What are the laws here?—Ask fate. As long as there are still bullets and zinc for coffins. Whether it's a mistake or not, whether someone's to blame or not—with a toothless smile War looks at us. She writhes and laughs, like a witch on the fire, and human blood pours into her bony palm. Don't waste time asking bullets for leniency—as long as you have luck and endurance and strength. Pour water from a mirage into an empty flask, and tramp step by step, unhurriedly, among the crags. March, soldier, march, your face set against the wind, and reckon your life in kilometre-tonnes. That's what the East is like, both malicious and sad, but someone keeps on about international duty. What do the tired soldiers owe anyone? As long as there is silence we don't need anything more.)

For several years little was made public in the Soviet Union about the undeclared war in Afghanistan. The extent of the casualties of this war, together with the fact that the campaign was unlikely to reach a successful resolution, tarnished the reputation of Soviet military power. Any implicit parallels between the Afghan war and the Soviet liberation of Eastern Europe in 1944–45 were now set in doubt. The war offered a focus for public discontent with the government. Like the war with Finland in 1939–40, events in Afghanistan threatened the authority of the state that embarked on them, and the true extent of losses in both campaigns was hidden from the public. Victory in the Second World War had ensured the survival of Stalin's Soviet Union, and became enshrined as the shining example of the unity of Party and people. A cult of memory was built up around a carefully edited version of the war's events, yet as these events receded into the past, the heroic version was increasingly questioned and amended to the extent that some among the younger generations have even asked whether it might not have been better had the Soviet Union been defeated. Rejection of the Soviet power entailed, for some, rejection of the victory so long represented as the system's greatest and undisputed achievement.

NOTES

1 'Voina', *Sobranie sochinenii*, 3 vols (Moscow, 1991), I, 230.

2 See Nina Tumarkin, 'Story of a War Memorial', in *World War Two and the Soviet People*, edited by John Garrard and Carol Garrard (London, 1993), pp. 125–146.

3 'Stikhi o sebe', *Sobranie sochinenii*, 3 vols (Leningrad, 1988–90), II, 89.

4 Pavel Antokol'skii, 'Preniia po dokladu Tikhonova', *Literaturnaia gazeta*, 22 May 1945, p. 1.

5 A.Nedogonov, *Flag nad sel'sovetom* (Moscow, 1951); N. Gribachev, 'Kolkhoz "Bol'shevik"', *Sobranie sochinenii*, 5 vols (Moscow, 1971–73), II, 337–393; 'Vesna v "Pobede"', II, 394–444; A.Iashin, 'Alena Fomina', *Sobranie sochinenii*, 3 vols (Moscow, 1984–86), I, 522–594.

For an account of wartime agriculture, see William Moskoff *The Bread of Affliction: the Food Supply in the USSR During World War Two* (Cambridge, 1990).

6 Nikolai Tikhonov, 'Pered novym pod"emom', *Literaturnaia gazeta*, 17 May 1945, p. 2.

7 See F. Levin, 'Zhizn' idet vpered', *Literaturnaia gazeta*, 5 October, 1946, p. 3; S. Gudzenko, M. Lukonin, 'Razgovor o molodykh', ibid., 26 October, 1946, p. 3; A. Tarasenkov, 'Replika kritiku', ibid., 12 October, 1946, p. 2; K. Simonov, 'Zametki pisatelia', *Novyi mir*, 1 (1947), 157–173 (p. 165).

8 'Druz'iam', *Izbrannoe* (Moscow, 1989), p. 467.

9 Ibid., pp. 489–490.

10 Quoted by S. I. Iaroslavtseva in her introduction to *Stikhi slagalis' na khodu* (Moscow, 1990), p. 11.

11 See 'Kak bez vesti propavshikh zhdut ...', *Stikhi slagalis' na khodu*, pp. 145–146; 'Ia prishel v shineli zhestko-seroi ...', pp. 120–122.

12 'Ia v garnizonnom klube za Karpatami...', ibid., pp. 129–130.

13 'Chto nam veseloiu vesnoi ...', p. 102.

14 'Bylo vsiakoe ...', ibid., p. 138.

15 *Izbrannoe*, p. 219.

16 'Chelovek zhivet na belom svete ...', p. 430.

17 'V otrezke ot shesti i do vos'mi ...', p. 285.

18 'Dom u dorogi', *Izbrannye proizvedeniia*, 3 vols (Moscow, 1990), II, 252.

19 II, 233.

20 *Istoriia russkoi sovetskoi poezii 1941-1980*, edited by V. V. Buznik, V. A. Kovalev, V. V. Timofeeva (Leningrad, 1984), p. 112.

21 'Aleksandr Matrosov', *Sobranie sochinenii*, 4 vols (Moscow, 1974–76), III, 266–312.

22 I, 311; 313.

23 I, 314.

24 'V tot den', kogda okonchilas' voina', *Izbrannye proizvedeniia*, I, 326–327.

25 I, 452.

26 Aleksandr Galich, 'Oshibka', *Pokolenie obrechennykh* (Frankfurt am Main, 1972), p. 47.

27 Sergei Narovchatov, 'Neizvestnyi soldat', *Stikhotvoreniia i poemy* (Leningrad, 1985), pp. 172–173; 'Koster', pp. 146–148; Aleksei Surkov, 'Londonskii nishchii', *Sobranie sochinenii*, 4 vols (Moscow, 1965–66), II, 70–71.

28 *Aleksandr Matrosov*, III, 295–296.

29 *Aleksandr Matrosov*, III, 273; 279. Matrosov's past is discussed in correspondence between Viktor Astaf'ev and Viacheslav Kondrat'ev, published under the title 'Pravda vyborochnoi ne byvaet', *Literaturnaia gazeta*, 26 October 1994, p. 3.

30 'Strannosti', I, 141.

31 'Kogda my vernulis' s voiny ...' I, 410.

32 'Skandal sorok shestogo goda', II, 425.

33 *Sobranie sochinenii*, 3 vols (Moscow, 1984–85), II, 19.

34 'O glavnom', pp. 252–253.

35 'Ia nikogda ne napishu takogo ...', II, 90.

36 'Ia idu po mestam boev ...', *Izbrannye proizvedeniia* (Leningrad, 1983), p. 359.

37 'Na sobran'e tselyi den' sidela ...', II, 97–98.

38 'My pod Kolpinom skopom stoim ...', pp. 561–562.

39 'Chto ty plachesh', staraia razvalina ...' p. 30.

40 'Vospominanie o poezdke v Vorkutu', *Rekviem: stikhi russkikh sovetskikh poetov* (Moscow, 1989), p. 213.

41 See 'Nevidimka', *Sobranie sochinenii*, 2 vols (Cheliabinsk, 1978–79), II, 22–35.

42 *Prusskie nochi* (Paris, 1977).

43 'Pristal'nost' pytlivuiu ne priacha ...', I, 144.

44 'Ia sudil liudei i znaiu tochno ...', I, 145.
45 'Otkaz', *Tvoreniia* (Moscow, 1986), pp. 172–173.
46 'Rasstrelivali Van'ku-vzodnogo ...', II, 320.
47 I, 146.
48 'Pervyi den' na peredovoi', *Stikhotvoreniia* (Moscow, 1985), pp. 7–8; 'Ia ukhozhu ot puli ...', pp. 37–38.
49 'Korol'', pp. 14–15; 'Dzhazisty', pp. 55–56.
50 'Bumazhnyi soldatik', pp. 72–73.
51 'Pesenka o soldatskikh sapogakh', pp. 16–17.
52 'Shestoe nebo', I, 484.
53 'Ne vechnaia pamiat'', *Znamia*, 8–9 (1946), p. 64; 'Ballada o rvakh', *Stikhi slagalis' na khodu*, pp. 142–143; 'Babii iar', *Sobranie sochinenii*, 3 vols, (Moscow, 1983–84), I, 316–318.
54 I, 213.
55 *Sobranie sochinenii*, 3 vols (Moscow, 1978–79), III, 258–419.
56 See 'Pekhota', *Okopnye stikhi* (Moscow, 1990), pp. 35–36; 'Nastupaem ...', p. 222; 'Vse bylo na voine—i tragizm, i samopozhertvovanie ...', p. 223.
57 'Naturalizm', p. 205.
58 'Svad'by', I, 51–52.
59 Iunna Morits, 'Posle voiny', in *Byla voina*, comp. V. Akatkin, L. Taganov (Moscow, 1984), p. 129.
60 'V blokadnykh dniakh ...', *Pobeda: poety o podvige Leningrada v Velikoi Otechestvennoi voine* (Leningrad, 1970), p. 124.
61 Iurii Kuznetsov, 'Otsu', *Izbrannoe* (Moscow, 1990), p. 112.
62 'Vozvrashchenie', p.146; see also 'Chetyresta', pp. 152–155.
63 See Arkadii L'vov's foreword to Vladimir Vysotskii, *Pesni i stikhi* (New York, 1981), p. 9.
64 Kseniia Mialo, 'Posviashchenie v nebytie', *Novyi mir*, 8 (1990), p. 231.
65 'Pesnia o novom vremeni', *Pesni i stikhi* (New York, 1981), pp. 91–92.
66 'Davno smolkli zalpy orudii ...', pp. 110–111.
67 Iu.Belichenko, 'Pomnit' imia svoe: zametki o molodoi geroiko-patrioticheskoi poezii 70-kh—nachala 80-kh godov', *Literatura velikogo podviga*, 4 (1985), 71–91 (p. 87).
68 Vladimir Mikhanovskii, 'Sviashchennye rubezhi', *Podvig*, 19 (1979), p. 164.
69 Feliks Chuev, 'Daetsia dorogo svoboda ...', ibid., 31 (1987), p. 18.
70 *Zvezda*, 7 (1989), p. 3.
71 Viktor Kutsenko, 'Idut v ataku molcha, stisnuv zuby ...', *Iz plameni Afganistana* (Moscow, 1990), p. 208.
72 Iuliia Drunina, 'Afgantsy', *Iz plameni Afganistana* (Moscow, 1990), p. 241; Aleksandr Stovba, 'U ofitserov i soldat ...'. ibid., p. 189; Vladimir Turkin, 'Zhestokii son', ibid., p. 216. The Vinokurov poem alluded to is 'V poliakh za Visloi sonnoi...' (1953), *Sobranie sochinenii*, 3 vols (Moscow, 1983–84), I, 41.
73 *Pesni i stikhi*, p. 196.
74 Viktor Verstakov, 'Mir prekrasen', *Iz plameni Afganistana*, p. 59.
75 Igor' Morozov, 'Kakie zdes' zakony?..', *Nikto ne sozdan dlia voiny* (Moscow, 1990), pp. 72–74.

Conclusion

Since 1945 poetry looking back on the war is largely divided between that of formal commemoration, which appeals to the reader not to forget past suffering and heroism, and that which deals with personal memories of wartime experience. The attitude Iurii Kuznetsov expresses towards the trappings of official commemoration in a poem of 1988 is most critical. The Eternal Flame, he reminds the reader, can go out if the gas is turned off, and the Unknown Soldier is an individual whose individuality has been nullified and forgotten:

> ... А вот другой обман перед глазами,
> С почетным караулом и цветами.
> Могила Неизвестного Солдата—
> К нему приходят люди на поклон.
> Его покой велик и место свято.
> Но почему он имени лишен?
> Кому он неизвестен? Близким людям?
> Сиротам? Овдовевшим матерям?
> О Боге всуе говорить не будем,
> Уж он-то знает всех по именам.
> Тут сатана, его расчет холодный:
> Заставить нас по нашей простоте
> Стирать черты из памяти народной
> И кланяться безликой пустоте.[1]

(And here's another deception before our eyes, with a guard of honour and flowers. The Tomb of the Unknown Soldier—people come to bow down to him. His rest is profound and his place is sacred. But why is he deprived of a name? To whom is he unknown? To those he loved? His orphan children? To widowed mothers? We shall not speak of God in vain, as he for one knows everyone by name. Here is Satan, his cold calculation: he forces us in our simplicity to remove the features from the people's memory and bow down to a faceless void.)

Those of the war generation, in whose name the commemoration of the war was established, had their own memories to draw upon; there was nothing anonymous about their experience. The work of Iurii Levitanskii, born in 1922, includes poems about his war memories which are intensely personal and tinged with the surreal. He recalls lying wounded under a red sky, on red snow like a warm field of poppies, dreaming of red tomatoes on a plate and red cobblestones under horses' hooves. In another poem Levitanskii remembers sharing a piece of lard—a great delicacy in those years—with other soldiers under fire. The lard seems almost human, like a rosy baby, freckled like the sergeant after a bath, a smiling fakir in a top hat.[2] In his more recent work, however, such individual details are rare. The entire experience of war, Levitanskii writes in a poem published in 1981, has become an organic, ineradicable part of his consciousness. This memory is strangely impersonal. Names and dates are forgotten, but the war still holds the poet in thrall:

... Я неопознанный солдат.
Я рядовой. Я имярек.
Я меткой пули недолет.
Я лед кровавый в январе.
Я прочно впаян в этот лед—
Я в нем, как мушка в янтаре.

(I am an unidentified soldier. I am a private soldier. I am N. or M. I'm the shortfall of the well-aimed bullet. I am bloody ice in January. I am firmly welded into this ice—I am in it like a fly in amber.)

Levitanskii here uses imagery reminiscent of that used by Berggol'ts in 'Tvoi put'' (Your Road). His involvement in the war is no longer personal and voluntary. Now the war is a part of him:

... Я не участвую в войне—
Она участвует во мне.[3]

(I don't take part in war—it takes part in me.)

These words seem to contradict what Gudzenko wrote in 1942:

Каждый помнит по-своему ...[4]

(Everyone remembers in their own way.)

Yet Levitanskii's memories have grown out of personal experience and individual perceptions. It is the passage of time which has brought about this change of perspective, together with the developments in literature which have made Gudzenko's plea for the unique qualities of individual memory less pressing. Gudzenko's early war poetry formed an account of the individual's experience at the front which represented a new departure in its honesty and immediacy. Wartime poetry, assisted by the more relaxed conditions regarding literary censorship at the time, moved away from focusing on the collective-minded New Soviet Man and focused instead on ordinary people's concerns and experiences. Poetry offered its readers ways of coping with the pressures imposed upon them by the war, all of which centred on seeking reassurance in thoughts of their immediate family and home, and so excluded a good deal of officially-inspired rhetoric which was largely irrelevant to their own perceptions of events. The record of individual experience was, however, too limited an objective for many poets, who, while not denying the value and truthfulness inherent in work written from a personal point of view, needed to place their accounts of the war in a broader, but equally truthful political and historical perspective. Work written and published during the post-Stalin thaws reflects this expanding horizon. At the same time, as the enormity of loss and destruction brought by the war became evident, poets needed to go beyond their immediate experiences to gain some understanding of the tragedy in which they had played their minor roles. These moves, each revealing new aspects of the war, were all countered by the elements among the literary establishment who wished to maintain a simple, uncontroversial picture of events.

The main achievement of Soviet wartime poetry was that, at its best, it freed itself from the dogma-led changes which had dominated literature during the pre-war decade, and reacted spontaneously to events. One former soldier recently described his sense of freedom during the war:

> It was genuine freedom, drawn from the air of history and of the inevitable future Victory. And Stalin had absolutely nothing to do with it. Those were years of unforgettable freedom from him. Although the fear of him didn't go away.[5]

The result was work which, in spite of remaining constraints, was truthful about the poets' and readers' shared experience of the war. In just under four years of war, a whole new generation of poets had appeared, while already published poets like Ol'ga Berggol'ts, Aleksandr Tvardovskii and Konstantin Simonov became genuinely and deservedly popular. Four years of war had shown the Soviet people, and its leaders, just what they were capable of. The country's poets had also gained in awareness of their own strength and independence, knowledge which was not permitted to be exploited immediately, but which proved its worth when the death of Stalin marked the end of a period of oppression in which the war was a brief respite.

NOTES

1 'Lozhnye sviatyni', *Izbrannoe* (Moscow, 1990), p. 307.

2 'Vospominanie o krasnom snege', *Izbrannoe* (Moscow, 1982), p. 201; 'Vospominanie o kuske sala', pp. 82–83.

3 'Nu chto s togo, chto ia tam byl ...', p. 349.

4 'Pamiat'', *Stikhi slagalis' na khodu ...* (Moscow, 1990), p. 83.

5 Daniil Danin, 'Strogo kak popalo', *Literaturnaia gazeta*, 12 July 1995, p. 3.

Bibliography

This bibliography is organised under the following headings: Primary Sources; Anthologies of Russian Second World War Poetry; Other Anthologies of Russian Poetry; Secondary Works on Soviet War Literature: Books; Secondary Works on Soviet War Literature: Articles; Secondary Works on Specific Authors; War Letters, Memoirs and Diaries; History of World War Two; Literature on the Afghan War; British Poetry of World War Two: Primary Texts; Secondary Literature; Literature in the Third Reich; Works on the History and Development of Soviet Literature; Other Works Cited.

For books published in Russia and the former USSR, only the place of publication is given.

Primary Sources

Akhmatova, A., *Sochineniia*, 2 vols (Moscow, 1986)
Aliger, M., *Sobranie sochinenii*, 3 vols (Moscow, 1984–85)
Antokol'skii, P., *Sobranie sochinenii*, 4 vols (Moscow, 1971–73)
Aseev, N., *Sobranie sochinenii*, 5 vols (Moscow, 1963–64)
Bagritskii, E., *Stikhotvoreniia i poemy* (Moscow–Leningrad, 1964)
Batiushkov, K., *Sochineniia*, 2 vols (Moscow, 1989)
Belash, Iu, *Okopnye stikhi* (Moscow, 1985)
Bednyi, D., *Sobranie sochinenii*, 8 vols (Moscow, 1963–65)
Berggol'ts, O., *Sobranie sochinenii*, 3 vols (Leningrad, 1988–90)
——— *Izbrannye proizvedeniia* (Leningrad, 1983)
——— *Uzel* (Moscow–Leningrad, 1965)
——— *Tvoi put'* (Leningrad, 1945)
Blok, A., *Sobranie sochinenii*, 6 vols (Leningrad 1980–83)
Chernyi, S., *Stikhotvoreniia* (Leningrad, 1960)
Chivilikhin, A., *Golos vremeni: stikhotvoreniia i poemy* (Moscow–Leningrad, 1964)
Dolmatovskii, E., *Sobranie sochinenii*, 3 vols (Moscow, 1978–79)
Drunina, Iu, *Izbrannoe*, 2 vols (Moscow, 1989)
——— *Ne byvaet liubvi neschastlivoi* (Moscow, 1977)
Dudin, M., *Sobranie sochinenii*, 4 vols (Moscow, 1987–88)
Dzhalil', M., *Izbrannoe* (Moscow, 1966)
Erenburg, I., *Stikhotvoreniia* (Moscow, 1982)

Evtushenko, E., *Sobranie sochinenii*, 3 vols (Moscow, 1983–84)
Galich, A., *Pokolenie obrechennykh* (Frankfurt am Main: Posev, 1972)
Gitovich, A., *Izbrannoe* (Leningrad, 1973)
Glazkov, N., *Izbrannoe* (Moscow, 1989)
Gribachev, N., *Sobranie sochinenii*, 5 vols (Moscow, 1971–73)
Gudzenko, S., *Odnopolchane* (Moscow, 1944)
——— *Stikhi* (Moscow, 1961)
——— *Stikhotvoreniia* (Moscow, 1985)
——— *Stikhi slagalis' na khodu* (Moscow, 1990)
Gumilev, N., *Stikhotvoreniia i poemy* (Leningrad, 1988)
Iashin, A., *Sobranie sochinenii*, 3 vols (Moscow, 1984–86)
Inber, V., *Dusha Leningrada* (Leningrad, 1979)
Isakovskii, M., *Sobranie sochinenii*, 5 vols (Moscow, 1981–82)
Khelemskii, Ia, *Izbrannoe* (Moscow, 1983)
Kedrin, D., *Izbrannoe* (Moscow, 1991)
——— *Stikhotvoreniia i poemy* (Moscow, 1974)
Khlebnikov, V., *Tvoreniia* (Moscow, 1986)
Kirsanov, S., *Sobranie sochinenii*, 4 vols (Moscow, 1974–76)
Kornilov, B., *Stikhotvoreniia i poemy* (Moscow–Leningrad, 1966)
Kuznetsov, Iu, *Izbrannoe* (Moscow, 1990)
Lebedev-Kumach, V., *Izbrannoe* (Moscow, 1984)
Lermontov, M., *Polnoe sobranie stikhotvorenii*, 2 vols (Leningrad, 1989)
Levitanskii, Iu, *Izbrannoe* (Moscow, 1982)
Lifshits, V., *Izbrannye stikhi* (Moscow, 1974)
Lipkin, S., *Volia: stikhi* (Ann Arbor: Ardis, 1981)
Lukonin, M., *Stikhotvoreniia i poemy* (Leningrad, 1985)
L'vov, M., *Sobranie sochinenii*, 3 vols (Moscow, 1987–88)
Maiakovskii, V., *Sobranie sochinenii*, 13 vols (Moscow, 1955–61)
Mandel'shtam, O., *Sochinenia*, 2 vols (Moscow, 1990)
Martynov, L., *Stikhotvoreniia* (Moscow, 1987)
Mezhirov, A., *Izbrannoe* (Moscow, 1989)
Narovchatov, S., *Stikhotvoreniia i poemy* (Leningrad, 1985)
Nedogonov, A., *Izbrannoe* (Moscow, 1958)
——— *Flag nad sel'sovetom* (Moscow, 1951)
Nikolaeva, G., *Sobranie sochinenii*, 3 vols (Moscow, 1987–88)
Okudzhava, B., *Stikhotvoreniia* (Moscow, 1985)
Orlov, S., *Izbrannoe* (Moscow, 1988)
Pasternak, B., *Sobranie sochinenii*, 5 vols (Moscow, 1989–92)
Petrovykh, M., *Izbrannoe* (Moscow, 1991)
Prokof'ev, A., *Stikhotvoreniia i poemy* (Leningrad, 1986)
Pushkin, A., *Sobranie sochinenii v odnom tome* (Moscow, 1984)
Ruch'ev, B., *Sobranie sochinenii*, 2 vols (Cheliabinsk, 1978–79)
Rylenkov, N., *Stikhotvoreniia i poemy* (Leningrad, 1981)
——— *Stikhotvoreniia i poemy*, 2 vols (Moscow, 1959)
Saianov, V., *Sochineniia*, 2 vols (Moscow, 1959)
Samoilov, D., *Izbrannye proizvedeniia*, 2 vols (Moscow, 1989)
Sel'vinskii, I., *Sobranie sochinenii*, 6 vols (Moscow, 1971–74)
——— *Stikhotvoreniia i poemy* (Leningrad, 1972)
——— *Lirika i drama* (Moscow, 1947)
Severianin, I., *Wictoria regia* (Moscow, 1915)
Shchipachev, S., *Sobranie sochinenii*, 3 vols (Moscow, 1976–77)
Shefner, V., *Lichnaia vechnost'* (Leningrad, 1984)

Shishova, Z., *Blokada* (Moscow, 1943)
Shubin, P., *Izbrannoe* (Moscow, 1988)
Shvedov, Ia, *Samoe zavetnoe: pesni, stikhi, poemy* (Moscow, 1976)
Simonov K, *Sobranie sochinenii*, 12 vols (Moscow, 1979–87)
——— *Stikhi, p'esy, rasskazy* (Leningrad, 1949)
Slutskii, B., *Sobranie sochinenii*, 3 vols (Moscow, 1991)
Smeliakov, Ia, *Stikhotvoreniia i poemy*, 2nd ed. (Leningrad, 1979)
Solzhenitsyn, A., *Prusskie nochi* (Paris: Y.M.C.A Press, 1977)
Surkov, A., *Sobranie sochinenii*, 4 vols (Moscow, 1965–6)
Svetlov, M., *Sobranie sochinenii*, 3 vols (Moscow, 1974–75)
Tikhonov, N., *Sobranie sochinenii*, 7 vols (Moscow, 1973–76)
Tsvetaeva, M., *Stikhotvoreniia i poemy*, 5 vols (New York: Russica, 1980–90)
Tvardovskii, A., *Izbrannye proizvedeniia*, 3 vols (Moscow, 1990)
——— *Sobranie sochinenii*, 6 vols (Moscow, 1976–83)
Ushakov, N., *Stikhotvoreniia* (Moscow, 1988)
Utkin, I., *Izbrannoe* (Moscow, 1975)
Vasil'ev, P., *Stikhotvoreniia i poemy* (Leningrad, 1968)
Vasil'ev, S., *Sobranie sochinenii*, 3 vols (Moscow, 1977–79)
Vinokurov, E., *Sobranie sochinenii*, 3 vols (Moscow, 1983–84)
Vishnevskii, V., *Stat'i, dnevniki, pis'ma* (Moscow, 1961)
Voloshin, M., *Izbrannye stikhotvoreniia* (Moscow, 1988)
Voronov, Iu, *Stikhotvoreniia* (Moscow, 1989)
Vysotskii, V., *Pesni i stikhi* (New York: Literaturnoe zarubezh'e, 1981)
Zharov, A., *Sobranie sochinenii*, 3 vols (Moscow, 1980–81)
Zhukovskii, V., *Izbrannye sochineniia* (Moscow, 1982)

Anthologies of Russian Second World War Poetry

Byla voina... comp. by V. Akatkin, L. Taganov (Moscow, 1984)
Do poslednego dykhaniia: stikhi sovetskikh poetov, pavshikh v Velikoi Otechestvennoi voine, comp. by I. Bogatko (Moscow, 1985)
Ia vernus' eshche k tebe, Rossiia: stikhi iz bloknota, naidennogo v kontslagere Zaksenkhauzen (Moscow, 1959)
Imena na poverke: stikhi voinov, pavshikh na frontakh Velikoi Otechestvennoi voiny, comp. by D. Kovalev, 3rd ed. (Moscow, 1975)
Iz frontovoi liriki: stikhi russkikh sovetskikh poetov, comp. by A. G. Kogan (Moscow, 1981)
Lirika voennykh let, comp. by V. A. Zaitsev, V. I. Fatiushenko (Moscow, 1985)
Ne zabyt' nam veki-naveki, ed. by E. I. Chichaeva (Moscow, 1944)
On vernulsia k tebe, Rossiia! Stikhi, naidennye v razvalinakh lageria smerti Zaksenkhauzena (Moscow, 1959)
Piat' obeliskov: Suvorov, Lebedev, Karim, Rogov, Pulkin (Moscow, 1968)
Pobeda: poety o podvige Leningrada v Velikoi Otechestvennoi voine (Leningrad, 1970)
Poeziia moia, ty iz okopa, comp. by A. M. Abramov, V. Avdeev (Moscow, 1985)
Poeziia v boiu, ed. by V. Azarov (Moscow, 1959)
Poeziia Velikoi Otechestvennoi voiny i antifashistskogo soprotivleniia, ed. by Iu. F. Bondarev (Moscow, 1980)
Pokolenie: sbornik stikhov (Moscow, 1975)
Porokhovaia pamiat': stikhi, pis'ma, vospominaniia, comp. by E. G. Rapoport (Irkutsk, 1975)

Radi zhizni na zemle: stikhotvoreniia o Velikoi Otechestvennoi voine, comp. by S. Podelkov (Moscow, 1975)
Skvoz' vremia: stikhi poetov P. Kogana, M.Kul'chitskogo, N. Maiorova, N. Otrady, comp. by V. Shveitser (Moscow, 1964)
Soldatskaia pesnia, ed. by A. Surkov (Moscow, 1945)
Sovetskie poety, pavshie na Velikoi Otechestvennoi voine (Moscow–Leningrad, 1965)
Stikhi ostaiutsia v stroiu, comp. by M. Matusovskii, 2nd ed. (Moscow, 1958)
Stikhi voennykh let 1941–1945, comp. by S. Narovchatov, Ia. Khelemskii (Moscow, 1985)
Stikhi za koliuchei provolokoi (Moscow, 1953)
Stroki, dobytye v boiiakh, comp. by L. Lazarev (Moscow, 1970)
Velikaia Otechestvennaia 1941–1945: stikhotvoreniia i poemy, ed. by S. Narovchatov, Ia. Khelemskii, 2 vols (Moscow, 1975)
Vesna pokhozha na pobedu (Omsk, 1985)

Other Anthologies of Russian Poetry

Antologiia russkoi sovetskoi poezii, ed. by V. A. Lugovskoi, V. O. Pertsov, A. A. Surkov, N. S. Tikhonov, 2 vols (Moscow, 1957)
Oborona: literaturno-khudozhestvennyi sbornik (Sverdlovsk–Moscow, 1933)
Oborona: stikhi krasnoarmeiskikh i krasnoflotskikh poetov, ed. by B. M. Likharev ([Moscow], 1939)
Prikaz o mobilizatsii, comp. by A. Prokof'ev, N. Braun, A. Gitovich ([Moscow], 1931)
Rekviem: stikhi russkikh sovetskikh poetov (Moscow, 1989)
Russkaia sovetskaia poezia: sbornik stikhov 1917–47, ed. by L. O. Belov, V. O. Pertsov, A. A. Surkov (Moscow, 1948)
Sbornik stikhov, comp. by V. Kazin, V. Pertsov (Moscow, 1943)
Stikhi i pesni o Krasnoi Armii, comp. by D. G. Ostrovskii (Leningrad, 1938)
Voina v russkoi poezii, ed. by A. Chebotarevskaia (Petrograd, 1915)

Secondary Works on Soviet War Literature: Books

Abramkin, V. M., *Frontovaia poeziia v gody grazhdanskoi voiny* (Moscow, 1938)
Abramov, A. M., *Lirika i epos Velikoi Otechestvennoi voiny*, 2nd ed. (Moscow, 1975)
Antokol'skii, P. G., *Ispytanie vremenem: stat'i* (Moscow, 1945)
Azadovskii, M. K., ed. *Frontovoi fol'klor* (Moscow, 1944)
Bakhtin, B., *Leningradskie pisateli-frontoviki: bio-bibliografiia* (Leningrad, 1985)
Dement'ev, V. V., *Ognennyi most: kniga o poezii*, 2nd ed. (Moscow, 1975)
Egolin, A. M., *Sovetskaia literatura v dni Otechestvennoi voiny* (Moscow, 1944)
Gudoshnikov, Ia. I., *Iazyk i stil' pesen Velikoi Otechestvennoi voiny* (Voronezh, 1959)
Gusev, V., ed., *Russkii fol'klor Velikoi Otechestvennoi voiny* (Moscow, 1964)
Iezuitov, A. N., A. I. Pavlovskii, V. A. Shoshin, eds., *Pobeda i mir: sbornik nauchnykh trudov* (AN SSSR IRLI, Leningrad, 1987)

Ivanova, L. V., *Velichie sovershaemogo: literatura o Velikoi Otechestvennoi voine i formirovanie sotsial'nogo soznaniia* (Moscow, 1981)
Kogan, A. G., *Uroki pamiati: literaturno-kriticheskie ocherki* (Moscow, 1988)
——— *Perechityvaia voinu: literaturno-kriticheskie ocherki* (Moscow, 1975)
——— *Zhivaia pamiat' pokoleniia* (Moscow, 1965)
——— *Skvoz' vremia* (Moscow, 1973)
——— *Stikhi i sud'by: frontovaia tema v sovetskoi poezii* (Moscow, 1977)
Komkov, G. D., V. A. Kumanev, *K shtyku priravniali pero: sovetskaia kul'tura v gody Velikoi Otechestvennoi voiny—tsifry i fakty* (Moscow, 1965)
Kosareva, L. A., *Velikaia Otechestvennaia voina v poeticheskom soznanii poslevoennogo pokoleniia* (Moscow, 1986)
Kovalenko, S. A., *Sovetskaia poeziia o Velikoi Otechestvennoi voine: k sorokaletiiu pobedy* (Moscow, 1985)
——— *Radi zhizni na zemle: sovetskaia literatura v bor'be za mir* (Moscow, 1980)
Kovalev, V. A., A. I. Pavlovskii, eds., *Literaturnyi Leningrad v dni blokady* (Leningrad, 1973)
Krupianskaia, V. Iu., S. I. Mints, *Materialy po istorii pesni Velikoi Otechestvennoi voiny* (Moscow, 1953)
Kuprianovskii, P., P. Shames, *Russkaia sovetskaia literatura perioda Otechestvennoi voiny: posobie dlia vuzovskogo spetsseminara*, 2nd ed. (Moscow, 1963)
Kuz'michev, I. K., *Zhanry russkoi literatury voennykh let* (Gor'kii, 1962)
——— *Bol' pamiati: Velikaia Otechestvennaia voina v sovetskoi literature* (Gor'kii, 1985)
Lavrov, V. A., A. N. Nikach, comps., *Radi zhizni na zemle: literaturno-kriticheskii sbornik* (Leningrad, 1986)
Lazarev, L. I., *Poeziia voennogo pokoleniia* (Moscow, 1966)
——— *Eto nasha sud'ba: zametki o literature, posviashchennoi Velikoi Otechestvennoi voine*, 2nd ed. (Moscow, 1983)
Lugovtsov, N. P., *Srazhaiushchaiasia muza: literaturno-kriticheskie stat'i i ocherki* (Leningrad, 1985)
Makedonov, A., *Poeziia narodnogo podviga* (Moscow, 1986)
Nikitina, E. P., *Poemy voennykh let* (Saratov, 1958)
Oborona SSSR i khudozhestvennaia literatura (Moscow, 1934)
Orochko, N. N., *Poeziia i voina* (Minsk, 1987)
Pantaleimonov, N. S., ed., *Narod-pobeditel': sovetskaia literatura o Velikoi Otechestvennoi voine* (Leningrad, 1985)
Pavlovskii, A. I., *Russkaia sovetskaia poeziia v gody Velikoi Otechestvennoi voiny* (Leningrad, 1967)
——— *Pamiat' i sud'ba* (Leningrad, 1982)
Pered boiiami: khudozhestvennaia literatura na oborone SSSR, sbornik statei (Leningrad, 1933)
Pertsov, V., *Podvig i geroi: etiudy o sovetskoi literature* (Moscow, 1946)
——— *Pisateli v Otechestvennoi voine: pis'ma chitatelei* (Moscow, 1946)
Plotkin, L. A., *Literatura i voina* (Moscow–Leningrad, 1957)
Porman, R. N., *Literaturnoe kraevedenie: iz istorii literaturnoi zhizni Tatarii i Bashkirii perioda Velikoi otechestvennoi voiny* (Ufa, 1987)
Prianshnikov, N., *Obraz sovetskoi patriotki v khudozhestvennoi literature* (Chkalov, 1943)
P'ianykh, M. F., *Russkaia lirika perioda Velikoi Otechestvennoi voiny 1941–1945* (Leningrad, 1960)
——— *Radi zhizni na zemle: poeziia perioda Velikoi Otechestvennoi voiny* (Leningrad, 1980)

——— *Radi zhizni na zemle: russkaia sovetskaia poeziia o Velikoi Otechestvennoi voine—kniga dlia uchitelei* (Moscow, 1985)
Rubashkin, A., *Golos Leningrada: leningradskoe radio v dni blokady* (Leningrad, 1975)
Samoilenko, G., *Stikhotvornaia satira i iumor perioda Velikoi Otechestvennoi voiny* (Kiev, 1977)
Shames, P. E., *Pisateli Velikoi Otechestvennoi voiny 1941–1945: pis'ma chitatelei* (Moscow, 1946)
Sheshukov, S. I., ed., *Velikaia Otechestvennaia voina v sovetskoi literature: mezhvuzovskii sbornik nauchnykh trudov* (Moscow, 1985)
Sovetskie pisateli na frontakh Velikoi Otechestvennoi voiny, ed. by I. I. Anisimov, D. D. Blagoi, A. S. Bushmin et al., Literaturnoe nasledstvo, 78, 2 vols (Moscow, 1966)
Spivak, I. A., *Sovetskaia poeziia perioda Velikoi Otechestvennoi voiny v zhanrovom razvitii* (L'vov, 1972)
Svirin, N., *Literatura i voina: sbornik kriticheskikh statei* (Leningrad, 1932)
Taganov, L. N., *Velikaia Otechestvennaia voina v sovetskoi poezii 40-kh—70-kh godov: uchebnoe posobie* (Ivanovo, 1978)
——— *Dolgoe ekho voiny* (Iaroslavl', 1983)
Tonkov, V., *Narodnoe tvorchestvo v dni Velikoi Otechestvennoi voiny* (Voronezh, 1945)
Tsekhnovitser, O., *Literatura i mirovaia voina 1914–1918* (Moscow, 1938)
Van Ackern, K. D., *Bulat Okudzava und die kritische Literatur über den Krieg*, Arbeiten und Texte zur Slawistik, 11 (Munich, 1976)
Volkov, A., *Poeziia russkogo imperializma* (Moscow, 1935)
Zamanskii, L. A., *Sovetskaia poeziia v voenno-patrioticheskom vospytanii 20-kh-30-kh gg.: uchebnoe posobie* (Cheliabinsk, 1987)
Zhukov, S., *Frontovaia pechat' v gody Velikoi Otechestvennoi voiny* (Moscow, 1968)

Secondary Works on Soviet War Literature: Articles

Abramov, A. M., 'Poeziia Velikoi Otechestvennoi voiny', *Russkaia literatura*, 3 (1960), 3–20
——— 'O stilevykh napravleniiakh poezii Velikoi Otechestvennoi voiny', *Russkaia literatura*, 3 (1969), 55–78
——— 'Klassicheskii stikh na sluzhbe sovremennosti: o poeticheskoi forme poem voennykh let', *Volga*, 2 (1966), 161–177
——— 'Bogatstvo krasok i golosov' (on 'Syn', 'Vasilii Terkin', 'Rossiia'), *Pod"em*, 3 (1965), 131–139
——— 'Molodye togda i—vsegda', *Literaturnaia Rossiia*, 18 February 1972, 17–18
Aleksandrova, V., 'Russia is changing: Wartime Plays, Poetry, Novels Provide Proof', *American Mercury*, 56 (1943), 311–318
——— 'Soviet Poetry and Poets', *Voices: a Quarterly of Poetry* (Maine), 124 (1946), 34–40
Alekseev, M., 'Nachalo: o tvorchestve sovetskikh pisatelei v gody Velikoi Otechestvennoi voiny', *Literaturnaia gazeta*, 9 May 1985, p. 5
Anninskii, L., 'Glubina fronta: eticheskaia tema v lirike voennogo pokoleniia', *Novyi mir*, 4 (1974), 216–236

——— 'Starshie brat'ia—obzor: tema "itoga" v stikhakh poetov "voennogo pokoleniia"—Slutskii, Vinokurov, Orlov', *Literaturnoe obozrenie*, 6 (1979), 44–45

Antokol'skii, P. G., 'Chuvstvo istorii', *Literatura i iskusstvo*, 10 April 1943, p. 2

——— 'Voina i kul'tura', *Literatura i iskusstvo*, 19 June 1943, p. 3

Apletin, M., 'Pisateli Anglii na boevom postu', *Krasnaia nov'*, 8 (1942), p. 88

Aseev, N., 'O chuvstve novogo', *Literatura i iskusstvo*, 3 April 1943, p. 3

Belichenko, Iu., 'Pomnit' imia svoe: zametki o molodoi geroiko-patrioticheskoi poezii 70-kh—nachala 80-kh godov', *Literatura velikogo podviga*, 4 (1985), 71–91

Belkina, N., 'Sovetskaia literatura v Otechestvennoi voine', *Pod znamenem marksizma*, 8–9 (1942), 125–135

Berggol'ts, O., 'Leningradskii opyt', *Oktiabr'*, 1–2 (1944), 150–153

——— 'Velikie temy sovremennosti', *Literatura i iskusstvo*, 12 February 1944, p. 3

——— 'Put' k zrelosti', *Literaturnaia gazeta*, 26 May 1945, p. 3

Bristol, E., 'World War Two and its Aftermath (1939–1955) in *A History of Russian Poetry* (Oxford: Oxford University Press, 1991), 267–278

Brodsky, J., 'Literature and War: the Soviet Union', *TLS*, 17 May 1985, 543–544

Brown, D., 'World War Two in Soviet Literature' in *The Impact of World War Two on the Soviet Union*, ed. by S. J. Linz (Totowa NJ: Rowman and Allanheld, 1985), 243–252

Bugovoi, M., 'Poeziia, rozhdennaia v okopakh: o soldatskom frontovom tvorchestve', *Neva*, 2 (1958), 204–207

Buznik, V. V., 'Poety tret'ego pokoleniia: Gudzenko, Orlov, Maksimov, Dudin', *Russkaia literatura*, 4 (1958), 139–162

Chashchina, L., 'Vzyskanie pogibshikh: literaturnaia khronika poslevoennykh let s kommentariiami', *Neva*, 10 (1990), 181–189

Danin, D., 'Voennaia lirika sorokovogo goda', *Krasnaia nov'*, 5 (1941), 189–204

Derevianko, N., 'Kto napisal "Sviashchennuiu voinu?"', *Argumenty i fakty*, 13 (1991), p. 7

Dobrenko, E., '"Stoi! Kto idet?": u istokov sovetskogo manikheistva', *Znamia*, 3 (1993), 180–189

Dudin, M., A. Mikhailov, 'Iz plameni i sveta rozhdennoe slovo', *Literaturnaia gazeta*, 7 May 1975, p. 4

Dudin, M., 'Pamiatnik nedolgoi pesne: vmesto retsenzii' (on anthology *Sovetskie poety, pavshie na Velikoi Otechestvennoi voine*), in *Den' poezii* (Moscow–Leningrad, 1965), 185–188

Erenburg, I., 'Muzy v pokhode', *Literatura i iskusstvo*, 13 January 1942, p. 1

——— 'Zrelost'', *Novyi mir*, 11–12 (1942), 202–205

——— 'Dolg pisatelia', *Novyi mir*, 9 (1943), 111–116

——— 'Rol' pisatelia v dni voiny', *Literatura i iskusstvo*, 3 July 1943, p. 4

——— 'V boevom poriadke', *Znamia*, 5–6 (1943), 235–238

——— 'Slovo—oruzhie', *Novyi mir*, 1–2 (1944), 210–214

Eventov, I., 'Stikhotvornye listovki', *Zvezda*, 5–6 (1942), 189–191

Evtushenko, E., 'O dvukh poeticheskikh pokoleniiakh', *Literaturnaia gazeta*, 25 January 1955, p. 3

Gitovich, A., 'Stikhi leningradskikh poetov, pogibshikh za rodinu', *Zvezda*, 6 (1947), 129–130

Glinkin, P., 'Byla mobilizatsiia: o deiatel'nosti LOKAF pervaia polovina 30-kh godov', *Volga*, 5 (1975), 180–188

Gnedich, T., 'Poety Krasnoi Armii ob Otechestvennoi voine', *Zvezda*, 5–6 (1943), 196–199

Gorodetskii, S., 'Stikhi i pesni Otechestvennoi voiny', *Literaturnaia gazeta*, 3 September 1941, p. 3
Grinberg, I., 'Tvorchestvo molodykh', *Literaturnaia gazeta*, 16 February 1946, p. 3
——— 'Vzgliad v budushchee', *Zvezda*, 7–8 (1944), 153–160
Gromov, P., 'O literature voennykh let', *Zvezda*, 2 (1945), 115–128; 3 (1945), 125–133
Gudzenko, S., 'Soldatskie pesni', *Literaturnaia gazeta*, 27 January 1945, p. 3
Gudzenko, S., M. Lukonin, 'Razgovor o molodykh', *Literaturnaia gazeta*, 26 October 1946, p. 3
Gusev, V., V. Ermilov, 'Literaturnyi dnevnik', *Novyi mir*, 11–12 (1941), 211–218
Gusev, V., 'Rastsvet sovetskoi poezii', *Literatura i iskusstvo*, 3 April 1943, p. 3
Inber, V., 'Boesposobnost' stikha', *Literatura i iskusstvo*, 3 April 1943, p. 3
——— 'Razgovor o poezii', *Literatura i iskusstvo*, 28 August 1943, p. 2
Isakovskii, M., 'O sovetskoi pesne', *Oktiabr'*, 9 (1944), 115–120
Iswolsky, H., 'Russian Emigré Literature in World War Two', *Russian Review*, 6, no.1 (1946), 69–76
Kapusto, Iu., 'Oni ostalis' molodymi', *Novyi mir*, 4 (1959), 260–264
Kardin, V., 'Poeziia podviga i podvig poezii', *Nedelia*, 12 (1964), 6–7
——— 'Prodolzhenie zhizni', in *Den' poezii* (Moscow, 1960), 150–153
Kedrina, Z., 'Ispytanie ognem', *Oktiabr'*, 12 (1942), 85–93
Kezhun, B., 'Stikhi na fronte', *Zvezda*, 12 (1966), 118–122
Khrenkov, D., 'Literatory perednego kraia', *Literatura i iskusstvo*, 16 January 1943, p. 2
King, B., 'Soviet Literature in War-Time', *Anglo-Soviet Journal*, 5, no.1 (1944), 28–33
Kireeva, A., 'Bessonnaia povest': o stikhakh na voennoi teme', *Pravda*, 21 June 1985, p. 3.
Knipovich, E., '"Krasivaia" nepravda o voine', *Znamia*, 9–10 (1944), 207–213
Kochetkov, V., 'Zhivaia pamiat' naroda: perechityvaia voennuiu liriku', *Moskva*, 5 (1971), 205–212
——— 'Poeziia velikoi voiny', *Nash sovremennik*, 5 (1985), 169–174
Kogan, A. G., 'Opyt zhizni i opyt iskusstva', *Voprosy literatury*, 5 (1975), 192–224
——— 'Pamiat' serdtsa: pisateli na Velikoi Otechestvennoi voine', *V mire knig*, 5 (1984), 9–12
——— 'Vospominanii vzryvchataia zona: iz nabliudenii nad frontovoi poeziei', *Novyi mir*, 4 (1979), 250–257
Kogan, A. G., M. A. Tseitlin, 'Pisateli vo frontovoi pechati', in *Istoriia russkoi sovetskoi literatury*, ed. by A. G. Dement'ev, 3 vols (Moscow, 1958–1961), III, 586–605
Kolpakova, E., 'Literatura na voine', *Voprosy literatury*, 8 (1957), 59–72
Kondratovich, A., 'Pamiati pavshikh', *Literaturnoe obozrenie*, 1 (1977), 21–23
Konstantinov, V., 'Pesni muzhestva: stikhi leningradskikh poetov', *Ogonek*, 10–11 (1943), p. 14
Kryshchuk, N., 'Molodye pishut o voine', *Sovetskaia kul'tura*, 6 May 1986, p. 4
Kuniaev, S., 'Radi zhizni na zemle: sovetskaia poeziia o Velikoi Otechestvennoi voine', *Molodaia gvardiia*, 8 (1987), 246–267
Kuzovleva, T., 'Stikhi ostalis', imena ostalis'', *Literaturnoe obozrenie*, 5 (1975), 36–37
Lapin, K., 'Pisateli na voine', *Literatura i zhizn'*, 23 February 1962, p. 4
Larikov, T. I., 'Literaturnoe ob"edinenie Krasnoi Armii i flota', *Voprosy russkoi literatury*, 3, no.18 (L'vov university, 1971), 60–67

Lavretskii, A., 'Sotsialisticheskii chelovek Velikoi Otechestvennoi voiny', *Znamia*, 11–12 (1943), 269–277
Lavrov, V., 'Pobed i bed nepovtorimyi opyt', *Den' poezii* (Leningrad, 1988), 168–186.
Lazarev, L. I., 'Iunoshi sorok pervogo goda', *Voprosy literatury*, 9 (1962), 42–58
——— 'Pered bessmertiem', *Iunost'*, 11 (1963), 73–80
——— 'Tovarishcham potomkam', *Znamia*, 12 (1958), 215–218
——— 'A ikh povybilo zhelezom', *Znamia*, 2 (1988), 215–225
Leites, A., 'Poeziia sviashchennoi voiny', *Literatura i iskusstvo*, 23 February 1943, p. 3
Leonov, B., 'Pamiat' ratnogo podviga: tvorchestvo pisatelei frontovogo pokoleniia', *Molodaia gvardiia*, 5 (1985), 235–247
Levin, F., 'Zhizn' idet vpered', *Literaturnaia gazeta*, 5 October 1946, p. 3
Lipkin, S., 'Narodnyi epos i sovremennost'', *Literatura i iskusstvo*, 8 July 1944, p. 3
'Literatura perioda Velikoi Otechestvennoi voiny', in *Istoriia russkoi sovetskoi literatury*, ed. by A. I. Metchenko, L. M. Poliak, 2 vols (Moscow, 1963), II, 5–87
'Literatura Velikoi Otechestvennoi voiny: na tvorcheskom soveshchanii v soiuze sovetskikh pisatelei', *Literatura i iskusstvo*, 3 April 1943, p. 3
Maiakovskii, V., 'Satiricheskie stikhi 1914 goda', *Zvezda*, 3–4 (1942), 153–154
Makagonenko, G., 'Leningradskaia tema', *Znamia*, 1 (1945), 212–218
Manuilov, V., 'Zhurnal Zvezda v gody blokady', *Zvezda*, 1 (1980), 163–170
Matskin, A., 'Ob ukrashatel'stve i ukrashateliakh', *Znamia*, 11–12 (1943), p. 278
——— 'Pisatel' v stroiu', *Znamia*, 11 (1942), 186–200
McMillin, A., 'The Second World War in Official and Unofficial Russian Prose', in *The Second World War in Literature: eight essays*, ed. by Ian Higgins (London–Edinburgh: Scottish Academic, 1986), 19–31
Messer, R., 'Iumor, smekalka, satira', *Zvezda*, 5–6 (1942), 187–188
'Mesto literatora v Otechestvennoi voine', *Literaturnaia gazeta*, 20 August 1941, p. 1
Metchenko, A., 'Literatura naroda-pobeditelia', *Vol'ga*, 2 (1945), 107–123
——— 'Obraz Rodiny v poezii Velikoi Otechestvennoi voiny', *Vol'ga*, 1 (1943), 59–70
Mialo, K., 'Posviashchenie v nebytie', *Novyi mir*, 8 (1990), 229–242
Miasnikov, A., 'Literatura i voina: 16 mesiatsev', *Oktiabr'*, 11 (1942), 136–144
——— 'Otechestvennaia voina i sovetskaia literatura', *Kommunisticheskii internatsional*, 7 (1942), 68–75
Mikhailov, A. A., 'Tri emblemy: iz zametok o poezii voennykh let', *Nash sovremennik*, 5 (1977), 178–184
——— 'Svetlaia radost' pobedy', *Novyi mir*, 5 (1975), 269–273
——— 'Kak na voine soldaty: o tvorchestve poetov-frontovikov', *Literaturnaia gazeta*, 1 May 1975, p. 6
Mokhirev, I., 'Russkie geroicheskie poemy perioda Velikoi Otechestvennoi voiny', in *O literaturnom masterstve* (Kirov, 1960), 43–91
Nikitin, N., 'Frontovye stikhi', *Znamia*, 3–4 (1942), 281–287
Nikonov, V., 'Poeticheskii dnevnik Otechestvennoi voiny', *Znamia*, 7 (1942), 157–159
Ortenberg, D. I., 'Muzhestvo', *Literaturnaia Rossiia*, 6 May 1966, 6–7
Ozerov, L., 'Pravda zhizni i literaturnye kanony', *Literatura i iskusstvo*, 26 August 1944, p. 3
Papkovskii, B., 'Chuvstvo edinoi Rodiny: zametki o sovetskoi poezii Otechestvennoi voiny', *Zvezda*, 9 (1941), 101–103
Pavlovskii, A. I., 'Prisiagaem pobedoi', *Neva*, 5 (1975), 196–206

——— 'Blokada i poeziia: tema blokady Leningrada v tvorchestve leningradskikh poetov', *Neva*, 1 (1973), 185–192

——— 'Poeticheskii epos blokadnykh let', in *Literaturnyi Leningrad v dni blokady*, ed. by A.I.Pavlovskii, V.A.Kovalev (Leningrad, 1973), 6–37

Pertsov, V., 'O lirike', *Literatura i iskusstvo*, 28 March 1942, p. 2

——— 'Zametki o sovetskoi poezii nashikh dnei', *Literatura i iskusstvo*, 14 March 1942, p. 2

——— 'Literaturnye zametki', *Znamia*, 3 (1944), 156–160

——— 'Podvig i geroi', *Znamia*, 9 (1945), 118–132

Piper, D., 'The Soviet Union', in *The Second World War in Fiction*, ed. by H. Klein, J. Flower, E. Homberger (London: Macmillan, 1984), 131–170

'Pisateli! Ovladevaite voennymi znaniiami!', *Literaturnaia gazeta*, 3 September 1941, p. 1

Poliak, L., 'O "liricheskom epose" Velikoi Otechestvennoi voiny', *Znamia*, 9–10 (1943), 292–299

Ponomarev, G. I., 'Obraz Lenina v russkoi sovetskoi poezii perioda Velikoi Otechestvennoi voiny', *Voprosy russkoi literatury*, 2, no.30 (1977), 52–57

'Preniia po dokladu Tikhonova "Pered novym pod"emom"', *Literaturnaia gazeta*, 22 May 1945, p. 1; 26 May 1945, p. 2

P'ianykh, M. F., 'Tvorchestvo gumanizma: k voprosu o edinstve lichnogo i obshchestvennogo v russkoi lirike 1941–1945', *Uchenye zapiski Kostromskogo gos. ped. in-ta*, vol.7 (Kostroma, 1960), 153–184

——— 'Obraz Rodiny v sovetskoi lirike 1941–1945', *Uchenye zapiski Leningradskogo gos. ped. in-ta*, 154, no.2 (Leningrad, 1957), 33–63

——— 'Voina i sovetskaia literatura', *Neva*, 12 (1978), p. 192.

——— 'Epos i lirika srazhaiushcheisia Rossii', *Vecherniaia sredniaia shkola*, 3 (1990), 43–47.

Radetskaia, M. M., 'Obraz pokoleniia v stikhakh o poetakh-uchastnikakh Velikoi Otechestvennoi voiny', in *Voprosy russkoi literatury*, vol.2, no.52 (L'vov University, 1988), 23–30

Rapina, O., 'Poety-frontoviki', *Literaturnaia Rossiia*, 12 August 1988, p. 17

Reizov, V., 'Il'ia Avramenko: Noch' nakanune bessmertiia', *Zvezda*, 4 (1943), 119–120

Reznik, O., 'Khudozhestvennaia publitsistika v gody voiny', *Novyi mir*, 11–12 (1945), 286–306

Rubashkin, A., 'Nikto ne zabyt', *Znamia*, 5 (1986), 230–232

Runin, B., 'Kniga pamiati', *Novyi mir*, 5 (1986), 247–250

——— 'Molodye golosa', *Novyi mir*, 12 (1947), 191–216

Saianov, V., 'Dnevnik pisatelia: Zvezda v 1945 godu', *Zvezda*, 7–8 (1944), 107–108

Sandomirsky, V., 'Soviet War Poetry', *Russian Review*, 4, no.1 (1944), 47–66

——— 'The Sad Armchair: Notes on Soviet War and Post-war Lyrical Poetry', *Harvard Slavonic Studies*, 3 (1957), 289–327

Segedi, I., 'Poets and Poetry in War–Time Russia', *Poetry Review* (Oct–Dec 1944), 311–319

Sergeev, A., 'Razgovor o poezii', *Literatura i iskusstvo*, 6 June 1942, p. 2

Shchipachev, S., 'Voennaia poeziia', *Literatura i iskusstvo*, 3 July 1943, p. 4

Shestinskii, O., 'Vechnaia kniga poezii: o tvorchestve poetov blokadnogo Leningrada', *Avrora*, 1 (1974), 62–64

Shklovskii, V., 'Sovremennost' i zlobodnevnost'', *Literatura i iskusstvo*, 10 April 1943, p. 3

——— 'Stikhi o blokade', *Znamia*, 4 (1943), 172–174

Shoshin, V., '"...I sodrognesh'sia, stikhom pronzennyi": k dvadtsatiletiiu proryva blokady', *Neva*, 1 (1963), 171–177

——— 'Vestniki velikoi pobedy: o leningradskoi poezii perioda Velikoi Otechestvennoi voiny', *Russkaia literatura*, 4 (1985), 142–149

Simmons, E. J., 'Soviet War Literature', *University of Toronto Quarterly*, (April 1944), 251–257

Simonov, K., 'Podumaem ob otsutstvuiushchikh', *Literatura i iskusstvo*, 19 August 1944, p. 3

——— 'Zametki pisatelia', *Novyi mir*, 1 (1947), 157–153

Siniavskii, A., M. I. Fetisov, 'Sovetskaia literatura v gody Velikoi Otechestvennoi voiny', in *Russkaia sovetskaia literatura*, ed. by L. I. Timofeeva (Moscow, 1955), 509–538

Siniavskii, A., 'Literatura perioda Velikoi Otechestvennoi voiny', in *Istoriia russkoi sovetskoi literatury*, ed. by A. G. Dement'ev, 3 vols (Moscow, 1958–1961), III, 5–53

Skosyrev, P., 'Otveta ne posledovalo: o kritike v nashi dni', *Novyi mir*, 4 (1943), 118–123

Slowchower, H., 'Fear, Tragedy and Humour in Soviet Literature', *Books Abroad*, 16 (1942), 246–251

Slutskii, B., 'Vozdukh frontovoi', *Znamia*, 9 (1982), 115–119

Smerdov, A., 'Molodye poety', *Sibirskie ogni*, 5 (1945), 256–265

Smith, F. D., 'The Spiritual Triumph of Russian Literature', *Southwest Review*, 31 (1945–46), 200–205

Solodar', Ts., 'Groznyi smekh', *Literatura i iskusstvo*, 19 January 1942, p. 2

Solov'ev, V., 'V dni voiny i mira: o poezii Orlova, Mezhirova, Slutskogo, Samoilova', *Neva*, 2 (1973), 181–189

'Sorok let nazad: iz podborki vystuplenii sovetskikh pisatelei po radio', *Druzhba narodov*, 5 (1985), 7–9

'Soveshchanie literaturovedov i kritikov', *Literatura i iskusstvo*, 28 February 1942, p. 4

Spasskii, S., 'Pis'ma o poezii: pis'mo pervoe', *Zvezda*, 1 (1945), 118–123

Spivak, I. A., 'Rodina v poezii Velikoi Otechestvennoi voiny 1943–44', *Voprosy russkoi literatury*, 1, no.10 (L'vov University, 1969), 40–46

——— 'Stikhotvornaia publitsistika nachal'nogo perioda Velikoi Otechestvennoi voiny', *Voprosy russkoi literatury*, 1, no.35 (L'vov University, 1980), 3–10

Stalin, I., Speech given 7 November on Red Square, *Novyi Mir*, 9–10 (1941), 14–16

Stepanov, N., 'Boris Lavrenev: Veter s moria', *Zvezda*, 9 (1941), 107

Subbotskii, L., 'Cherty kharaktera bol'shevika v khudozhestvennoi literature', *Partiinoe stroitel'stvo*, 20 (1945), 43–47

——— 'Oruzhie pobedy', *Znamia*, 5–6 (1945), 161–167

——— 'Sovetskii ofitser v khudozhestvennoi literature', *Voennyi vestnik*, 5 (1945), 27–34

Surkov, A., 'Tovarishcham kritikam', *Literatura i iskusstvo*, 8 March 1942, p. 2

——— 'Molodye golosa', *Literaturnaia gazeta*, 2 December 1944, p. 3

——— 'Predchuvstvie pobedy', *Literaturnaia gazeta*, 7 November 1944, p. 3

——— 'Poeziia naroda-pobeditelia', *Literaturnaia gazeta*, 17 May 1945, p. 2

——— 'Tvorcheskii otchet na zasedanii voennoi komissii Soiuza Pisatelei 12.7.43', in *Sovetskie pisateli na frontakh Velikoi Otechestvennoi voiny*, Literaturnoe nasledstvo, 78, 2 vols (Moscow, 1966), I, 331–343

Taganov, L. N., 'Velikaia Otechestvennaia voina i literatura', *Voprosy literatury*, 6 (1967), 19–25

Tarasenkov, A., 'Poeziia v dni voiny', in *Idei i obrazy sovetskoi literatury* (Moscow, 1949), 175–200

——— 'Replika kritiku', *Literaturnaia gazeta*, 12 October 1946, p. 2

Tikhonov, N., 'Boevaia molodost'', *Literatura i iskusstvo*, 5 September 1942, p. 2

——— 'V ogne ispytanii', *Literatura i iskusstvo*, 14 February 1942, p. 2

——— 'Slovo o literature', *Leningrad*, 13–14 (1943), 4–5

——— 'Boevaia pereklichka', *Literaturnaia gazeta*, 7 November 1944, p. 3

——— 'Otechestvennaia voina i sovetskaia literatura', *Novyi mir*, 1–2 (1944), 180–189

——— 'Pered novym pod"emom: sovetskaia literatura v 1944–1945 gody', *Literaturnaia gazeta*, 17 May 1945, p. 2

Timofeev, L., 'Sovetskaia literatura i voina', *Znamia*, 11 (1942), 178–185

Tolstoi, A., 'Chetvert' veka sovetskoi literatury', *Novyi mir*, 11–12 (1942), 206–218

——— 'O literature i voine', *Literatura i iskusstvo*, 5 December 1942, p. 1

Tregub, S., 'Mesto poeta', *Literatura i iskusstvo*, 5 December 1942, p. 2

Troshchenko, E., 'Poeziia molodykh', *Literatura i iskusstvo*, 11 September 1943, p. 3

Tumanovskii, R., '1941–1945: front v pisatel'skoi sud'be. Materialy', *Knizhnoe obozrenie*, 19 (1988), p. 8

Urban, A., 'Trudnye budni poezii', *Literaturnoe obozrenie*, 4 (1988), 20–25

——— 'Sviashchennaia voina', *Zvezda*, 2 (1984), 181–197

Utkin, I., 'Poeziia v dni voiny', in *Den' poezii* (Moscow, 1973), 262–264

——— 'Pisatel' i chuvstva naroda', *Literatura i iskusstvo*, 17 April 1943, p. 2

Veresov, L., 'Oboronnaia poeziia v 1932 g.', *Zalp*, 2 (1933), p. 47

Vikulov, S., 'Imia etomu oruzhiiu: zametki o russkoi sovetskoi poezii nachala Velikoi Otechestvennoi voiny', *Nash sovremennik*, 5 (1980), 167–176

Vykhodtsev, P. S., 'Iz opyta raboty sovetskikh poetov nad poemami v gody Velikoi Otechestvennoi voiny',in *Voprosy sovetskoi literatury*, 6 (Moscow, 1957), 202–254

'Za rubezhom: angliiskaia voennaia poeziia', *Literatura i iskusstvo*, 5 September 1942, p. 3

Zaitsev, V. A., 'Russkaia sovetskaia poeziia epokhi Velikoi Otechestvennoi voiny: zhanrovo-stilevye tendentsii', *Vestnik moskovskogo universiteta*, seriia 9, filologiia, no.3 (Moscow, 1980), 3–15

Secondary Works on Specific Authors

Akhmatova

Bazhenov, M. N., '"I my sokhranim tebia, russkaia rech'": o stikhotvorenii A.Akhmatovoi "Muzhestvo"', *Russkaia rech'*, 1 (1982), 41–42

Nekrasova, E. A., 'Shedevr grazhdanskoi liriki: o stikhotvorenii A.Akhmatovoi "Muzhestvo"', *Russkaia rech'*, 1 (1982), 43–47

P'ianykh, M. F., '"Menia, kak reku, surovaia epokha povernula": o poezii A.Akhmatovoi vtoroi poloviny 1930-kh—pervoi poloviny 1940-kh godov', *Zvezda*, 6 (1989), 195–201

Reeder, R., *Anna Akhmatova: Poet and Prophet* (London: Alison and Busby, 1994)

Serebrovskii, E., 'Doch' svoei Rodiny', *Zvezda*, 1 (1988), 178–183

Sluzhevskii, I., 'Tak vot ty takoi, vostok!', *Zvezda vostoka*, 5 (1982), 96–100

Aliger

Kedrina, Z., 'Schast'e', *Znamia*, 2–3 (1943), 224–229

Lotman, L., 'Margarita Aliger: Stikhi i poemy 1935–1943', *Zvezda*, 7–8 (1944), 191
Troshchenko, E., 'Poeziia pokoleniia, sozrevshego na voine', *Novyi mir*, 9 (1943), 102–119

Antokol'skii

Afanas'ev, V., 'Istoriia i sovremennost'', *Novyi mir*, 1–2 (1942), 242–244
Bank, N., 'Moi syn byl komsomol'tsem', *Avrora*, 5 (1982), 129–134
Khelemskii, Ia., 'Chtob drugim dyshalos' goriacho: o poezii P. Antokol'skogo', *Oktiabr'*, 7 (1976), 195–206
Nikolaev, V., 'Stikhi pervogo polugodiia', *Literatura i iskusstvo*, 18 July 1942, p. 3
Ozerov, L., 'Synov'ia i otsy', *Literatura i iskusstvo*, 26 June 1943, p. 2
Potapova, G. V., 'Vsia zhizn' moia, vsia bol' moia—k oruzhiiu!: o poeme Antokol'skogo "Syn"', *Russkaia rech'*, 3 (1985), 56–65
Vasil'ev, S., 'Golos poeta', *Literatura i iskusstvo*, 21 March 1942, p. 2
Vengrov, N., 'Syn', *Novyi mir*, 3 (1944) 130–134

Berggol'ts

Abramov, A. M., 'Poema Ol'gi Berggol'ts "Tvoi put'"', in *Metod i masterstvo*, ed. by V. V. Gura, vol.3, Sovetskaia literatura (Vologda, 1971), 162–176
Ar'ev, A., 'Litsom k Leningradu', *Zvezda*, 5 (1985), 184–189
Bank, N., *Ol'ga Berggol'ts* (Leningrad, 1962)
——— 'Zapominai vse eto...', *Zvezda*, 2 (1978), 183–199
——— 'Liricheskie poemy O.Berggol'ts voennykh let', in *Filologicheskii sbornik studencheskogo nauchnogo obshchestva* (Leningrad, 1957), 63–86
Chashchina, L., 'Vse shlo k tebe, torzhestvennaia zrelost'', *Literaturnaia ucheba*, 3 (1985), 116–126
Danilin, Iu., 'Poemy Ol'gi Berggol'ts', *Oktiabr'*, 2 (1943), 111–113
Danin, D., 'Preodolenie stradaniia', *Znamia*, 7 (1946), 179–183
Dobin, E., 'Pereklichka serdets', *Zvezda*, 5–6 (1945), 146–152
Dudin, M., 'Po pravu razdelennoi sud'by: o poezii O.Berggol'ts', *Avrora*, 1 (1976), 34–36
Fiedler-Stolz, E. M., *Ol'ga Berggol'c: Aspekte ihres lyrischen Werkes*, Arbeiten und Texte zur Slawistik, 13 (München, 1976)
Gruzdev, I., 'Leningradskaia poema', *Literatura i iskusstvo*, 16 January 1943, p. 3
Gubko, N., 'Put' k vershinam', *Neva*, 5 (1961), 190–194
Kalitin, N., 'Leningradskaia tetrad'', *Novyi mir*, 4 (1943), 125–127
Khmel'nitskaia, T., 'Soprichastnost' vremeni: tvorchestvo Ol'gi Berggol'ts', in *Golosa vremeni* (Moscow–Leningrad, 1963), 125–150
Khrenkov, D., *Ot serdtsa k serdtsu*, 2nd ed. (Leningrad, 1982)
Levin, L., 'Zhestokii rastsvet', *Novyi mir*, 4 (1979), 170–191
Maklina, E., 'Leningradskaia poema', *Leningrad*, 15–16 (1943), p. 32
Moldavskii, D., 'Stikhi, prorvavshie blokadu', *Literaturnaia gazeta*, 7 March 1973, p. 5
Pavlovskii, A. I., 'Poeziia narodnogo muzhestva i gneva', *Russkaia literatura*, 3 (1959), 79–88
——— *Stikh i serdtse* (Leningrad, 1962)
——— 'Tak verila, tak pela', *Zvezda*, 5 (1988), 187–199
——— 'Blokadnaia rapsodiia', in *Poety-sovremenniki* (Moscow–Leningrad, 1966), 53–102
Rubashkin, A., 'Bol'she, chem vospominaniia', *Neva*, 5 (1979), 185–189
——— 'Vspominaia blokadnuiu muzu', *Neva*, 1 (1980), 193–194
——— 'Dva golosa', *Neva*, 3 (1973), 183–190

Sidorovskii, L., '"Ot serdtsa k serdtsu. Tol'ko etot put'...": Ol'ga Berggol'ts, poeziia i sud'ba', *Literaturnaia Rossiia*, 25 March 1988, 16–17
Siniavskii, A., 'Poeziia i proza O.Berggol'ts', *Novyi mir*, 5 (1960), 225–236
Tschöpl, C., *Die sowjetische Lyrik-Diskussion: Ol'ga Berggol'c Leningrader Blockadedichtung als Paradigma* (München: Fink, 1988)
Zlatova, E., 'Orden stoikikh', *Literatura i iskusstvo*, 24 October 1942, p. 2

Dolmatovskii
Antokol'skii, P., 'Voennye stikhi Dolmatovskogo', *Literaturnaia gazeta*, 7 April 1945, p. 3
Azarov, V., 'Stikhi moikh tovarishchei', *Znamia*, 3 (1945), 169–175
Kedrina, Z., 'Geroi spravedlivoi voiny', *Oktiabr'*, 4 (1941), 215–223
Makarov, A., 'Po stranitsam zhurnalov', *Novyi mir*, 5–6 (1945), 172–182
Troshchenko, E., 'Poeziia pokoleniia, sozrevshego na voine', *Novyi mir*, 10–11 (1943), 164–171
——— 'Stikhi o voine', *Literatura i iskusstvo*, 23 February 1944, p. 3

Drunina
Slutskii, B., 'Sred' ognia', foreword to Iu.Drunina, *Ne byvaet liubvi neschastlivoi* (Moscow, 1977), 3–5

Dudin
Dymshits, A., 'Soldatskaia lirika', *Znamia*, 5–6 (1945), 188–191
Khmel'nitskaia, T., 'Stikhi Mikhaila Dudina', *Zvezda*, 5–6 (1943), 192–195
——— 'Mikhail Dudin, Koster na perekrestke', *Zvezda*, 7–8 (1944), 193–194
Lapshin, M., 'Poeziia ataki', *Krasnaia zvezda*, 21 November 1986, p. 4.
L'vov, M., 'K shtyku prirovniav pero', *Sovetskaia kul'tura*, 20 November 1986, p. 3
Solov'ev, B., 'Nepreodelennoe uchenichestvo', *Literaturnaia gazeta*, 16 June 1945, p. 3

Erenburg
Goldberg, A., *Ilya Ehrenburg: Writing, Politics and the Art of Survival* (London: Weidenfeld and Nicolson, 1984)
Laychuk, J. L., 'The Lyric Verse of I. I. Erenburg during the Great Patriotic War', *Canadian Slavic Papers*, XIX, 1, 64–75
Marcou, L., *Ilya Ehrenbourg: un homme dans son siècle* (Paris: Plon, 1992)
Oksenov, I., 'Vernost' chelovechestvu', *Zvezda*, 9 (1941), 89–92
Stupples, P., 'Il'ia Erenburg and the Jewish Anti-Fascist Committee', *New Zealand Slavonic Journal*, 2 (1977), 13–28

Grossman
Ellis, F., *Vasiliy Grossman: the Genesis and Evolution of a Russian Heretic* (Oxford: Berg, 1994)
——— 'Army and Party in Conflict: Soldiers and Commissars in the Prose of Vasiliy Grossman' in J and C Garrard, eds., *World War Two and the Soviet People*(London: Macmillan, 1993), 180–201
Lamont, R. C., 'Vassili Grossman's "Zhizn' i sud'ba": the "Life and Fate" of the First Dissident Novel', *World Literature Today*, 59, no.1 (1985), 46–48
Lipkin, S., *Zhizn' i sud'ba Vasiliia Grossmana* (Moscow, 1990)
Voinovich, V., 'The "Life and Fate" of Vasily Grossman', *Index on Censorship*, 14, no.5 (1985), 9–10

Gudzenko
Antokol'skii, P., '6 prostykh istin: grazhdanskaia poeziia', *Literaturnaia gazeta*, 19 February 1969, p. 6
Aronov, A., 'Shagnut'-i raspriamit'sia', *Literaturnoe obozrenie*, 5 (1985), 68–70
Bazhov, V., 'Posle ataki' (parody), *Smena*, 9 (1947), p. 13
Erenburg, I., 'Stikhi soldata', *Znamia*, 5–6 (1944), 219–221
——— 'O poete Gudzenko', *Sovetskie pisateli na frontakh Velikoi Otechestvennoi voiny*, ed. by I. I. Anisimov, D. D. Blagoi, A. S. Bushmin et al, Literaturnoe nasledstvo, 78, 2 vols (Moscow, 1966), I, 96
Golovanivskii, S., 'Pevets soldatskogo muzhestva', *Literaturnaia gazeta*, 10 March 1982, p. 5
Gromov, P., 'S.Gudzenko, Odnopolchane', *Zvezda*, 7–8 (1944), 192–193
Kardin, V., 'Chelovek tvoego pokoleniia', in *Den' poezii* (Moscow, 1971), p. 168
Khelemskii, Ia., 'Rasskaz o tovarishche',in *Den' poezii* (Moscow, 1960), 177–181
——— 'Po starym pylaiushchim dorogam', *Znamia*, 3 (1969), 202–218
Kutler, S., 'Byt' nuzhnym—eto schast'e', *Vecherniaia Moskva*, 8 June 1962, p. 3
Leont'ev, A., 'Cherty pokoleniia', *Novyi mir*, 12 (1962), 256–258
Levitanskii, Iu., 'Poety ostaiutsia v stroiu', *Literaturnaia gazeta*, 27 February 1960, p. 3
Osetrov, E., 'Zhivaia krov' sobytii: obzor voennoi poezii', *Vechernii Leningrad*, 20 March 1970, p. 3
Ozerov, L., 'Zhizn' poeta prodolzhaetsia', *Literaturnaia gazeta*, 6 February 1962, p. 3
Pozdniaev, K., 'Nadezhnyi drug', *Literaturnaia Rossiia*, February 1963, p. 17
Shister, E., 'Po sledam podviga: zapiski', *Sovetskaia kul'tura*, 16 March 1973, p. 3
Solov'ev, V., 'Vroven' s istoriei', *Neva*, 11 (1975), 189–191
Strashnov, S. L., 'Pravda nastroieniia: Odnopolchane', *Literaturnaia ucheba*, 2 (1984), 130–137

Iashin
Khabarova, A., 'Skvoz' dushu poeta' *Vol'ga*, 2 (1979), 182–184
Mal'chukov, L., 'Voennaia strada poeta', *Sever*, 6 (1978), 123–125
Reshetnikov, L., 'Bol' i sila sovesti: o poezii Aleksandra Iashina', *Sibirskie ogni*, 12 (1985), 148–155
Rudenko, G. G., 'Poeziia A.Iashina nachala voiny', *Voprosy russkoi literatury*, vol.2, no.37 (L'vov University, 1981), 21–28

Inber
'Dusha Leningrada', *Zvezda*, 5–6 (1942), p. 194
Gruzdev, I., 'Leningradskaia poema', *Literatura i iskusstvo*, 16 January 1943, p. 3
Poliak, L., 'Vera Inber: o Leningrade', *Znamia*, 4 (1944), 150–153

Isakovskii
Derman, A., 'Stikhi Isakovskogo', *Literatura i iskusstvo*, 9 January 1943, p. 3
Kamnev, A., 'Novye stikhi Isakovskogo', *Literatura i iskusstvo*, 24 October 1942, p. 4
Smirnova, V., 'Avtor pesni', *Znamia*, 5–6 (1943), 246–248

Kedrin
Evtushenko, E., 'Vossozdatel' pamiati: perechityvaia D.Kedrina', *Literaturnaia Rossiia*, 4 August 1978, p. 18
Kasack, W., 'Dmitrii Kedrin', *Osteuropa*, 11 (1978), 947–948

Levin, L., 'Na mnogo let vpered', *Novyi mir*, 12 (1984), 237–241
Ozerov, L., 'Od pisat' ne umeiu', *Literaturnaia gazeta*, 11 March 1987, p. 6
Petrunin, Iu., 'V etoi bitve pobedim my', *Bibliotekar'*, 2 (1982), 37–38
Sel'vinskii, I., 'Stikhi D.Kedrina', *Novyi mir*, 8 (1957), 233–236
Smeliakov, Ia., 'Stroi grazhdanskoi liry: masterstvo pisatelia', *Voprosy literatury*, 4 (1966), 123–129
Soloukhin, V., 'Ubit ne na voine', *Literaturnaia gazeta*, 13 January 1959, p. 2
Stesin, S., 'Poet sverkaiushchego talanta', *Molodaia gvardiia*, 2 (1977), 296–300
Tartakovskii, P., *Dmitrii Kedrin: zhizn' i tvorchestvo* (Moscow, 1963)
Urban, A., 'Otkryvaia knigu stikhov: zametki', *Zvezda*, 1 (1975), 189–209
Voronova, O., 'Obnazhennost' serdtsa', *V mire knig*, 2 (1967), 34–35
Znatnov, A., 'Moia sud'ba, tvoia sud'ba, Rossiia!', *Literaturnaia Rossiia*, 30 January 1987, p. 18

Kirsanov

Mineralov, Iu., *Poeziia, poetika, poet* (Moscow, 1984)
Nikonov, V., 'S.Kirsanov: Poema fronta', *Znamia*, 8 (1942), 179–181

Kogan

Narovchatov, S., 'Tol'ko chutochki prishuriv glaza', *Literaturnaia gazeta*, 18 September 1974, p. 7
Panchenko, O. N., 'Prizyv okhripshei polkovoi truby: obraz trubacha v poezii P. Kogana i N. Maiorova', *Russkaia rech'*, 4 (1985), 69–76
Samoilov, D., 'Est' v nashikh dniakh takaia tochnost'', *Literaturnaia gazeta*, 15 May 1985, p. 5
——— 'V filibusterskom dal'nem more', *Komsomol'skaia pravda*, 22 May 1974, p. 4

Kul'chitskii

L'vov, M., 'Naveki prav: o M.Kul'chitskom', *Literaturnaia gazeta*, 10 April 1985, p. 3
Narovchatov, S., 'Moe, sovetskoe do kornei', *Literaturnaia gazeta*, 19 June 1974, p. 6

Lebedev-Kumach

Derevianko, N., 'Kto napisal "Sviashchennuiu voinu?"', *Argumenty i fakty*, 13 (1991), p. 7

Lifshits

Azarov, V., 'Vozmuzhanie poeta', *Zvezda*, 3 (1943), p. 100
——— 'Stikhi moikh tovarishchei', *Znamia*, 3 (1945), 169–175
Bukhshtab, B., 'Vladimir Lifshits, Zarevo nad zalivom', *Zvezda*, 3 (1945), 142–143
Kedrina, Z., 'Geroi spravedlivoi voiny', *Oktiabr'*, 4 (1941), 215–223

Lukonin

Anninskii, L., 'Pervyi ozhog; o stikhotvorenii M. Lukonina "Kole Otrade"', *Literaturnaia ucheba*, 3 (1980), 78–84
Pechenko, S., 'Poety odnogo pokoleniia', *Voprosy literatury*, 2 (1984), 215–221

L'vov

Erenburg, I., 'Stikhi Mikhaila L'vova', *Literaturnaia gazeta*, 25 November 1944, p. 2

Martynov
Bukhshtab, B., 'Leonid Martynov, Zhar–tsvet', *Zvezda*, 7–8 (1944), 194–195
Leites, A., 'O mysli i dvumyslii v poezii', *Literaturnaia gazeta*, 16 June 1945, p. 3

Mezhirov
Lapshin, M., 'Pole boia poeta', *Moskva*, 5 (1983), 191–193
P'ianykh, M. F., 'Chelovek na belom svete', *Voprosy literatury*, 11 (1983), 46–75

Narovchatov
Mikhailov, A., 'On iz frontovoi pleiady', *Oktiabr'*, 9 (1979), 217–219
Rzhevskaia, E., 'Starinnaia udacha', in *Znaki prepinaniia* (Moscow, 1989), 224–250
Starshinov, N., 'Vernost' teme: tema Velikoi Otechestvennoi voiny v tvorchestve S.Narovchatova', *Pravda*, 23 June 1981, p. 6.
Vospominaniia o Sergee Narovchatove (Moscow, 1990)

Nikolaeva
Aleksandrova, A., 'Vsia zhizn'—bitva v puti', *Znamia*, 5 (1984), 217–223
Makarov, A., 'Po stranitsam zhurnalov', *Novyi mir*, 5–6 (1945), 172–182

Pasternak
Antokol'skii, P., 'Boris Pasternak', *Znamia*, 9–10 (1943), 312–314
Durylin, S., 'Zemnoi prostor: pis'ma B. L. Pasternaku', *Literaturnaia ucheba*, 6 (1988), 111–114
Fleishman, L., *Boris Pasternak: the Poet and His Politics* (Cambridge, MA–London: Harvard University Press, 1990)
Gromov, P., 'Boris Pasternak: Zemnoi prostor', *Zvezda*, 5–6 (1945), 157–158
Margvelashvili, G., 'Dnei sviazyvaiushchaia nit': o tvorchestve B.Pasternaka v 1941–1945', *Literaturnaia Gruziia*, 11 (1980), 142–156
'O novykh stikhakh Borisa Pasternaka', *Novyi mir*, 7–8 (1943), 157–160
Simonov, K., 'Pravil'nyi put'', *Ogonek*, 34–35 (1943), p. 13
Tarasenkov, A., 'Novye stikhi Borisa Pasternaka', *Znamia*, 4 (1945), 136–139

Prokof'ev
Dobin, E., 'Liricheskaia tema Aleksandra Prokof'eva', *Zvezda*, 1 (1944), 119–124
Grinberg, I., 'Pesn' o rodine', *Literatura i iskusstvo*, 13 November 1943, p. 3
Grinberg, I., E. Dobin, *Klinkami pesen boevykh: poeziia A.Prokof'eva* (Moscow, 1966)
Kondrashov, G., 'V dni blokady: vstrechi s A. Prokof'evym', *Zvezda*, 1 (1974), 189–195
Zolotnitskii, D., 'Oruzhie agitatora-pesnotvortsa', *Zvezda*, 5–6 (1942), 183–185

Rylenkov
Danilin, Iu., 'Stikhi N.Rylenkova', *Literatura i iskusstvo*, 19 June 1943, p. 4
Gromov, P., 'Nikolai Rylenkov, Otchii dom', *Zvezda*, 2 (1945), p. 140

Sel'vinskii
Aseev, N., 'Litoe slovo', *Znamia*, 10 (1945), p. 175
Ozerov, L., 'Voennaia lirika Sel'vinskogo', *Literatura i iskusstvo*, 25 July 1942, p. 3
Petrovskii, V. I., 'Ballada o leninizme I.Sel'vinskogo', *Voprosy russkoi literatury*, 1, no.25 (L'vov University, 1975), 18–21

Shchipachev
Vengrov, N., 'Lirika S Shchipacheva', *Novyi mir*, 1–2 (1944), 219–221

Shefner
Azarov, V., 'Stikhi moikh tovarishchei', *Znamia*, 3 (1945), 169–175
Khmel'nitskaia, T., 'Voennye stikhi Shefnera', *Zvezda*, 4 (1944), 118–121

Shishova
Shklovskii, V, 'Stikhi o blokade', *Znamia*, 4 (1943), 172–174

Shubin
Kogan, A. G., *Pavel Shubin* (Moscow, 1974)
Serova, E., 'Odin iz geroicheskoi pleiady', *Neva*, 6 (1975), p. 193
Shevelev, A., 'Vernost'. Vera. Rodina. Sud'ba', *Zvezda*, 7 (1983), 203–204

Simonov
Aleksandrov, V., 'Pis'mo v Moskvu', *Znamia*, 1 (1943), 149–160
Gekht S, 'Frontovoi bloknot K.Simonova', *Literaturnaia gazeta*, 1 October 1941, p. 3
Golubkov, M. M., 'Grazhdanin svoego vremeni: lirika Simonova voennykh let', *Literatura v shkole*, 6 (1985), 12–15
Kedrina Z, 'Geroi spravedlivoi voiny', *Oktiabr'*, 4 (1941), 215–223
——— 'Ispytanie kharakterom', *Oktiabr'*, 5–6 (1942), 138–143
Kostrov, V., 'Ty pomnish', Alesha', *Literaturnaia gazeta*, 10 April 1985, p. 3
Lazarev, L. I., 'Dolg i muzhestvo: poeziia Simonova', *Novyi mir*, 1 (1982), 232–245
Papernyi, Z., 'Stikhi i sud'ba: poeziia K. Simonova', *Znamia*, 5 (1981), 246–247
Sadovskii, E.,'Pisateli na fronte', *Literaturnaia gazeta*, 30 July 1941, p. 2
Seemann, K.-D., 'Rezeptionswandel eines Kriegsgedichts: Konstantin Simonows Zdi menia in der sowjetischen Kritik', *Welt der Slaven*, 22, 1 (1977), 370–390
Tregub, S., 'Liricheskii dnevnik K. Simonova', *Literatura i iskusstvo*, 4 July 1942, p. 2
Troshchenko, E., 'Poeziia pokoleniia, sozrevshego na voine', *Novyi mir*, 7–8 (1943), 124–138

Slutskii
Boldyrev, Iu., 'Boris Slutskii: esse', *Ogonek*, 20 (1989), 24–26
Smith, G. S., 'Epitaph for the Soviet Experience', *TLS*, 19 June 1992, p. 22
Urban, A., 'Stikh vstaet, kak soldat', *Zvezda*, 4 (1984), 188–200
——— 'Sud'ba voiny, sud'ba stikhov', *Zvezda*, 6 (1970), 193–202

Surkov
Abramov, A. M., 'Stikhi Surkova v gody voiny', *Trudy Voronezhskogo universiteta*, 59 (Voronezh, 1957), 29–42
Antokol'skii, P., 'Stikhi Alekseia Surkova', *Literatura i iskusstvo*, 8 May 1943, p. 2
Borovkova, O., 'Stikhi A. Surkova', *Novyi mir*, 8 (1945), 127–128
Kedrina, Z., 'Poet v boevom stroiu', *Oktiabr'*, 9 (1945), 155–159
Leites, A., 'Novye stikhi A. Surkova', *Novyi mir*, 3–4 (1942), 241–245
Kostrov, V., 'Ty pomnish', Alesha', *Literaturnaia gazeta*, 10 April 1985, p. 3
Sadovskii, E., 'Pisateli na fronte', *Literaturnaia gazeta*, 30 July 1941, p. 2
Shapiro, Z., 'Pisateli-frontoviki', *Literatura i iskusstvo*, 1 January 1942, p. 3
Troinov, P., 'Stikhi A Surkova', *Literatura i iskusstvo*, 23 September 1944, p. 3

Vasil'evskaia, E. A., 'Poeziia grazhdanstvennosti: o voennykh stikhakh A. Surkova', *Russkaia rech'*, 1 (1976), 44–50
Vengrov, N., 'Poet na fronte', *Znamia*, 7–8 (1941), 186–188
——— 'Zrenie i masterstvo poeta', *Znamia*, 8 (1945), 175–183
Verkin, A., 'Tsennoe oruzhie', *Literatura i iskusstvo*, 17 October 1942, p. 2

Suvorov
Khmel'nitskaia, T., 'Georgii Suvorov, Slovo soldata', *Zvezda*, 1 (1945), 150–151
Khrenkov, D., 'Kak bystro nashe vremia proshlo', *Literaturnaia gazeta*, 26 June 1985, p. 7
Narovchatov, S., 'Poet na fronte', *Literatura i iskusstvo*, 8 May 1974, p. 6

Svetlov
Ozerov, L., 'Poemy Mikhaila Svetlova', *Literatura i iskusstvo*, 22 August 1942, p. 2
Tochenyi, O., 'Ia obnimaiu armiiu svoiu', *Krasnaia zvezda*, 17 June 1983, p. 4

Tikhonov
Afanas'ev, V., 'Stikhi o geroizme i muzhestve', *Novyi mir*, 10 (1942), p. 127
Antokol'skii, P., 'Nikolai Tikhonov', *Krasnaia nov'*, 3–4 (1942), 139–144
Kalitin, N., 'Poeziia muzhestva', *Oktiabr'*, 2 (1943), 104–107
Reznik, O., 'Rozhdenie sovremennogo eposa', *Novyi mir*, 1–2 (1942), 222–228
Rozen, A., 'Poet geroicheskogo Leningrada', *Leningrad*, 1–2 (1946), p. 5
Simonov, K., 'Soldatskoe serdtse', *Literatura i iskusstvo*, 16 April 1942, p. 2
Tolstoi, A., 'Nikolai Tikhonov', *Sobranie sochinenii*, 10 vols (Moscow, 1958–61), X, 520–522
Zenkevich, M., 'Nikolai Tikhonov: Ognennyi god', *Znamia*, 8 (1942), p. 178

Tsvetaeva
Belkina, M., *Skreshchenie sudeb*, 2nd ed. (Moscow, 1992)
Kudrova, I., 'Tret'ia versiia: eshche raz o poslednikh dniakh Mariny Tsvetaevoi', *Novyi mir*, 2 (1994), 205–229

Tvardovskii
Akatkin, V. M., *Doroga i pamiat': o Tvardovskom* (Voronezh, 1989)
Belozertsev, A., 'Tsvet frontovoi druzhby', *Literaturnaia Rossiia*, 31 July 1987, 6–7
Danin, D., 'Obraz russkogo voina', *Literatura i iskusstvo*, 3 October 1942, p. 2
Dement'ev, V., 'Poet na velikoi voine', *Moskva*, 5 (1975), 196–206
Ermilov, V., 'Russkii voin Vasilii Terkin', *Literatura i iskusstvo*, 31 October 1942, p. 2
Gorbov, A., 'Voennye stikhi Tvardovskogo', *Novyi mir*, 11–12 (1942), p. 252
Il'in, V. V., ed., *Velikaia otechestvennaia voina v tvorchestve A. T. Tvardovskogo, M. V. Isakovskogo, N. I. Rylenkova* (Smolensk, 1989)
Kolesnikova, V. P., 'Tema rodiny v frontovoi lirike A. Tvardovskogo', *Russkii iazyk v shkole*, 3 (1985), 55–60
Levin, D., 'Tvardovsky's "Everyman"', *Nation*, 211 (1970), 248–249
Makarov, A., 'Aleksandr Tvardovskii i ego kniga pro boitsa', *Novyi mir*, 3 (1946), 191–204.
Makedonov, A. V., *Tvorcheskii put' Tvardovskogo: doma i dorogi* (Moscow, 1981)
Marshak, S., *Radi zhizni na zemle: ob A.Tvardovskom* (Moscow, 1961)
Mokhirev, I., 'O fabule i siuzhete Vasiliia Terkina', in *Uchenye zapiski Kirovskogo gos. ped. in-ta*, vol.11 (Kirov, 1957), 69–84

Pakhareva, K. M., 'Tema voiny v lirike A. Tvardovskogo', *Voprosy russkoi literatury*, 2, no.36, (L'vov University, 1980), 20–26
——— 'K tvorcheskoi istorii poemy A. Tvardovskogo "Dom u dorogi"', *Voprosy russkoi literatury*, 1, no.49 (L'vov University, 1987), 22–29
Pankov, A., 'V trudnoi zhizni boevoi: Vasilii Terkin A. Tvardovskogo i literatura voennogo vremeni', *Znamia*, 6 (1985), 220–231
Pervushin, N., 'Les deux Vasili Tiorkine de la littérature russe', *Canadian Slavic Studies*, 1 (1967), 113–116
'Pis'ma frontovikov o Vasilie Terkine', *Znamia*, 12 (1944), 199–200
Strashnov, S., 'V toske i slave etikh let: voina v khudozhestvennom razvitii A.Tvardovskogo', *Literaturnoe obozrenie*, 6 (1985), 45–50
Tarasenkov, A., 'O Vasilii Terkine A. Tvardovskogo', *Zvezda*, 5–6 (1945), 145–147
Turkov, A., 'Pevets pravdy sushchei', *Kul'tura i zhizn'*, 2 (1958), 29–34
Tvardovskii, A., 'Otvet chitateliam Vasiliia Terkina', *Novyi mir*, 11 (1951), 204–228
Ulaev, G., *V dni godiny gor'koi* (Voronezh, 1986)
Vasilii Terkin A.Tvardovskogo: narodnaia epopeia (Voronezh, 1981)

Utkin
Kirpotin, V., 'Vintovkoi, molotom, perom', *Literaturnaia gazeta*, 24 September 1941, p. 3
Sel'vinskii, I., 'Poeziia I.Utkina', *Literaturnaia gazeta*, 2 December 1944, p. 4

Vinokurov
Urban, A., 'Sud'ba voiny, sud'ba stikhov', *Zvezda*, 6 (1970), 193–202

War Memoirs, Letters and Diaries

Adamovich, A., Bryl', Ia., Kolesnik, V., *Ia iz ognennoi derevni*
Adamovich, A., Granin, D., *Blokadnaia kniga* (Moscow, 1991)
Aleksievich, S. A., *U voiny nezhenskoe litso* (Moscow, 1989)
Antokol'skii, P., '"U menia mnogo raboty": pis'ma poeta k rodnym 1941–1942', *Literaturnaia Rossiia*, 27 July 1986, 16–17
Bank, N., '"Zdes' ostavleno serdtse moe": iz vospominanii Ol'gi Berggol'ts', *Voprosy literatury*, 3 (1985), 28–46
Beilin, A. M., comp., *Riadom s geroiiami* (Leningrad, 1967)
Berggol'ts, O. F., 'Blokadnyi dnevnik', *Aprel'*, 4 (1991), 128–144
——— *Dnevnye zvezdy* (Leningrad, 1960)
——— 'Dnevnye zvezdy, vtoraia chast'—extracts, *Ogonek*, 19 (1990), 15–16
——— 'Iz dnevnikov Ol'gi Berggol'ts', *Vremia i my*, 6, no.57 (1980), 276–302
——— 'Iz dnevnikov Ol'gi Berggol'ts, *Zvezda*, 6 (1990), 153–174
——— 'Pobedonosnoe terpen'e: pis'ma k rodnym vremeni blokady v Leningrade', *Literaturnoe obozrenie*, 5 (1979), 100–112
——— 'Sviatoe eto vremia navsegda s nami: stranitsy dnevnika', *Literaturnaia gazeta*, 23 January 1974, p. 3
Chukovskii, N., 'V osade: iz vospominanii', *Iunost'*, 1 (1966), 8–92
Czapski, J., 'Oblaka i golubi: vstrechi s Akhmatovoi v Tashkente 1942-ogo goda', *Vestnik russkogo khristianskogo dvizheniia*, 2 (1989), 157–164.
Erenburg, I., *Liudi, gody, zhizn'*, 3 vols (Moscow, 1990)
Filips-Juswigg, E., *Nemtsy o russkikh v memuarnoi literature perioda vtoroi mirovoi voiny* (New York; Slavica, 1976)

Freidenberg, O., 'Osada cheloveka', *Minuvshee*, 3 (1987), 7–44.
Ginzburg, L., 'Zapiski blokadnogo cheloveka', *Chelovek za pis'mennym stolom* (Leningrad, 1989), 517–178
Grossman, V., 'Treblinskii ad', *Znamia*, 11–12 (1945), 121–144
Gudzenko, S., *Armeiskie zapisnye knizhki* (Moscow, 1962)
——— *Zaveshchanie muzhestva: stikhi, zapisnye knizhki, vospominaniia druzei* (Moscow, 1971)
Iashin, A., *Dnevniki 1941–45* (Moscow, 1977)
Isakovskii, M., 'Dva goda v Chistopole: iz pisem 1942–1943', *Voprosy literatury*, 5 (1982), 150–166
Kedrin, D., 'Bessmertie: pis'ma s fronta. Iz arkhiva pisatelia', *Ogonek*, 30 (1988), p. 9
——— 'V oboronnuiu komissiiu SSP ot chlena SSP D. Kedrina—zaiavlenie', *Literaturnaia Rossiia*, 21 February 1969, p. 5
——— 'Dmitrii Kedrin pishet s fronta', *Literaturnaia Rossiia*, 8 January 1971, p. 10
——— 'Pis'ma zhene, 24;26.6.43', *Literaturnaia gazeta*, 23 February 1957, p. 2
——— 'Iz nalsediia: iz zapisnykh knizhek, iz pisem rodnym', *Voprosy Literatury*, 3 (1979), 204–225
Kogan, P., 'Iz pisem k rodnym i druz'iam', in *Den' poezii* (Moscow, 1960), p. 161
Kopelev, L., *Khranit' vechno*, 2nd ed. (Ann Arbor: Ardis, 1978)
Kosterina, N., 'Dnevniki, 1936–1941', *Novyi mir*, 12 (1962), 31–105.
Lipkin, S., *Stalingrad Vasiliia Grossmana* (Ann Arbor: Ardis, 1986)
Losievskii, I., 'V arkhive D. Kedrina', *Moskva*, 2 (1982), 193–195
Luknitskii, P. N., *Skvoz' vsiu blokadu* (Leningrad, 1988)
Makagonenko, G., 'Pis'ma Ol'gi Berggol'ts 1941–1942', *Voprosy literatury*, 5 (1978), 196–224
Mukhanov, G. S., 'V dolgu pered temoi: Chistopol' v istorii sovetskoi literatury perioda Velikoi otechestvennoi voiny 1941–1943', in *Chistopol'skie stranitsy* (Kazan', 1987), 3–14
Narovchatov, S., 'Pis'ma s fronta: S. Narovchatov—N.Aseevu 1944', *Voprosy literatury*, 7 (1982), 174–179
——— *My vkhodim v zhizn': kniga molodosti* (Moscow, 1980)
Negretov, P. I., *Vse dorogi vedut na Vorkutu* (Benson, VT: Chalidze, 1985)
Pasternak, B., 'Khochu zhit' s toboi khorosho dolgo, dolgo...', (wartime letters), *Literaturnaia gazeta*, 5 August 1992, p. 6
——— *Perepiska Borisa Pasternaka* (Moscow, 1990)
——— *Vtoroe rozhdenie: pis'ma k Z. N. Pasternak* (Moscow, 1993)
Pavlov, B., 'Smelogo pulia boitsia', *Literaturnaia Rossiia*, 11 September 1961, p. 10
'Poety-frontoviki Il'e Erenburgu', *Voprosy literatury*, 1 (1993), 270–282
Romanchik, L., 'Nash sotrudnik M. Svetlov: po stranitsam voennogo dnevnika 1944–45', *Neman*, 9 (1983), 146–151
Romazneva, V., 'V pamiati i v serdtse navsegda: dokumenty TsGALI rasskazyvaiut', *Literaturnaia gazeta*, 23 February 1988, p. 3 (Gudzenko)
Rozhdestvenskii, V., 'Iz frontovykh pisem 1942–44', *Voprosy literatury*, 5 (1985), 244–256
Rubashkin, A., '10 pisem: k 60-letiiu Ol'gi Berggol'ts', *Zvezda*, 5 (1970), 173–180
Sel'vinskii, I., 'Na voine: iz dnevnikov i pisem rodnym, 1941–1945', *Novyi mir*, 12 (1984), 163–175
Simonov, K., *Raznye dni voiny: dnevnik pisatelia*, 2 vols (Moscow, 1977)
——— 'V kontse voiny', in *Den' poezii* (Moscow, 1971), 169–174
——— 'Glavnaia tsel'' (letters 1943–1978), *Voprosy literatury*, 5 (1985), 182–227
Suprunenko, P., 'Voina ubivaet pravdu', *Iunost'*, 6 (1991), 16–17

Terkel, S., *The Good War: an Oral History of World War Two* (London: Hamilton, 1985)
Tomashevskaia, Z., 'Ia—kak peterburgskaia tumba', in *Ob Anne Akhmatovoi*, ed. by M. M. Kralin and I. I. Slobozhan (Leningrad, 1990), 417–438
Tvardovskii, A., 'S Karel'skogo peresheika' (war diaries 1939–40), *Novyi mir*, 2 (1969), 116–160
1418 dnei voiny: iz vospominanii o Velikoi Otechestvennoi, comp. by E. N. Tsvetaev, V. S. Iarovikov (Moscow, 1990)
Vishnevskii, V., *Dnevniki voennykh let: 1943, 1945 gg.* (Moscow, 1974)
——— 'Dva pis'ma Ol'gi Berggol'ts 21.1.43; 17.5.45', *Avrora*, 5 (1970), p. 62
Volkova, N. B., 'Fond no.1814 TsGALI', *Ogonek*, 49 (1985), 28–29 (Simonov)
Vospominaniia o Borise Pasternake, comp. by E. V. Pasternak, M. I. Feinberg (Moscow, 1993)
Zamotaev, A., 'Materi nashi za nami' (interview with Gudzenko's mother), *Literaturnaia Rossiia*, 15 May 1972, 10–11

History of World War Two

Andreyev, C., *Vlasov and the Russian Liberation Movement: Soviet Reality and Emigre Theories* (Cambridge: Cambridge University Press, 1987)
Astaf'ev, V., V. Kondrat'ev, 'Pravda vyborochnoi ne byvaet', *Literaturnaia gazeta*, 26 October 1994, p. 3
Barber, J., 'The Twenty-Eight Panfilovtsy and the Battle of Dubosekovo Siding: the Making of a Soviet Myth', unpublished paper, CREES, University of Birmingham, March 1993.
Barber, J., Harrison, M., *The Soviet Home Front 1941–1945: a Social and Economic History of the USSR in World War II* (London: Longman, 1991)
Danin, D., 'Strogo kak popalo', *Literaturnaia gazeta*, 12 July 1995, p. 3.
Erenburg, I., Grossman, V., eds., *Chernaia kniga: o zlodeiskom povsemestnom ubiistve evreev nemetsko-fashistskimi zakhvatchikami* (Jerusalem: Tarbut, 1980)
Fröhlich, S., *General Wlassow: Russen und Deutsche zwischen Hitler und Stalin* (Köln: Markus Verlag, 1987)
Garrard, J. and C., eds., *World War Two and the Soviet People*, Selected Papers from the Fourth World Congress for Soviet and East European Studies, Harrogate, 1990 (London: Macmillan, 1993)
Hoffmann, J., *Die Geschichte der Wlasov–Armee*, 2nd ed. (Freiburg: Rombach, 1984)
Granin, D., 'Daty, kotorye vsegda s nami', *Literaturnaia gazeta*, 23 June 1993, p. 1
Leetz, A., ed., *Blockade Leningrad 1941–1944: Dokumente und Essays von Russen und Deutschen* (Hamburg: Rowohlt, 1992)
Liddell-Hart, B. H., *History of the Second World War* (London: Cassell, 1970)
Lyons, G., ed., *The Russian Version of the Second World War as Taught to Schoolchildren* (London: Leo Cooper, 1976)
Moskoff, W., *The Bread of Affliction: the Food Supply in the USSR during World War Two* (Cambridge: Cambridge University Press, 1990)
Nekrich, A. M., 'Stalin i natsistskaia Germaniia', *Kontinent*, 24 (1980), 239–262
Palladin, P. A., Zeger, M. K., V'iunik, A. A., *Leningradskoe radio: ot blokady do 'ottepeli'* (Moscow, 1991)
Rapoport, V., Iu. Alekseev, *Izmena Rodine: ocherki po istorii Krasnoi Armii* (London: Overseas Publications Interchange, 1988)

Redlich, S., *Propaganda and Nationalism in Wartime Russia: the Jewish Antifascist Committee in the USSR 1941–1948* (Boulder, CO: East European Quarterly, 1982)
Salisbury, H., *The Siege of Leningrad* (London: Secker and Warburg, 1969)
Samsonov, A. M., ed., *Velikaia pobeda: istoricheskii primer geroizma sovetskogo naroda. Sovetskaia istoriografiia Velikoi Otechestvennoi voiny 1941–1945* (Moscow, 1985)
Schulte, T. J., *The German Army and Nazi Policies in Occupied Russia* (Oxford: Berg, 1989)
Seniavskaia, E. S., *1941–1945. Frontovoe pokolenie: istoriko-psikhologicheskoe issledovanie* (Moscow, 1995)
Shapiro, G., *Under Fire: the Stories of Jewish Heroes of the Soviet Union* (Jerusalem: Yad Vashem, 1988)
Streit, C., *Keine Kameraden: die Wehrmacht und die sowjetischen Kriegsgefangenen 1941–1945* (Bonn: Deutsche Verlags–Anstalt, 1991)
Topitsch, E., *Stalin's War* (London: Fourth Estate, 1987)
Udal'tsov, A., 'Vechnaia voina posle Velikoi Pobedy', *Literaturnaia gazeta*, 9 May 1995, p. 1
Werth, A., *Leningrad* (London: Hamish Hamilton, 1944)
——— *The Year of Stalingrad: an historical record and a study of Russian mentality, methods and policies* (London: Hamish Hamilton, 1946)
——— *Russia At War* (London: Barrie and Rockliff, 1964)

Literature on the Afghan War

Aladinov, M., '"Why Must We Die Here?": Six Poems by Former "Afgantsy"', *Freedom At Issue*, 81 (November–December 1984), 28–30
Aleksievich, S., *Zinky Boys: Soviet Voices from a Forgotten War*, trans. Julia and Robin Whitby (London: Chatto and Windus, 1992)
Dynin, I. M., *Posle Afganistana: 'Afgantsy' v pis'makh, dokumentakh, svidetel'st-vakh ochevidtsev* (Moscow, 1990)
Ekho afganskikh gor: povesti i rasskazy, comp. by N. P. Kuz'min (Moscow, 1987)
Iz plameni Afganistana (Moscow, 1990)
Smirnov, O., *Nikto ne sozdan dlia voiny* (Moscow, 1990)
Uchebnaia trevoga (Moscow, 1988)

British Poetry of World War Two: Primary Texts

Chaos of the Night: Women's Poetry and Verse of the Second World War, ed. by Catherine Reilly (London: Virago, 1984)
Douglas, K., *The Complete Poems* (Oxford: Oxford University Press, 1978)
Poems from the Forces, ed. by K. Rhys (London: George Routledge & Sons, 1941)
Poems of the Second World War: the Oasis Selection (London: Dent), 1985
Selected Poems of Alun Lewis (London: Unwin, 1981)
The Terrible Rain: The War Poets 1939–1945, comp. by B. Gardner (London: Methuen, 1966)
War Poems from the Sunday Times, printed for private circulation (1945)

Secondary Literature

Comfort, A., 'English Poetry and the War', *Partisan Review*, 10, 2 (March 1943), 191–193
Connolly, C., 'Comment', *Horizon*, 1, no.5 (May 1940), 309–314
Currey, R. N., *Poets of the 1939–1945 War* (London: Longmans, Green & Co., 1960)
Daiches, D., 'Contemporary Poetry in Britain', *Poetry (Chicago)*, 62 (1943), 150–164
Deutch, B., 'War Poetry Then and Now', *New Republic*, 21 April 1941, 565–567
Douglas, K., *Alamein to Zem-Zem* (London: Editions Poetry London, 1946)
Graves, R., 'War Poetry in this War', *Listener*, 23 October 1941, p. 566
Hughes, T., 'The Poetry of Keith Douglas', *Critical Quarterly*, 5, 1 (Spring 1963), 43–48
Jones, G., 'Alun Lewis', *Welsh Review*, 3, 2 (June 1944), 118–121
Murdoch, B., *Fighting Songs and Warring Words: Popular Lyrics of the Two World Wars* (London: Routledge, 1990)
Orwell, G., 'English Writing in Total War', *New Republic*, 17 July 1941, 57–58
Reed, H., 'Poetry in Wartime: the Younger Poets', *Listener*, 25 January 1945, 100–101
Rees, G., 'Letter from a Soldier', *Horizon*, 1, no.7 (July 1940), 467–471
Ross, J. M., 'Second Lieutenant Alun Lewis', *Penguin New Writing*, 27 (April 1946), 78–80
Ross, A., 'The Poetry of Keith Douglas', *TLS*, 6 August 1984, p. xxii
Scannell, V., *Not Without Glory: Poets of the Second World War* (London: Woburn Press, 1976)
Shires, L. M., *British Poetry of the Second World War* (London: Macmillan, 1985)
Spender, S., 'Poetry in 1941', *Horizon*, 5, 26 (February 1942), 96–111
Stonier, G., 'Poetry and the War', *New Statesman and Nation*, 2 September 1944, p. 155
Williams, J. S., 'The Poetry of Alun Lewis', *Anglo-Welsh Review*, 14, 33 (1964), 59–70

Literature in the Third Reich

Lamprecht, H., *Deutschland, Deutschland* (Bremen: Carl Schünemann Verlag, 1969)
Loewy, E., *Literatur unterm Hakenkreuz: Das Dritte Reich und seine Dichtung. Eine Dokumentation*, 2nd ed. (Frankfurt am Main: Europäische Verlagsanstalt, 1969)
Schöne, A., *Uber politische Lyrik im zwanzigsten Jahrhundert* (Göttingen: Vandenhoeck & Ruprecht, 1972)
Wulf, J., *Literatur und Dichtung im Dritten Reich* (Gütersloh: Sigbert Mohn Verlag, 1963)

Works on the History and Development of Soviet Literature

Babichenko, D., *Pisateli i tsenzory: sovetskaia literatura 1940-kh godov pod politicheskim kontrolem Ts.K* (Moscow, 1994)

——— 'Zhdanov, Malenkov i delo leningradskikh zhurnalov, *Voprosy literatury*, 3 (1993), 201–214

Buznik, V. V., V. A. Kovalev, V. V. Timofeeva, eds., *Istoriia russkoi sovetskoi poezii 1941–1980* (Leningrad, 1984)

Clark, K., *The Soviet Novel: History as Ritual*, 2nd ed. (Chicago–London: University of Chicago Press, 1985)

Dobrenko, E., 'Levoi! Levoi! Levoi! Metamorfozy revoliutsionnoi kul'tury', *Novyi mir*, 3 (1992), 228–240

Etkind, E., *Russische Lyrik von der Oktoberrevolution bis zur Gegenwart: Versuch einer Darstellung* (Munich: Beck, 1984)

Ermolaev, H., *Soviet Literary Theory 1917–1934: The Genesis of Socialist Realism*, University of California Publications in Modern Philology, volume LXIX (Berkeley–Los Angeles: University of California Press, 1963)

Geller, M., *Kontsentratsionnyi mir i sovetskaia literatura* (London: Overseas Publications Interchange, 1974)

Grois, B., *The Total Art of Stalinism: Avant-Garde, Aesthetic Dictatorship and Beyond* (Princeton: Princeton University Press, 1992)

Günther, H., *Die Verstaatlichung der Literatur: Entstehung und Funktionsweise des sozialistisch-realistischen Kanons in der sowjetischer Literatur der dreissiger Jahre* (Stuttgart: Metzler, 1984)

James, C. V., *Soviet Socialist Realism: Origins and Theory* (London: Macmillan, 1973)

Kasack, W., *Entsiklopedicheskii slovar' russkoi literatury s 1917 goda* (London: Overseas Publications Interchange, 1988)

Kulinich, A., *Russkaia sovetskaia poeziia: ocherki istorii* (Moscow, 1963)

Marsh, R., *Images of Dictatorship: Stalin in Literature* (London: Routledge, 1989)

Ocherki istorii russkoi sovetskoi zhurnalistiki, ed. by A. G. Dement'ev, 2 vols (Moscow, 1966–68)

Pervyi vsesoiuznyi s"ezd sovetskikh pisatelei: stenograficheskii otchet, facsimile reprint of 1934 Moscow edition (Moscow, 1990)

Rais, E., 'Sorokaletie sovetskoi poezii', *Grani*, 49, 94–136; 50, 144–163; 51, 140–148

Reavey, G., *Soviet Literature To-day* (London: Lindsay Drummond, 1946)

Robin, R., *Le réalisme socialiste: une esthétique impossible* (Paris: Payot, 1986)

Smith, G. S., *Songs to Seven Strings: Russian Guitar Poetry and Soviet 'Mass Song'* (Bloomington: Indiana University Press, 1984)

Terts, A. (pseudonym of A. Siniavskii), 'Chto takoe sotsialisticheskii realizm?', in *Fantasticheskii mir Abrama Tertsa* (New York: Inter-Language Literary Associates, 1967), 399–446

Vykhodtsev, P. S., *Istoriia russkoi sovetskoi literatury* (Moscow, 1970)

Zhukov, Iu., 'Preliudiia', *Literaturnaia gazeta*, 28 July 1993, p. 6

Other works cited

Aleksievich, S., 'Zacharovannye smert'iu', *Druzhba narodov*, 4 (1993), 15–75
Bakhtin, M., *Voprosy literatury i estetiki* (Moscow, 1975)
Brooke, R., *The Poems of Rupert Brooke* (London: Black Swan, 1987)
Dostoevskii, F. M., *Diary of a Writer*, trans. Boris Brasol (Haslemere: Ianmead, 1984)
Gor'kii, M., *Sobranie sochinenii*, 30 vols (Moscow, 1949–55)
Eliade, M., *Le mythe de l'éternel retour: archétypes et répétition*, 2nd ed. (Paris: Gallimard, 1949)
Elshtain, J. B., *Women and War* (Brighton: Harvester Press, 1987)
El'vin, I., 'Kannibaly', *Oktiabr'*, 7–8 (1941), 190–197
Engel, B. A., *Mothers and Daughters: Women of the Intelligentsia in Nineteenth Century Russia* (Cambridge: Cambridge University Press, 1983)
Golant, V., 'Korichnevaia chuma nad Evropoi', *Zvezda*, 7–8 (1941), 143–151
Gollerbakh, E., 'Iskusstvo v okovakh', *Zvezda*, 7–8 (1941), 66–74
Grossman, V., *Zhizn' i sud'ba* (Lausanne: L'Age d'Homme, 1980)
Heldt, B., *Terrible Perfection: Women and Russian Literature* (Bloomington, Indiana: Indiana University Press, 1987)
Howlett, J., R. Mengham, eds., *The Violent Muse: Violence and the Artistic Imagination in Europe 1910–1949* (Manchester: Manchester University Press, 1994)
'Kak nemetskie okkupanty grabili Ukrainu v 1918 god', *Novyi mir*, 7–8 (1941), 179–184
Khmel'nitskaia, T., 'Smert' kul'tury', *Zvezda*, 7–8 (1941), 152–153
Kononeko, N., 'Women as Performers of Oral Literature: a Re-examination of Epic and Lament' in *Women Writers in Russian Literature*, ed. by T. Clyman and D. Greene (Westport, CT: Greenwood Press, 1994), 17–28
Korotnev, M., 'Sterilizatsiia dukha', *Znamia*, 7–8 (1941), 158–163
Likhachev, D. S., *Chelovek v literature drevnei Rusi* (Moscow–Leningrad, 1958)
Ozhegov, S. I., *Slovar' russkogo iazyka* (Moscow, 1978)
Pamiatniki literatury drevnei Rusi: XII vek, ed. by D. S. Likhachev, L. A. Dmitrieva (Moscow, 1981)
Pamiatniki literatury drevnei Rusi XIV—seredina XV veka, ed. by D. S. Likhachev, L. A. Dmitrieva (Moscow, 1981)
Pasternak, B., *Doctor Zhivago*, trans. Max Hayward and Manya Harari (London: Collins Harvill, 1988)
Popova, L., *Women in the Land of Socialism* (Moscow, 1949)
Rabinovich, Z., 'Protiv fashistskogo varvarstva', *Novyi mir*, 7–8 (1941), 169–178
Rozman, M., 'Germanskii narod pod igom fashizma', *Oktiabr'*, 7–8 (1941), 198–204
Solzhenitsyn, A., *Bodalsia telenok s dubom* (Paris: YMCA Press, 1975)
——— *Arkhipelag GULag*, 3 vols (Paris: YMCA Press, 1989)
Tolstoi, A., *Sobranie sochinenii*, 10 vols (Moscow, 1958–61)
Zil'berfarb, I., 'Germaniia Gitlera protiv Germanii Gete', *Novyi mir*, 9–10 (1941), 158–173

Index